WITHDRAWN
CHARLESTON COUNTY LIBRARY

D1039158

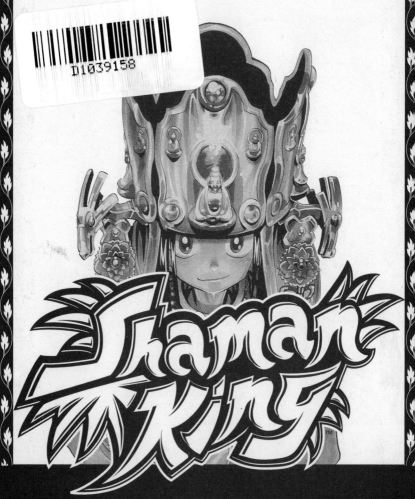

VOL. 3
THE LIZARD MAN

STORY AND ART BY
HIROYUKI TAKEI

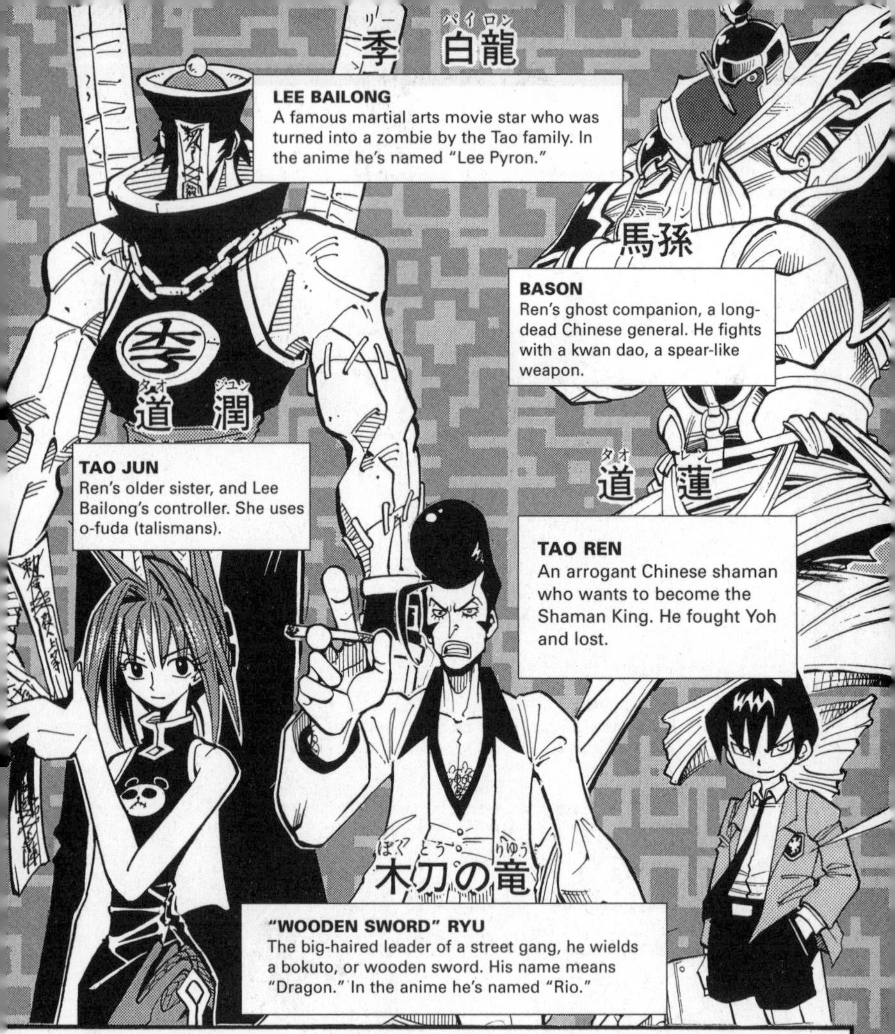
李 白龍
LEE BAILONG
A famous martial arts movie star who was turned into a zombie by the Tao family. In the anime he's named "Lee Pyron."
馬孫
BASON
Ren's ghost companion, a long-dead Chinese general. He fights with a kwan dao, a spear-like weapon.
道 潤
TAO JUN
Ren's older sister, and Lee Bailong's controller. She uses o-fuda (talismans).
道 蓮
TAO REN
An arrogant Chinese shaman who wants to become the Shaman King. He fought Yoh and lost.
木刀の竜
"WOODEN SWORD" RYU
The big-haired leader of a street gang, he wields a bokuto, or wooden sword. His name means "Dragon." In the anime he's named "Rio."

THE STORY SO FAR...

Yoh Asakura is a *shaman*...one of the gifted few who, thanks to training or natural talent, can speak to spirits that most people can't even see. He can even channel them and use their powers! But a modern-day shaman faces great responsibilities. With the help of his fiancée Anna, Yoh is in training for the ultimate shaman sports event: the "Shaman Fight in Tokyo," the once-every-500-years tournament to see who can channel the "King of Spirits" and become the *Shaman King*. Already Yoh has defeated two opponents, the brother-sister pair of Ren and Jun...what dangers await him next?

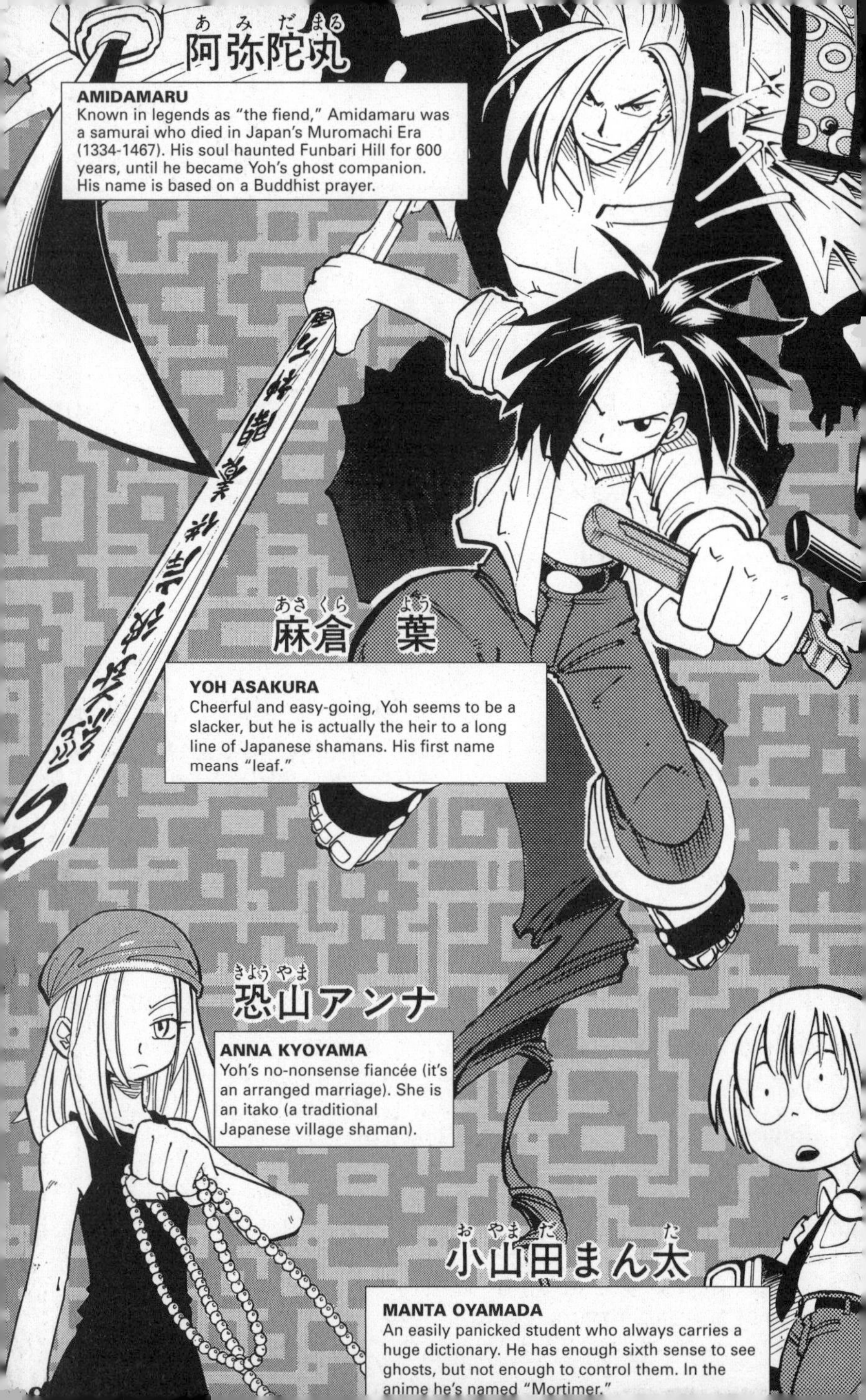
あみだまる
阿弥陀丸
AMIDAMARU
Known in legends as "the fiend," Amidamaru was a samurai who died in Japan's Muromachi Era (1334-1467). His soul haunted Funbari Hill for 600 years, until he became Yoh's ghost companion. His name is based on a Buddhist prayer.
あさくら よう
麻倉 葉
YOH ASAKURA
Cheerful and easy-going, Yoh seems to be a slacker, but he is actually the heir to a long line of Japanese shamans. His first name means "leaf."
きょうやま
恐山アンナ
ANNA KYOYAMA
Yoh's no-nonsense fiancée (it's an arranged marriage). She is an itako (a traditional Japanese village shaman).
おやまだ た
小山田まん太
MANTA OYAMADA
An easily panicked student who always carries a huge dictionary. He has enough sixth sense to see ghosts, but not enough to control them. In the anime he's named "Mortimer."

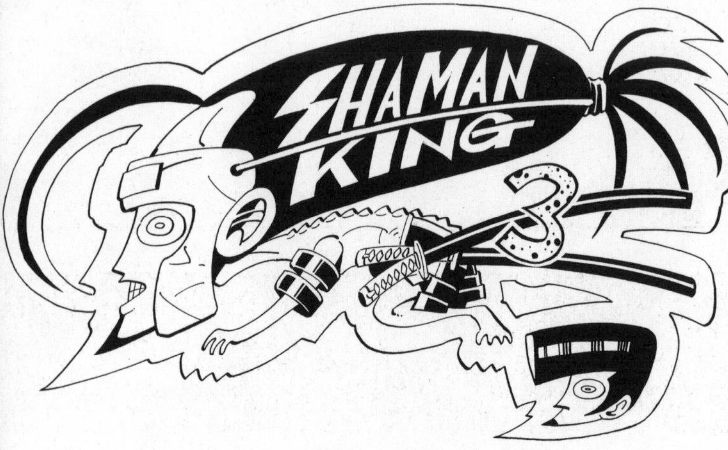
SHAMAN KING
3

VOL. 3: THE LIZARD MAN

CONTENTS

READ THIS WAY

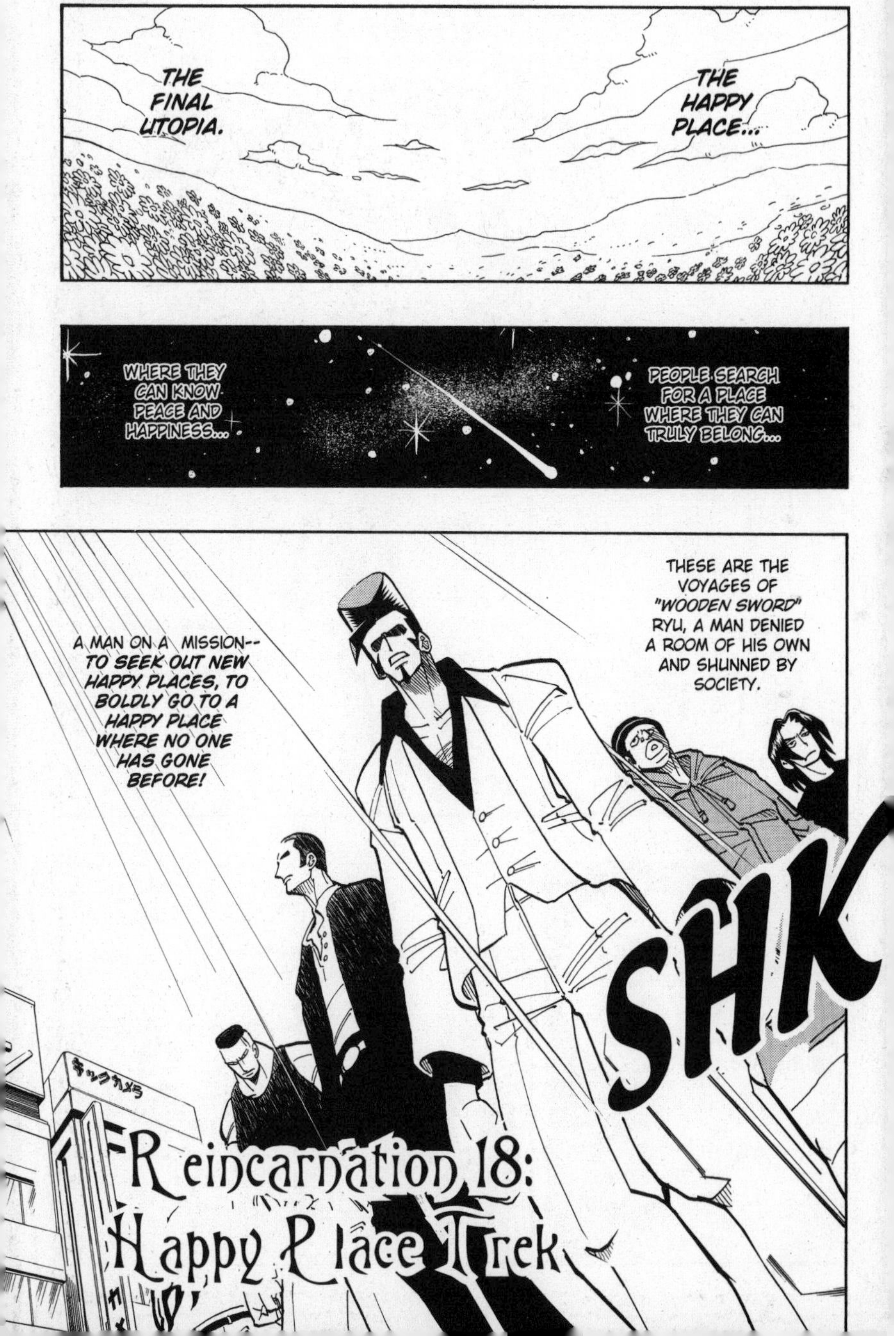
THE HAPPY PLACE...
THE FINAL UTOPIA.
PEOPLE SEARCH FOR A PLACE WHERE THEY CAN TRULY BELONG...
WHERE THEY CAN KNOW PEACE AND HAPPINESS...
THESE ARE THE VOYAGES OF "WOODEN SWORD" RYU, A MAN DENIED A ROOM OF HIS OWN AND SHUNNED BY SOCIETY.
A MAN ON A MISSION-- TO SEEK OUT NEW HAPPY PLACES, TO BOLDLY GO TO A HAPPY PLACE WHERE NO ONE HAS GONE BEFORE!
SHK
Reincarnation 18: Happy Place Trek

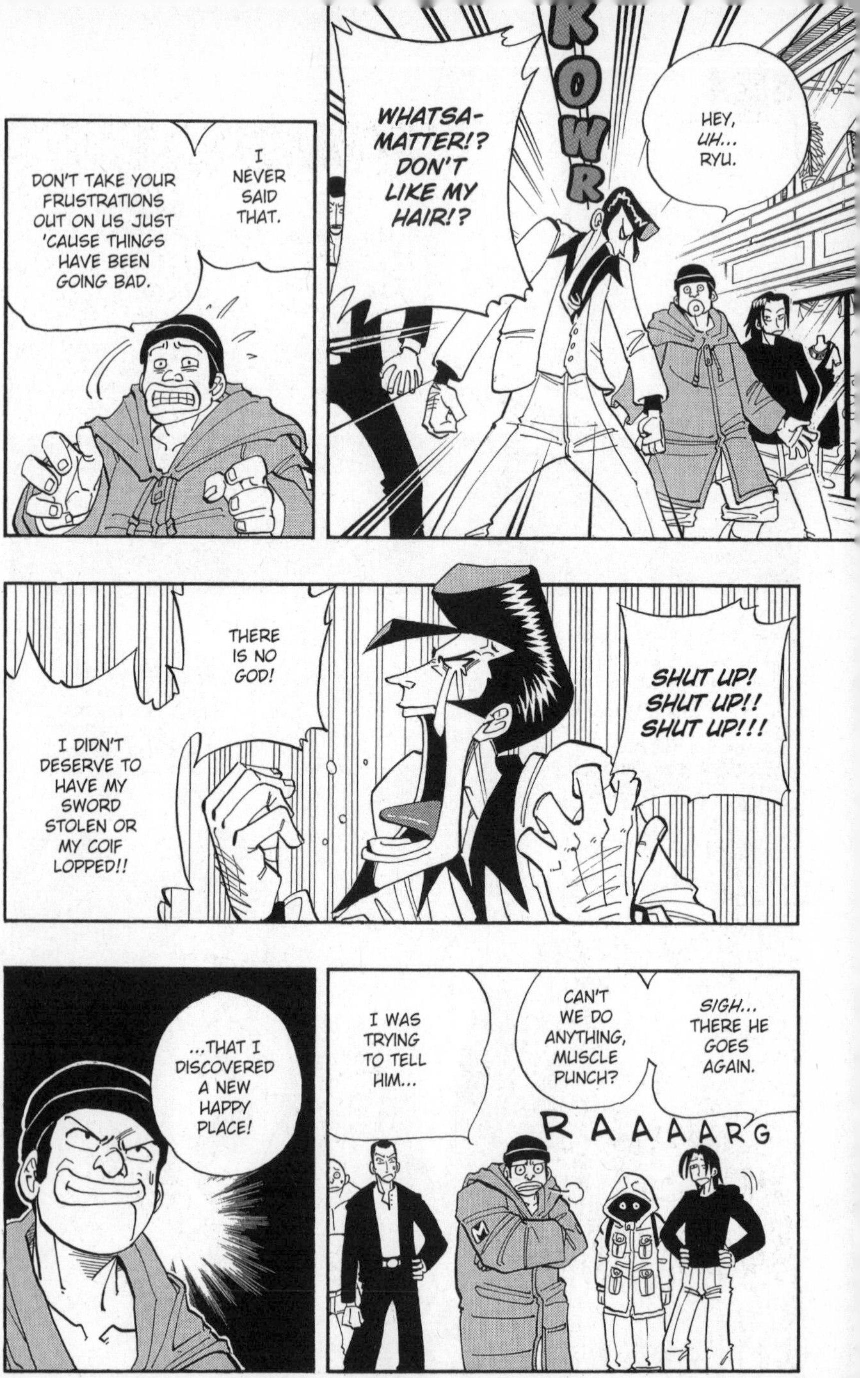
HEY, UH... RYU.
KOWR
WHATSA-MATTER!? DON'T LIKE MY HAIR!?
I NEVER SAID THAT.
DON'T TAKE YOUR FRUSTRATIONS OUT ON US JUST 'CAUSE THINGS HAVE BEEN GOING BAD.
SHUT UP! SHUT UP!! SHUT UP!!!
THERE IS NO GOD!
I DIDN'T DESERVE TO HAVE MY SWORD STOLEN OR MY COIF LOPPED!!
SIGH... THERE HE GOES AGAIN.
CAN'T WE DO ANYTHING, MUSCLE PUNCH?
I WAS TRYING TO TELL HIM...
RAAAARG
...THAT I DISCOVERED A NEW HAPPY PLACE!

READ THIS WAY

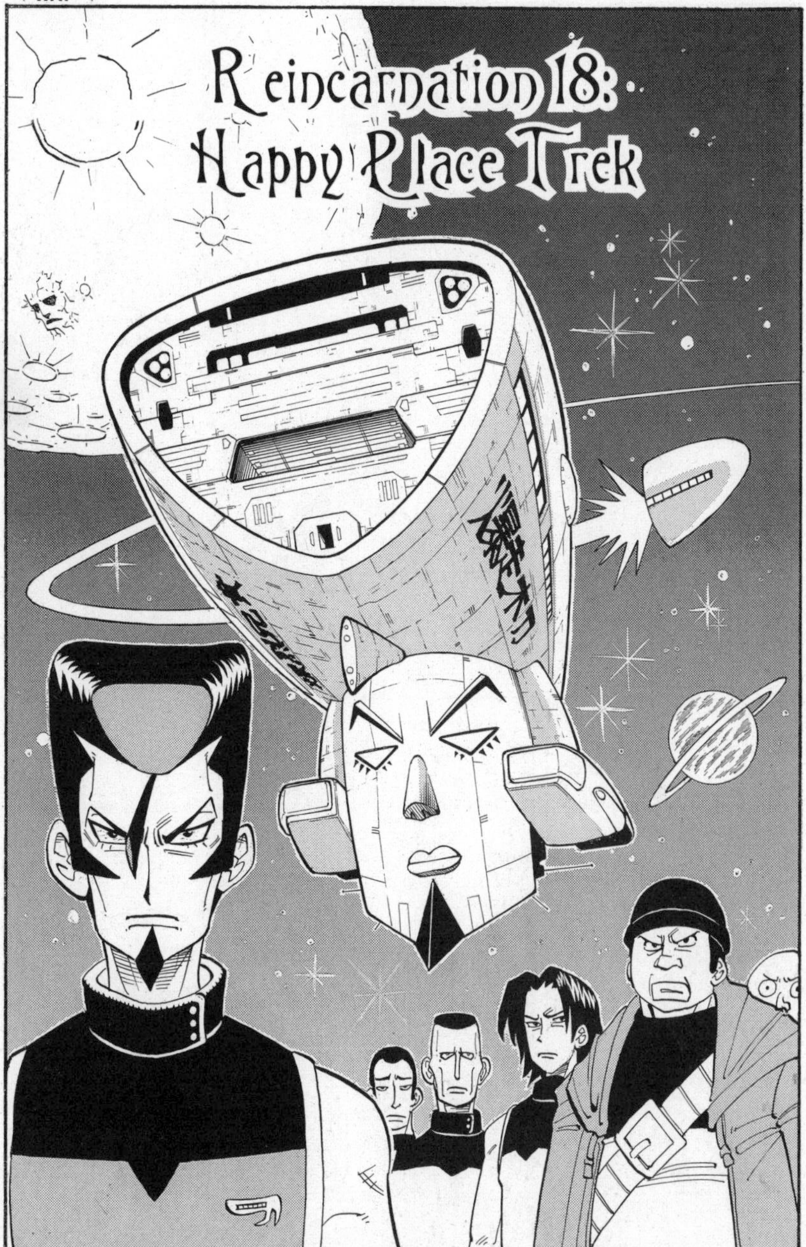
Reincarnation 18:
Happy Place Trek

READ THIS WAY

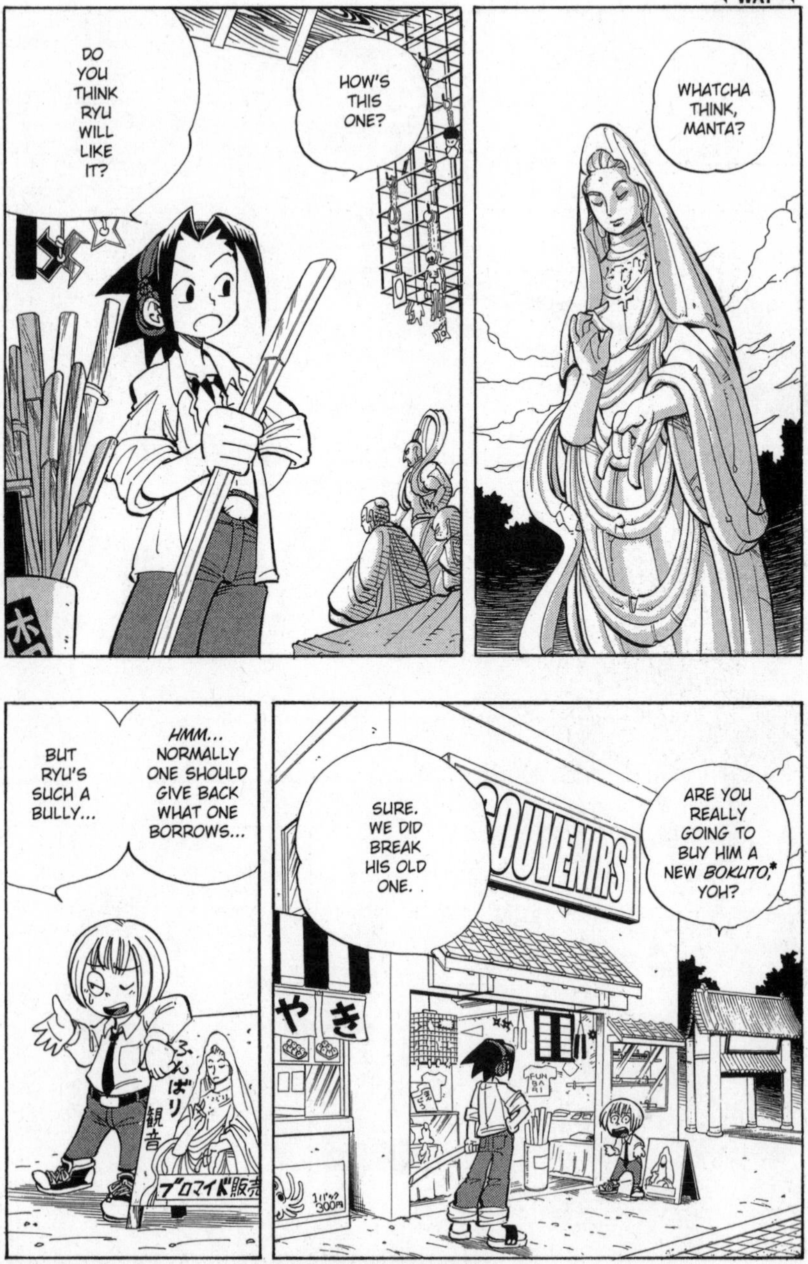
WHATCHA THINK, MANTA?
HOW'S THIS ONE?
DO YOU THINK RYU WILL LIKE IT?
ARE YOU REALLY GOING TO BUY HIM A NEW *BOKUTO*,* YOH?
SOUVENIRS
SURE. WE DID BREAK HIS OLD ONE.
やき
FUN BA RI
HMM... NORMALLY ONE SHOULD GIVE BACK WHAT ONE BORROWS...
BUT RYU'S SUCH A BULLY...
ふんばり観音
ブロマイド販売

**BOKUTO=WOODEN SWORD*

READ THIS WAY

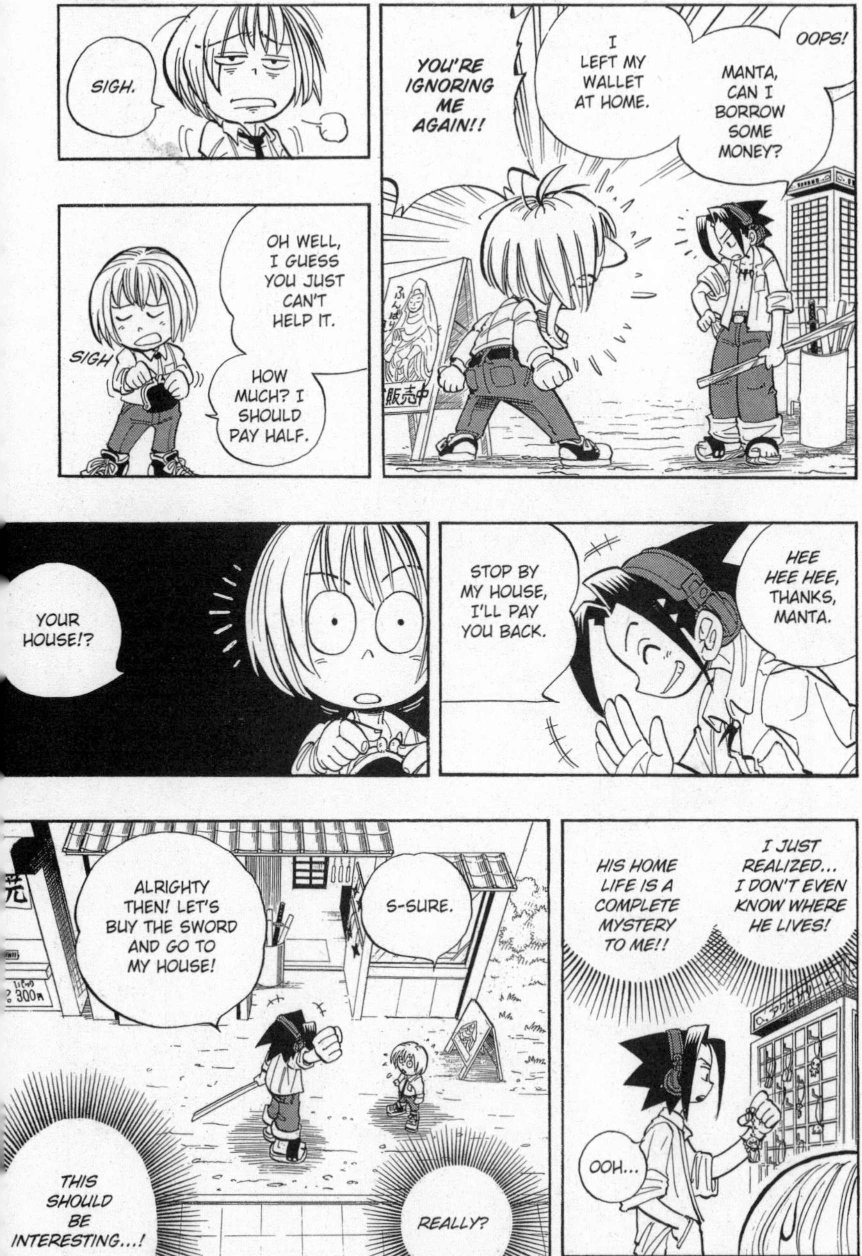
OOPS!
I LEFT MY WALLET AT HOME.
MANTA, CAN I BORROW SOME MONEY?
YOU'RE IGNORING ME AGAIN!!
SIGH.
OH WELL, I GUESS YOU JUST CAN'T HELP IT.
HOW MUCH? I SHOULD PAY HALF.
SIGH
HEE HEE HEE, THANKS, MANTA.
STOP BY MY HOUSE, I'LL PAY YOU BACK.
YOUR HOUSE!?
I JUST REALIZED... I DON'T EVEN KNOW WHERE HE LIVES!
HIS HOME LIFE IS A COMPLETE MYSTERY TO ME!!
OOH...
ALRIGHTY THEN! LET'S BUY THE SWORD AND GO TO MY HOUSE!
S-SURE.
REALLY?
THIS SHOULD BE INTERESTING...!

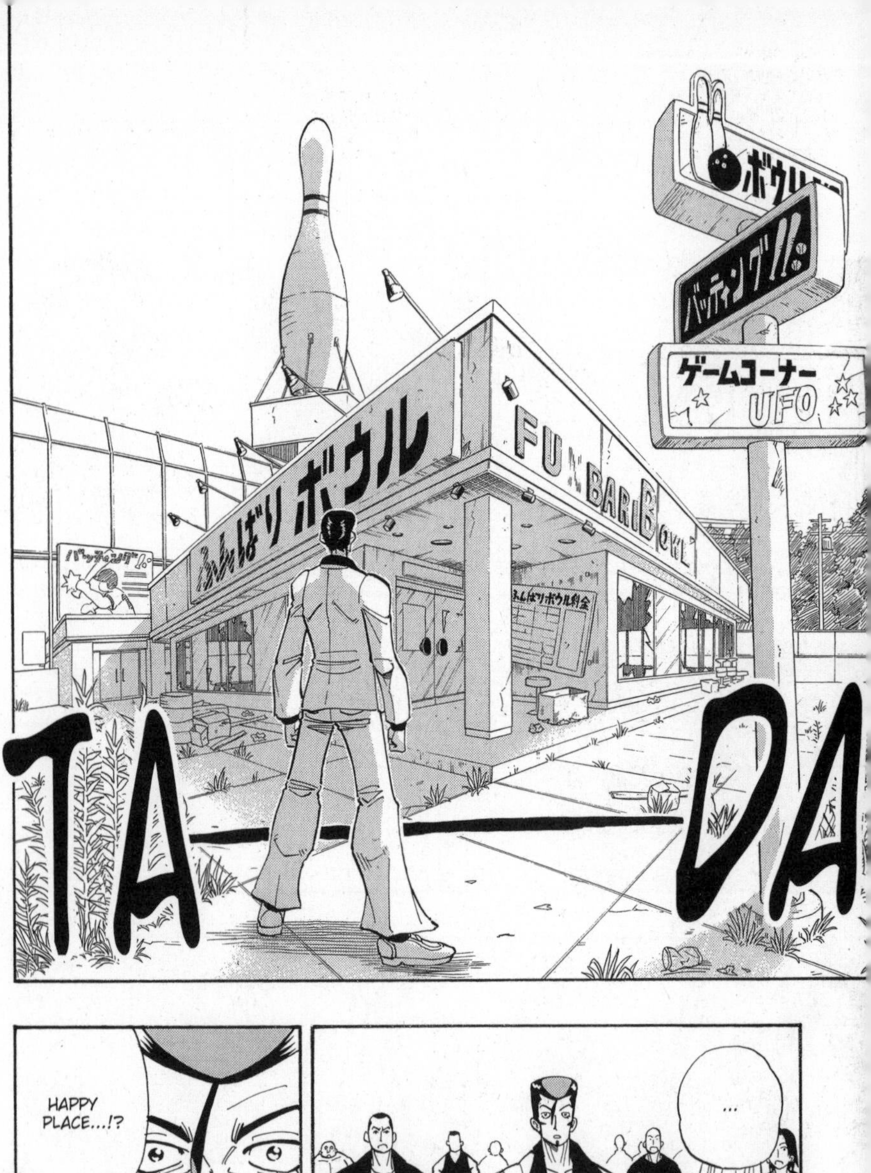
バッティング!!
ゲームコーナー
UFO
ふんばりボウル
FUNBARI BOWL
ふんばりボウル料金
TA
DA
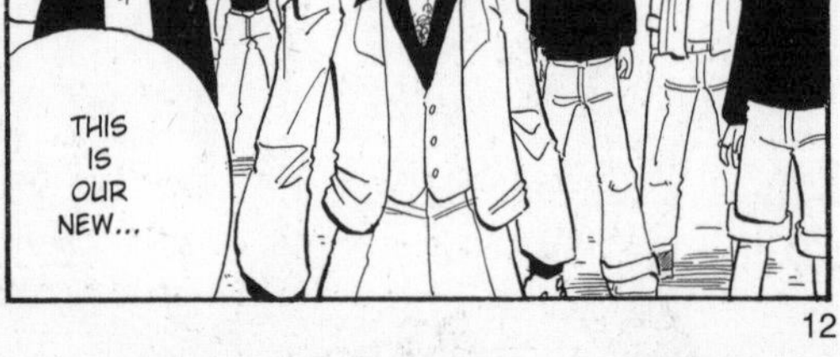
...
THIS IS OUR NEW...
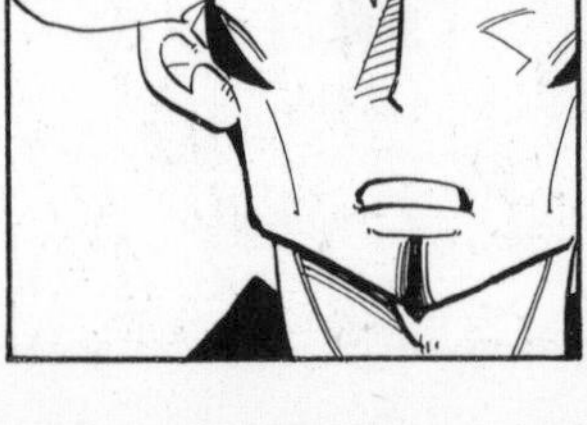
HAPPY PLACE...!?

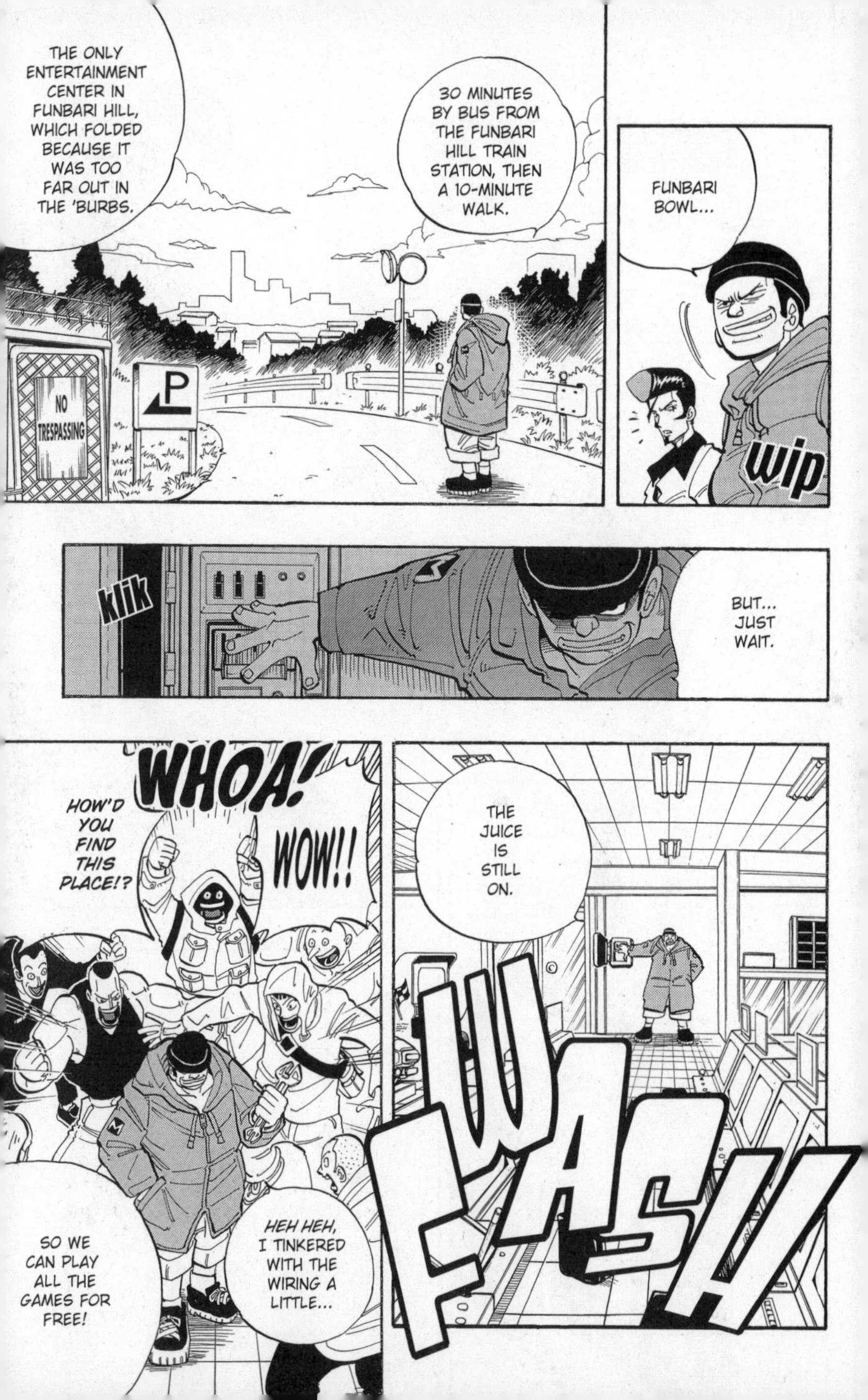
FUNBARI BOWL...
wip
THE ONLY ENTERTAINMENT CENTER IN FUNBARI HILL, WHICH FOLDED BECAUSE IT WAS TOO FAR OUT IN THE 'BURBS.
30 MINUTES BY BUS FROM THE FUNBARI HILL TRAIN STATION, THEN A 10-MINUTE WALK.
NO TRESPASSING
P
BUT... JUST WAIT.
klik
THE JUICE IS STILL ON.
FWASH!!
WHOA!
WOW!!
HOW'D YOU FIND THIS PLACE!?
HEH HEH, I TINKERED WITH THE WIRING A LITTLE...
SO WE CAN PLAY ALL THE GAMES FOR FREE!

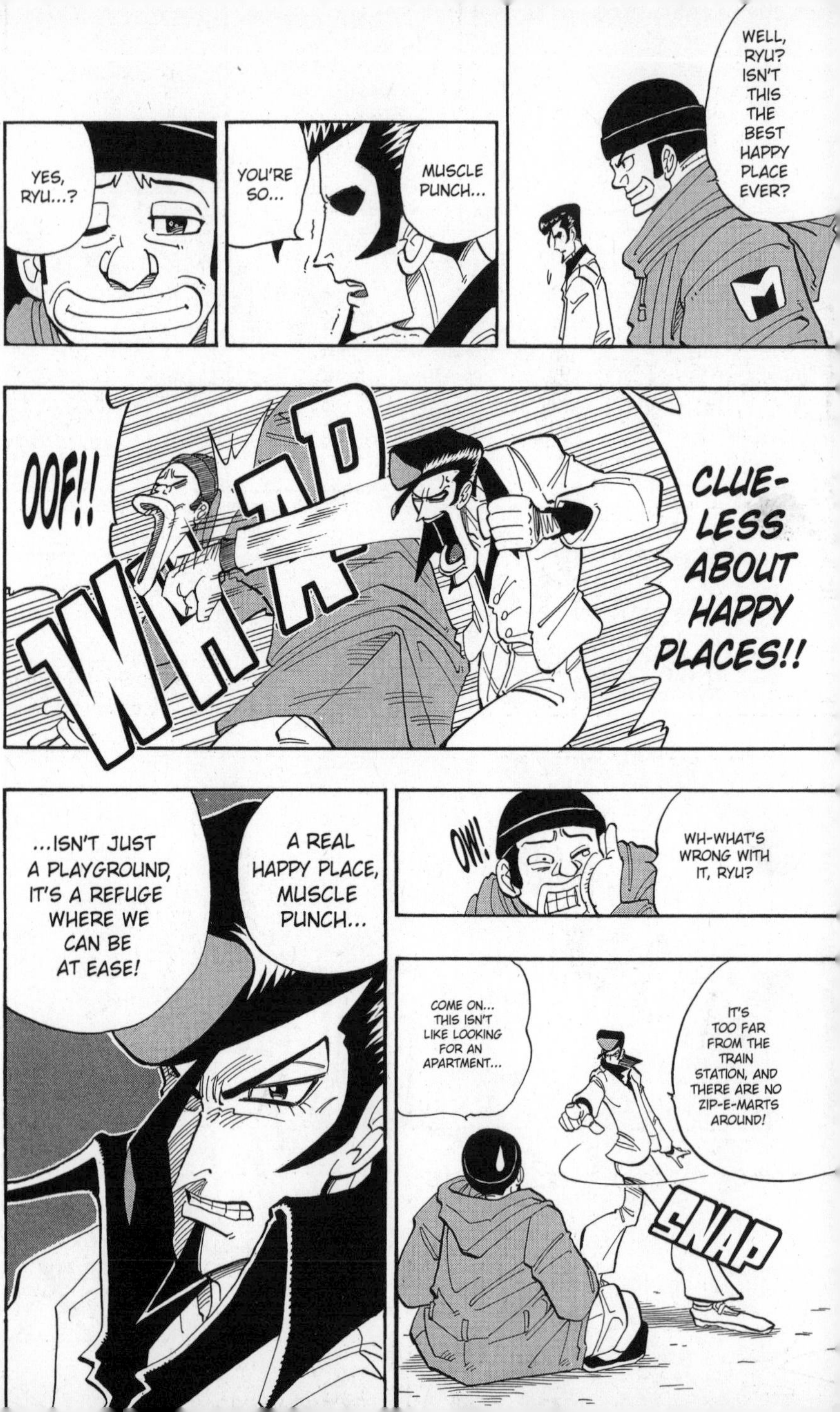
WELL, RYU? ISN'T THIS THE BEST HAPPY PLACE EVER?
MUSCLE PUNCH...
YOU'RE SO...
YES, RYU...?
CLUE-LESS ABOUT HAPPY PLACES!!
WHAP
OOF!!
WH-WHAT'S WRONG WITH IT, RYU?
OW!
IT'S TOO FAR FROM THE TRAIN STATION, AND THERE ARE NO ZIP-E-MARTS AROUND!
SNAP
COME ON... THIS ISN'T LIKE LOOKING FOR AN APARTMENT...
A REAL HAPPY PLACE, MUSCLE PUNCH...
...ISN'T JUST A PLAYGROUND, IT'S A REFUGE WHERE WE CAN BE AT EASE!

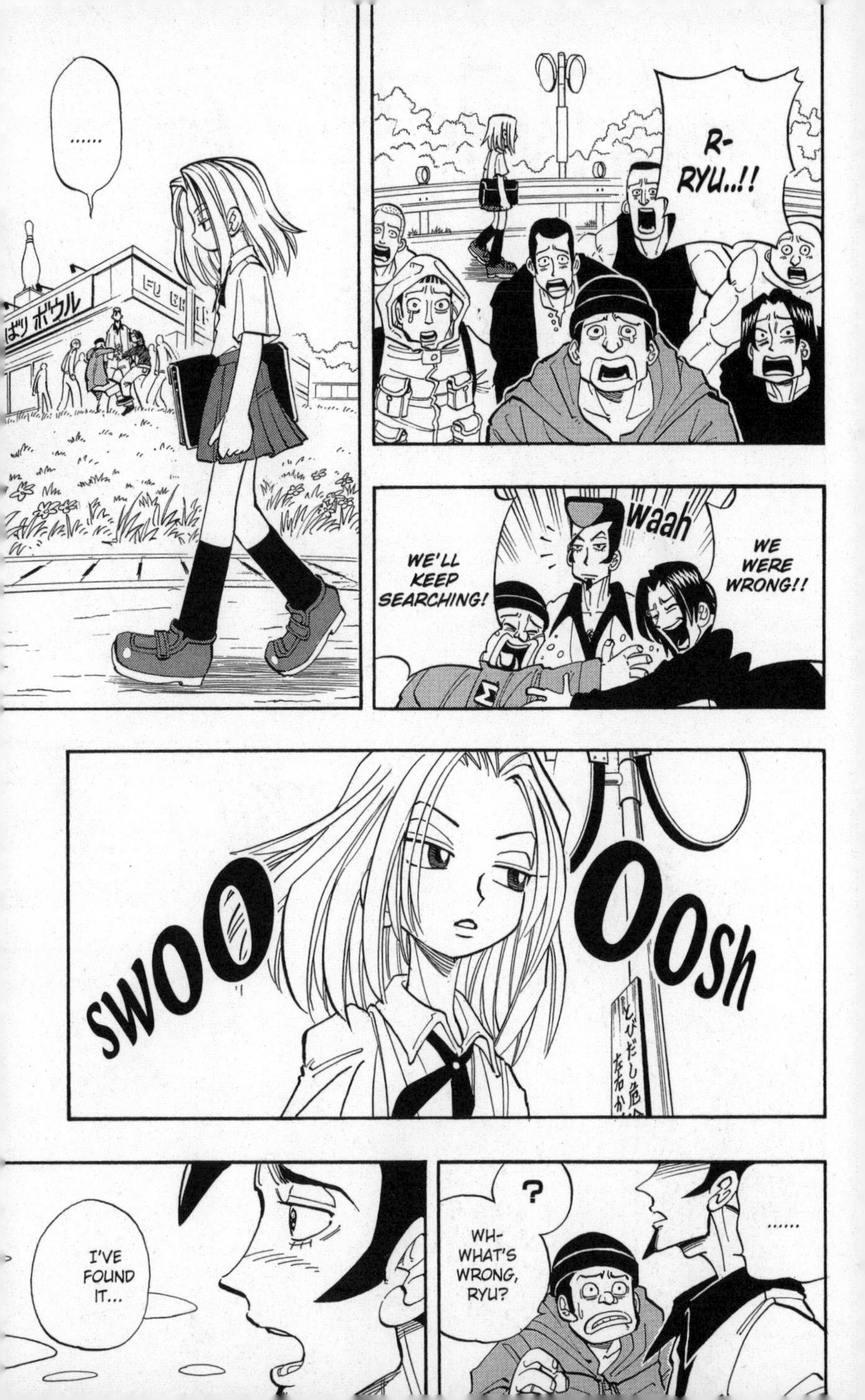
R-RYU..!!
WE WERE WRONG!!
waah
WE'LL KEEP SEARCHING!
......
SWOOOOSH
......
?
WH-WHAT'S WRONG, RYU?
I'VE FOUND IT...

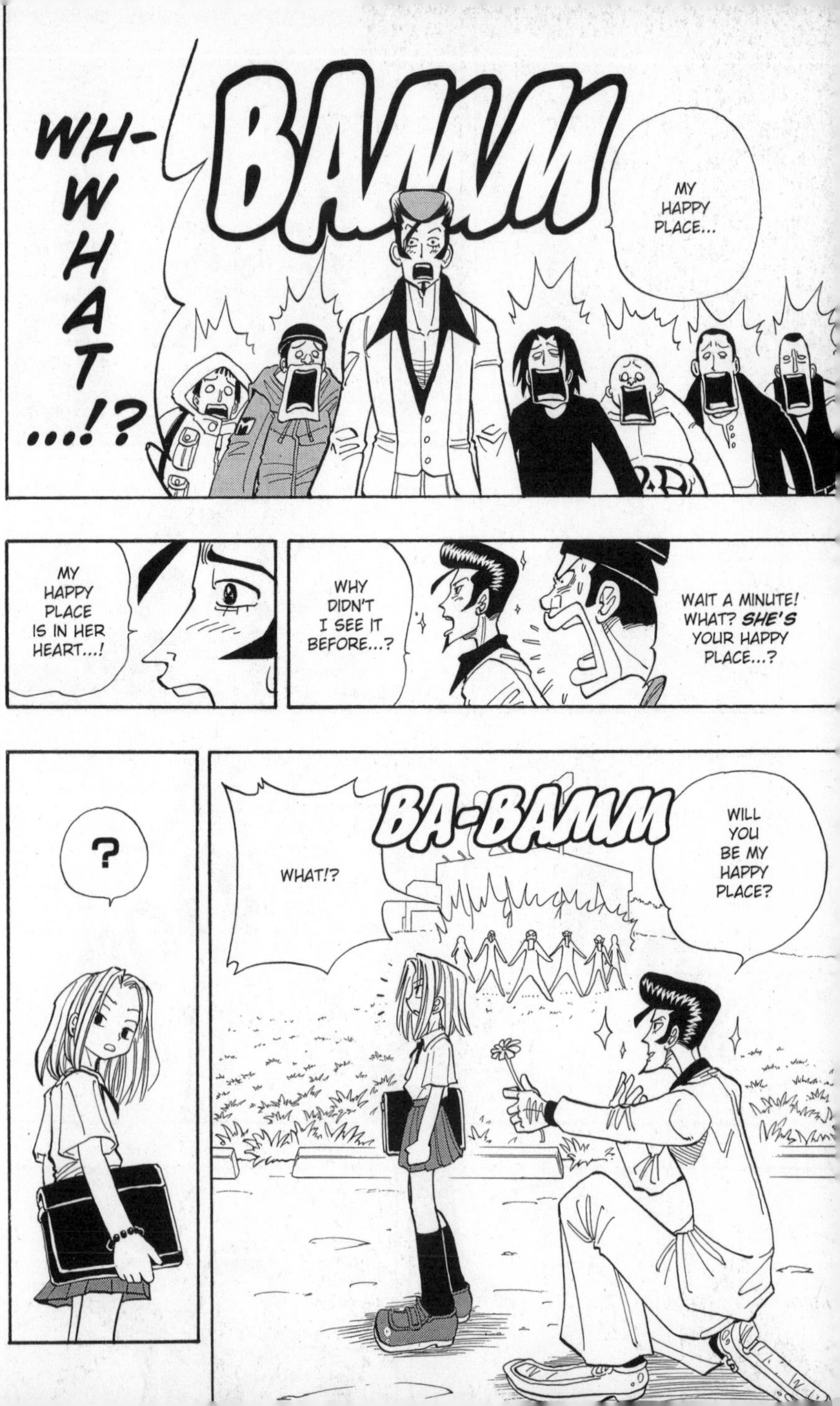
MY HAPPY PLACE...
BAMM
WH-WHAT...!?
WAIT A MINUTE! WHAT? SHE'S YOUR HAPPY PLACE...?
WHY DIDN'T I SEE IT BEFORE...?
MY HAPPY PLACE IS IN HER HEART...!
WILL YOU BE MY HAPPY PLACE?
BA-BAMM
WHAT!?
?

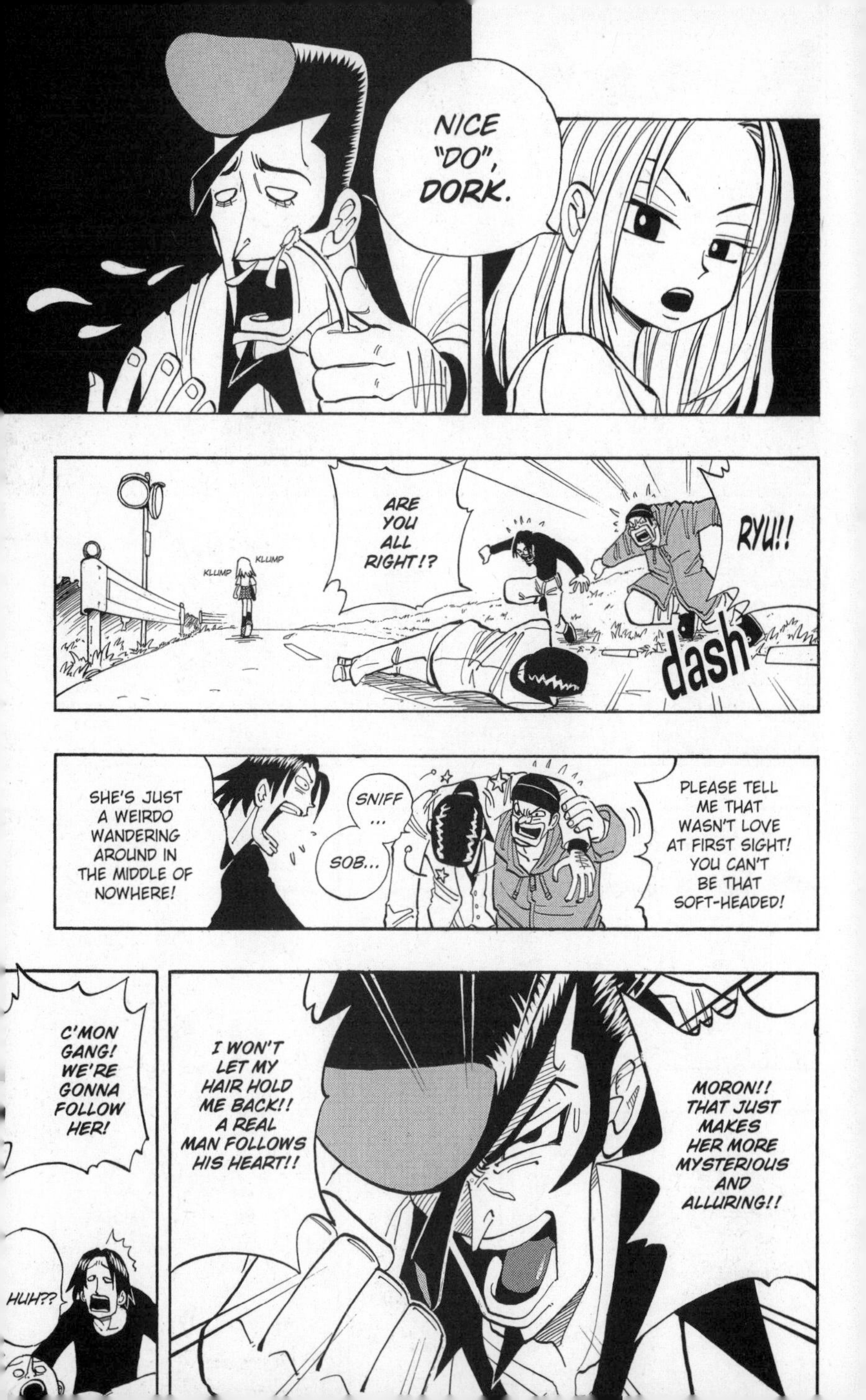
NICE "DO", DORK.
RYU!!
dash
ARE YOU ALL RIGHT!?
KLUMP
KLUMP
PLEASE TELL ME THAT WASN'T LOVE AT FIRST SIGHT! YOU CAN'T BE THAT SOFT-HEADED!
SNIFF ...
SOB...
SHE'S JUST A WEIRDO WANDERING AROUND IN THE MIDDLE OF NOWHERE!
MORON!! THAT JUST MAKES HER MORE MYSTERIOUS AND ALLURING!!
I WON'T LET MY HAIR HOLD ME BACK!! A REAL MAN FOLLOWS HIS HEART!!
C'MON GANG! WE'RE GONNA FOLLOW HER!
HUH??

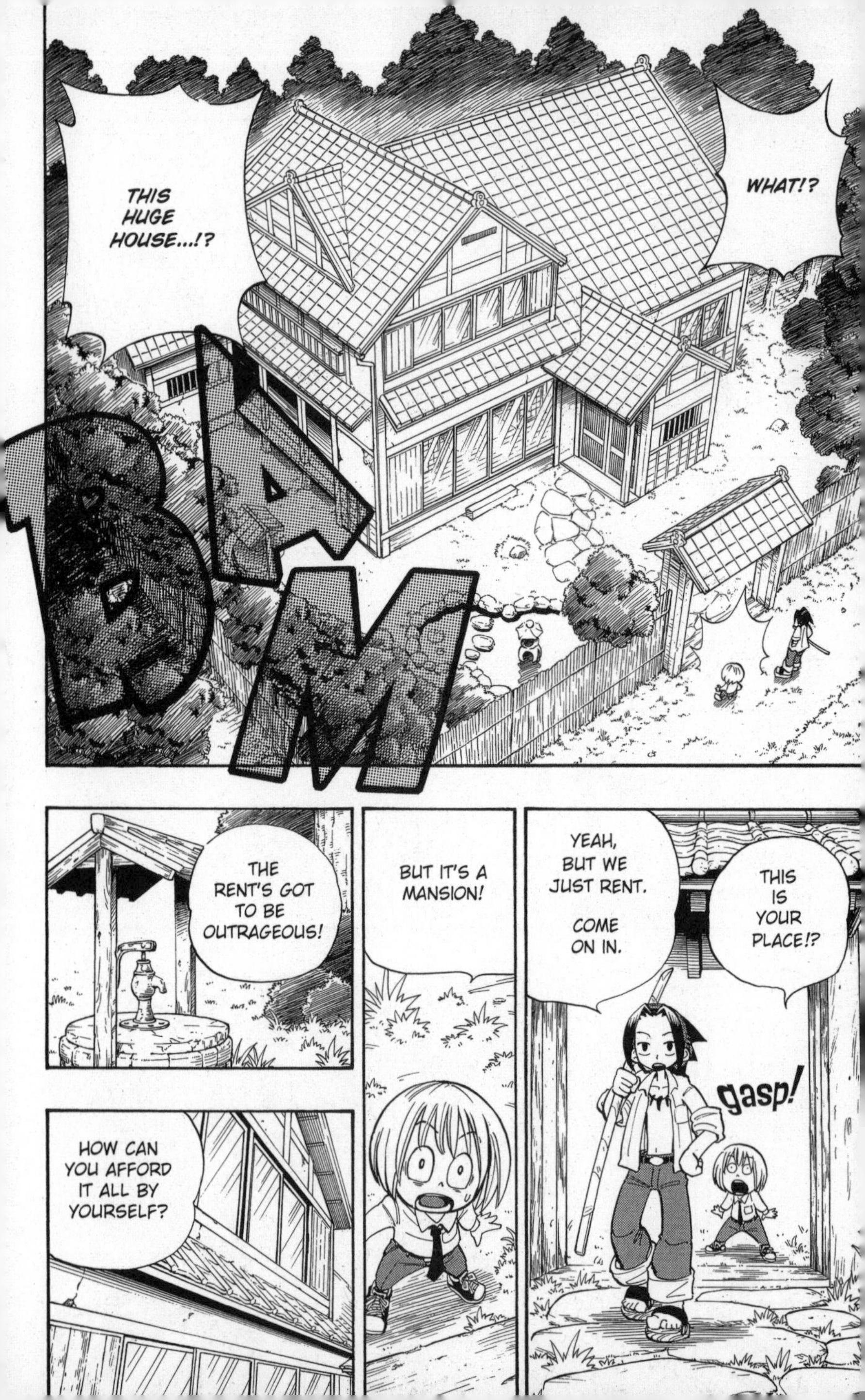
WHAT!?
THIS HUGE HOUSE...!?
BAM
THIS IS YOUR PLACE!?
YEAH, BUT WE JUST RENT.
COME ON IN.
gasp!
BUT IT'S A MANSION!
THE RENT'S GOT TO BE OUTRAGEOUS!
HOW CAN YOU AFFORD IT ALL BY YOURSELF?

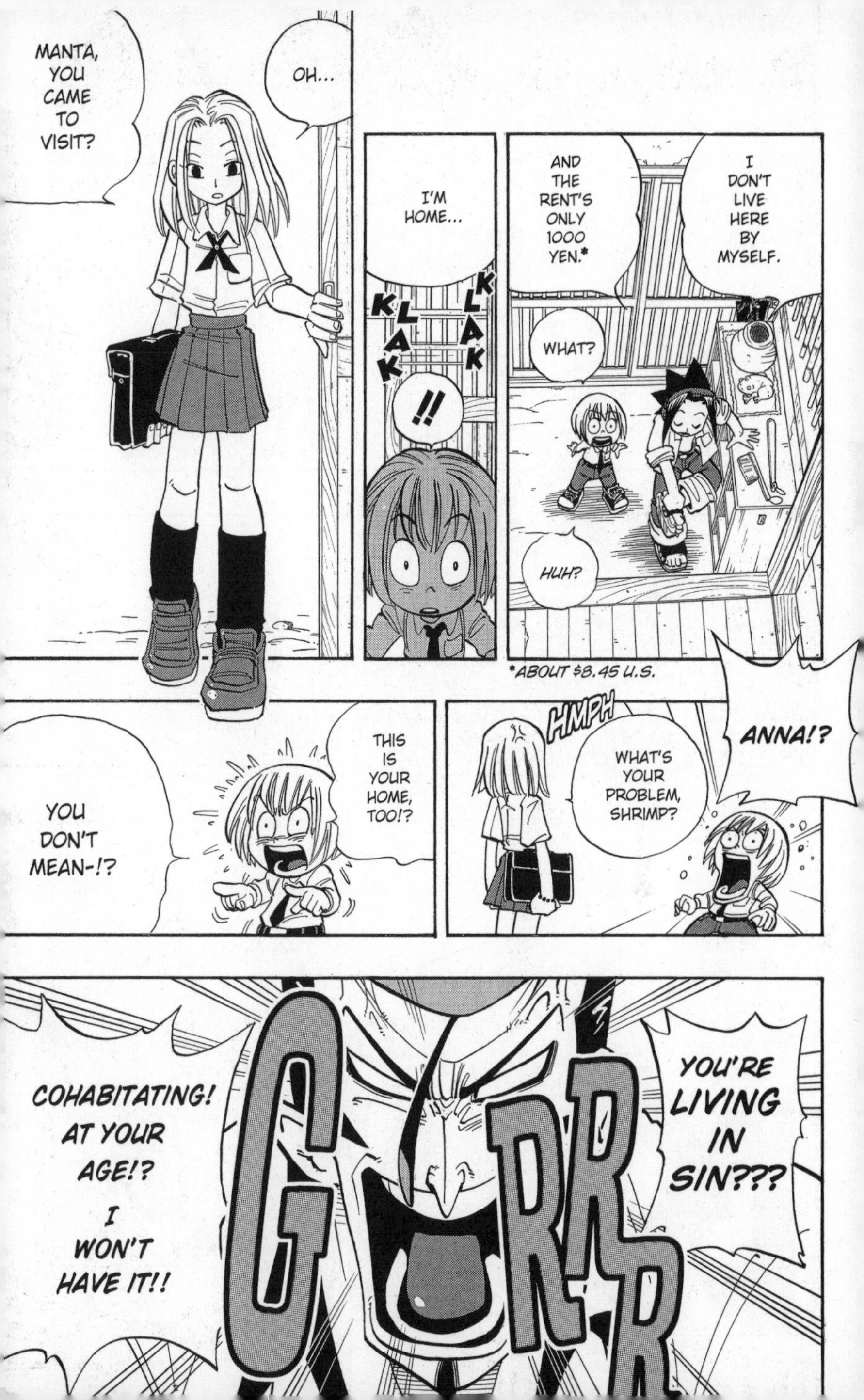
I DON'T LIVE HERE BY MYSELF.
AND THE RENT'S ONLY 1000 YEN.*
WHAT?
HUH?
I'M HOME...
KLAK KLAK
!!
OH...
MANTA, YOU CAME TO VISIT?
ANNA!?
HMPH
WHAT'S YOUR PROBLEM, SHRIMP?
THIS IS YOUR HOME, TOO!?
YOU DON'T MEAN-!?
YOU'RE LIVING IN SIN???
GRRR
COHABITATING! AT YOUR AGE!?
I WON'T HAVE IT!!

*ABOUT $8.45 U.S.

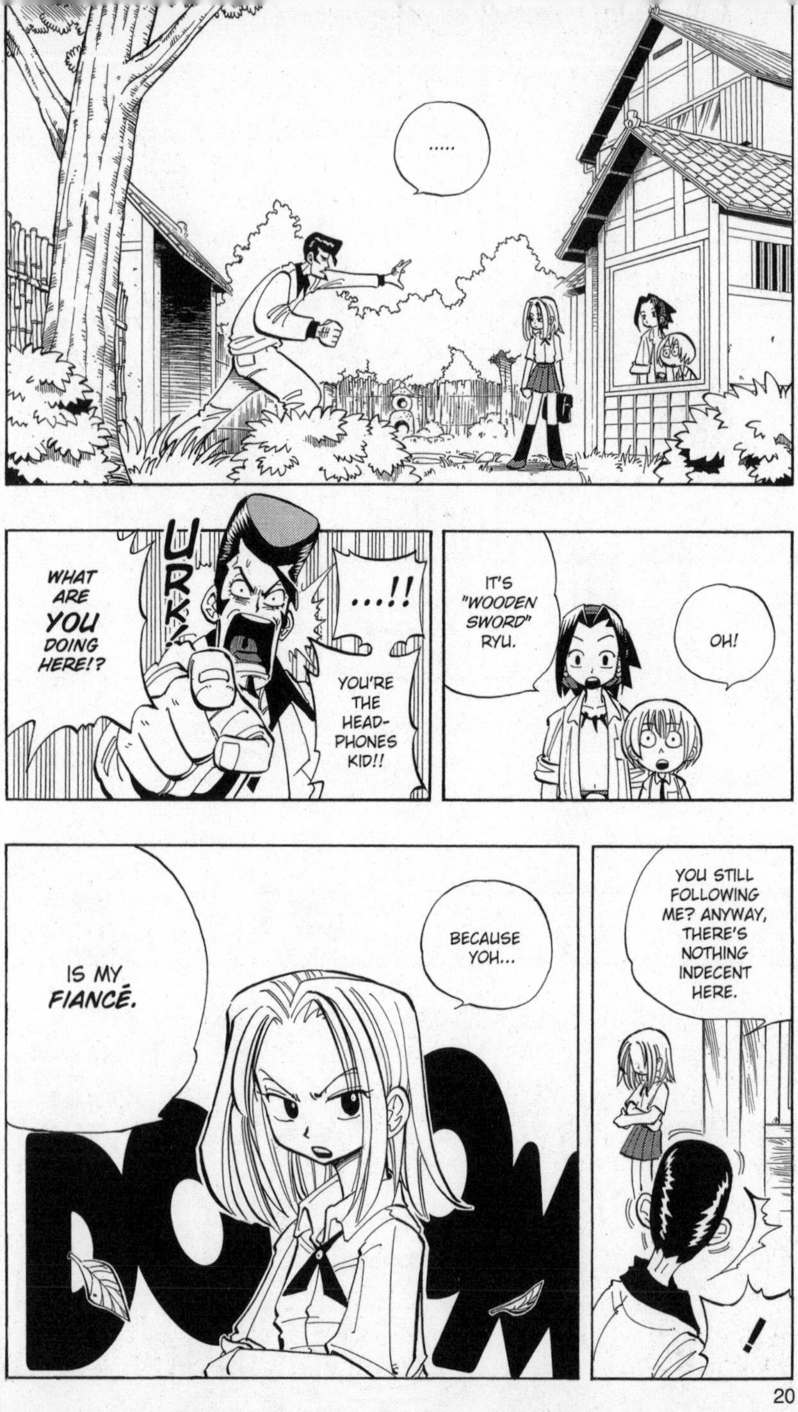
.....
IT'S "WOODEN SWORD" RYU.
OH!
URK!
...!!
YOU'RE THE HEAD-PHONES KID!!
WHAT ARE YOU DOING HERE!?
YOU STILL FOLLOWING ME? ANYWAY, THERE'S NOTHING INDECENT HERE.
!
BECAUSE YOH...
IS MY FIANCÉ.

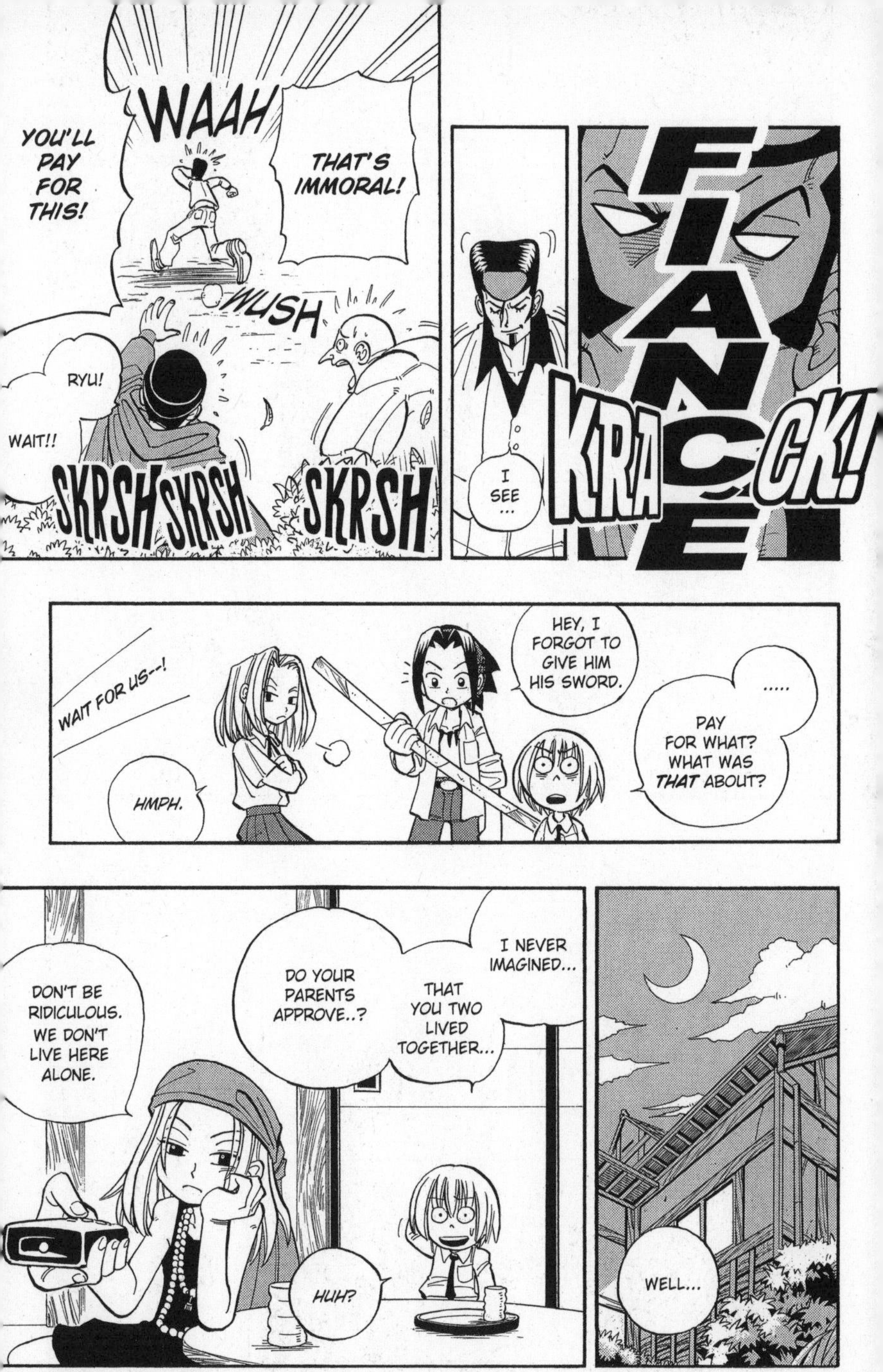
FIANCÉE
KRACK!
I SEE ...
THAT'S IMMORAL!
WAAH
YOU'LL PAY FOR THIS!
WUSH
RYU!
WAIT!!
SKRSH SKRSH
SKRSH
HEY, I FORGOT TO GIVE HIM HIS SWORD.
.....
PAY FOR WHAT? WHAT WAS *THAT* ABOUT?
WAIT FOR US--!
HMPH.
WELL...
I NEVER IMAGINED...
THAT YOU TWO LIVED TOGETHER...
DO YOUR PARENTS APPROVE..?
DON'T BE RIDICULOUS. WE DON'T LIVE HERE ALONE.
HUH?

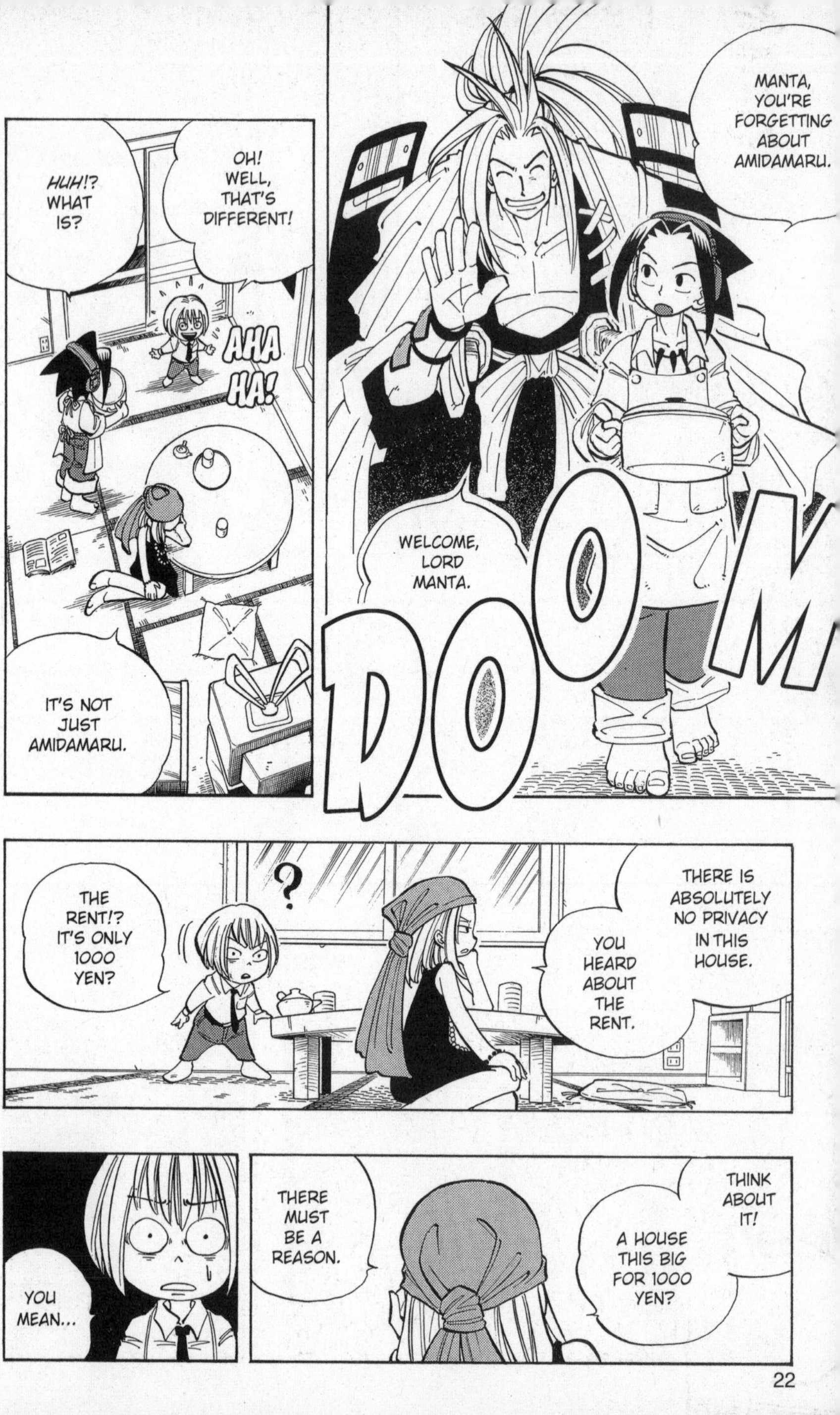
MANTA, YOU'RE FORGETTING ABOUT AMIDAMARU.
WELCOME, LORD MANTA.
DOOM
OH! WELL, THAT'S DIFFERENT!
AHA HA!
HUH!? WHAT IS?
IT'S NOT JUST AMIDAMARU.
THERE IS ABSOLUTELY NO PRIVACY IN THIS HOUSE.
YOU HEARD ABOUT THE RENT.
?
THE RENT!? IT'S ONLY 1000 YEN?
THINK ABOUT IT!
A HOUSE THIS BIG FOR 1000 YEN?
THERE MUST BE A REASON.
YOU MEAN...

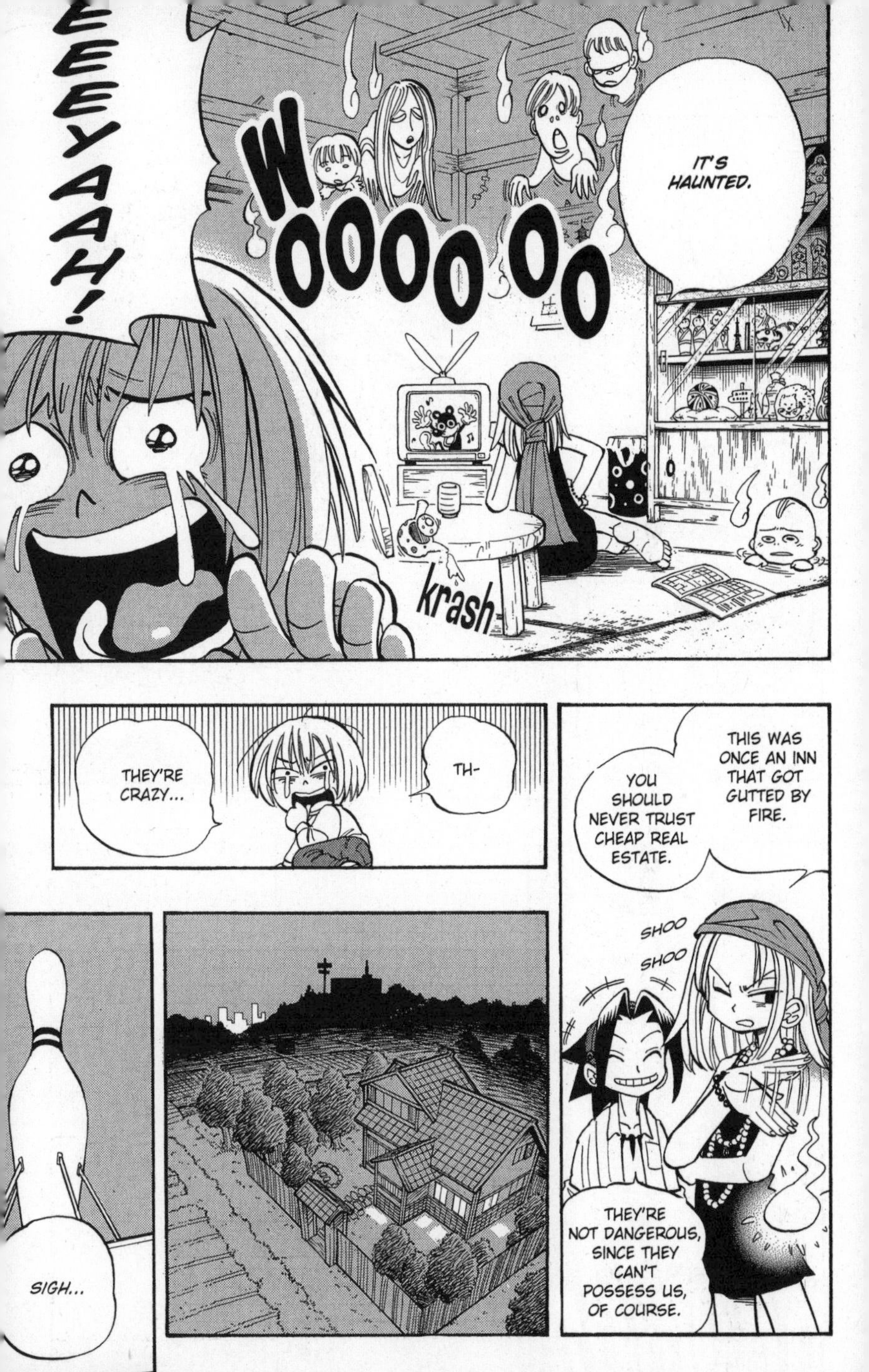
IT'S HAUNTED.
WOOOOOO
EEEEYAAAH!
krash
THIS WAS ONCE AN INN THAT GOT GUTTED BY FIRE.
YOU SHOULD NEVER TRUST CHEAP REAL ESTATE.
SHOO SHOO
THEY'RE NOT DANGEROUS, SINCE THEY CAN'T POSSESS US, OF COURSE.
TH-
THEY'RE CRAZY...
SIGH...

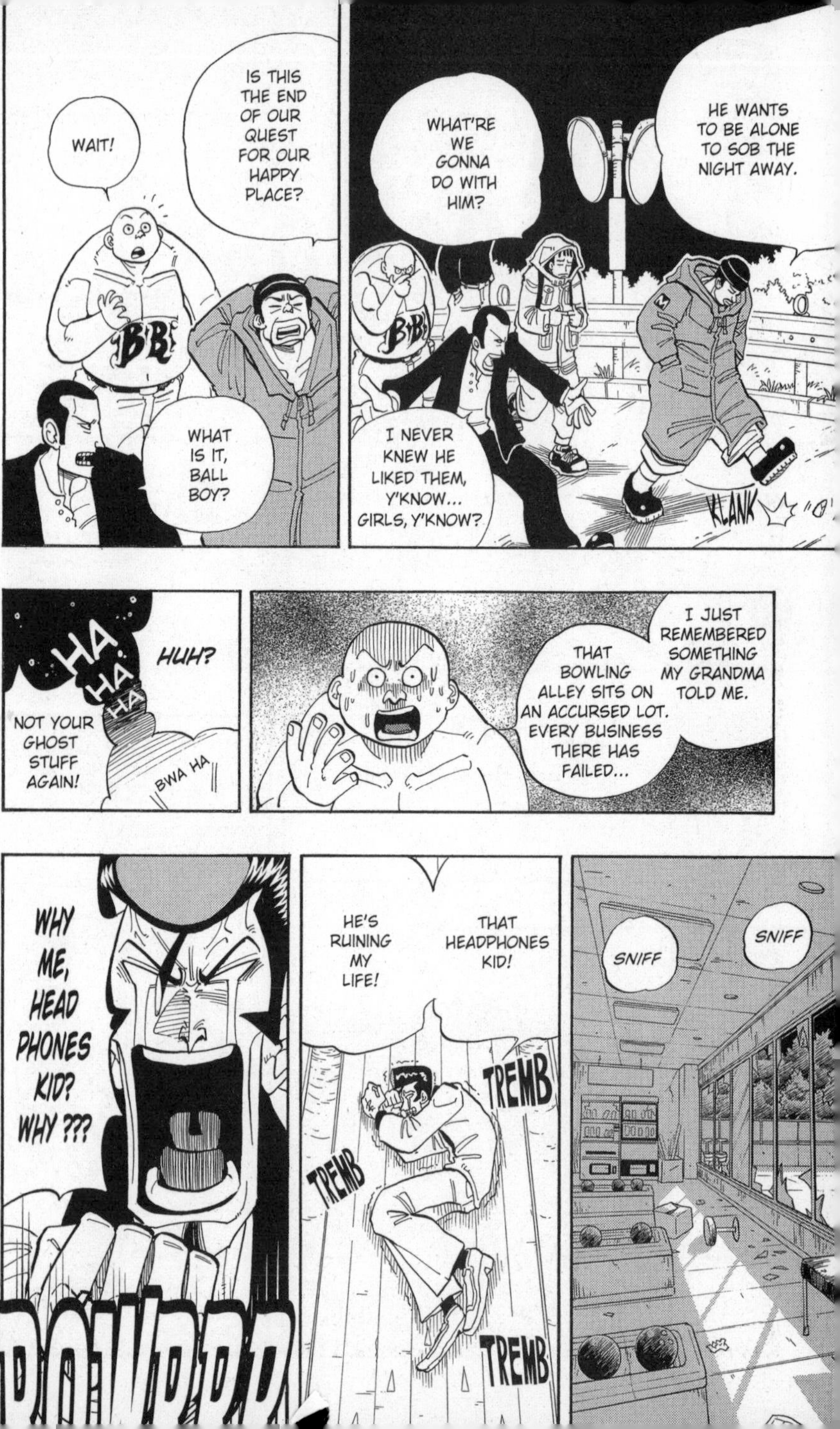
HE WANTS TO BE ALONE TO SOB THE NIGHT AWAY.
WHAT'RE WE GONNA DO WITH HIM?
I NEVER KNEW HE LIKED THEM, Y'KNOW... GIRLS, Y'KNOW?
KLANK
IS THIS THE END OF OUR QUEST FOR OUR HAPPY PLACE?
WAIT!
WHAT IS IT, BALL BOY?
I JUST REMEMBERED SOMETHING MY GRANDMA TOLD ME.
THAT BOWLING ALLEY SITS ON AN ACCURSED LOT. EVERY BUSINESS THERE HAS FAILED...
HUH?
HA HA HA
NOT YOUR GHOST STUFF AGAIN!
BWA HA
SNIFF
SNIFF
THAT HEADPHONES KID!
HE'S RUINING MY LIFE!
TREMB
TREMB
TREMB
WHY ME, HEAD PHONES KID? WHY ???

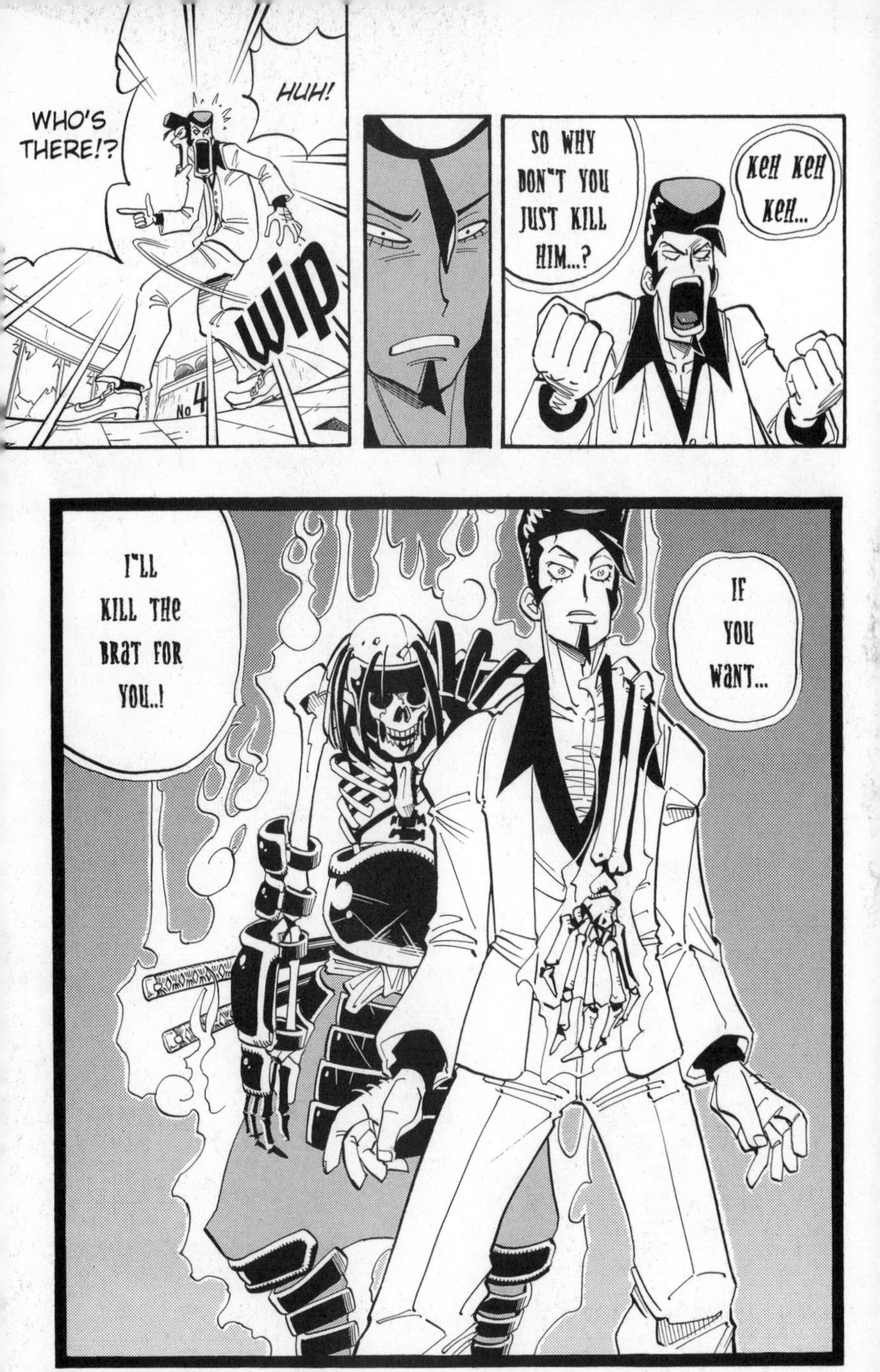
KEH KEH KEH...
SO WHY DON'T YOU JUST KILL HIM...?
HUH!
WHO'S THERE!?
WIP
No 4
IF YOU WANT...
I'LL KILL THE BRAT FOR YOU..!

SHAMAN KING CHARACTER FILE No.10

麻倉 葉
YOH ASAKURA
1989

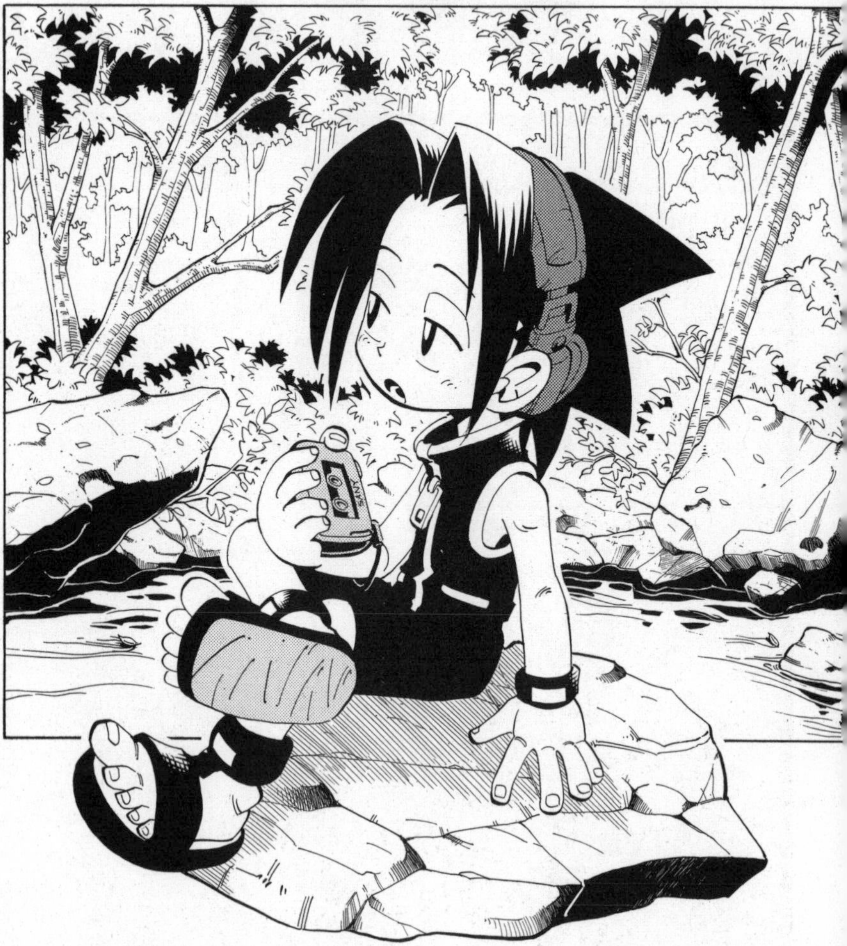
SANY

Reincarnation 19: The 600-Year Curse

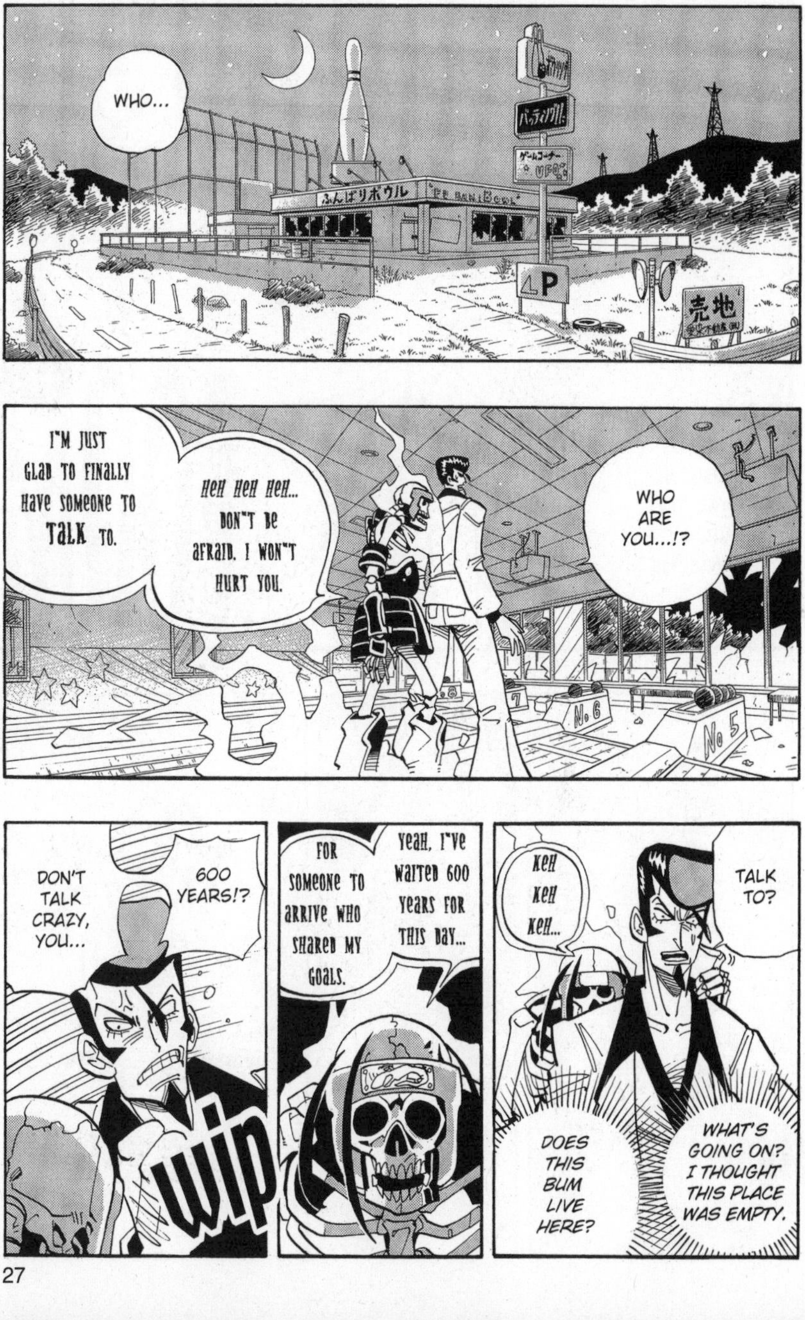
WHO...
ふんばりボウル
P
売地
WHO ARE YOU...!?
HEH HEH HEH... DON'T BE AFRAID. I WON'T HURT YOU.
I'M JUST GLAD TO FINALLY HAVE SOMEONE TO TALK TO.
No 5
No 6
TALK TO?
KEH KEH KEH...
WHAT'S GOING ON? I THOUGHT THIS PLACE WAS EMPTY.
DOES THIS BUM LIVE HERE?
YEAH, I'VE WAITED 600 YEARS FOR THIS DAY...
FOR SOMEONE TO ARRIVE WHO SHARED MY GOALS.
600 YEARS!?
DON'T TALK CRAZY, YOU...
wip

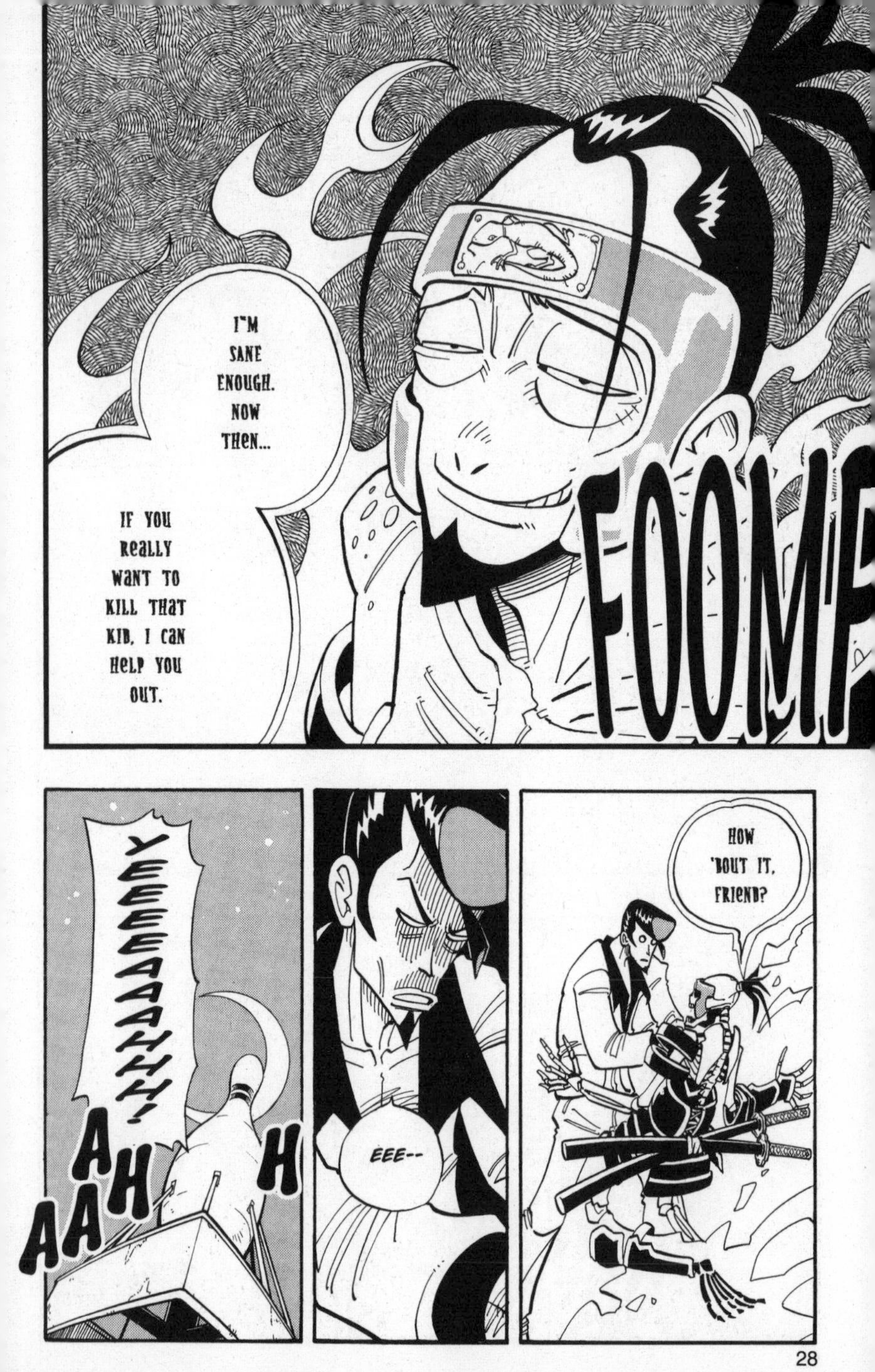
I'M SANE ENOUGH. NOW THEN...
IF YOU REALLY WANT TO KILL THAT KID, I CAN HELP YOU OUT.
FOOMP
HOW 'BOUT IT, FRIEND?
EEE--
YEEEEAAAHHH!
AAAHH

READ THIS WAY

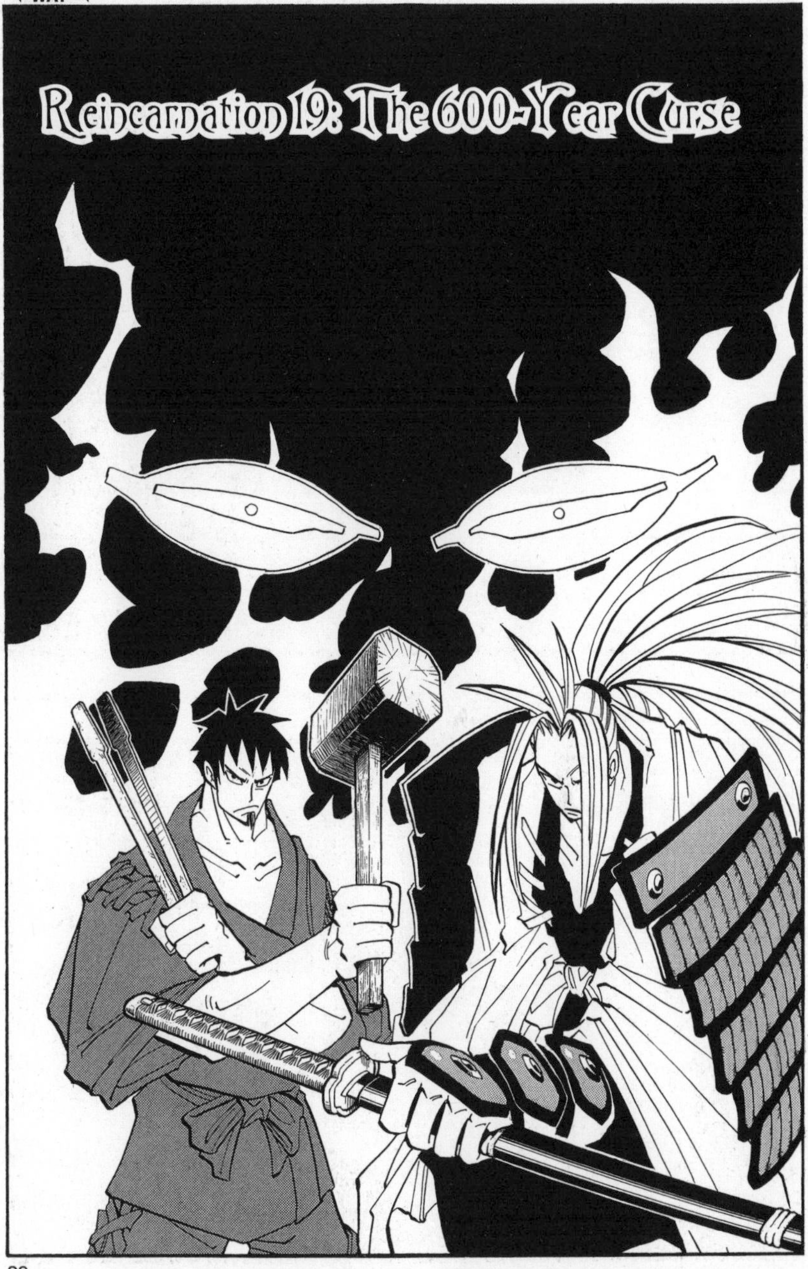
Reincarnation 19: The 600-Year Curse

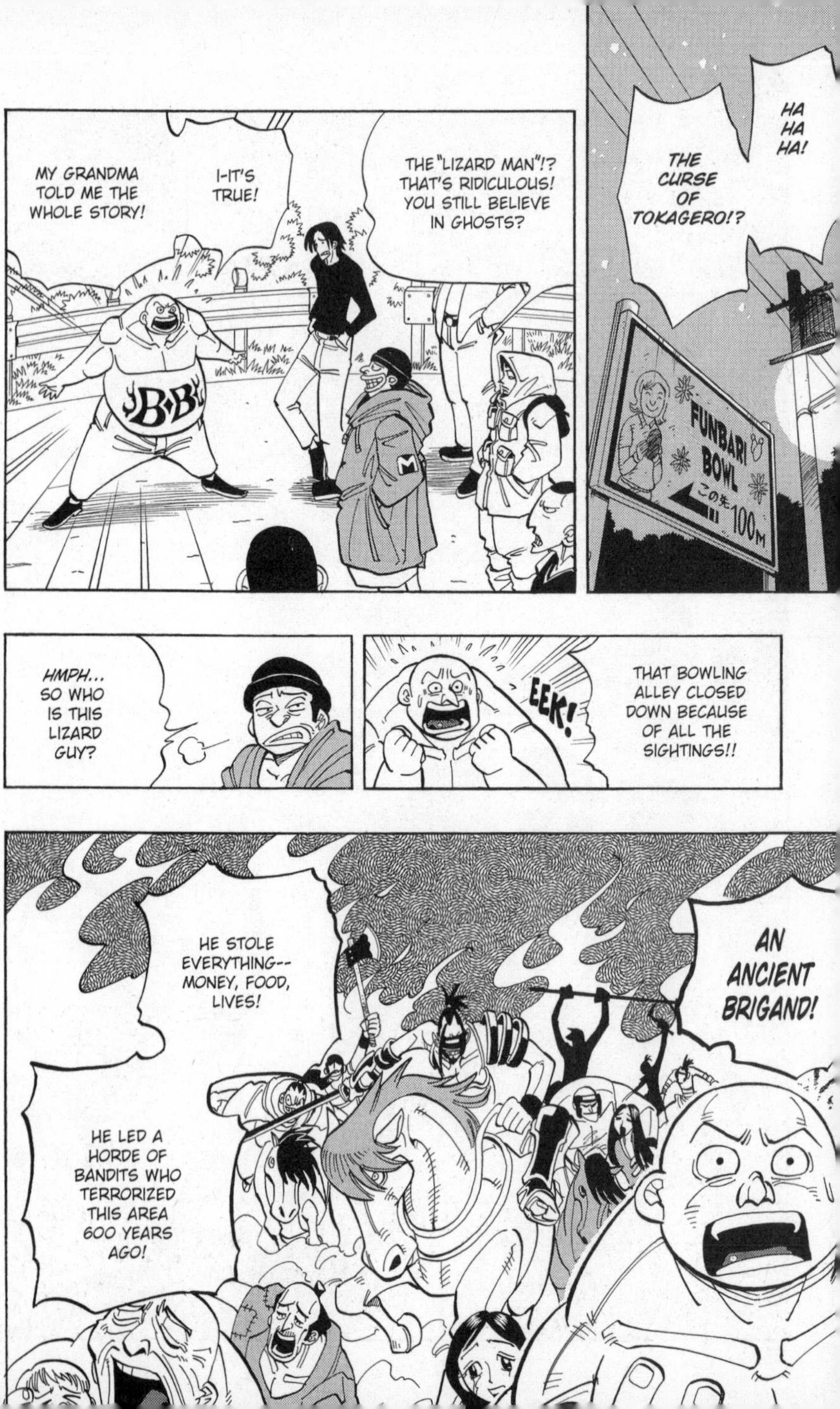
HA HA HA!
THE CURSE OF TOKAGERO!?
FUNBARI BOWL
この先 100M
THE "LIZARD MAN"!? THAT'S RIDICULOUS! YOU STILL BELIEVE IN GHOSTS?
I-IT'S TRUE!
MY GRANDMA TOLD ME THE WHOLE STORY!
B·B
EEK!
THAT BOWLING ALLEY CLOSED DOWN BECAUSE OF ALL THE SIGHTINGS!!
HMPH... SO WHO IS THIS LIZARD GUY?
AN ANCIENT BRIGAND!
HE STOLE EVERYTHING-- MONEY, FOOD, LIVES!
HE LED A HORDE OF BANDITS WHO TERRORIZED THIS AREA 600 YEARS AGO!

READ THIS WAY

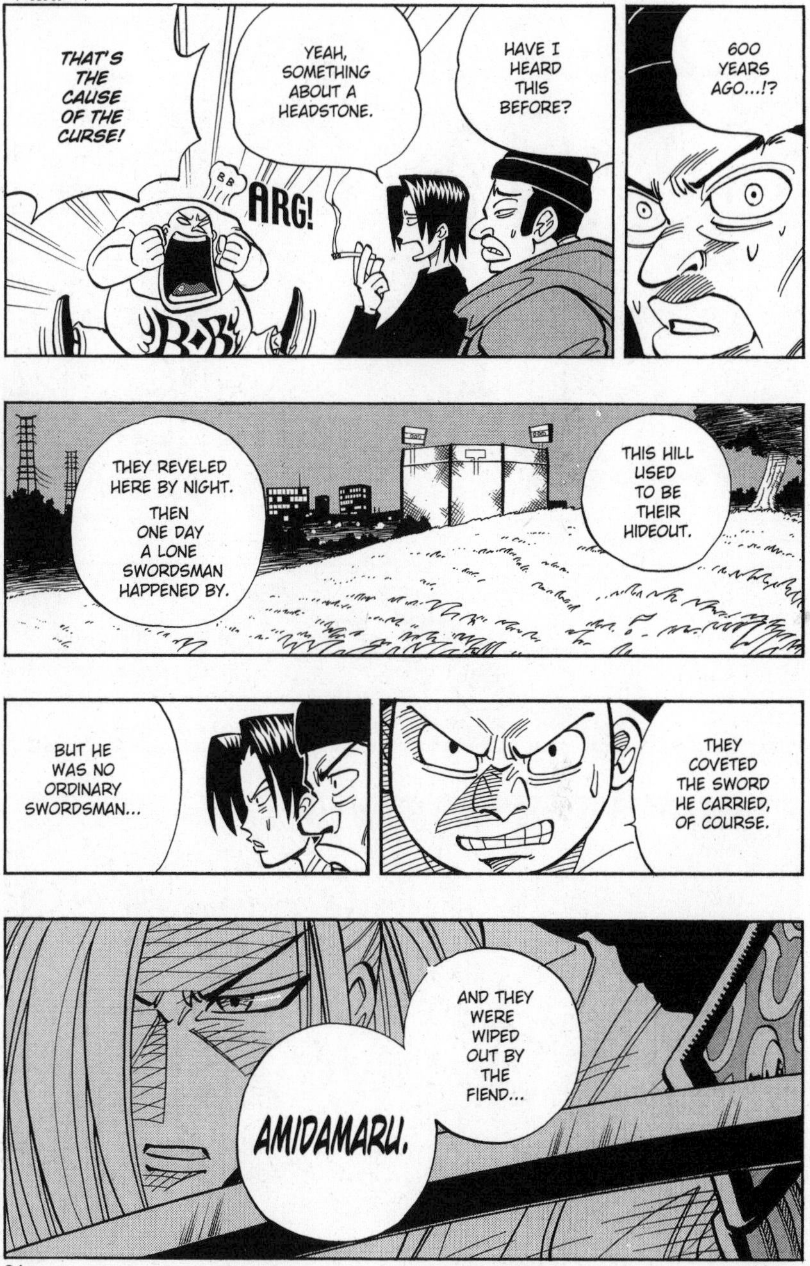
600 YEARS AGO...!?
HAVE I HEARD THIS BEFORE?
YEAH, SOMETHING ABOUT A HEADSTONE.
THAT'S THE CAUSE OF THE CURSE!
ARG!
THIS HILL USED TO BE THEIR HIDEOUT.
THEY REVELED HERE BY NIGHT.
THEN ONE DAY A LONE SWORDSMAN HAPPENED BY.
THEY COVETED THE SWORD HE CARRIED, OF COURSE.
BUT HE WAS NO ORDINARY SWORDSMAN...
AND THEY WERE WIPED OUT BY THE FIEND...
AMIDAMARU.

READ THIS WAY

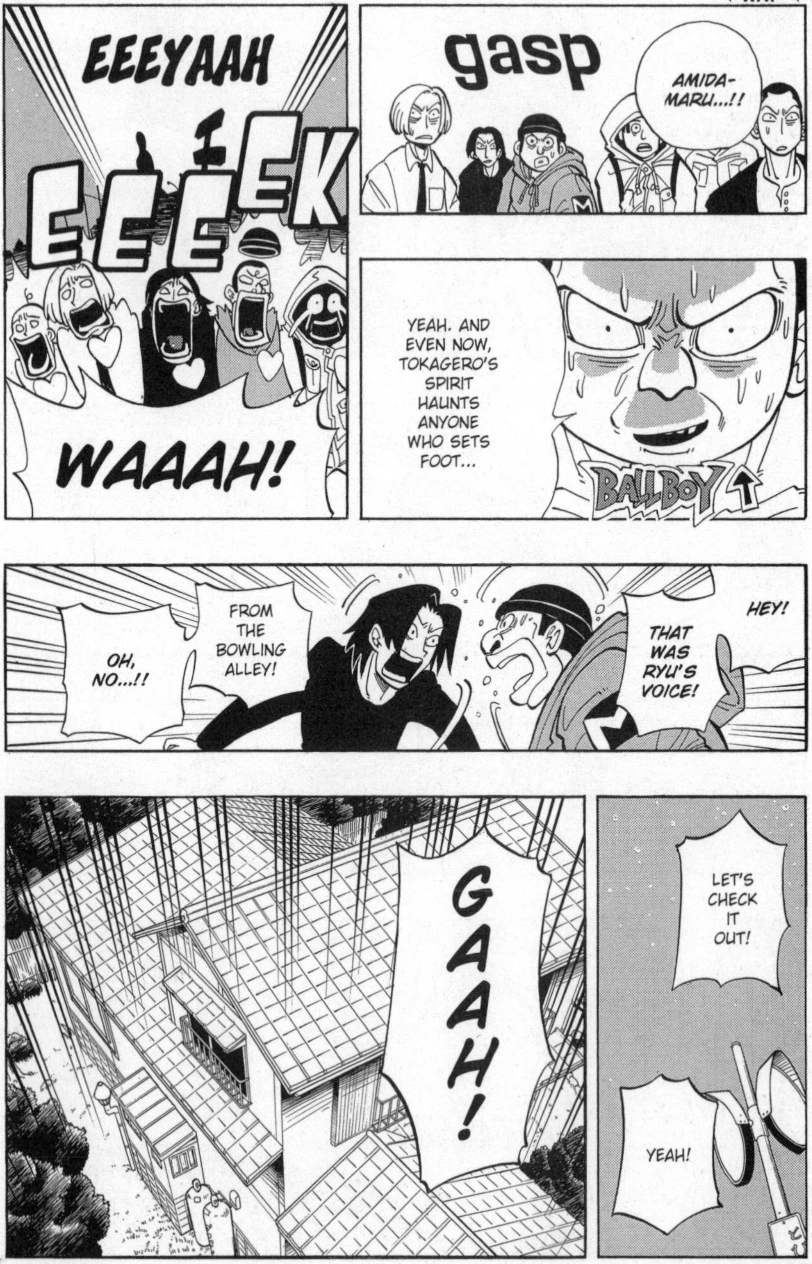
gasp
AMIDA-MARU...!!
YEAH. AND EVEN NOW, TOKAGERO'S SPIRIT HAUNTS ANYONE WHO SETS FOOT...
BALLBOY
EEEYAAH
EEEEK
WAAAH!
HEY!
THAT WAS RYU'S VOICE!
FROM THE BOWLING ALLEY!
OH, NO...!!
LET'S CHECK IT OUT!
YEAH!
GAAAH!

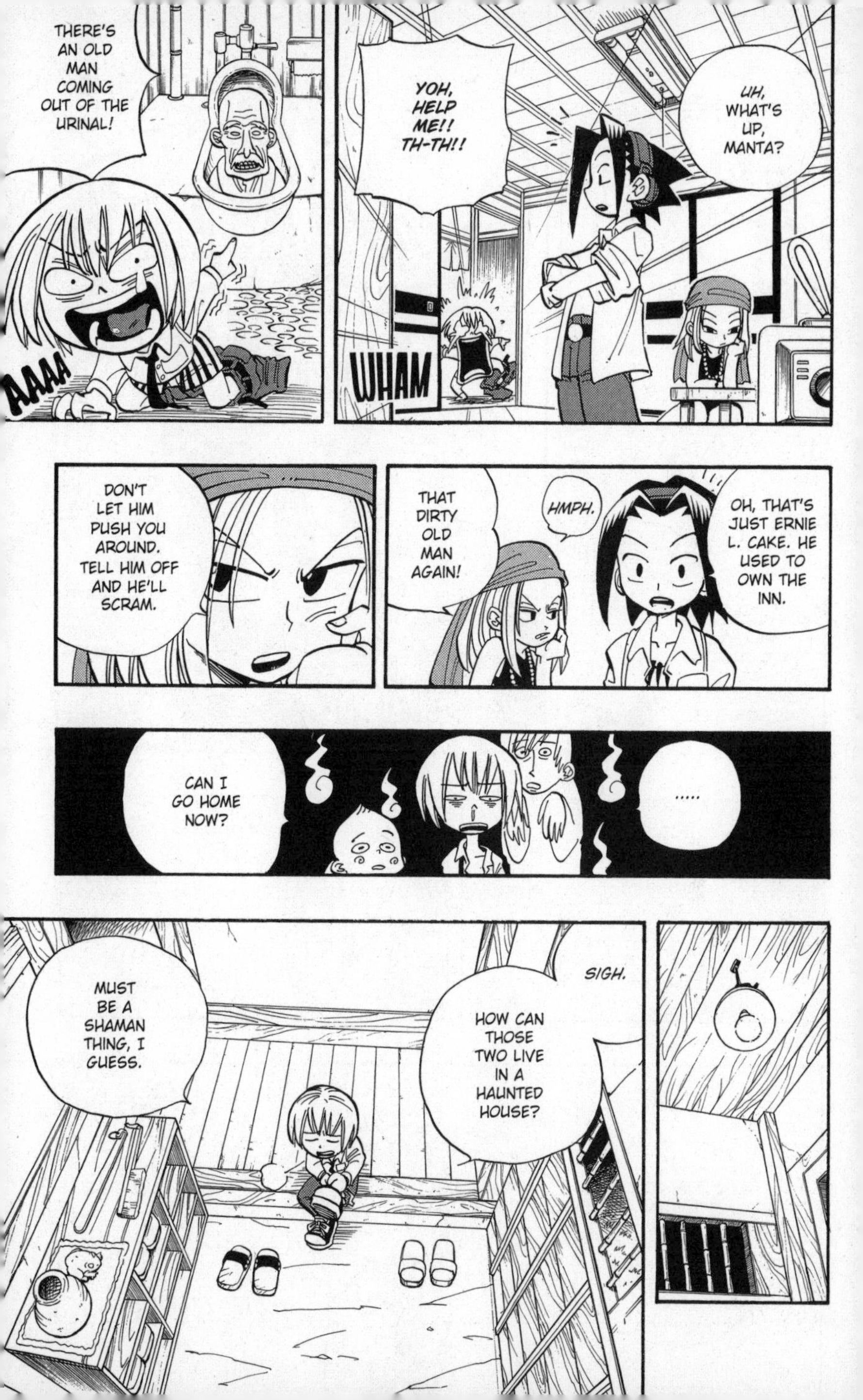

UH, WHAT'S UP, MANTA?
YOH, HELP ME!! TH-TH!!
WHAM
THERE'S AN OLD MAN COMING OUT OF THE URINAL!
AAAA
OH, THAT'S JUST ERNIE L. CAKE. HE USED TO OWN THE INN.
HMPH.
THAT DIRTY OLD MAN AGAIN!
DON'T LET HIM PUSH YOU AROUND. TELL HIM OFF AND HE'LL SCRAM.
.....
CAN I GO HOME NOW?
SIGH.
HOW CAN THOSE TWO LIVE IN A HAUNTED HOUSE?
MUST BE A SHAMAN THING, I GUESS.

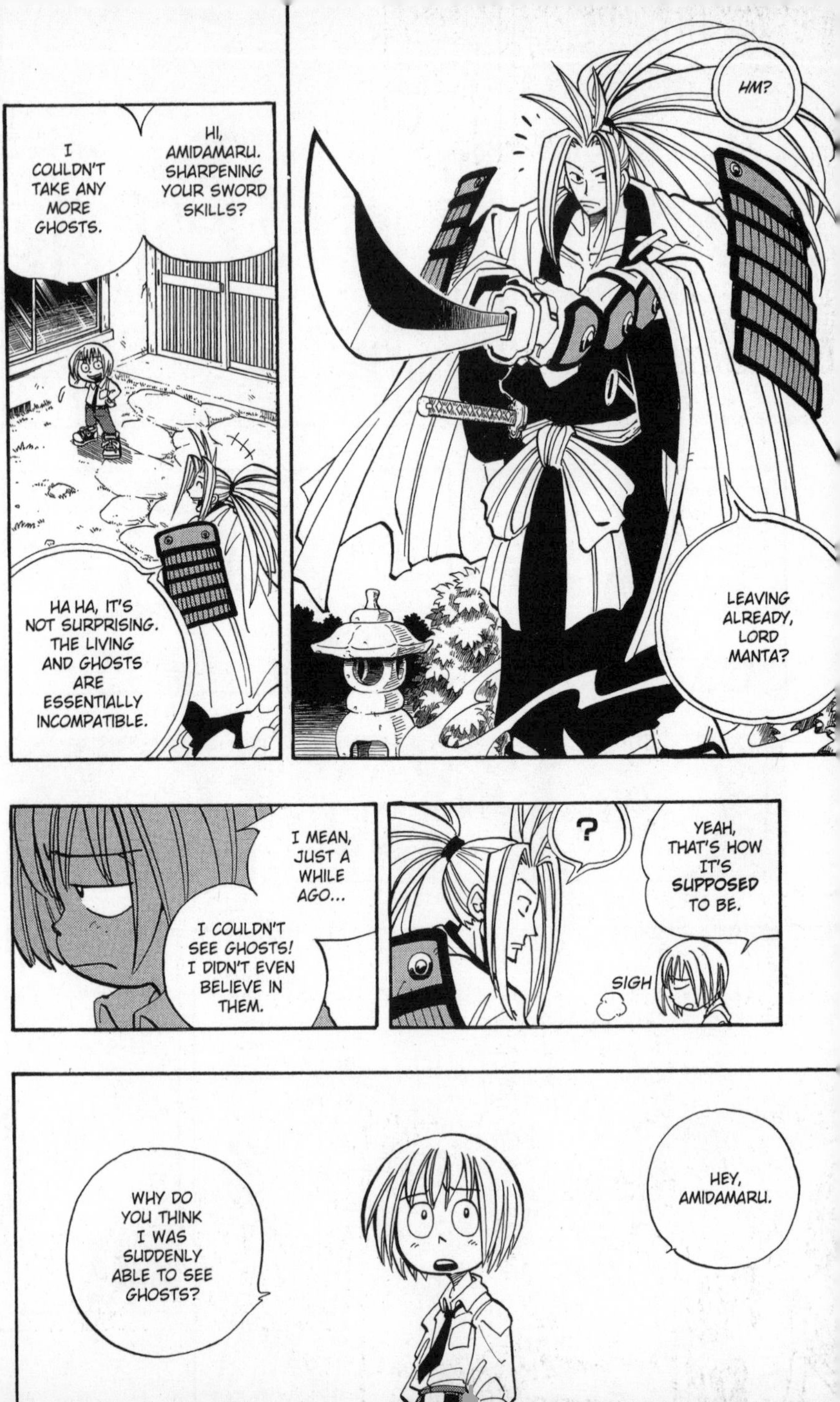
HM?
LEAVING ALREADY, LORD MANTA?
HI, AMIDAMARU. SHARPENING YOUR SWORD SKILLS?
I COULDN'T TAKE ANY MORE GHOSTS.
HA HA, IT'S NOT SURPRISING. THE LIVING AND GHOSTS ARE ESSENTIALLY INCOMPATIBLE.
YEAH, THAT'S HOW IT'S SUPPOSED TO BE.
?
SIGH
I MEAN, JUST A WHILE AGO...
I COULDN'T SEE GHOSTS! I DIDN'T EVEN BELIEVE IN THEM.
HEY, AMIDAMARU.
WHY DO YOU THINK I WAS SUDDENLY ABLE TO SEE GHOSTS?

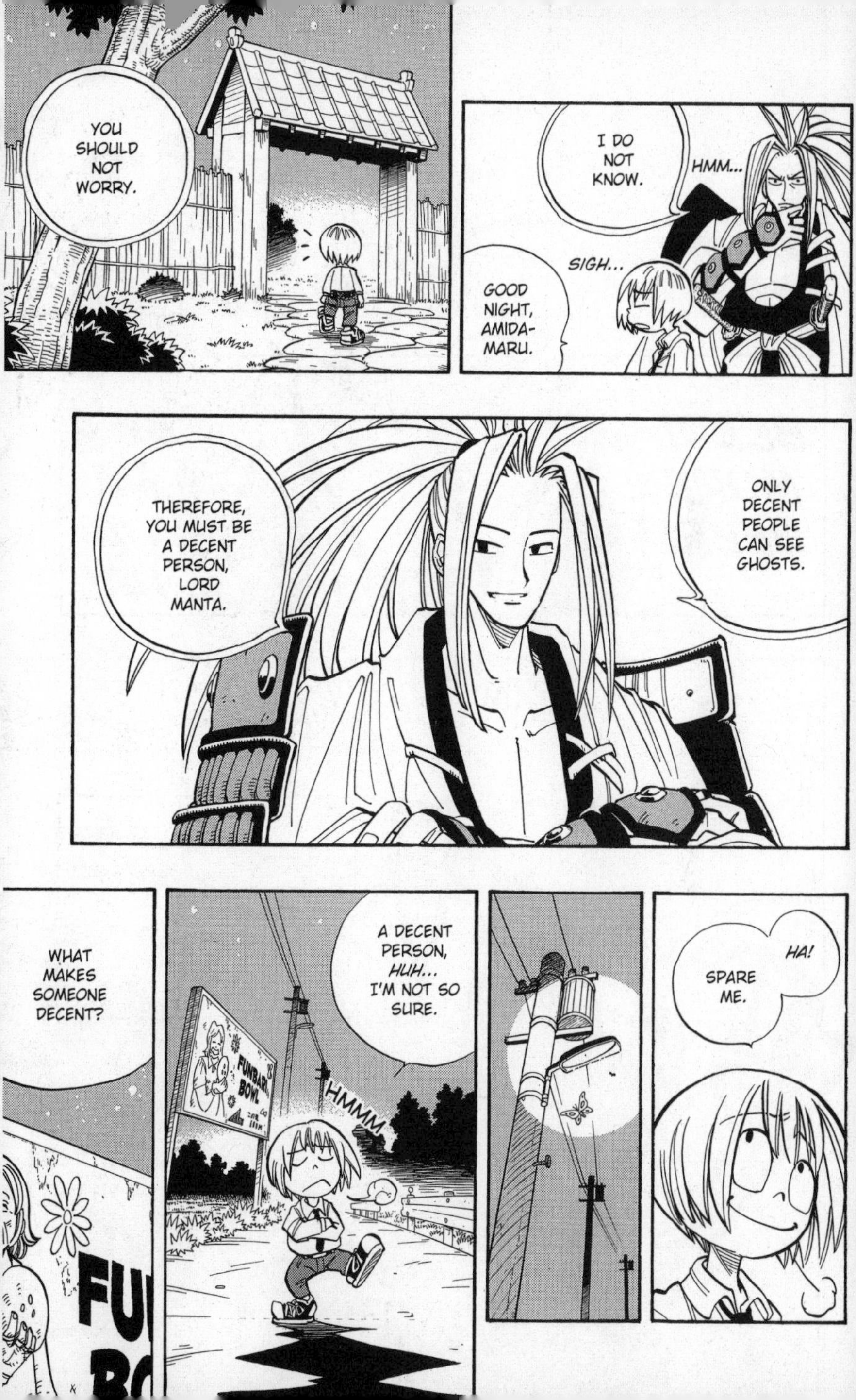
HMM...
I DO NOT KNOW.
SIGH...
GOOD NIGHT, AMIDA-MARU.
YOU SHOULD NOT WORRY.
ONLY DECENT PEOPLE CAN SEE GHOSTS.
THEREFORE, YOU MUST BE A DECENT PERSON, LORD MANTA.
HA!
SPARE ME.
A DECENT PERSON, *HUH*... I'M NOT SO SURE.
HMMM
FUNBARI BOWL
WHAT MAKES SOMEONE DECENT?

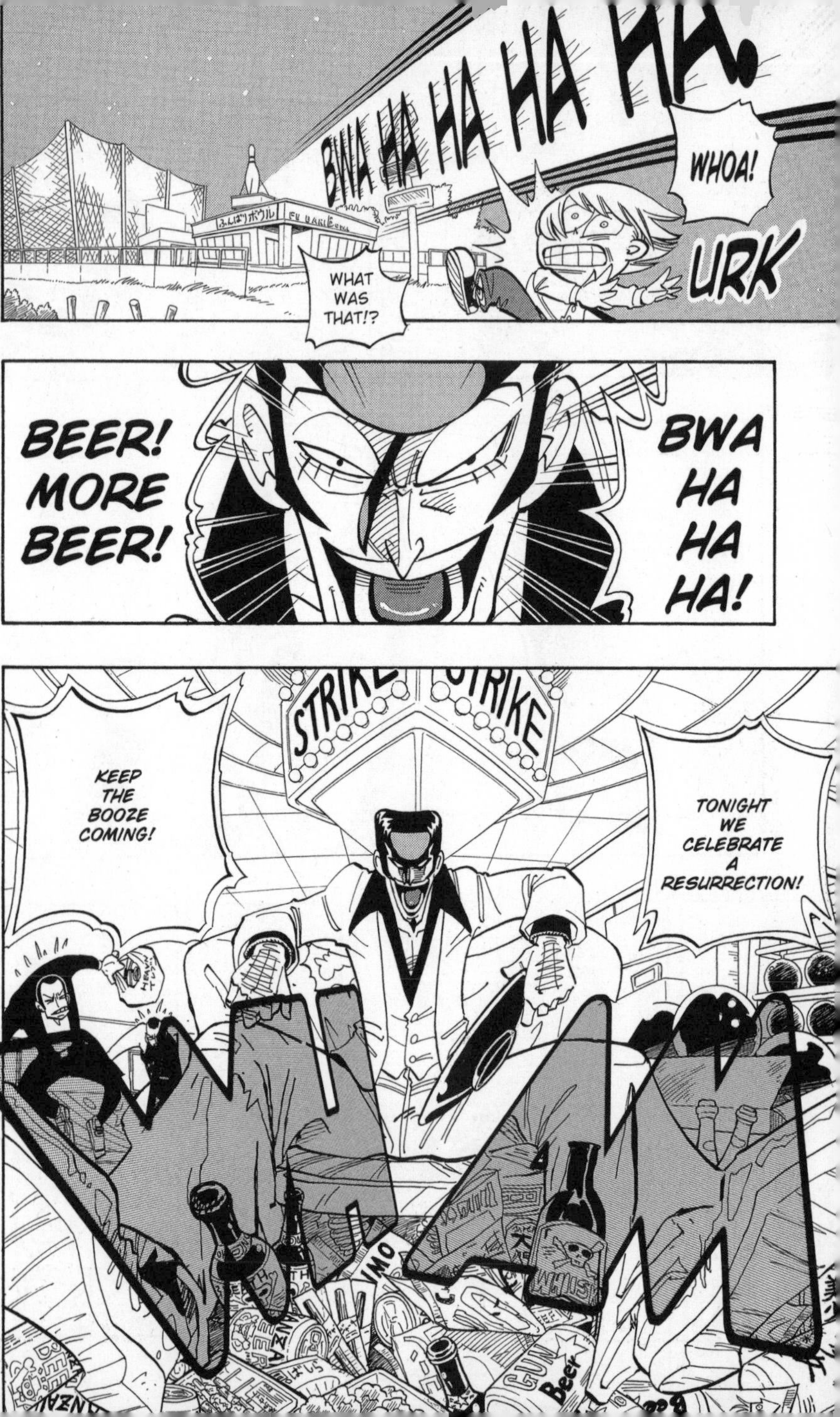
BWA HA HA HA HA.
WHOA!
URK
WHAT WAS THAT!?
BWA HA HA HA!
BEER! MORE BEER!
STRIKE
STRIKE
TONIGHT WE CELEBRATE A RESURRECTION!
KEEP THE BOOZE COMING!

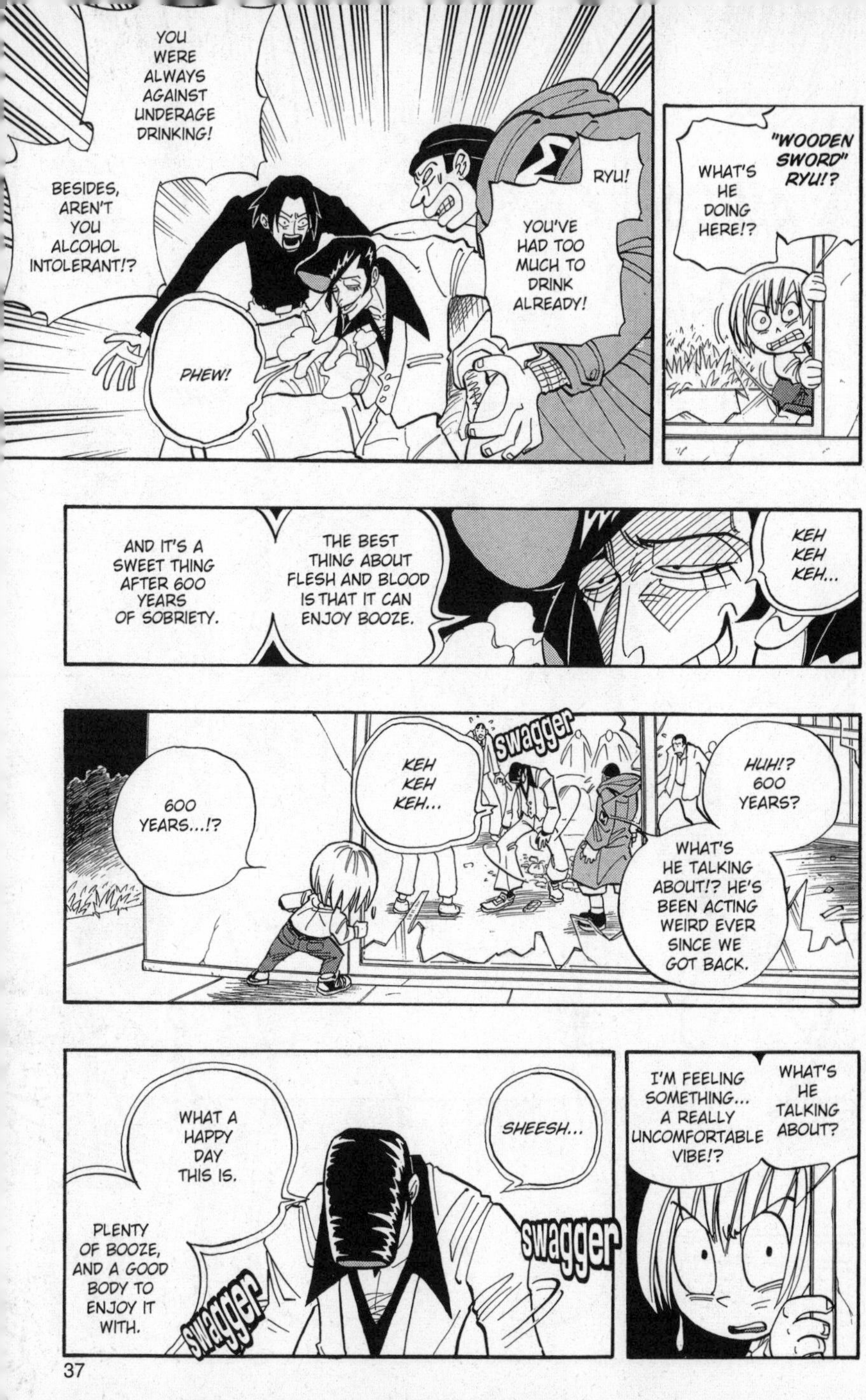
"WOODEN SWORD" RYU!?
WHAT'S HE DOING HERE!?
RYU!
YOU'VE HAD TOO MUCH TO DRINK ALREADY!
YOU WERE ALWAYS AGAINST UNDERAGE DRINKING!
BESIDES, AREN'T YOU ALCOHOL INTOLERANT!?
PHEW!
KEH KEH KEH...
THE BEST THING ABOUT FLESH AND BLOOD IS THAT IT CAN ENJOY BOOZE.
AND IT'S A SWEET THING AFTER 600 YEARS OF SOBRIETY.
HUH!? 600 YEARS?
WHAT'S HE TALKING ABOUT!? HE'S BEEN ACTING WEIRD EVER SINCE WE GOT BACK.
swagger
KEH KEH KEH...
600 YEARS...!?
WHAT'S HE TALKING ABOUT?
I'M FEELING SOMETHING... A REALLY UNCOMFORTABLE VIBE!?
SHEESH...
swagger
WHAT A HAPPY DAY THIS IS.
PLENTY OF BOOZE, AND A GOOD BODY TO ENJOY IT WITH.
swagger

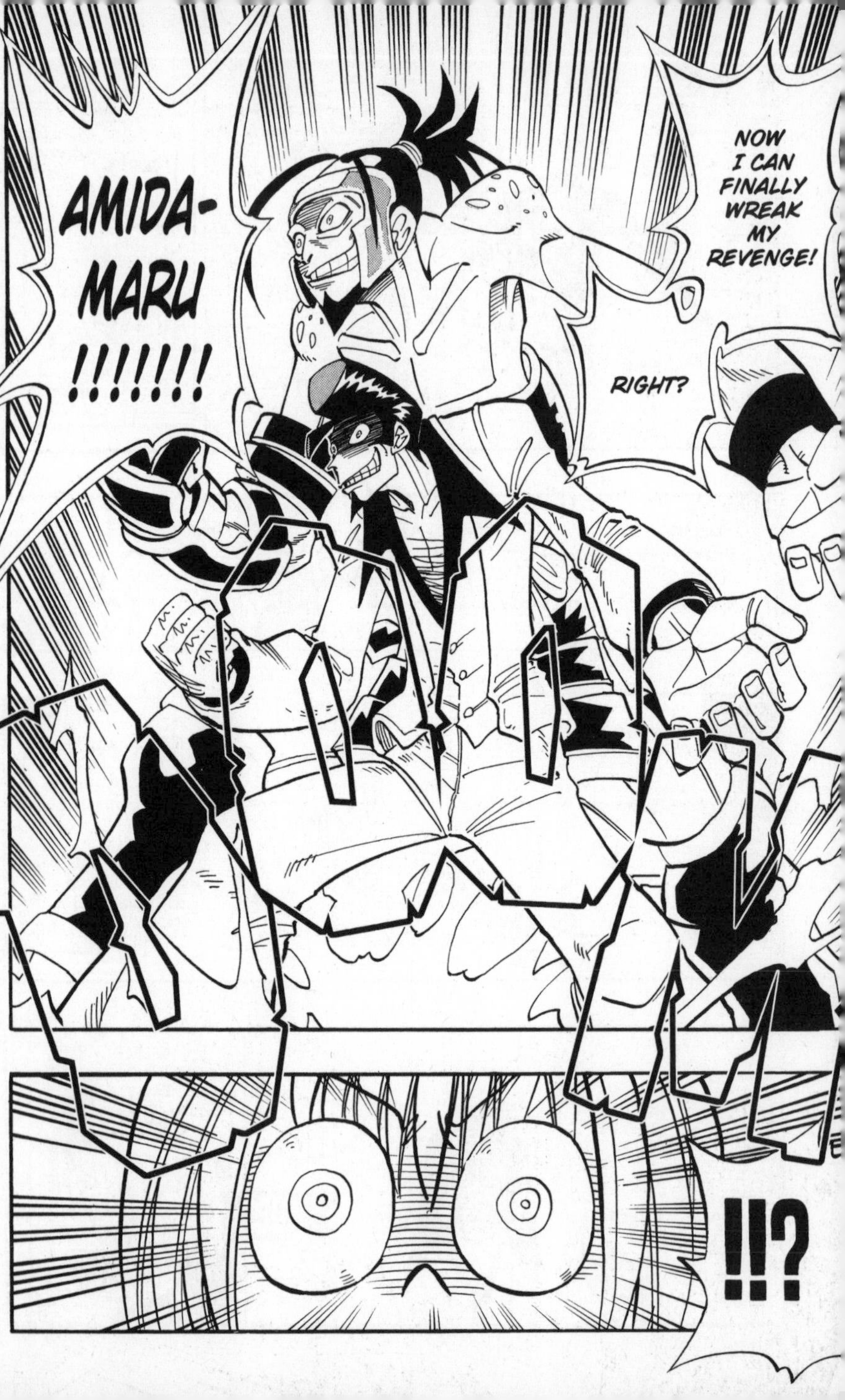
NOW I CAN FINALLY WREAK MY REVENGE!
RIGHT?
AMIDA-MARU !!!!!!!
!!?

READ THIS WAY

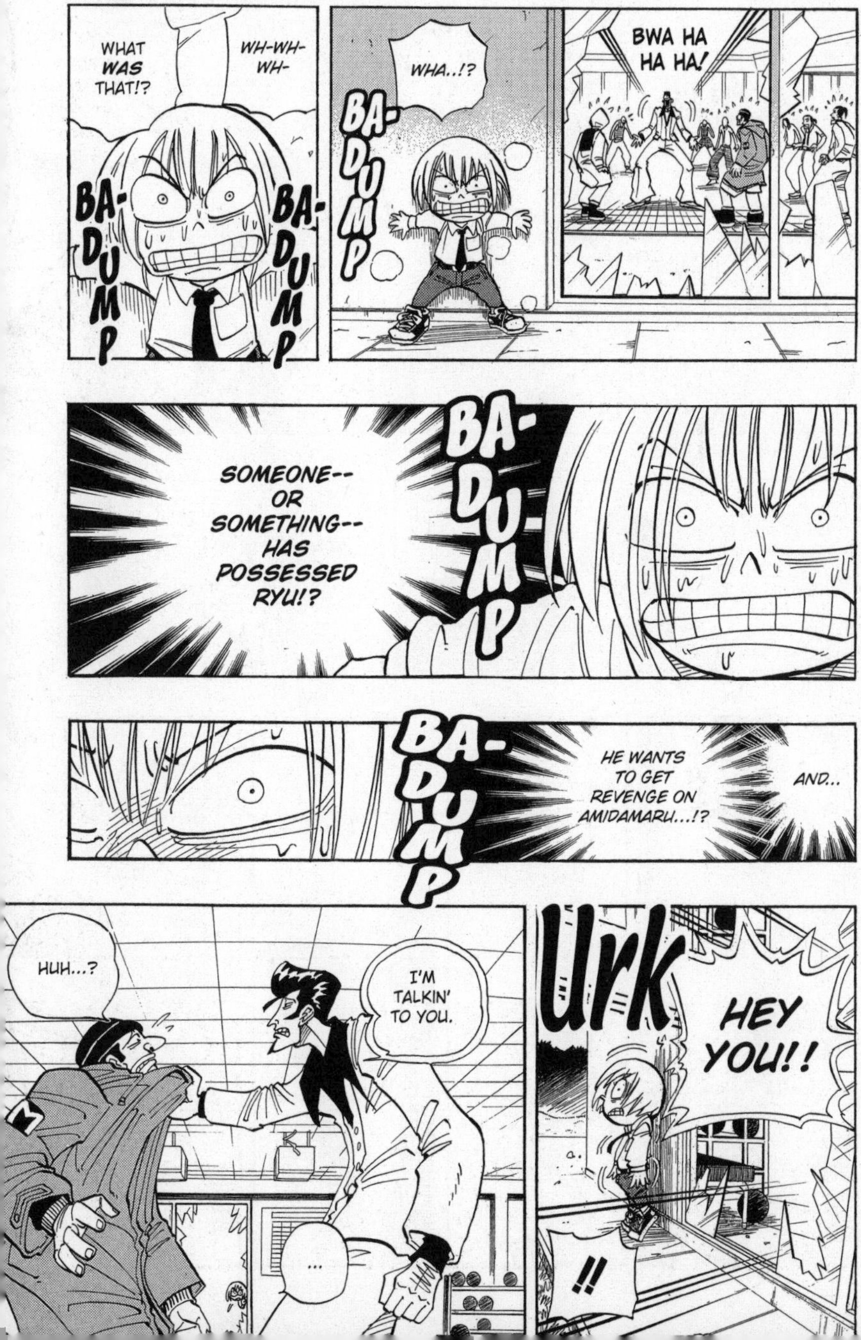

BWA HA HA HA!
WHA..!?
BA-DUMP
WH-WH-WH-
WHAT WAS THAT!?
BA-DUMP
BA-DUMP
BA-DUMP
SOMEONE-- OR SOMETHING-- HAS POSSESSED RYU!?
AND...
HE WANTS TO GET REVENGE ON AMIDAMARU...!?
BA-DUMP
Urk
HEY YOU!!
!!
I'M TALKIN' TO YOU.
HUH...?
...

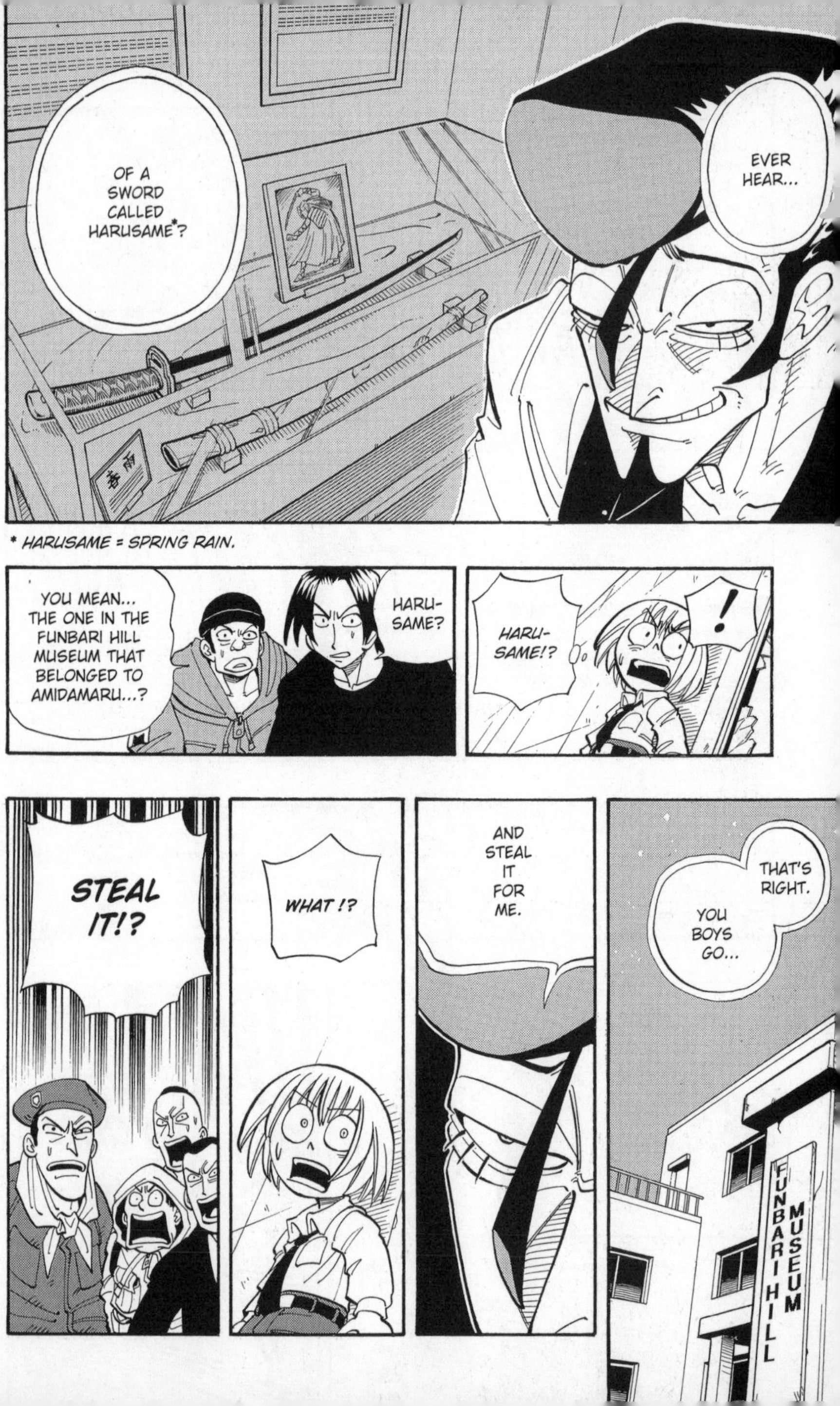
EVER HEAR...
OF A SWORD CALLED HARUSAME*?
春雨
HARU-SAME!?
!
HARU-SAME?
YOU MEAN... THE ONE IN THE FUNBARI HILL MUSEUM THAT BELONGED TO AMIDAMARU...?
THAT'S RIGHT.
YOU BOYS GO...
FUNBARI HILL MUSEUM
AND STEAL IT FOR ME.
WHAT !?
STEAL IT!?

* HARUSAME = SPRING RAIN.

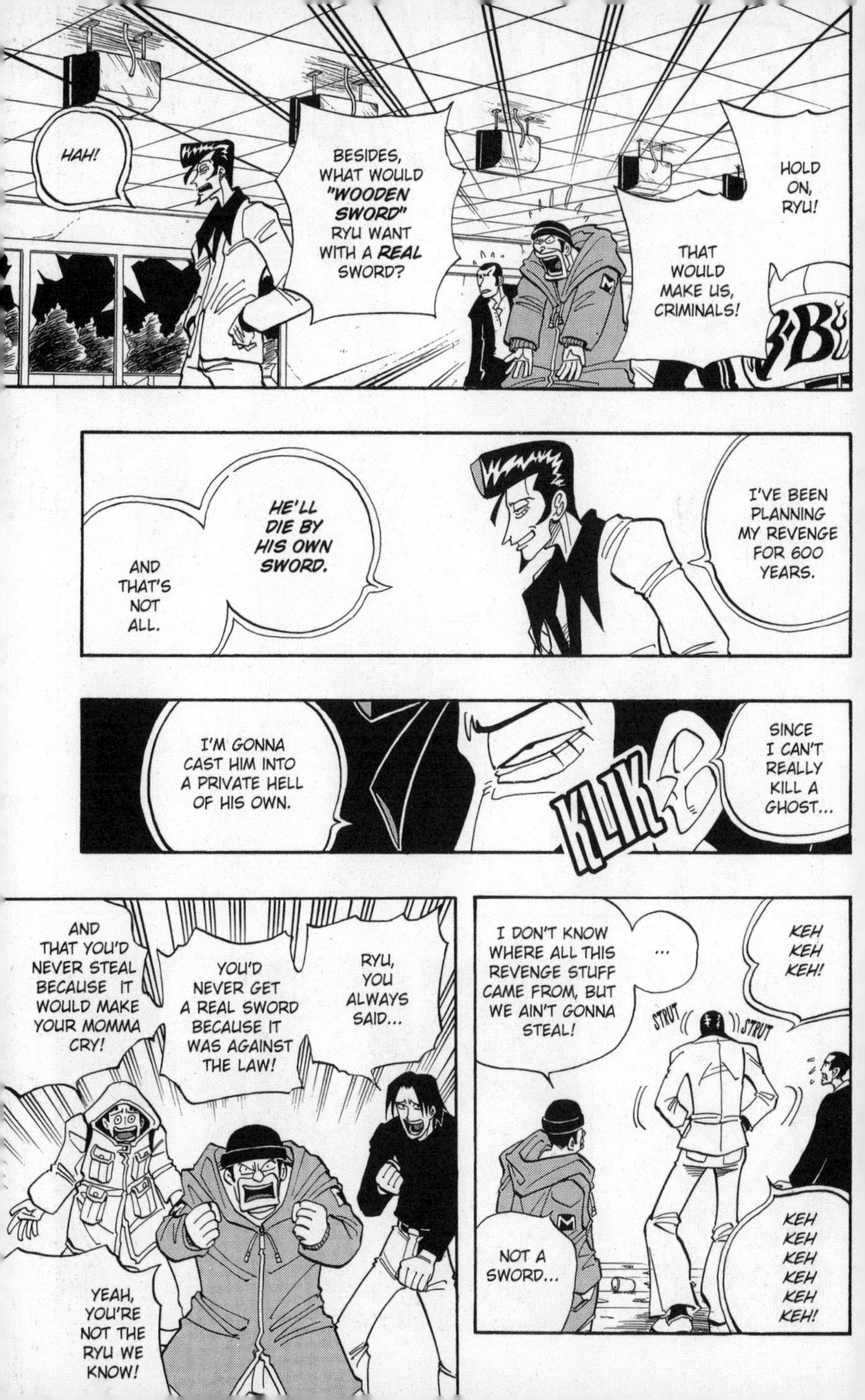
HOLD ON, RYU!
THAT WOULD MAKE US, CRIMINALS!
BESIDES, WHAT WOULD "WOODEN SWORD" RYU WANT WITH A REAL SWORD?
HAH!
I'VE BEEN PLANNING MY REVENGE FOR 600 YEARS.
HE'LL DIE BY HIS OWN SWORD.
AND THAT'S NOT ALL.
SINCE I CAN'T REALLY KILL A GHOST...
KLIK
I'M GONNA CAST HIM INTO A PRIVATE HELL OF HIS OWN.
KEH KEH KEH!
...
I DON'T KNOW WHERE ALL THIS REVENGE STUFF CAME FROM, BUT WE AIN'T GONNA STEAL!
STRUT STRUT
KEH KEH KEH KEH KEH KEH!
NOT A SWORD...
RYU, YOU ALWAYS SAID...
YOU'D NEVER GET A REAL SWORD BECAUSE IT WAS AGAINST THE LAW!
AND THAT YOU'D NEVER STEAL BECAUSE IT WOULD MAKE YOUR MOMMA CRY!
YEAH, YOU'RE NOT THE RYU WE KNOW!

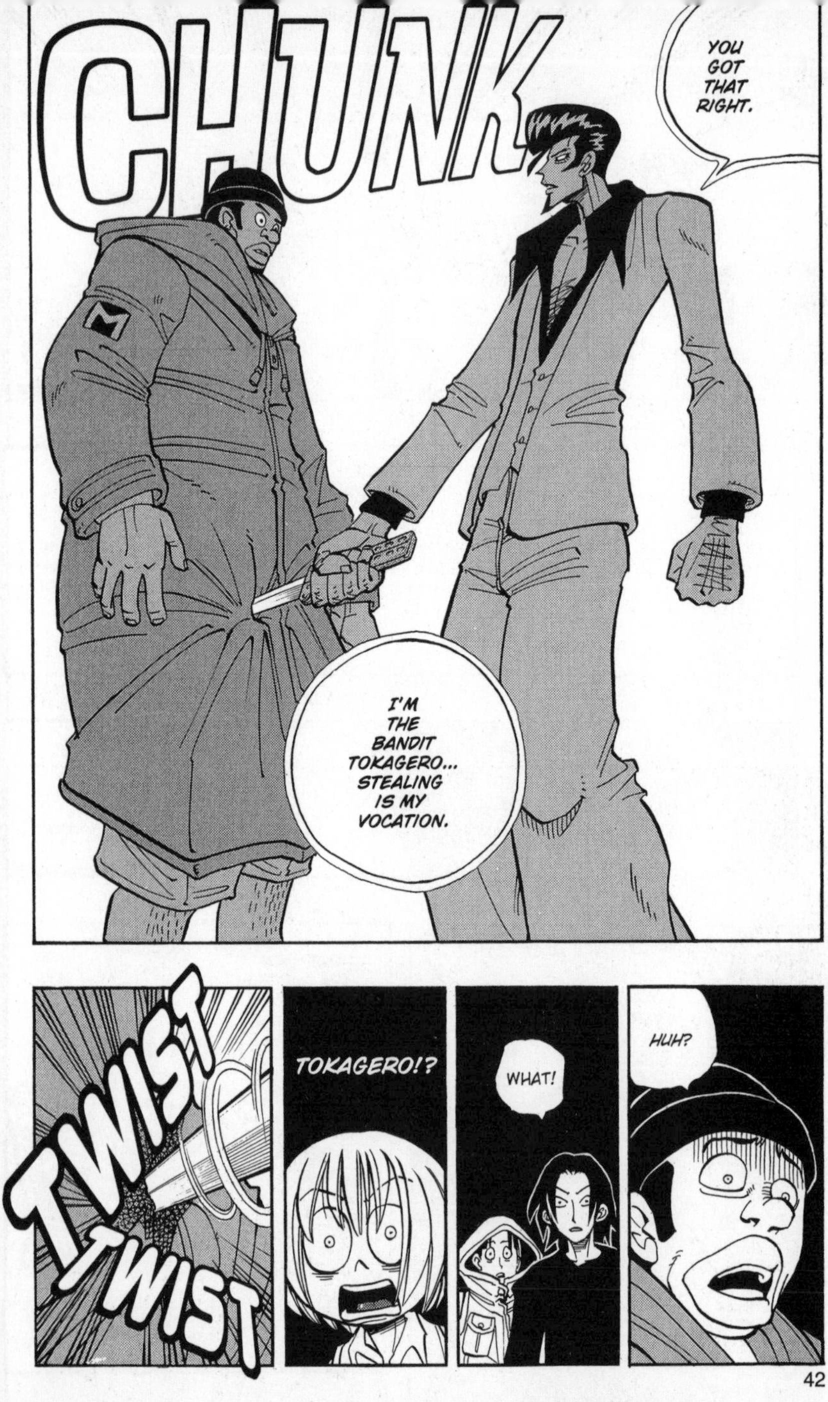
CHUNK
YOU GOT THAT RIGHT.
I'M THE BANDIT TOKAGERO... STEALING IS MY VOCATION.
HUH?
WHAT!
TOKAGERO!?
TWIST TWIST

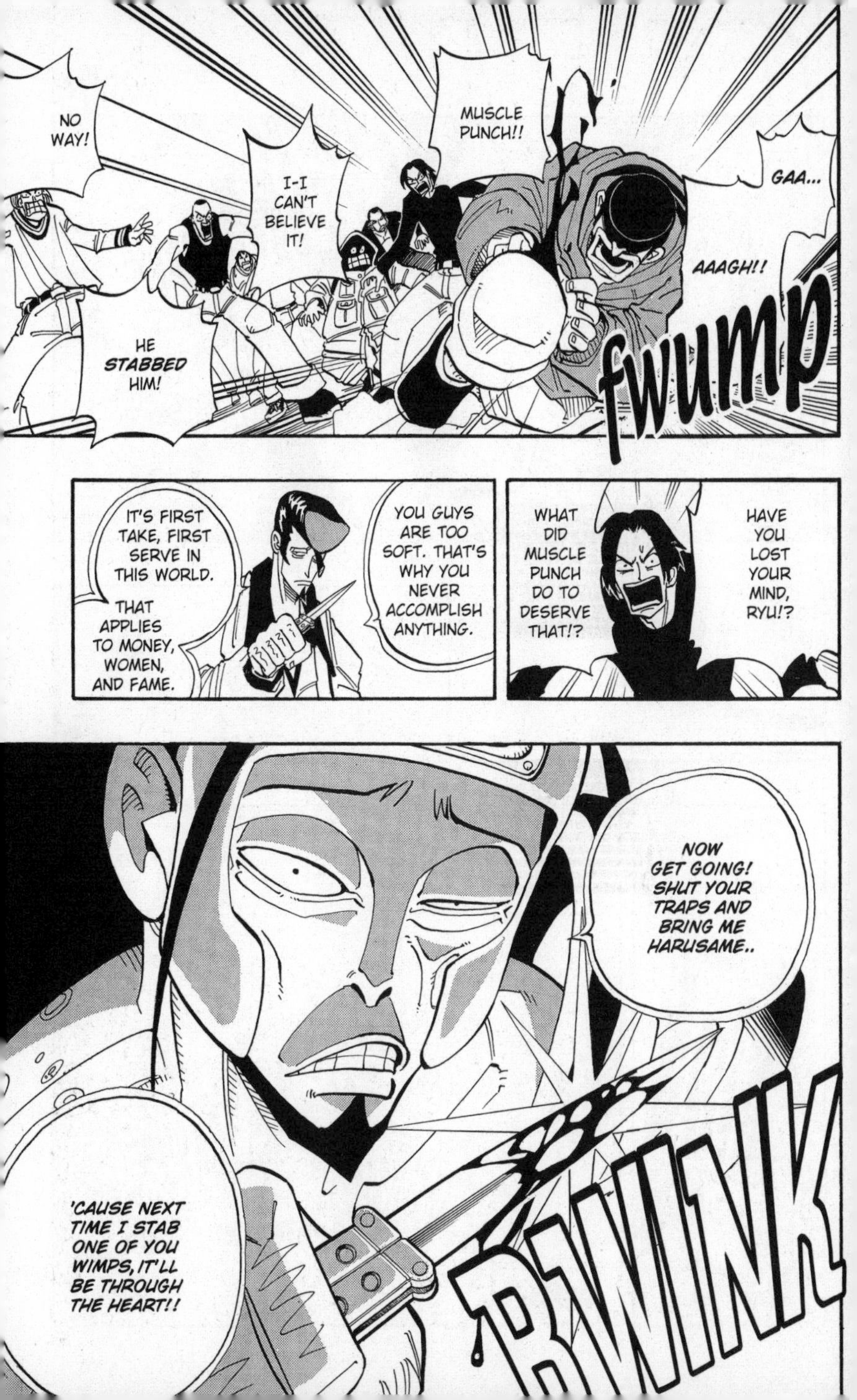
GAA...
AAAGH!!
fwump
MUSCLE PUNCH!!
I-I CAN'T BELIEVE IT!
NO WAY!
HE STABBED HIM!
HAVE YOU LOST YOUR MIND, RYU!?
WHAT DID MUSCLE PUNCH DO TO DESERVE THAT!?
YOU GUYS ARE TOO SOFT. THAT'S WHY YOU NEVER ACCOMPLISH ANYTHING.
IT'S FIRST TAKE, FIRST SERVE IN THIS WORLD.
THAT APPLIES TO MONEY, WOMEN, AND FAME.
NOW GET GOING! SHUT YOUR TRAPS AND BRING ME HARUSAME..
'CAUSE NEXT TIME I STAB ONE OF YOU WIMPS, IT'LL BE THROUGH THE HEART!!

READ THIS WAY

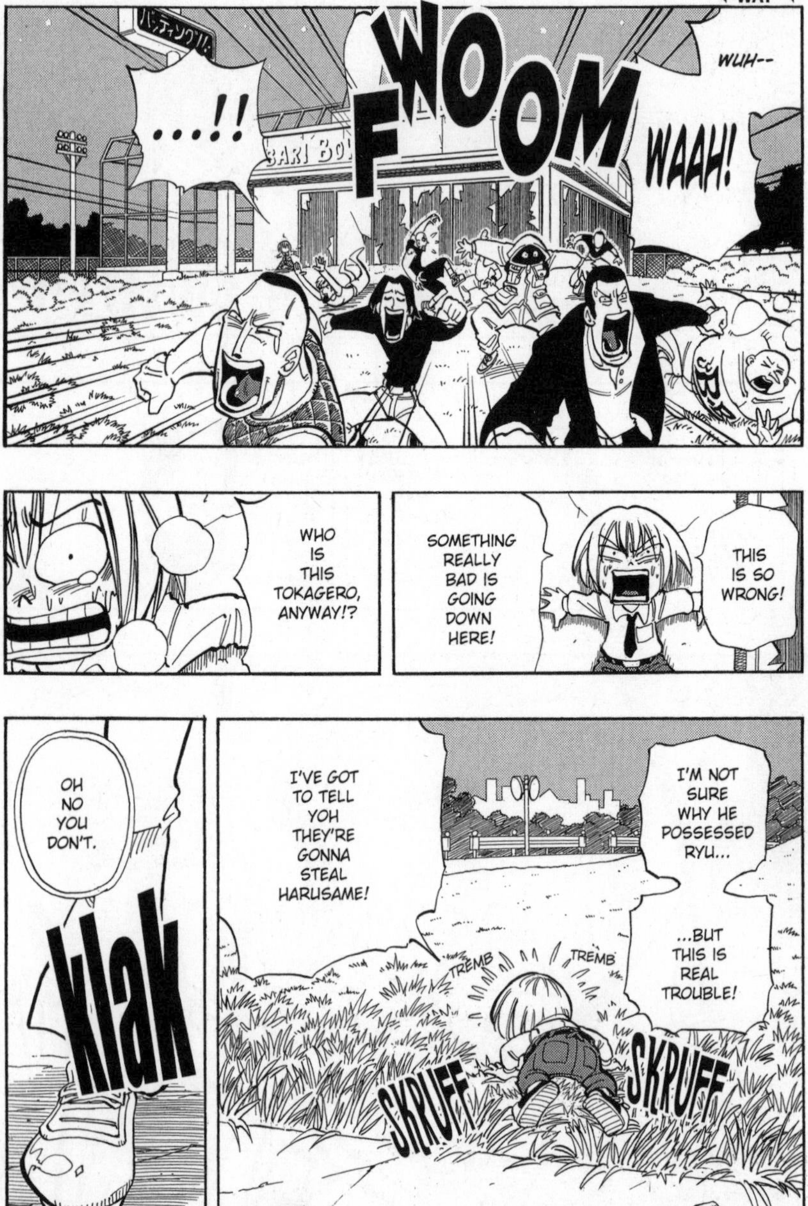
WUH--
WAAH!
FWOOM
....!!
THIS IS SO WRONG!
SOMETHING REALLY BAD IS GOING DOWN HERE!
WHO IS THIS TOKAGERO, ANYWAY!?
I'M NOT SURE WHY HE POSSESSED RYU...
...BUT THIS IS REAL TROUBLE!
I'VE GOT TO TELL YOH THEY'RE GONNA STEAL HARUSAME!
TREMB
TREMB
SKRUFF
SKRUFF
OH NO YOU DON'T.
KLAK

READ THIS WAY

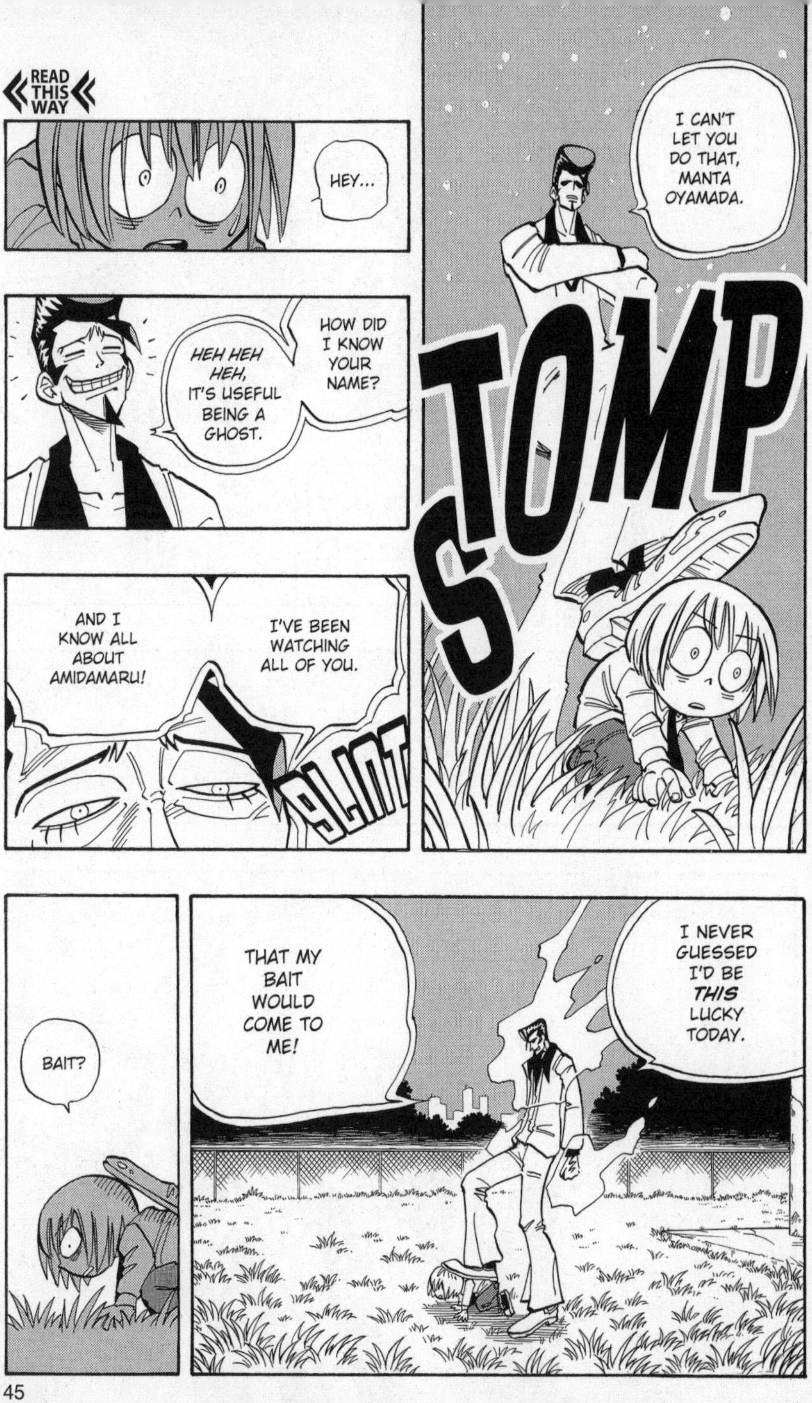
I CAN'T LET YOU DO THAT, MANTA OYAMADA.
STOMP
HEY...
HOW DID I KNOW YOUR NAME?
HEH HEH HEH, IT'S USEFUL BEING A GHOST.
I'VE BEEN WATCHING ALL OF YOU.
AND I KNOW ALL ABOUT AMIDAMARU!
I NEVER GUESSED I'D BE THIS LUCKY TODAY.
THAT MY BAIT WOULD COME TO ME!
BAIT?

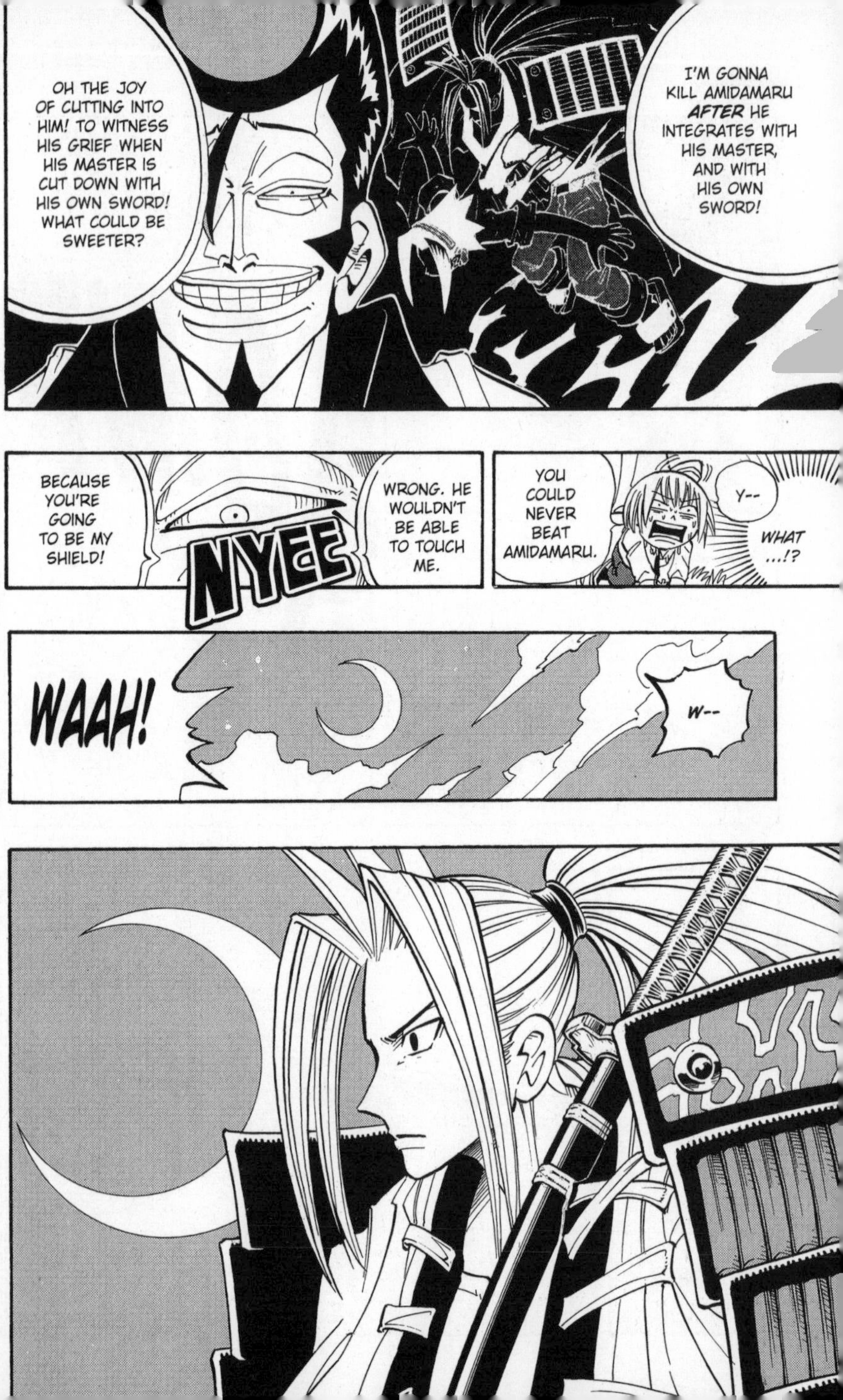
I'M GONNA KILL AMIDAMARU AFTER HE INTEGRATES WITH HIS MASTER, AND WITH HIS OWN SWORD!
OH THE JOY OF CUTTING INTO HIM! TO WITNESS HIS GRIEF WHEN HIS MASTER IS CUT DOWN WITH HIS OWN SWORD! WHAT COULD BE SWEETER?
Y--
WHAT ...!?
YOU COULD NEVER BEAT AMIDAMARU.
WRONG. HE WOULDN'T BE ABLE TO TOUCH ME.
NYEE
BECAUSE YOU'RE GOING TO BE MY SHIELD!
W--
WAAH!

READ THIS WAY

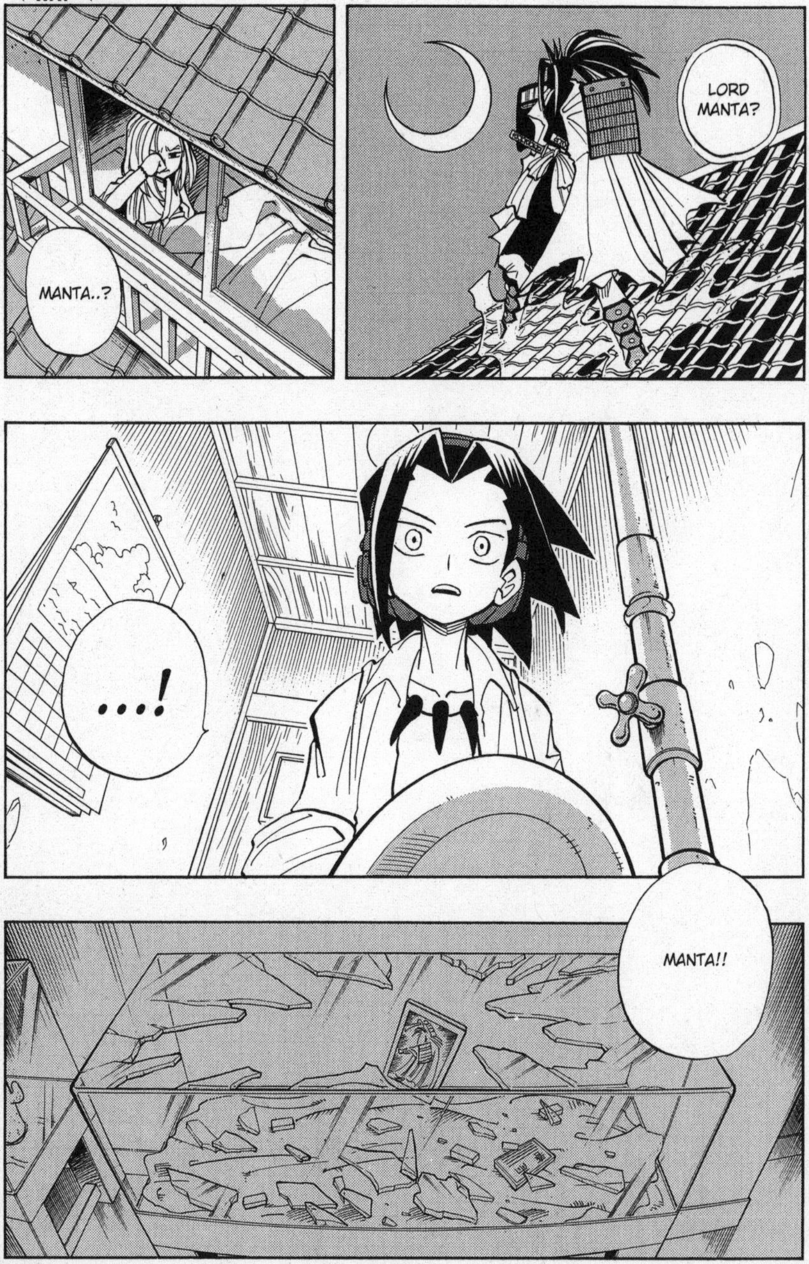
LORD MANTA?
MANTA..?
...!
MANTA!!

SHAMAN
KING
3

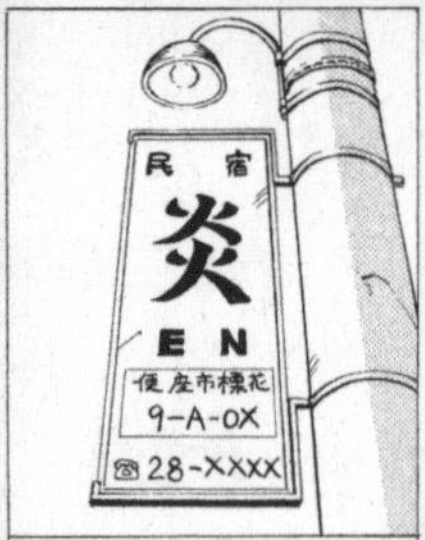
民宿
炎
EN
9-A-0X
28-XXXX

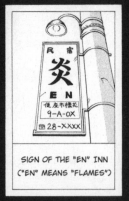

SIGN OF THE "EN" INN
("EN" MEANS "FLAMES")

READ THIS WAY

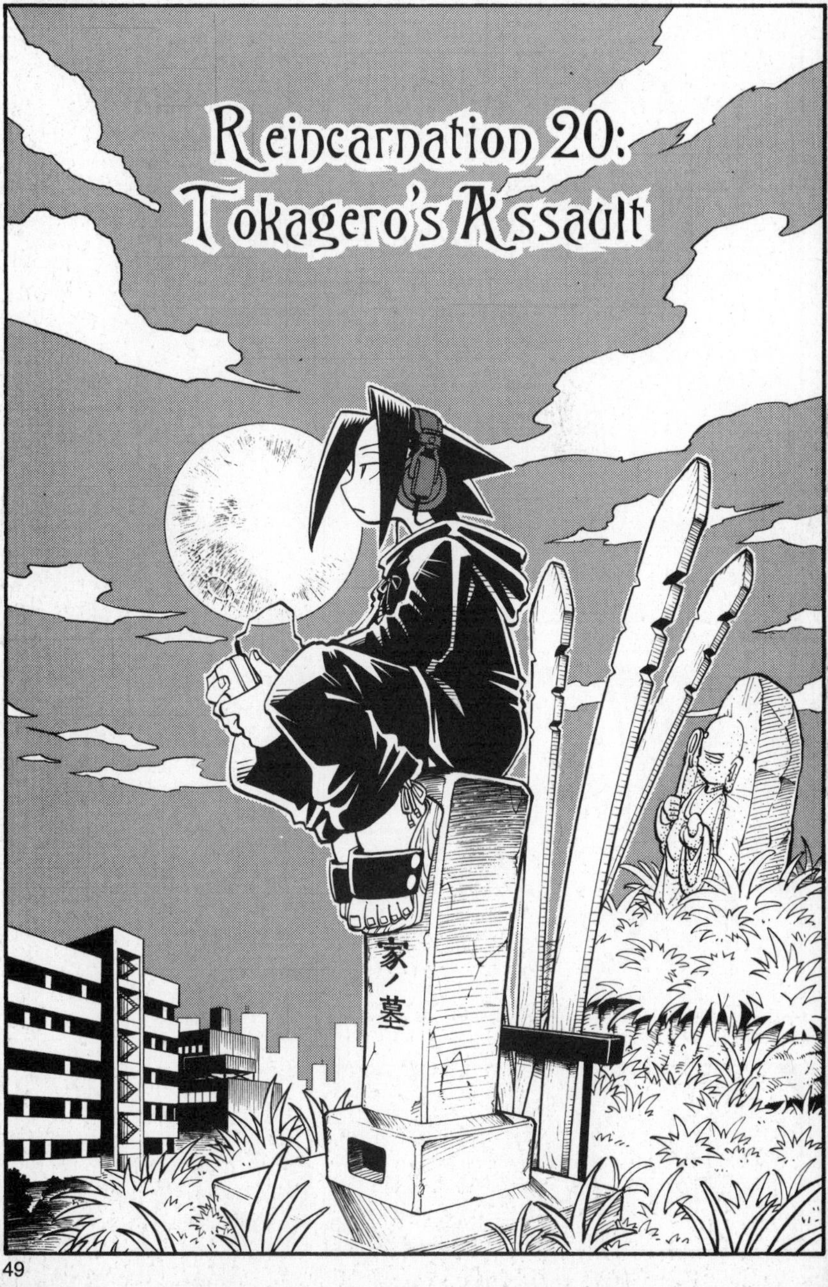
Reincarnation 20:
Tokagero's Assault
家ノ墓

READ THIS WAY

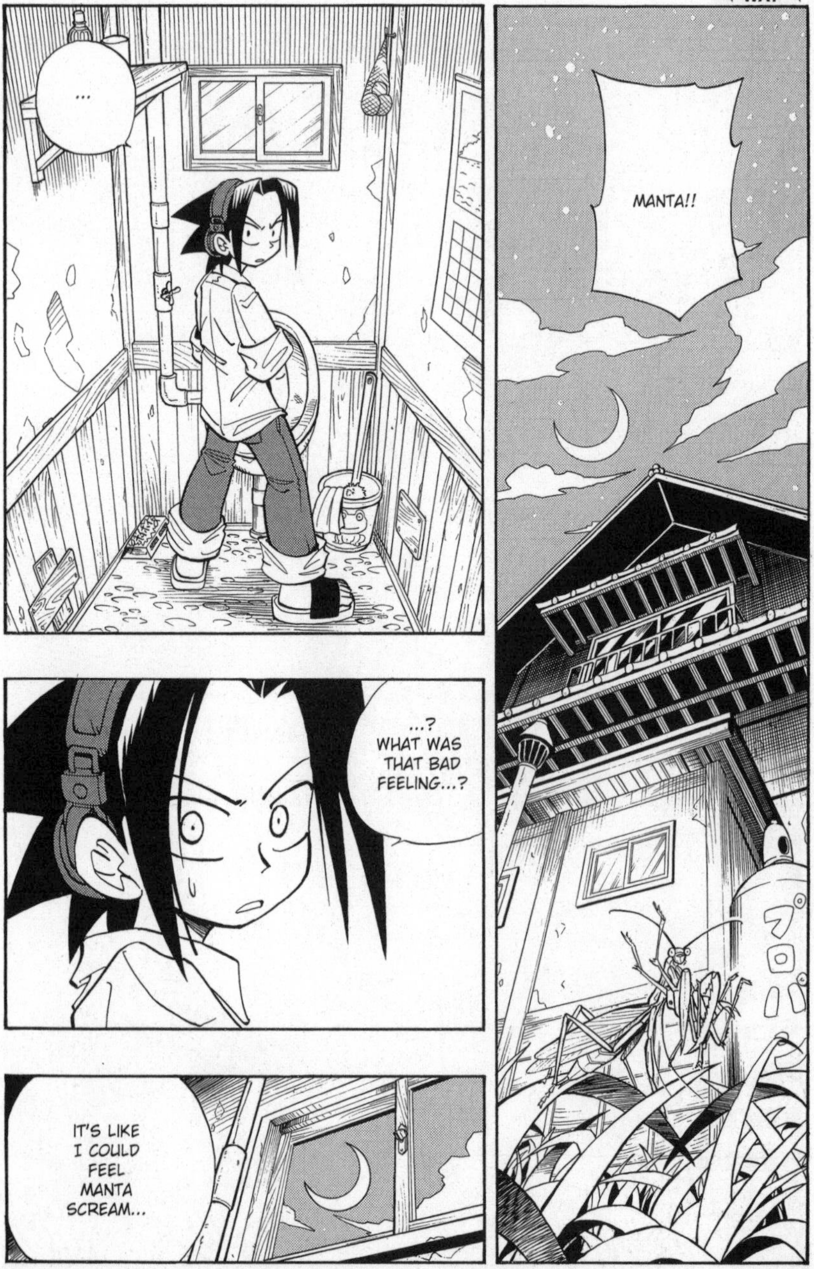
MANTA!!
プロパ
...
...? WHAT WAS THAT BAD FEELING...?
IT'S LIKE I COULD FEEL MANTA SCREAM...

READ THIS WAY

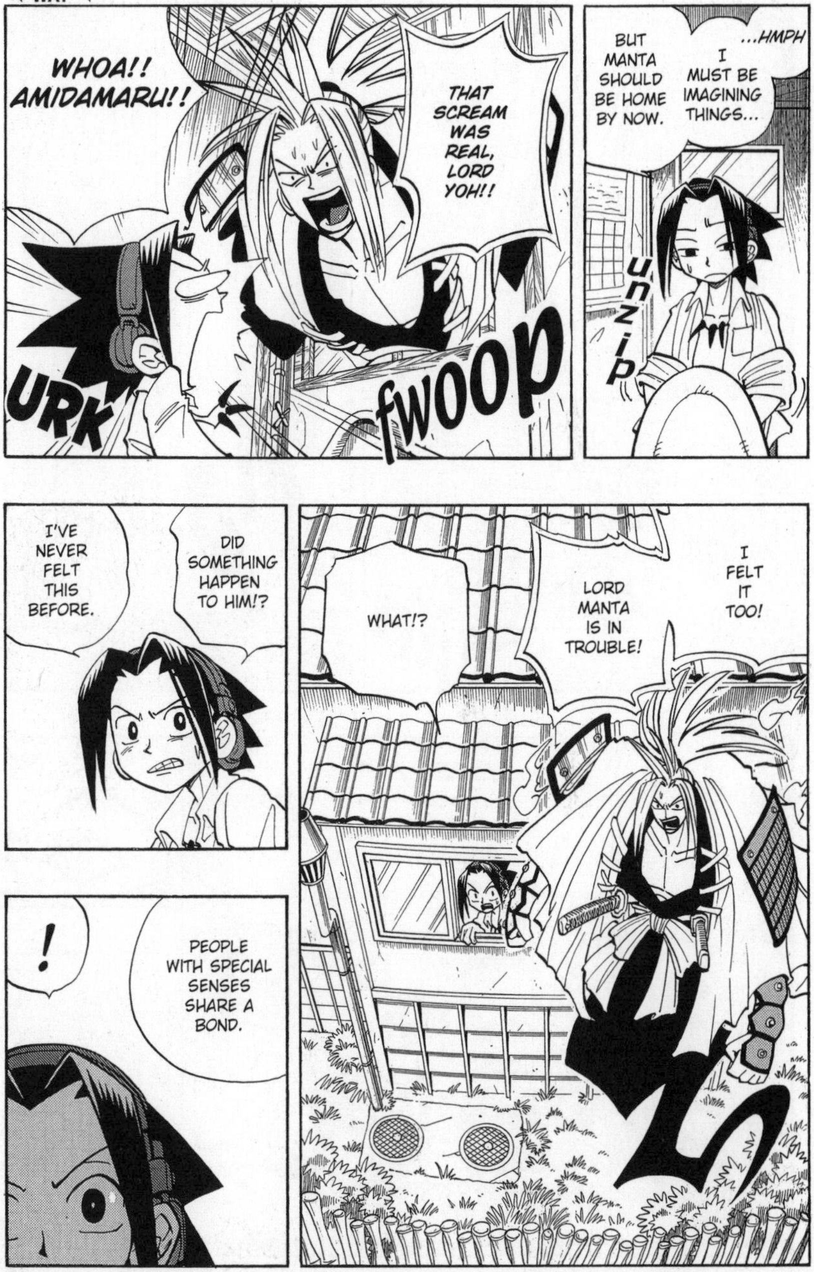

...HMPH
I MUST BE IMAGINING THINGS...
BUT MANTA SHOULD BE HOME BY NOW.
unzip
THAT SCREAM WAS REAL, LORD YOH!!
WHOA!! AMIDAMARU!!
fwoop
URK
I FELT IT TOO!
LORD MANTA IS IN TROUBLE!
WHAT!?
DID SOMETHING HAPPEN TO HIM!?
I'VE NEVER FELT THIS BEFORE.
PEOPLE WITH SPECIAL SENSES SHARE A BOND.
!

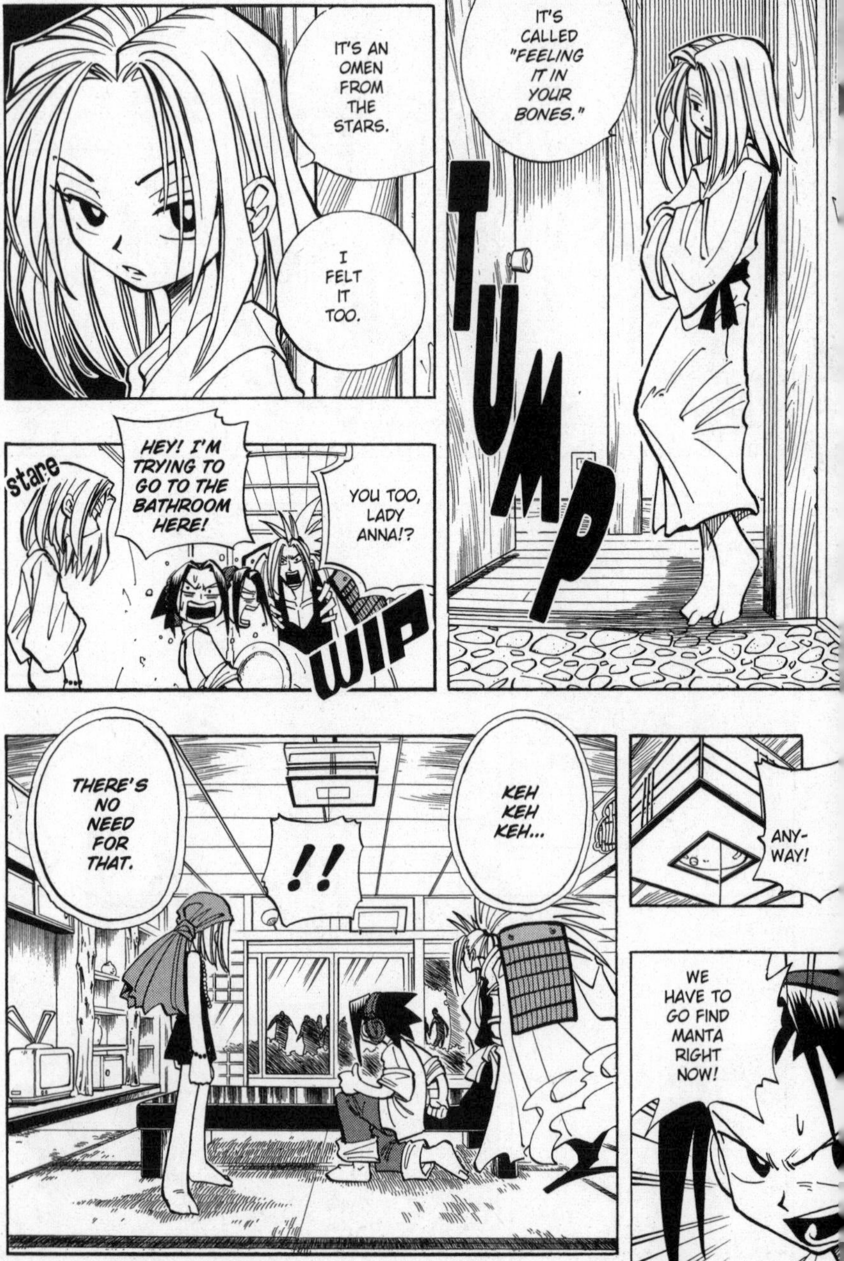
IT'S CALLED "FEELING IT IN YOUR BONES."
TUMP
IT'S AN OMEN FROM THE STARS.
I FELT IT TOO.
YOU TOO, LADY ANNA!?
HEY! I'M TRYING TO GO TO THE BATHROOM HERE!
stare
WIP
ANY-WAY!
WE HAVE TO GO FIND MANTA RIGHT NOW!
KEH KEH KEH...
!!
THERE'S NO NEED FOR THAT.

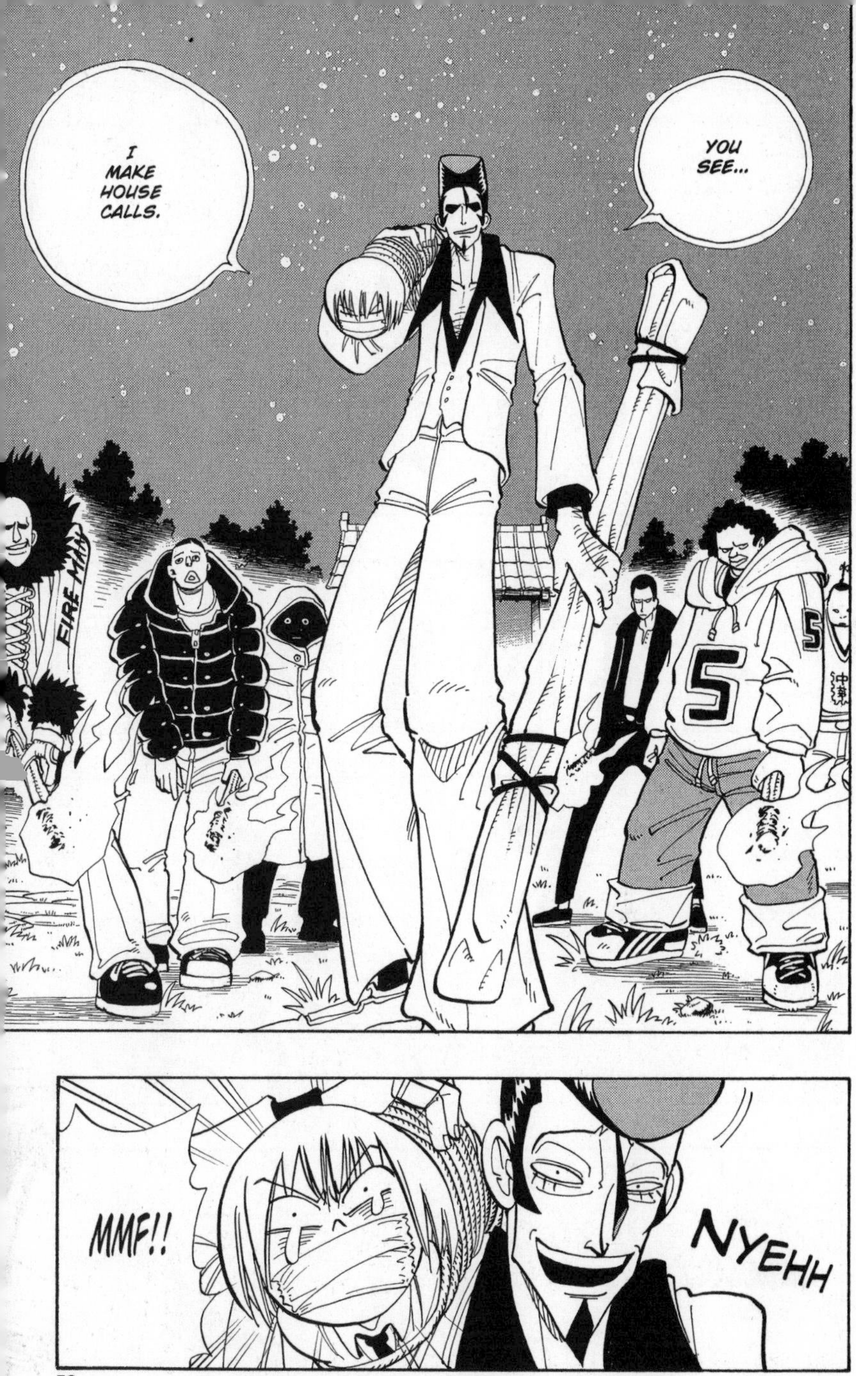
YOU SEE...
I MAKE HOUSE CALLS.
FIRE MAN
NYEHH
MMF!!

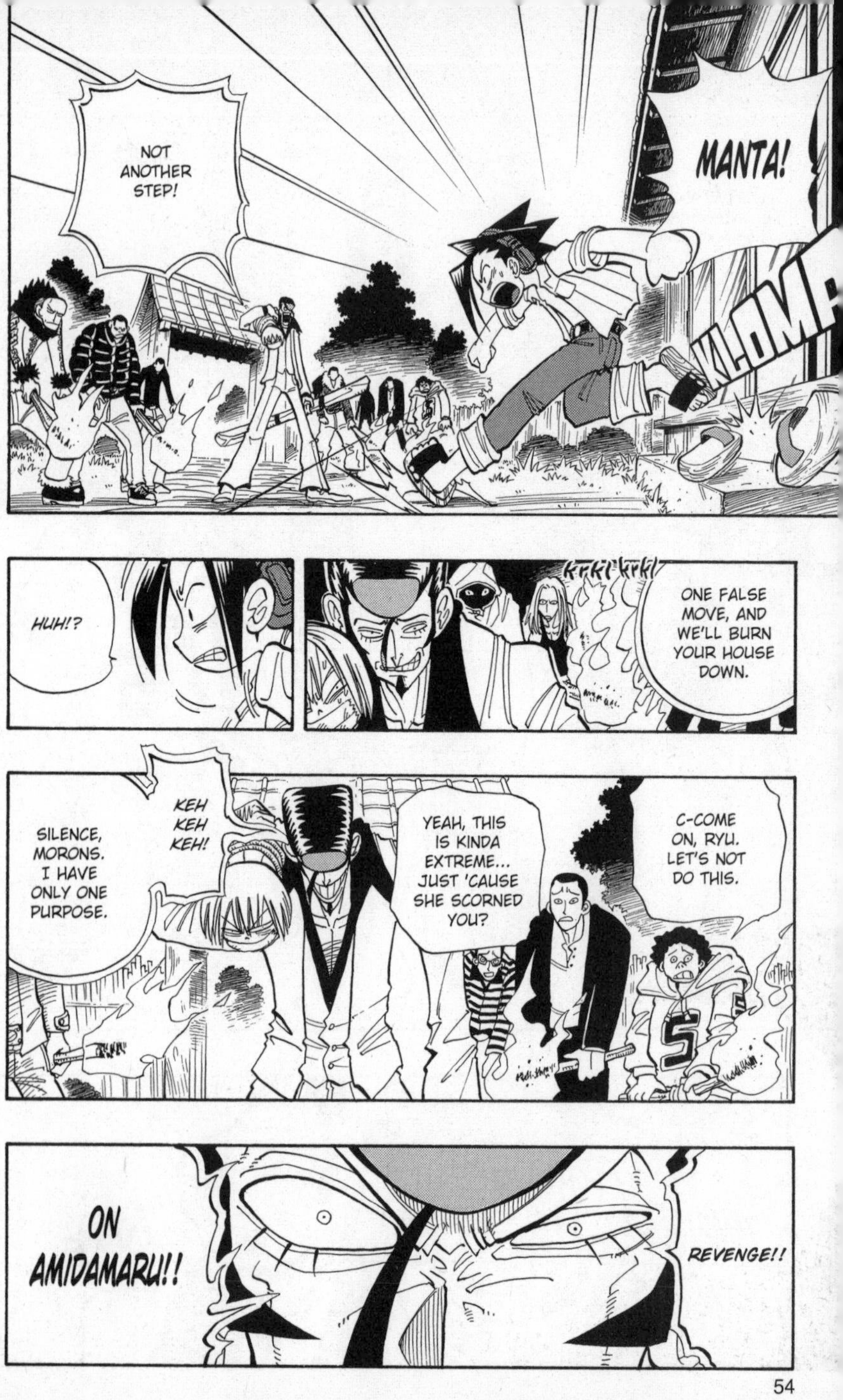
MANTA!
NOT ANOTHER STEP!
krkl krkl
ONE FALSE MOVE, AND WE'LL BURN YOUR HOUSE DOWN.
HUH!?
C-COME ON, RYU. LET'S NOT DO THIS.
YEAH, THIS IS KINDA EXTREME... JUST 'CAUSE SHE SCORNED YOU?
KEH KEH KEH!
SILENCE, MORONS. I HAVE ONLY ONE PURPOSE.
REVENGE!!
ON AMIDAMARU!!

READ THIS WAY

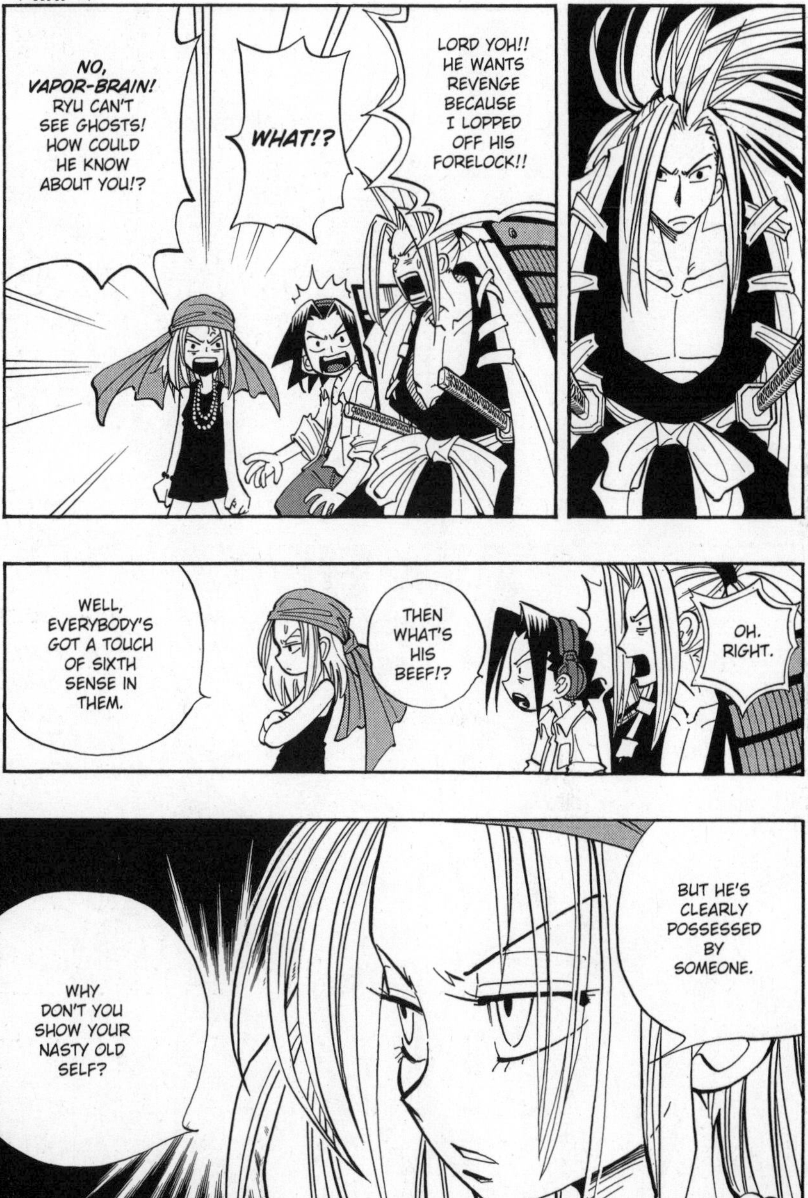
LORD YOH!! HE WANTS REVENGE BECAUSE I LOPPED OFF HIS FORELOCK!!
WHAT!?
NO, VAPOR-BRAIN! RYU CAN'T SEE GHOSTS! HOW COULD HE KNOW ABOUT YOU!?
OH. RIGHT.
THEN WHAT'S HIS BEEF!?
WELL, EVERYBODY'S GOT A TOUCH OF SIXTH SENSE IN THEM.
BUT HE'S CLEARLY POSSESSED BY SOMEONE.
WHY DON'T YOU SHOW YOUR NASTY OLD SELF?

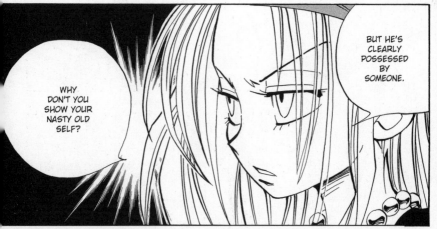

READ THIS WAY

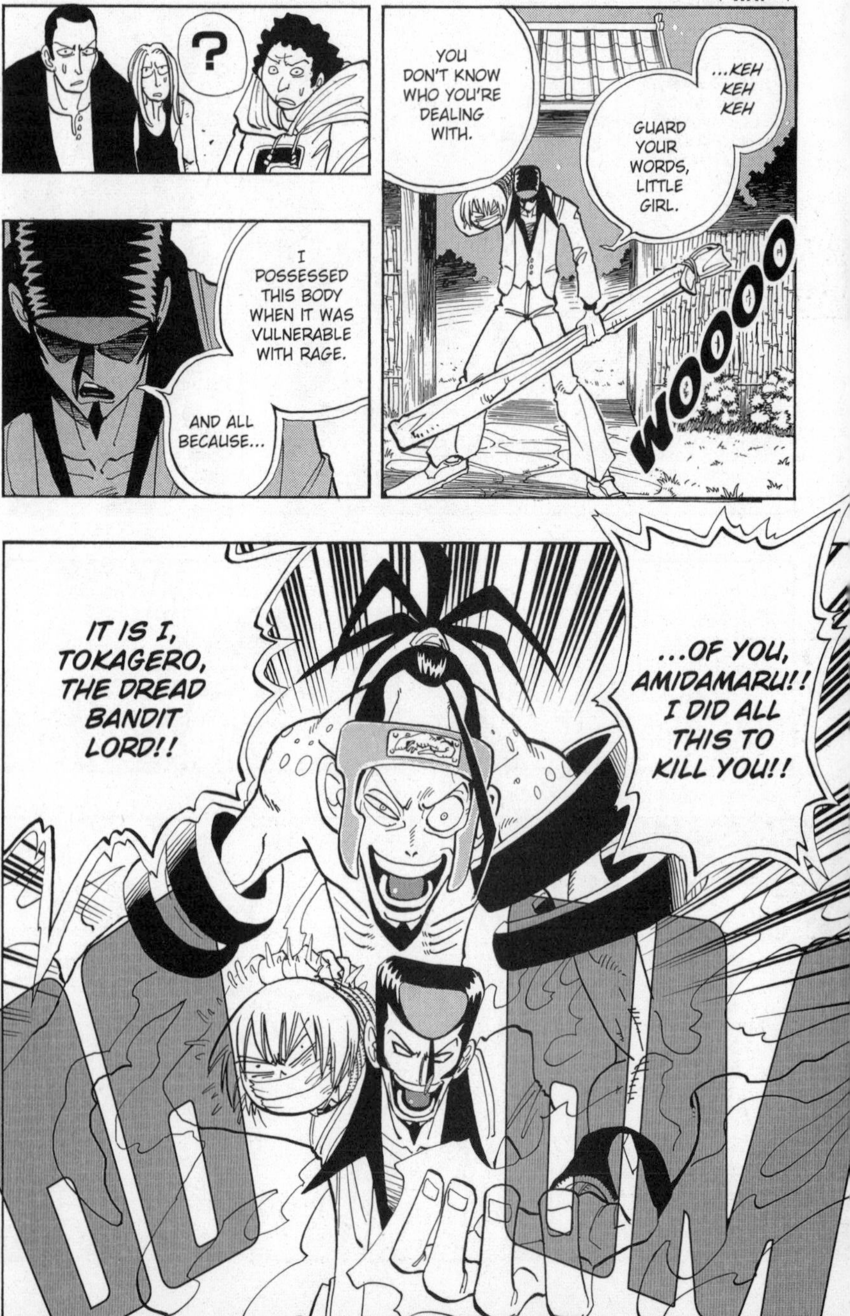

...KEH KEH KEH
GUARD YOUR WORDS, LITTLE GIRL.
YOU DON'T KNOW WHO YOU'RE DEALING WITH.
WOOOOO
?
I POSSESSED THIS BODY WHEN IT WAS VULNERABLE WITH RAGE.
AND ALL BECAUSE...
...OF YOU, AMIDAMARU!! I DID ALL THIS TO KILL YOU!!
IT IS I, TOKAGERO, THE DREAD BANDIT LORD!!

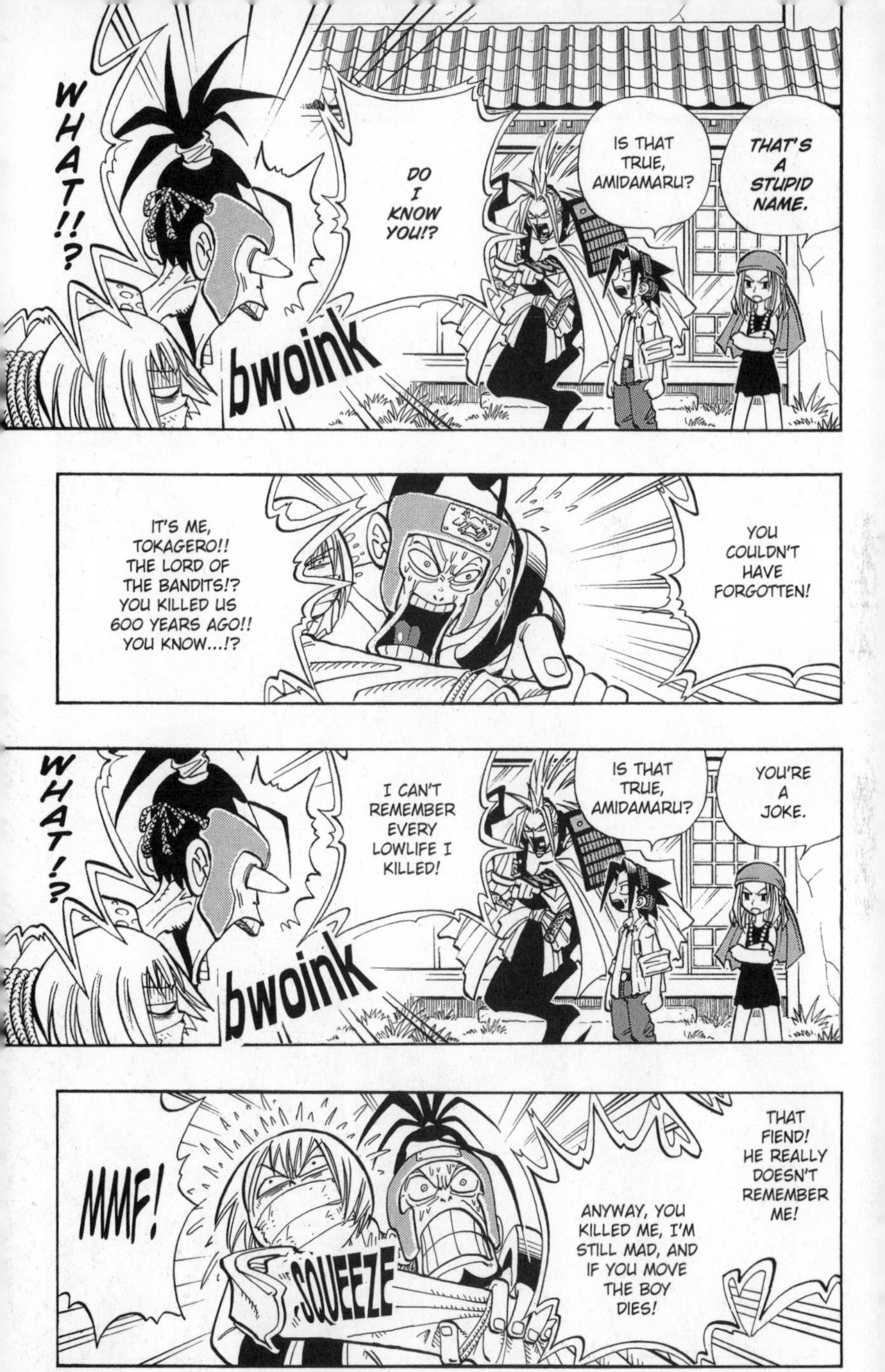
THAT'S A STUPID NAME.
IS THAT TRUE, AMIDAMARU?
DO I KNOW YOU!?
WHAT!!?
bwoink
YOU COULDN'T HAVE FORGOTTEN!
IT'S ME, TOKAGERO!! THE LORD OF THE BANDITS!? YOU KILLED US 600 YEARS AGO!! YOU KNOW...!?
YOU'RE A JOKE.
IS THAT TRUE, AMIDAMARU?
I CAN'T REMEMBER EVERY LOWLIFE I KILLED!
WHAT!?
bwoink
THAT FIEND! HE REALLY DOESN'T REMEMBER ME!
ANYWAY, YOU KILLED ME, I'M STILL MAD, AND IF YOU MOVE THE BOY DIES!
MMF!
SQUEEZE

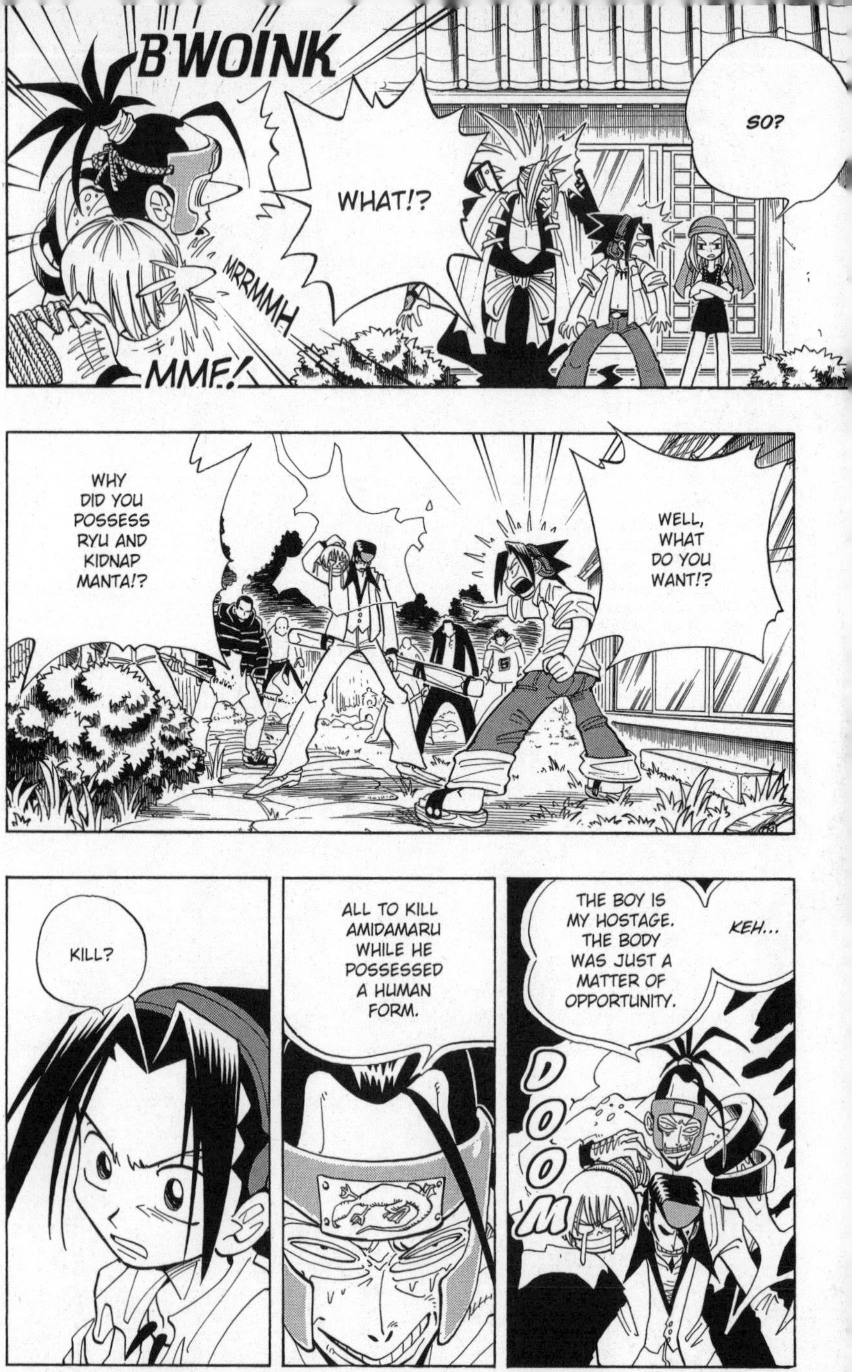
SO?
WHAT!?
B'WOINK
MRRMMH
MMF!
WELL, WHAT DO YOU WANT!?
WHY DID YOU POSSESS RYU AND KIDNAP MANTA!?
KEH...
THE BOY IS MY HOSTAGE. THE BODY WAS JUST A MATTER OF OPPORTUNITY.
DOOOM
ALL TO KILL AMIDAMARU WHILE HE POSSESSED A HUMAN FORM.
KILL?

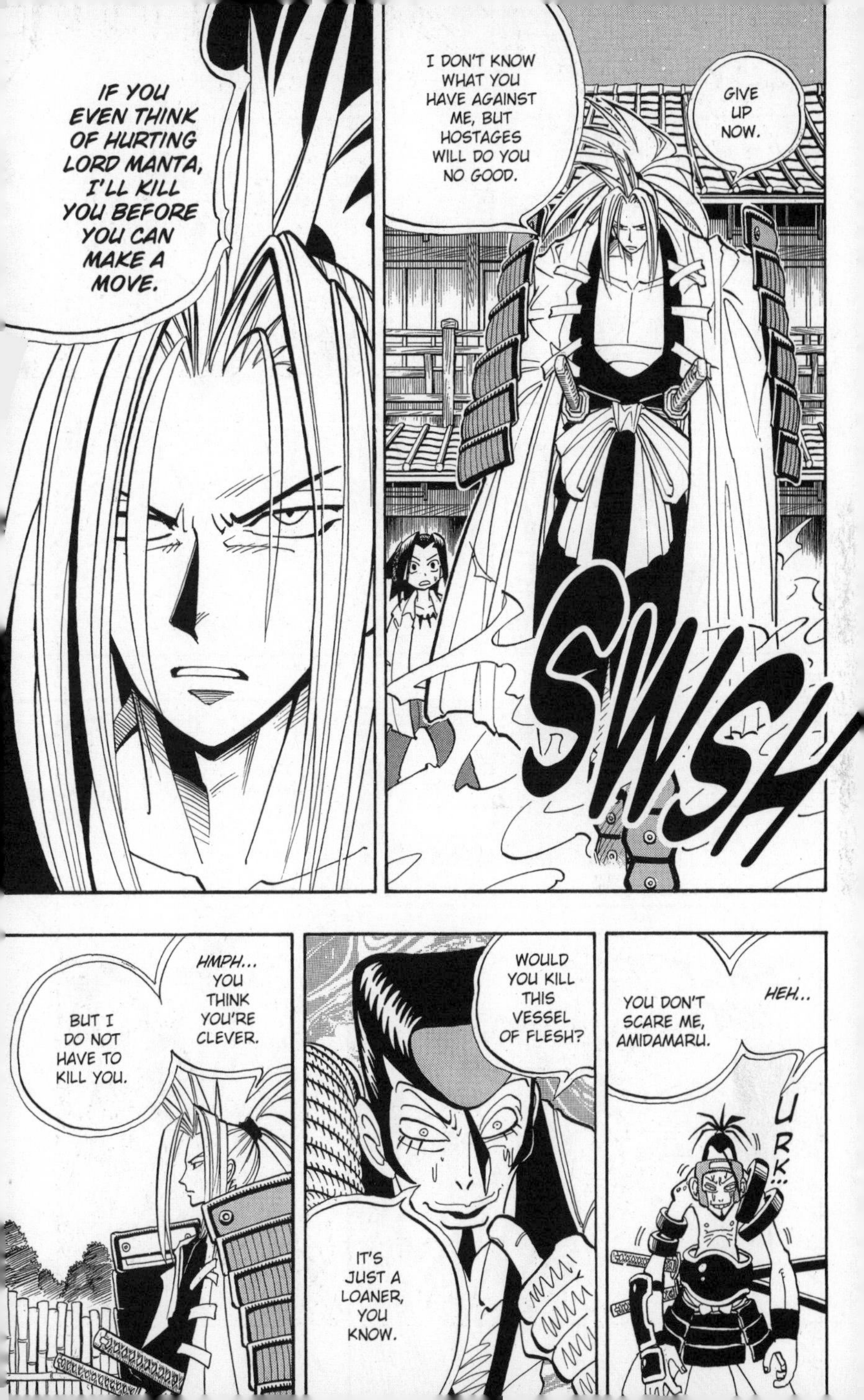
I DON'T KNOW WHAT YOU HAVE AGAINST ME, BUT HOSTAGES WILL DO YOU NO GOOD.
GIVE UP NOW.
SWSH
IF YOU EVEN THINK OF HURTING LORD MANTA, I'LL KILL YOU BEFORE YOU CAN MAKE A MOVE.
HEH...
YOU DON'T SCARE ME, AMIDAMARU.
URK...
WOULD YOU KILL THIS VESSEL OF FLESH?
IT'S JUST A LOANER, YOU KNOW.
HMPH... YOU THINK YOU'RE CLEVER.
BUT I DO NOT HAVE TO KILL YOU.

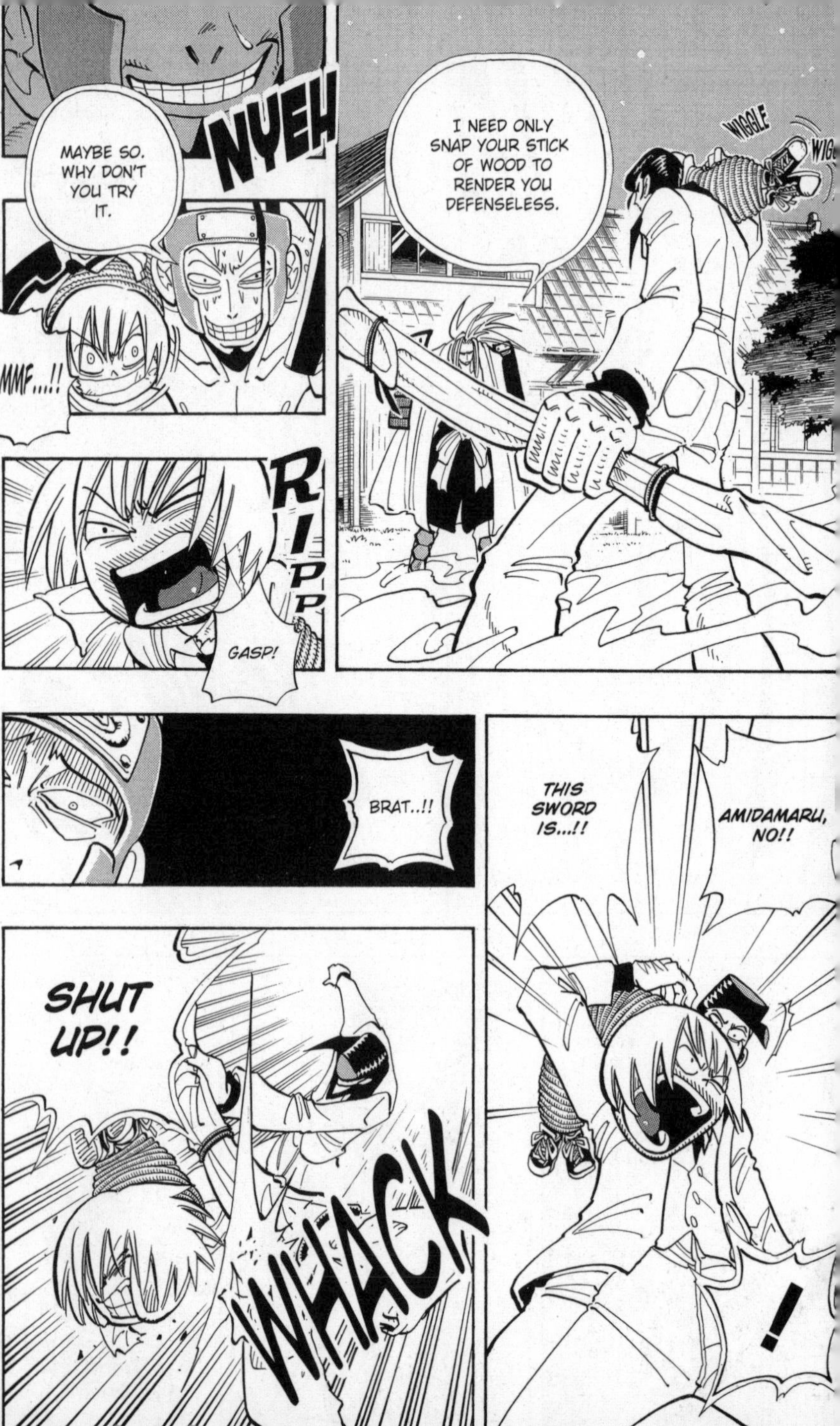
I NEED ONLY SNAP YOUR STICK OF WOOD TO RENDER YOU DEFENSELESS.
WIGGLE
NYEH
MAYBE SO. WHY DON'T YOU TRY IT.
MMF...!!
RIPP
GASP!
AMIDAMARU, NO!!
THIS SWORD IS...!!
!
BRAT..!!
SHUT UP!!
WHACK

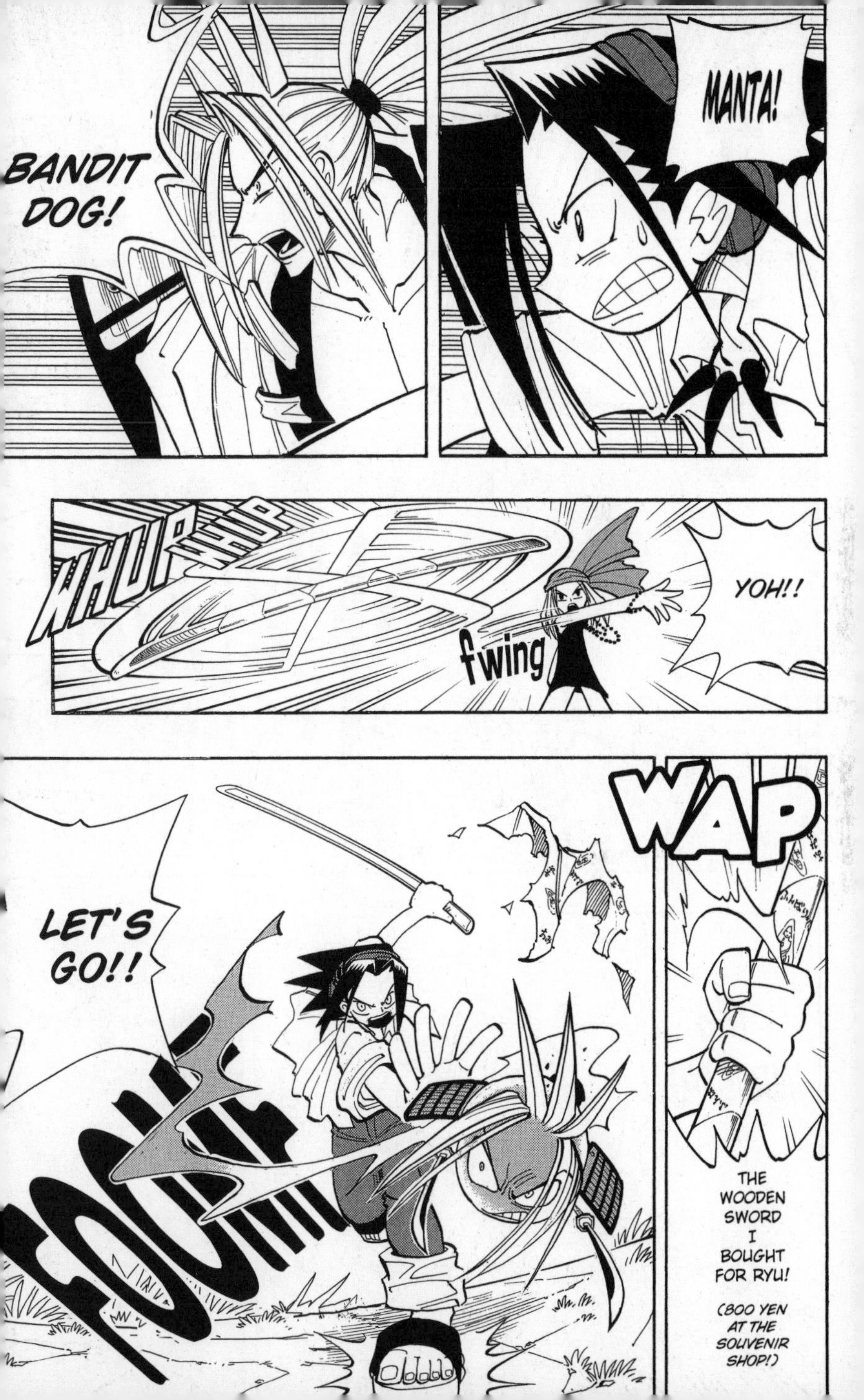
MANTA!
BANDIT DOG!
YOH!!
fwing
WHUP
WAP
THE WOODEN SWORD I BOUGHT FOR RYU!
(800 YEN AT THE SOUVENIR SHOP!)
LET'S GO!!

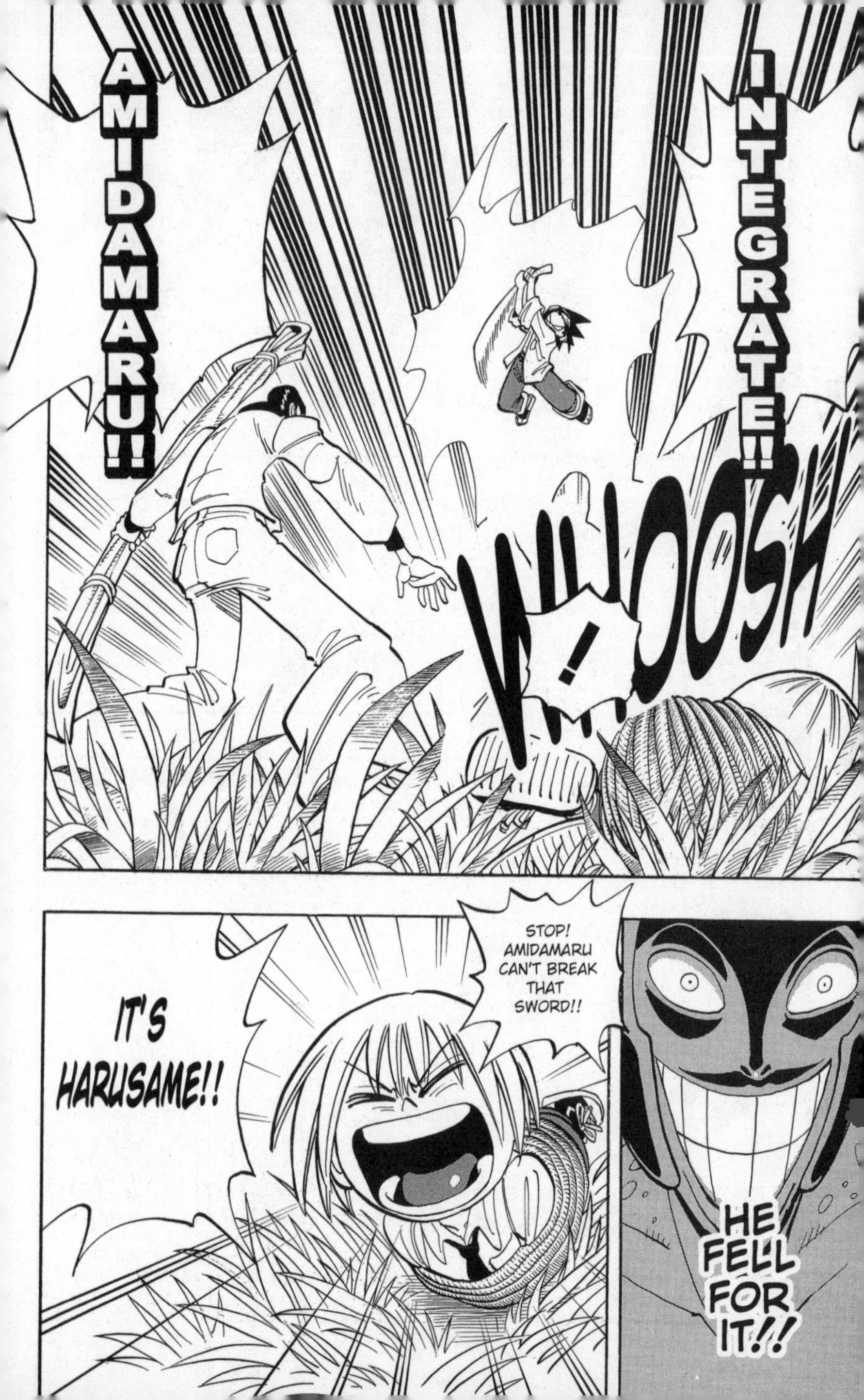
INTEGRATE!!
AMIDAMARU!!
KWOOSH
!
HE FELL FOR IT!!
STOP! AMIDAMARU CAN'T BREAK THAT SWORD!!
IT'S HARUSAME!!

READ THIS WAY

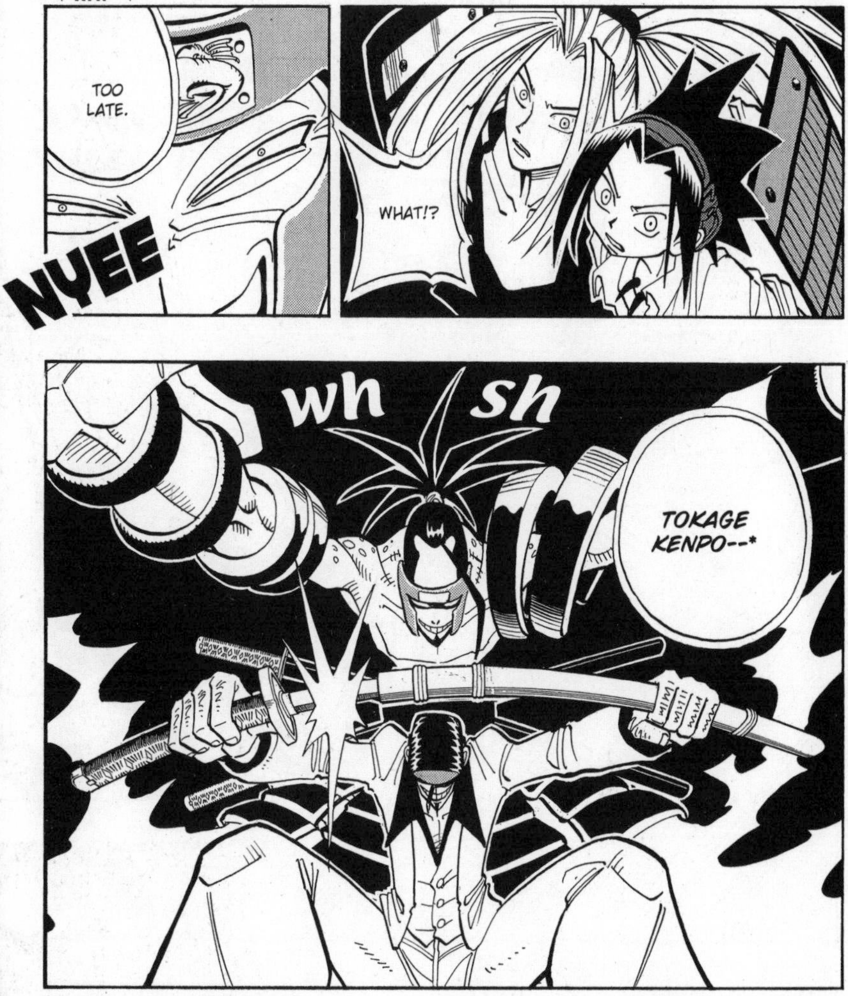
WHAT!?
TOO LATE.
NYEE
wh sh
TOKAGE KENPO--*

*TOKAGE KENPO = LIZARD STYLE

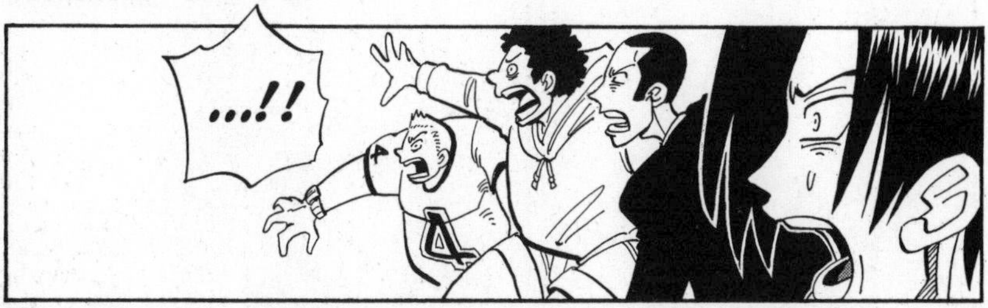
...!!

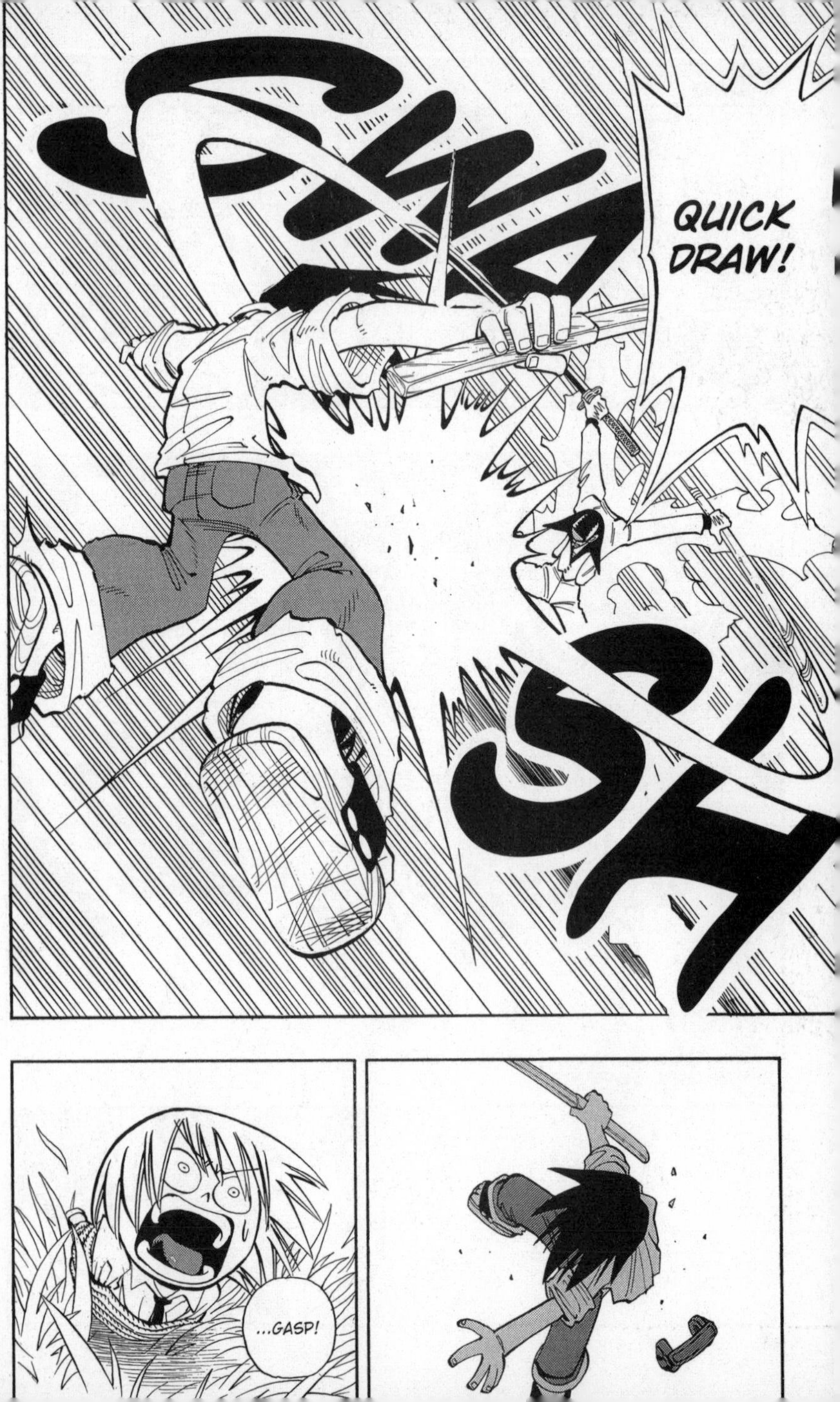
QUICK DRAW!
...GASP!

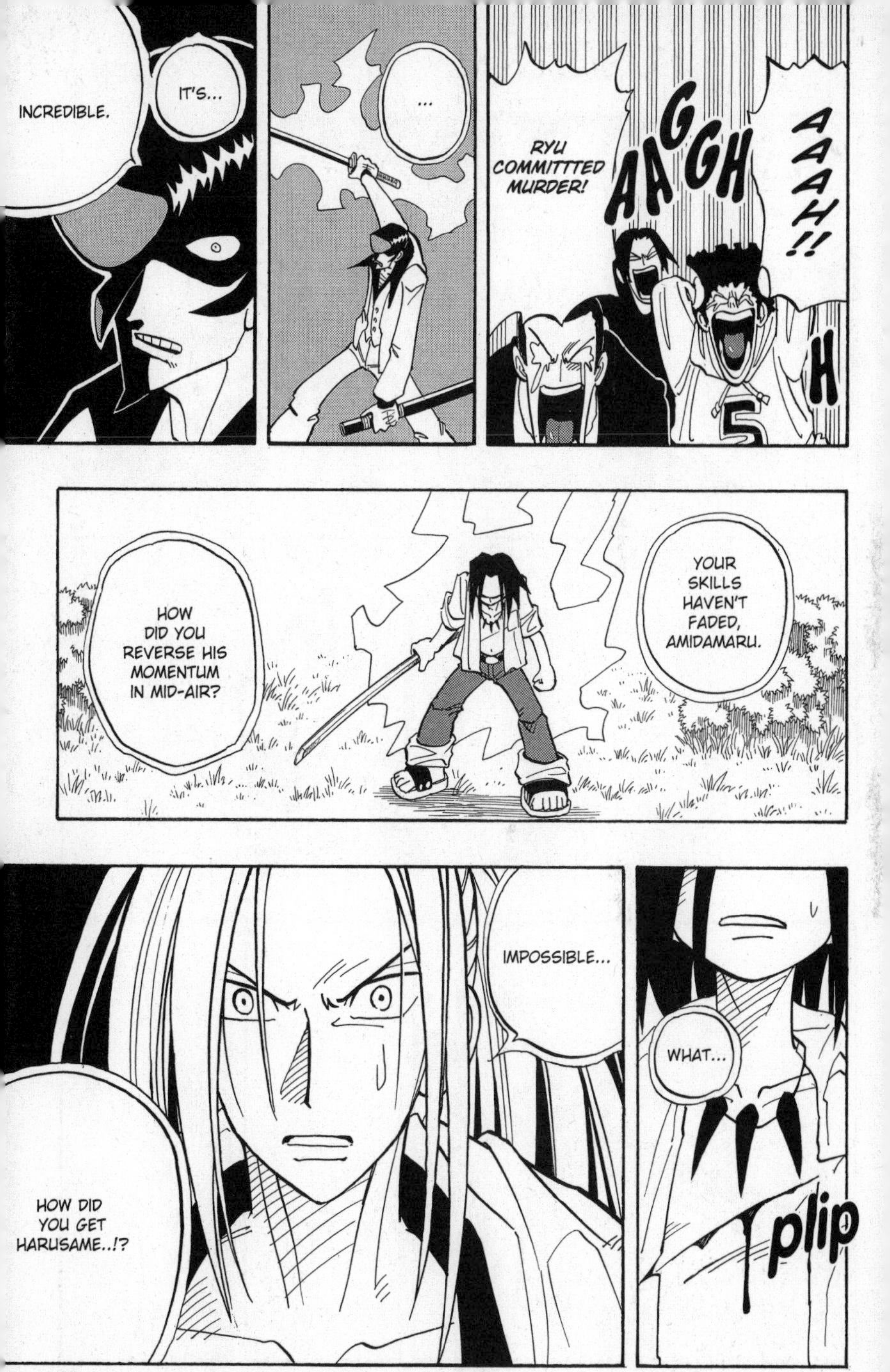
RYU COMMITTTED MURDER!
AAGGH
AAAAH!!
H
...
IT'S...
INCREDIBLE.
YOUR SKILLS HAVEN'T FADED, AMIDAMARU.
HOW DID YOU REVERSE HIS MOMENTUM IN MID-AIR?
WHAT...
plip
IMPOSSIBLE...
HOW DID YOU GET HARUSAME..!?

READ THIS WAY

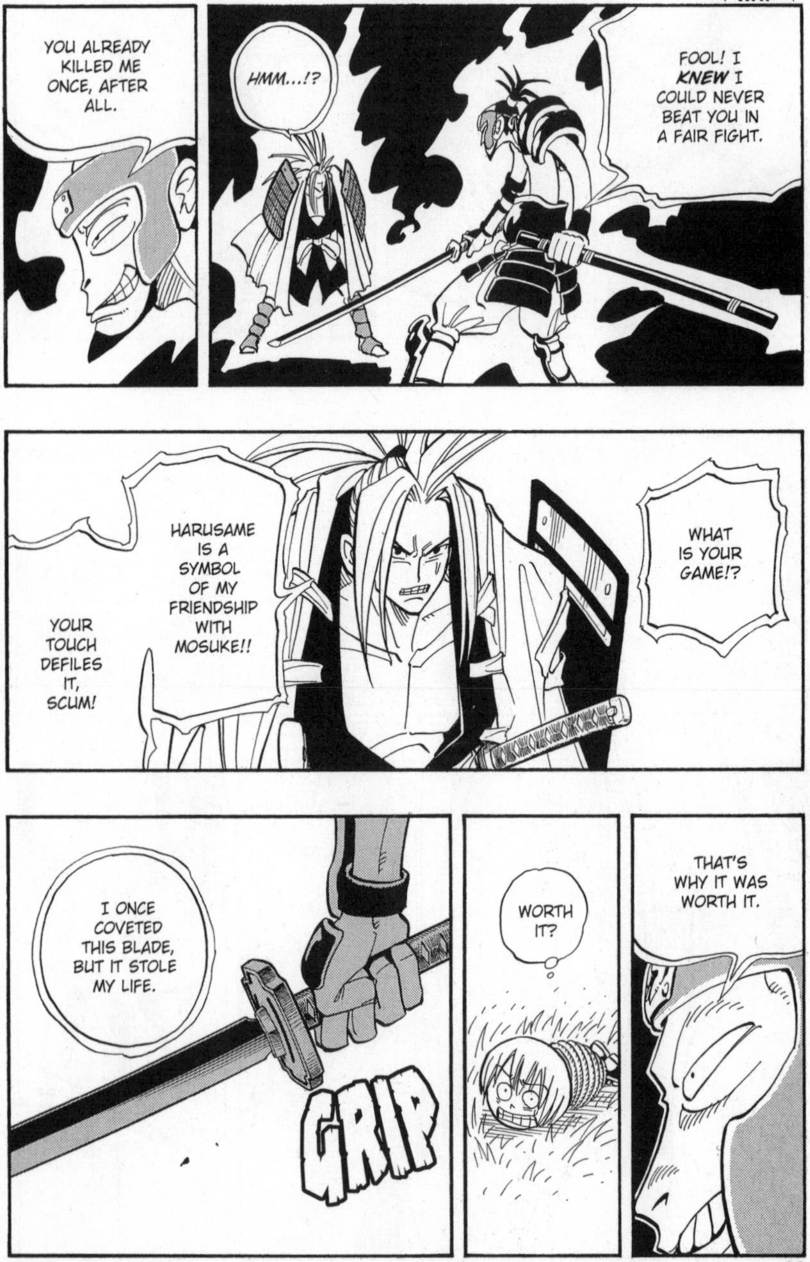
FOOL! I ***KNEW*** I COULD NEVER BEAT YOU IN A FAIR FIGHT.
HMM...!?
YOU ALREADY KILLED ME ONCE, AFTER ALL.
WHAT IS YOUR GAME!?
HARUSAME IS A SYMBOL OF MY FRIENDSHIP WITH MOSUKE!!
YOUR TOUCH DEFILES IT, SCUM!
THAT'S WHY IT WAS WORTH IT.
WORTH IT?
I ONCE COVETED THIS BLADE, BUT IT STOLE MY LIFE.
GRIP

READ THIS WAY

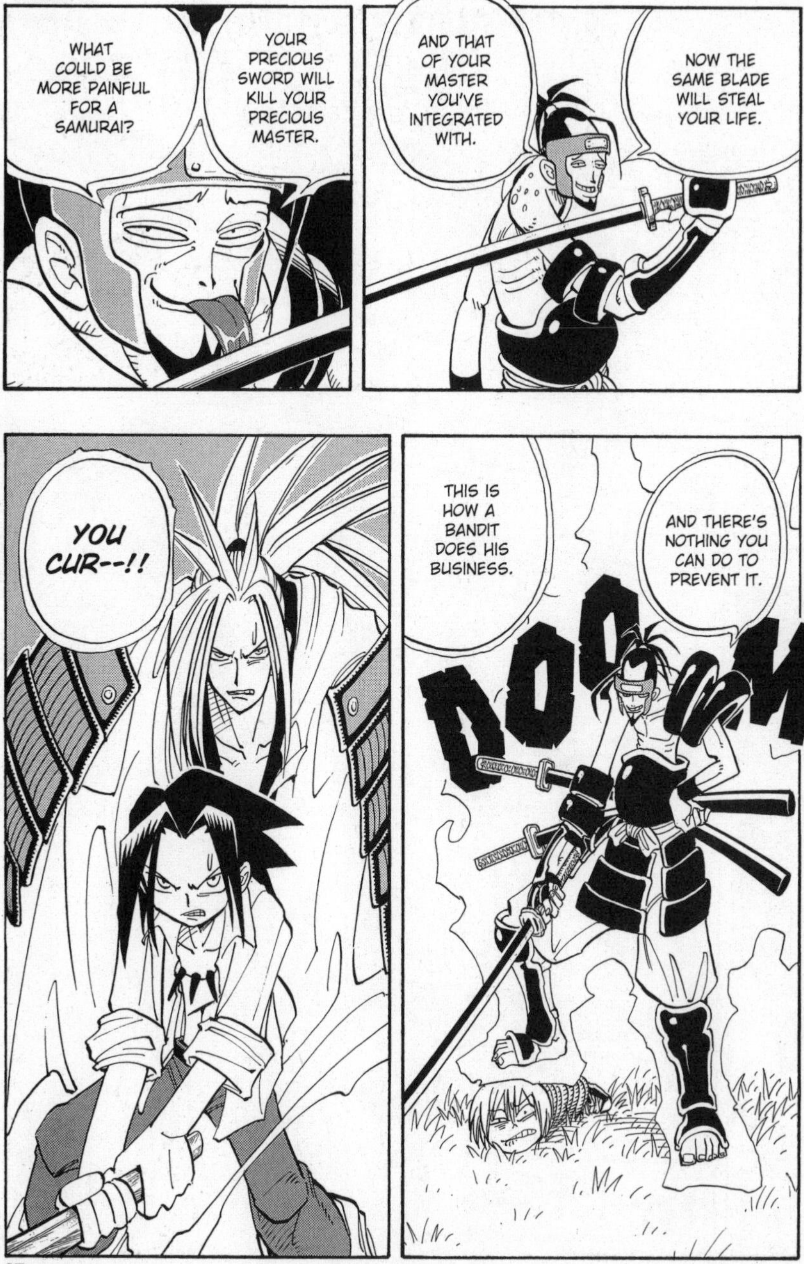
WHAT COULD BE MORE PAINFUL FOR A SAMURAI?
YOUR PRECIOUS SWORD WILL KILL YOUR PRECIOUS MASTER.
AND THAT OF YOUR MASTER YOU'VE INTEGRATED WITH.
NOW THE SAME BLADE WILL STEAL YOUR LIFE.
YOU CUR--!!
THIS IS HOW A BANDIT DOES HIS BUSINESS.
AND THERE'S NOTHING YOU CAN DO TO PREVENT IT.
DOOOM

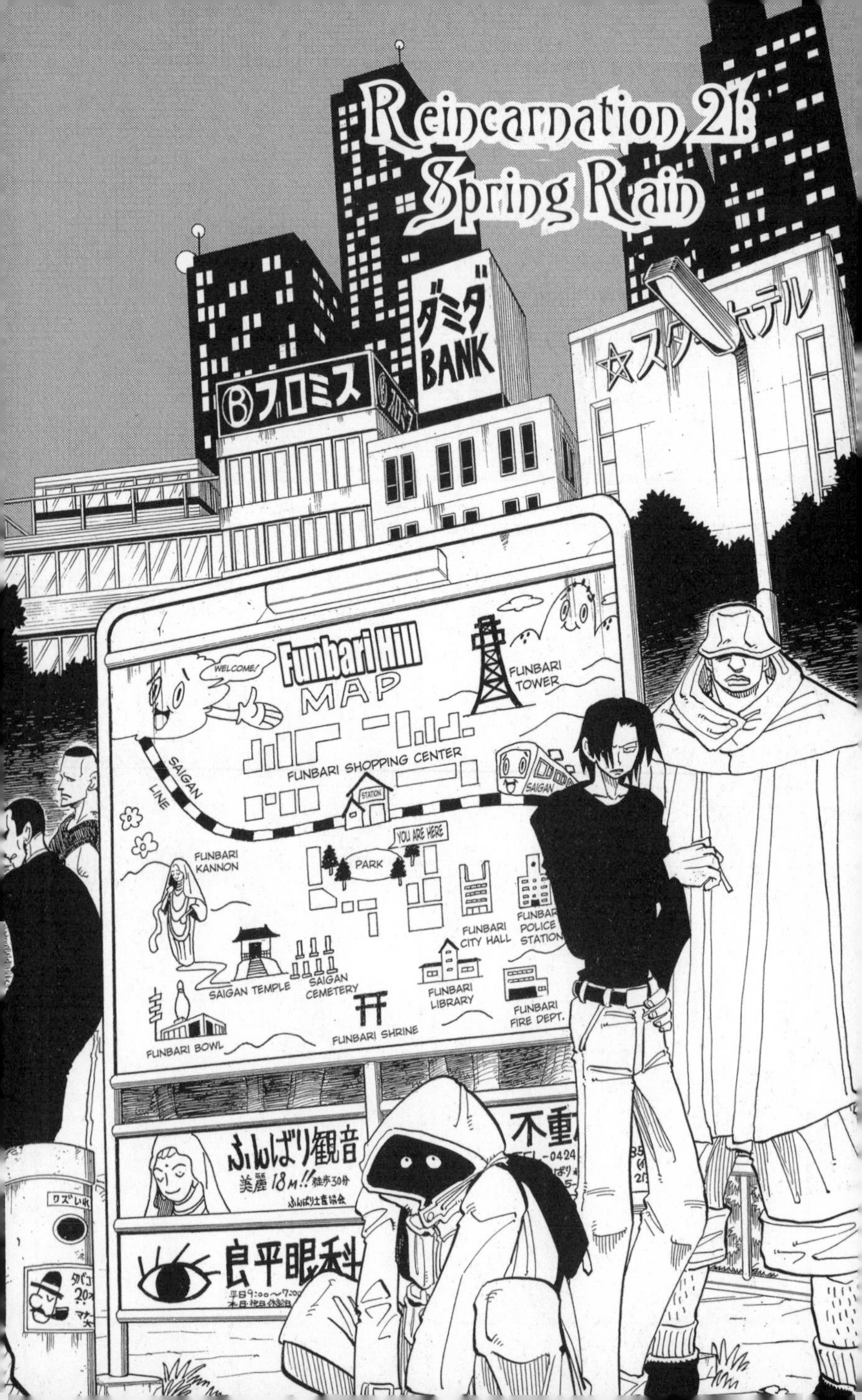
Reincarnation 21:
Spring Rain
ダミダ
BANK
Ⓑフロミス
Funbari Hill
MAP
WELCOME!
FUNBARI TOWER
SAIGAN LINE
FUNBARI SHOPPING CENTER
STATION
SAIGAN
YOU ARE HERE
PARK
FUNBARI KANNON
FUNBARI CITY HALL
FUNBARI POLICE STATION
SAIGAN TEMPLE
SAIGAN CEMETERY
FUNBARI LIBRARY
FUNBARI FIRE DEPT.
FUNBARI BOWL
FUNBARI SHRINE
ふんばり観音
美麗 18M!!
良平眼科

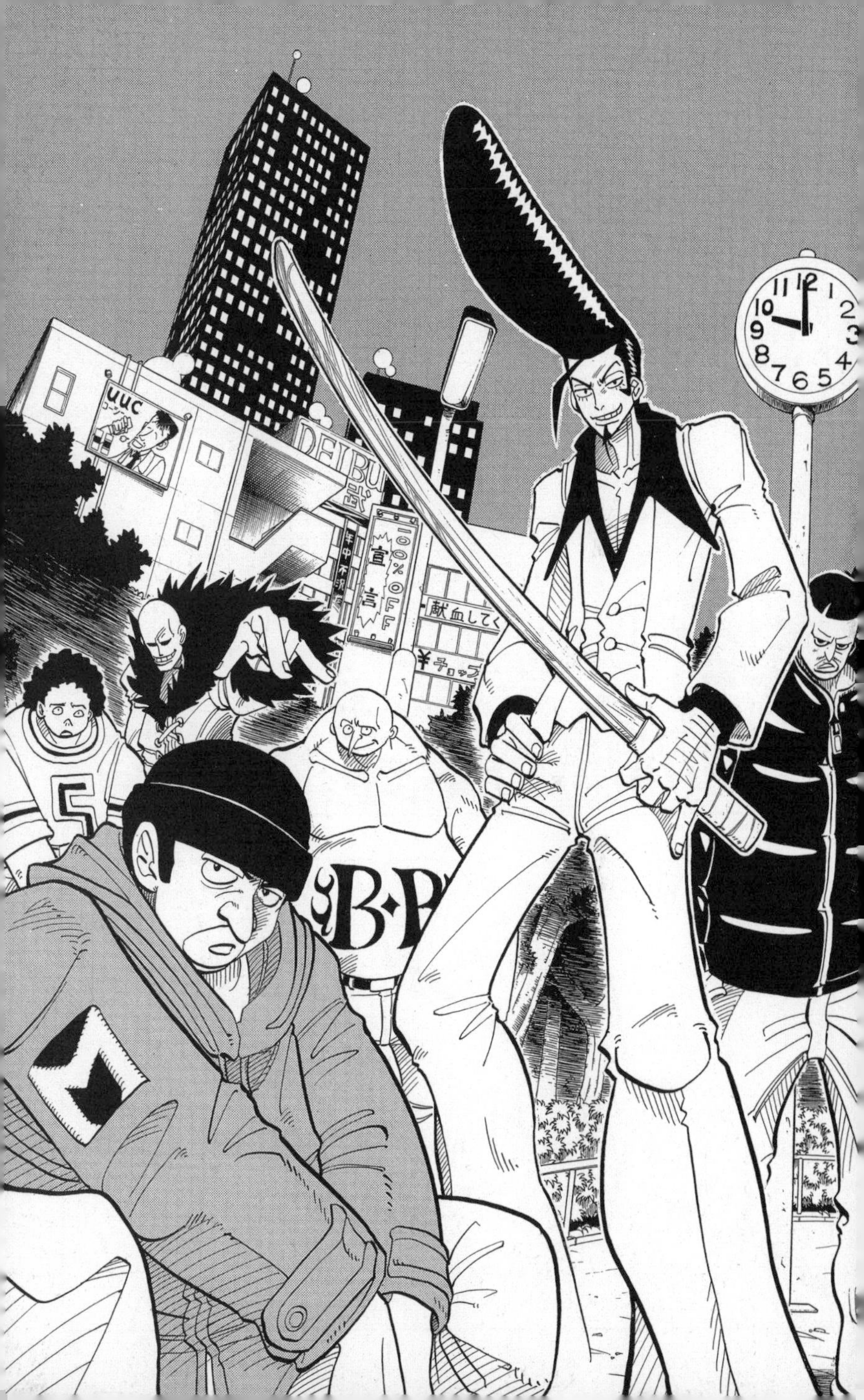
UUC
DEIBU
武
宣言
100%OFF
献血してく
¥チョップ
B・B

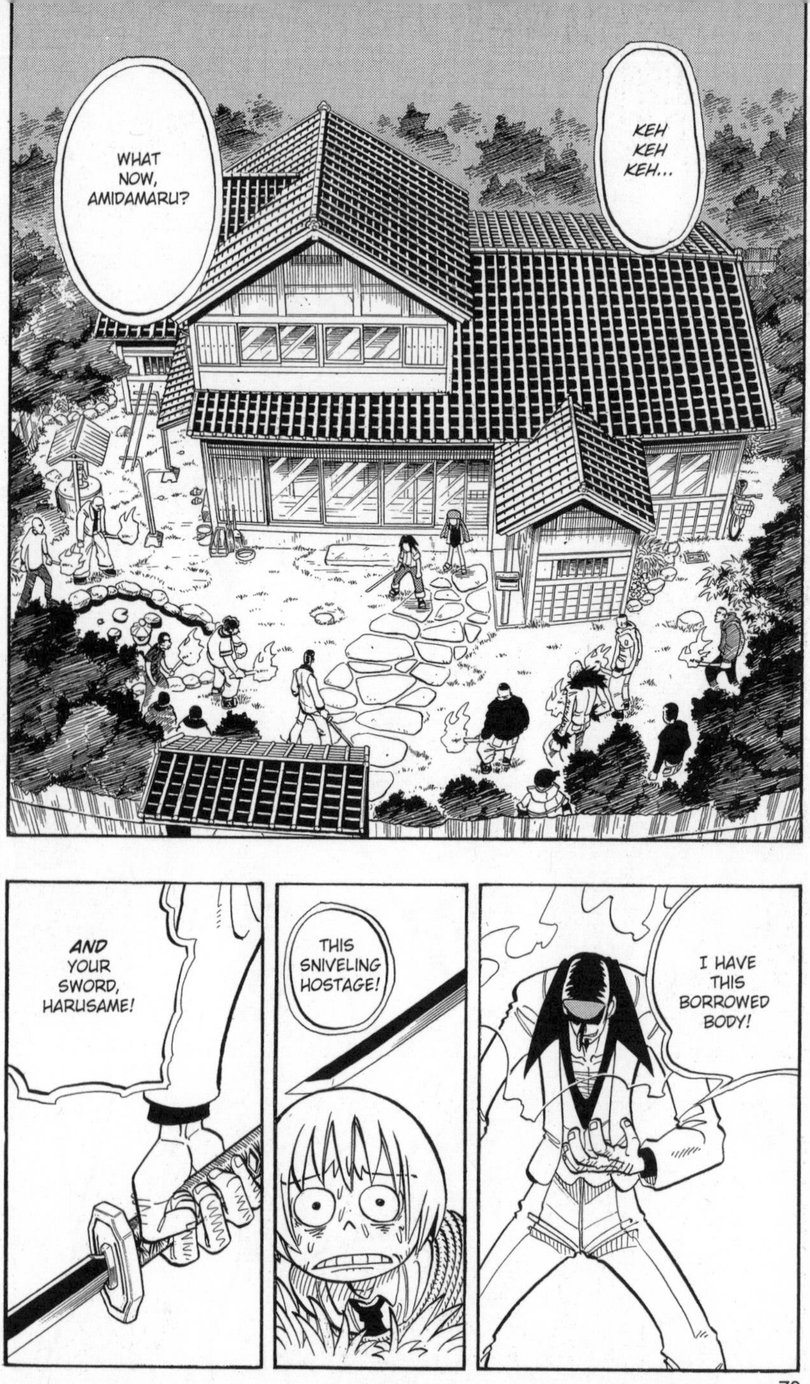
KEH KEH KEH...
WHAT NOW, AMIDAMARU?
I HAVE THIS BORROWED BODY!
THIS SNIVELING HOSTAGE!
AND YOUR SWORD, HARUSAME!

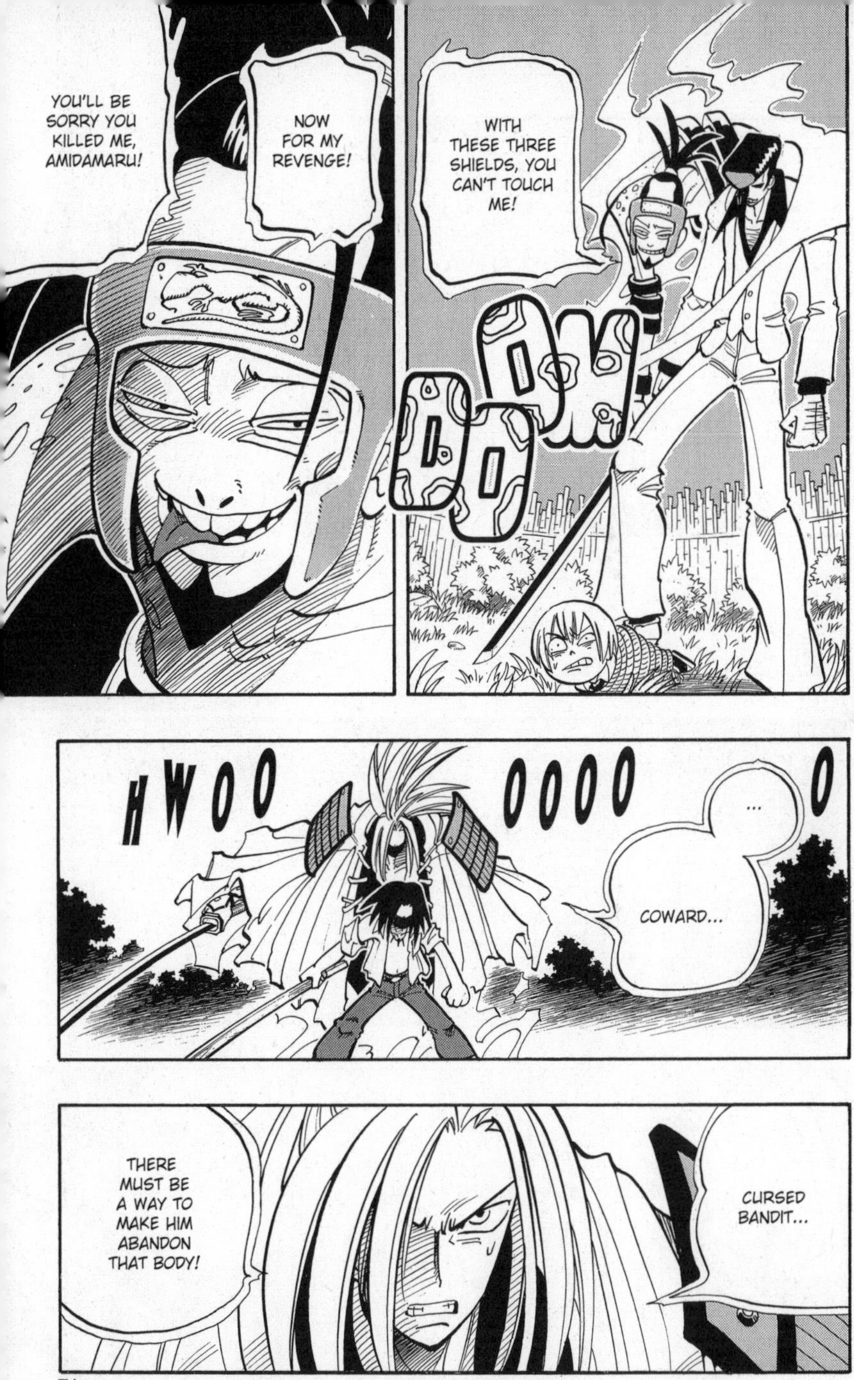
WITH THESE THREE SHIELDS, YOU CAN'T TOUCH ME!
DOOOM
NOW FOR MY REVENGE!
YOU'LL BE SORRY YOU KILLED ME, AMIDAMARU!
... COWARD...
HWOOOOOOO
CURSED BANDIT...
THERE MUST BE A WAY TO MAKE HIM ABANDON THAT BODY!

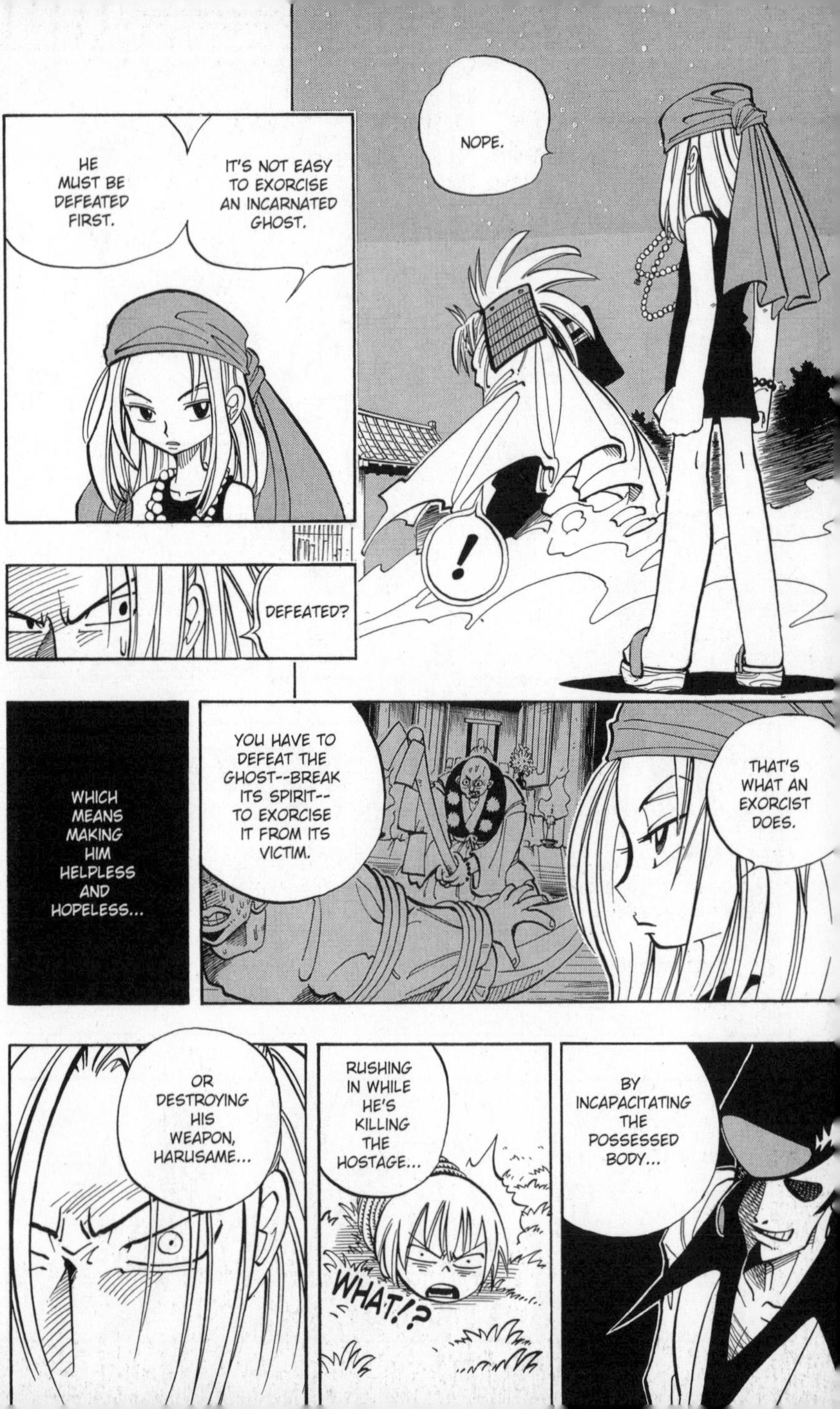
NOPE.
!
IT'S NOT EASY TO EXORCISE AN INCARNATED GHOST.
HE MUST BE DEFEATED FIRST.
DEFEATED?
YOU HAVE TO DEFEAT THE GHOST--BREAK ITS SPIRIT-- TO EXORCISE IT FROM ITS VICTIM.
THAT'S WHAT AN EXORCIST DOES.
WHICH MEANS MAKING HIM HELPLESS AND HOPELESS...
BY INCAPACITATING THE POSSESSED BODY...
RUSHING IN WHILE HE'S KILLING THE HOSTAGE...
WHAT!?
OR DESTROYING HIS WEAPON, HARUSAME...

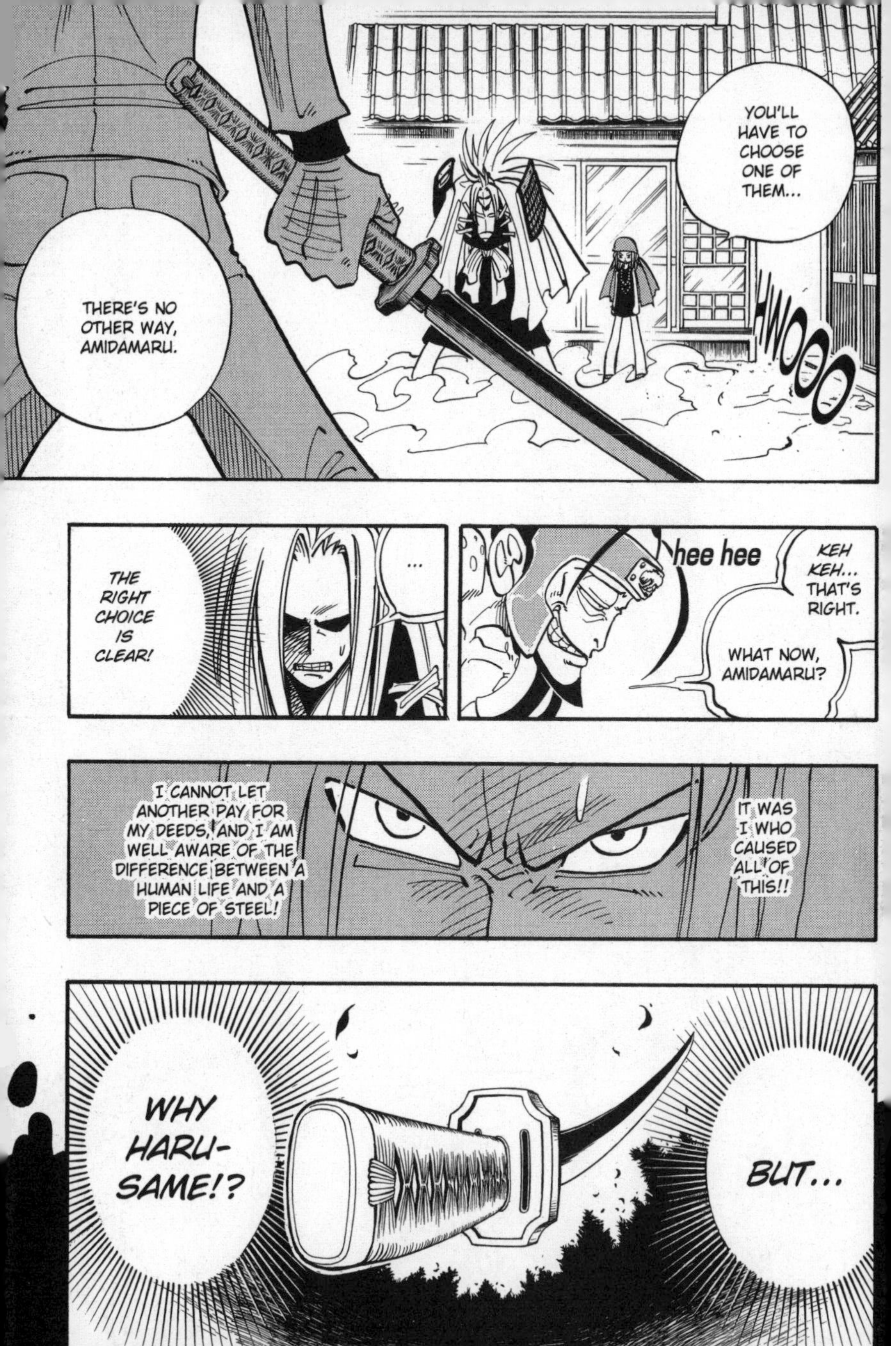
YOU'LL HAVE TO CHOOSE ONE OF THEM...
HWOOO
THERE'S NO OTHER WAY, AMIDAMARU.
hee hee
KEH KEH... THAT'S RIGHT.
WHAT NOW, AMIDAMARU?
...
THE RIGHT CHOICE IS CLEAR!
IT WAS I WHO CAUSED ALL OF THIS!!
I CANNOT LET ANOTHER PAY FOR MY DEEDS, AND I AM WELL AWARE OF THE DIFFERENCE BETWEEN A HUMAN LIFE AND A PIECE OF STEEL!
BUT...
WHY HARU-SAME!?

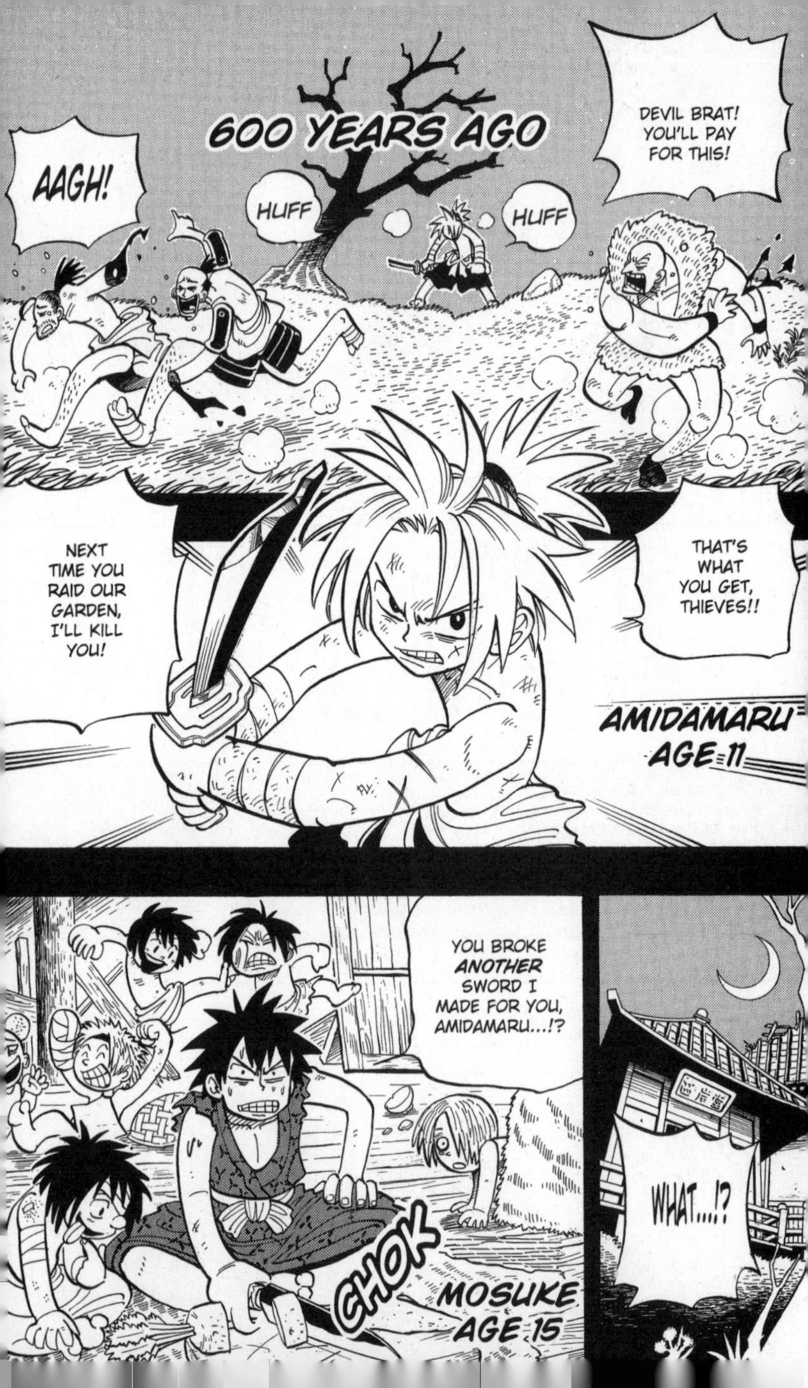
DEVIL BRAT! YOU'LL PAY FOR THIS!
600 YEARS AGO
HUFF
HUFF
AAGH!
THAT'S WHAT YOU GET, THIEVES!!
AMIDAMARU AGE 11
NEXT TIME YOU RAID OUR GARDEN, I'LL KILL YOU!
WHAT...!?
YOU BROKE ANOTHER SWORD I MADE FOR YOU, AMIDAMARU...!?
CHOK
MOSUKE AGE 15

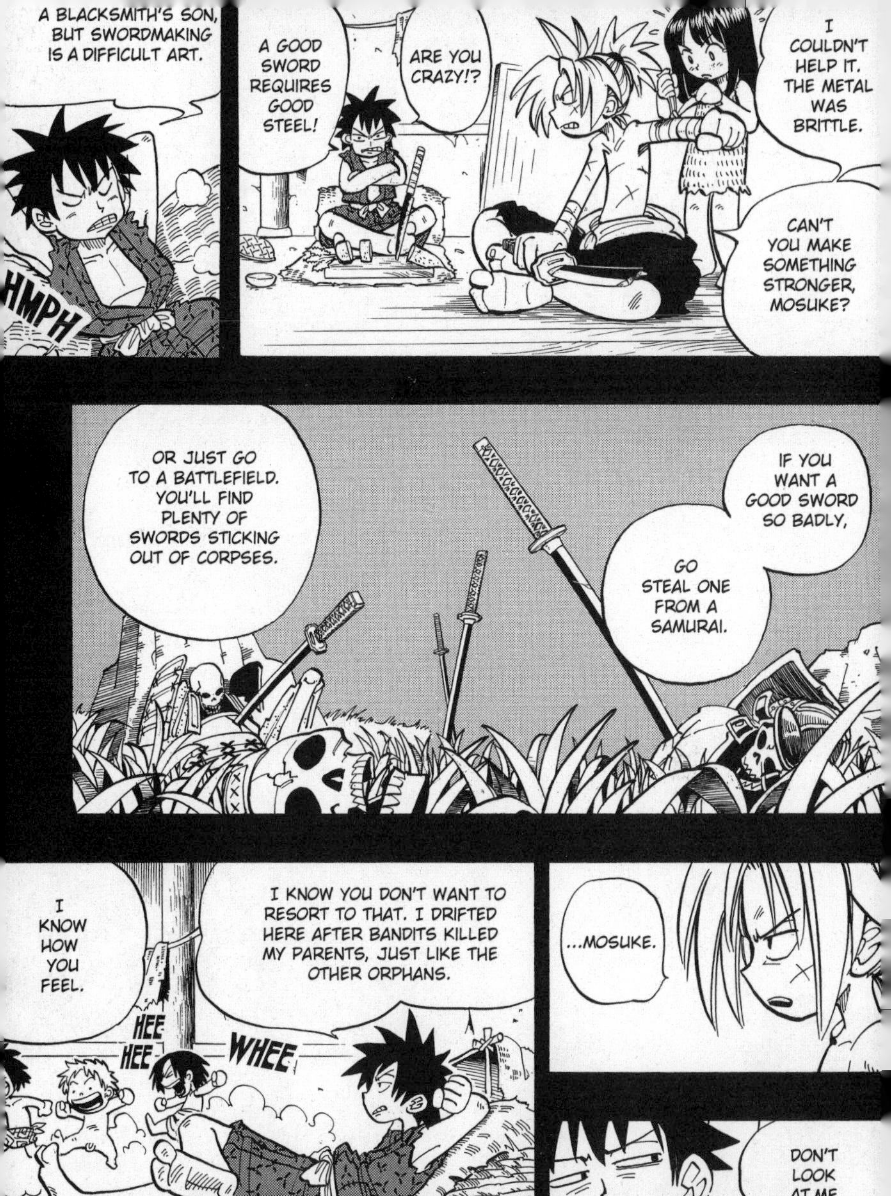
I COULDN'T HELP IT. THE METAL WAS BRITTLE.
CAN'T YOU MAKE SOMETHING STRONGER, MOSUKE?
ARE YOU CRAZY!?
A GOOD SWORD REQUIRES GOOD STEEL!
A BLACKSMITH'S SON, BUT SWORDMAKING IS A DIFFICULT ART.
HMPH
IF YOU WANT A GOOD SWORD SO BADLY,
GO STEAL ONE FROM A SAMURAI.
OR JUST GO TO A BATTLEFIELD. YOU'LL FIND PLENTY OF SWORDS STICKING OUT OF CORPSES.
...MOSUKE.
DON'T LOOK AT ME LIKE THAT.
I KNOW YOU DON'T WANT TO RESORT TO THAT. I DRIFTED HERE AFTER BANDITS KILLED MY PARENTS, JUST LIKE THE OTHER ORPHANS.
I KNOW HOW YOU FEEL.
WHEE
HEE HEE

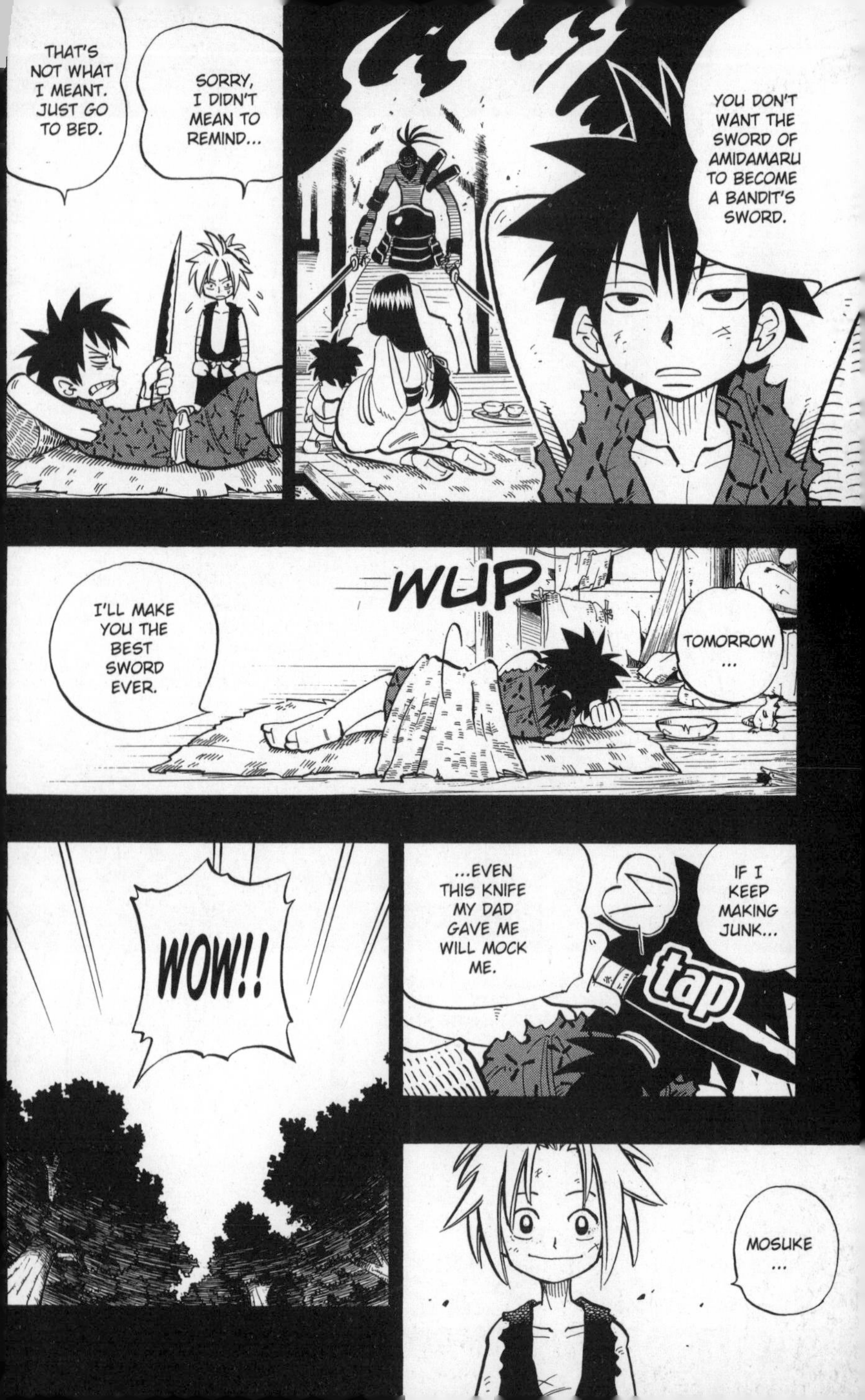
YOU DON'T WANT THE SWORD OF AMIDAMARU TO BECOME A BANDIT'S SWORD.
SORRY, I DIDN'T MEAN TO REMIND...
THAT'S NOT WHAT I MEANT. JUST GO TO BED.
WUP
TOMORROW ...
I'LL MAKE YOU THE BEST SWORD EVER.
IF I KEEP MAKING JUNK...
...EVEN THIS KNIFE MY DAD GAVE ME WILL MOCK ME.
tap
MOSUKE ...
WOW!!

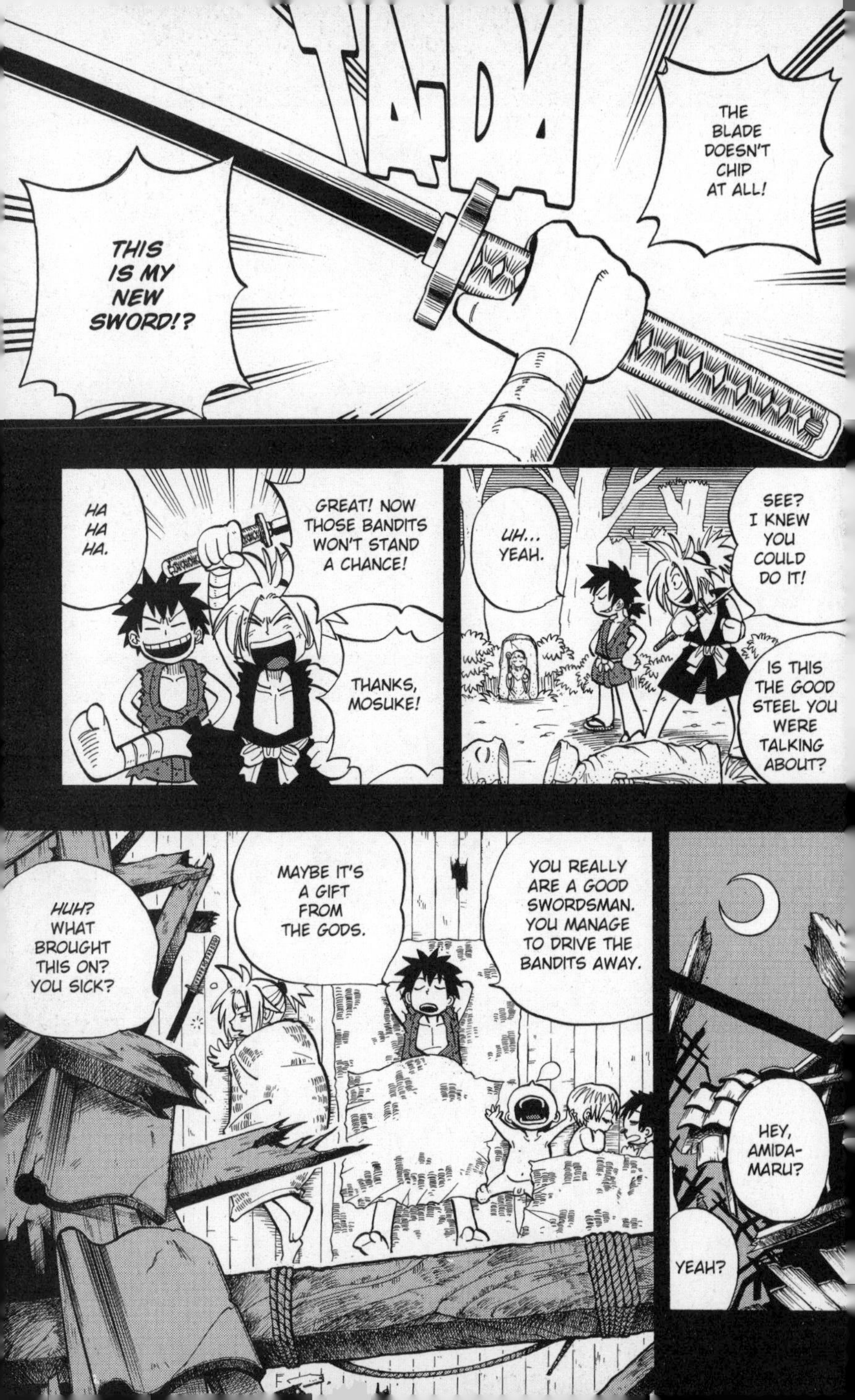
TADA
THE BLADE DOESN'T CHIP AT ALL!
THIS IS MY NEW SWORD!?
SEE? I KNEW YOU COULD DO IT!
UH... YEAH.
IS THIS THE GOOD STEEL YOU WERE TALKING ABOUT?
GREAT! NOW THOSE BANDITS WON'T STAND A CHANCE!
HA HA HA.
THANKS, MOSUKE!
HEY, AMIDA-MARU?
YEAH?
YOU REALLY ARE A GOOD SWORDSMAN. YOU MANAGE TO DRIVE THE BANDITS AWAY.
MAYBE IT'S A GIFT FROM THE GODS.
HUH? WHAT BROUGHT THIS ON? YOU SICK?

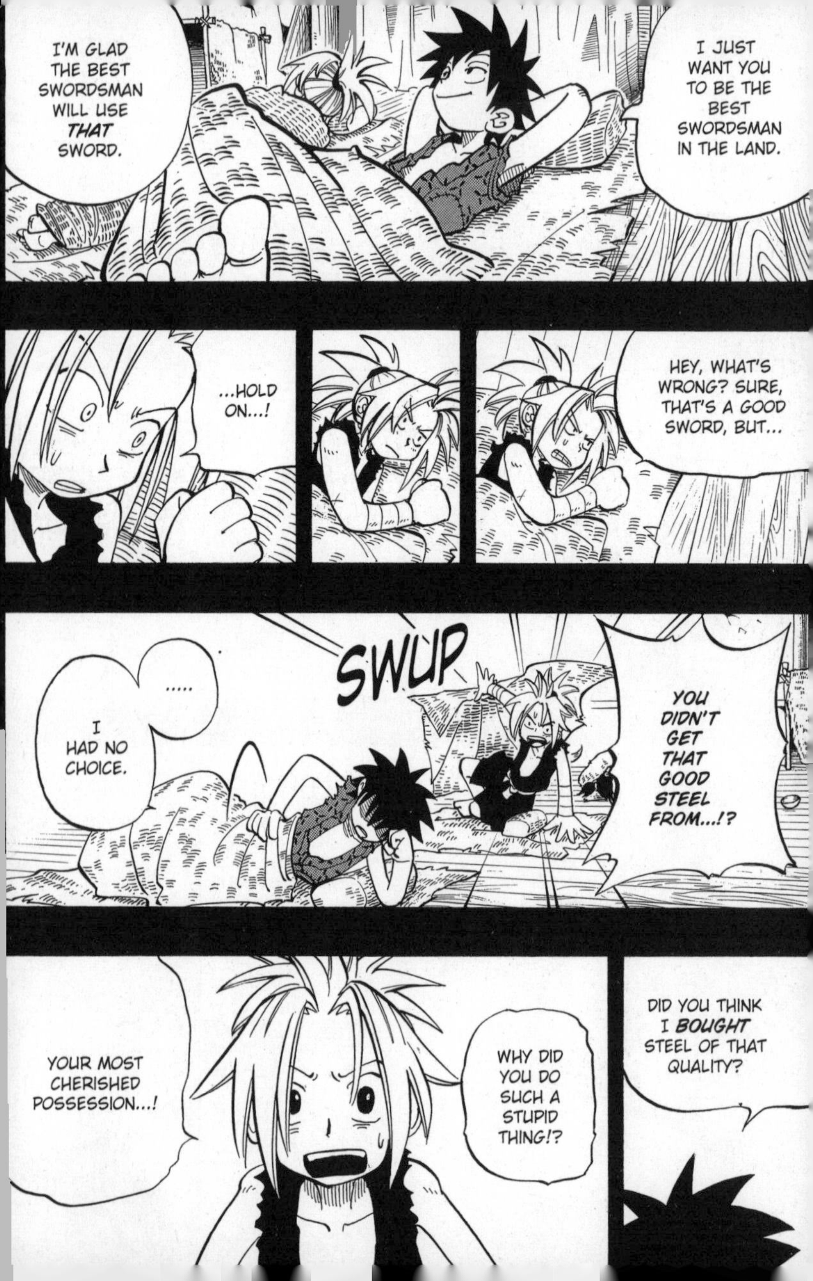
I JUST WANT YOU TO BE THE BEST SWORDSMAN IN THE LAND.
I'M GLAD THE BEST SWORDSMAN WILL USE *THAT* SWORD.
HEY, WHAT'S WRONG? SURE, THAT'S A GOOD SWORD, BUT...
...HOLD ON...!
YOU DIDN'T GET THAT GOOD STEEL FROM...!?
SWUP
.....
I HAD NO CHOICE.
DID YOU THINK I *BOUGHT* STEEL OF THAT QUALITY?
WHY DID YOU DO SUCH A STUPID THING!?
YOUR MOST CHERISHED POSSESSION...!

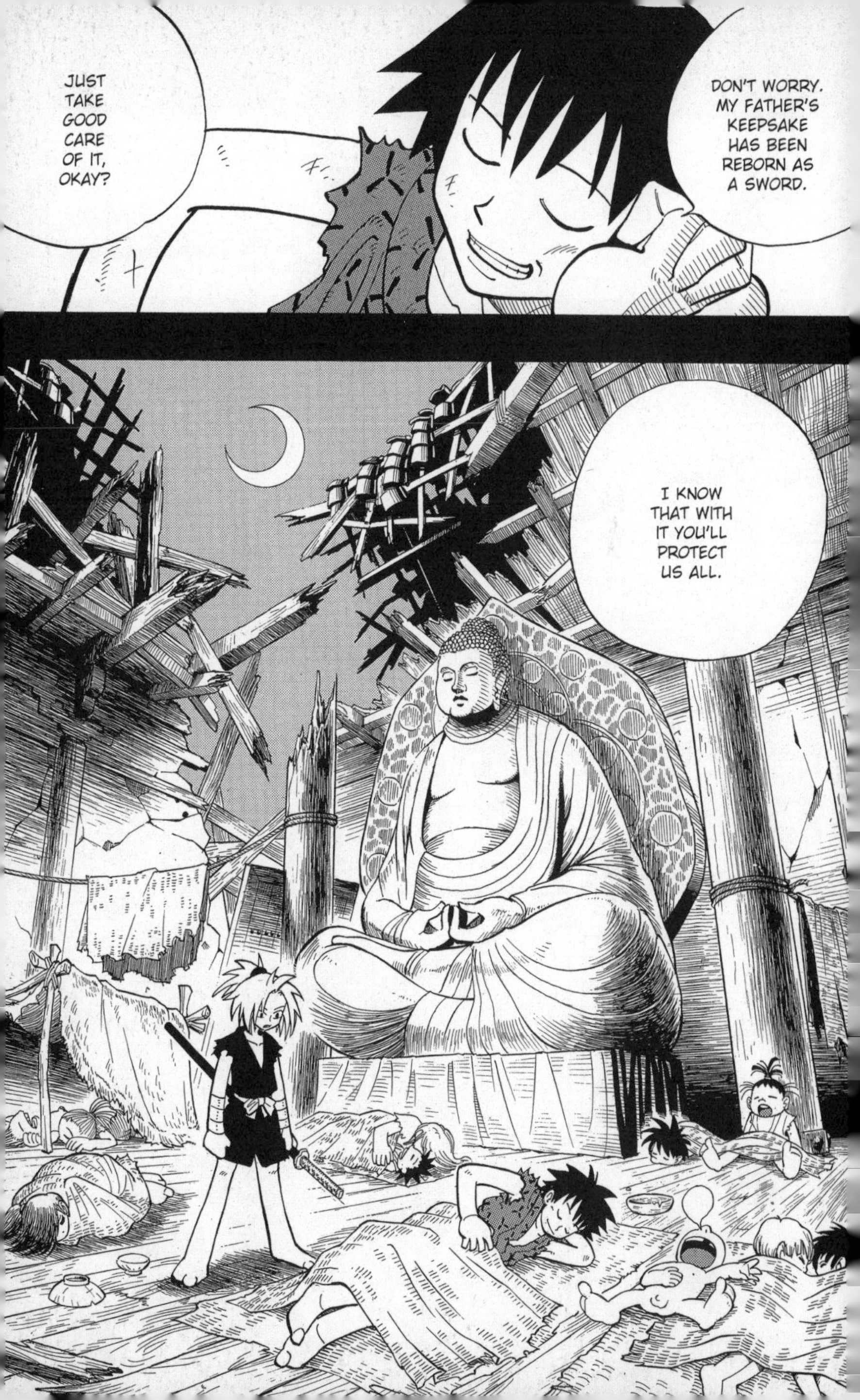
DON'T WORRY. MY FATHER'S KEEPSAKE HAS BEEN REBORN AS A SWORD.
JUST TAKE GOOD CARE OF IT, OKAY?
I KNOW THAT WITH IT YOU'LL PROTECT US ALL.

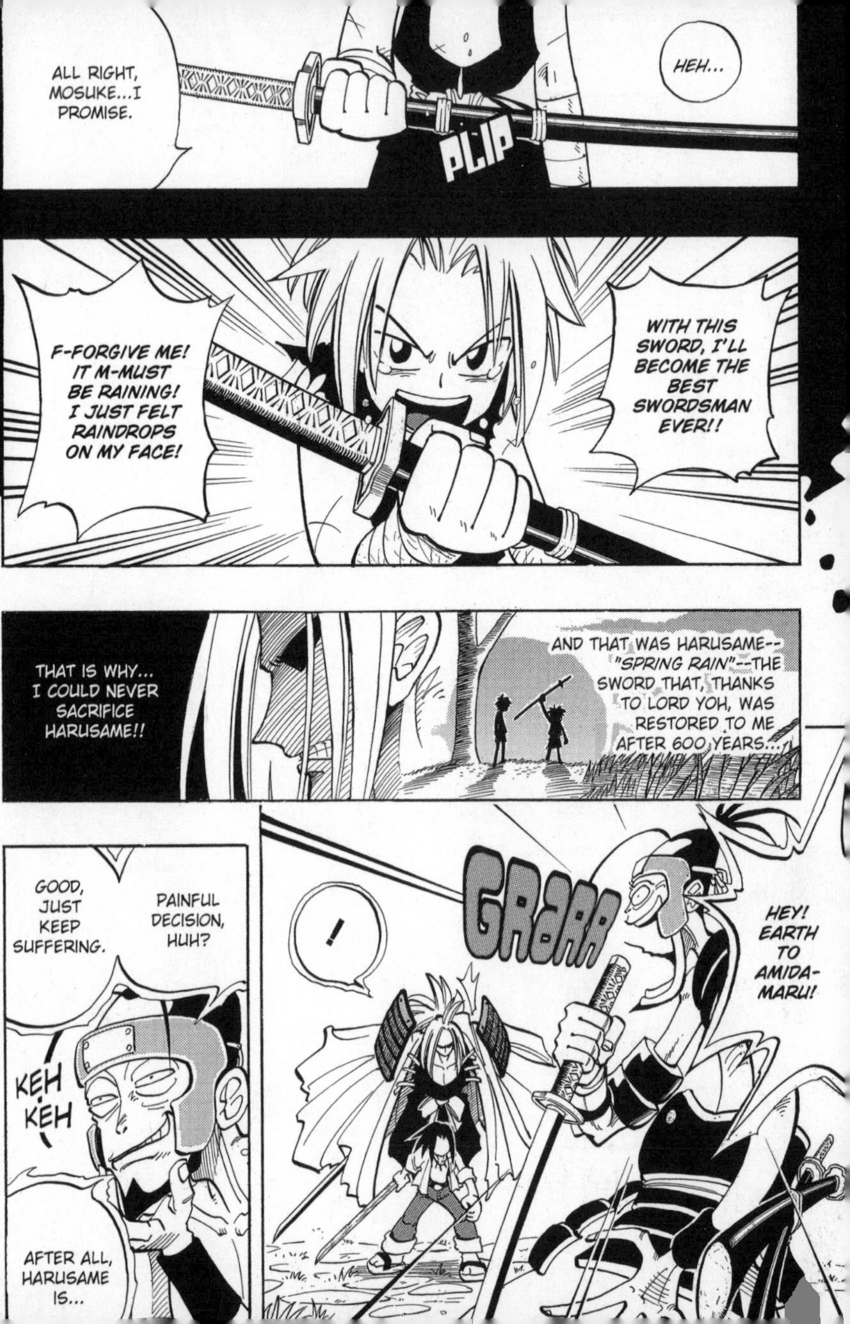
HEH...
PLIP
ALL RIGHT, MOSUKE...I PROMISE.
WITH THIS SWORD, I'LL BECOME THE BEST SWORDSMAN EVER!!
F-FORGIVE ME! IT M-MUST BE RAINING! I JUST FELT RAINDROPS ON MY FACE!
AND THAT WAS HARUSAME--"SPRING RAIN"--THE SWORD THAT, THANKS TO LORD YOH, WAS RESTORED TO ME AFTER 600 YEARS...
THAT IS WHY... I COULD NEVER SACRIFICE HARUSAME!!
HEY! EARTH TO AMIDA-MARU!
GRAAR
!
PAINFUL DECISION, HUH?
GOOD, JUST KEEP SUFFERING.
KEH KEH
AFTER ALL, HARUSAME IS...

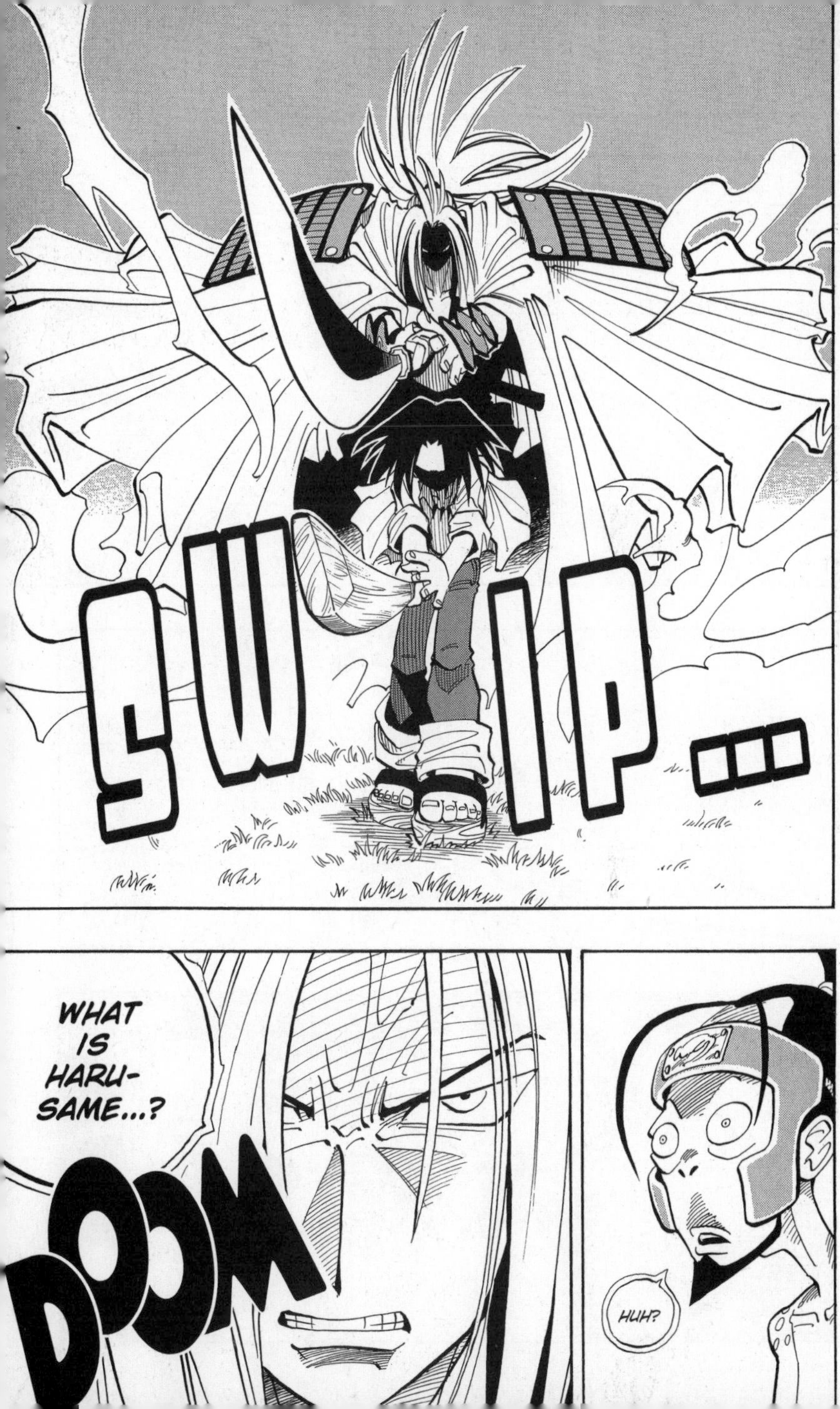
SWIP...
HUH?
WHAT IS HARU-SAME...?
DOOM

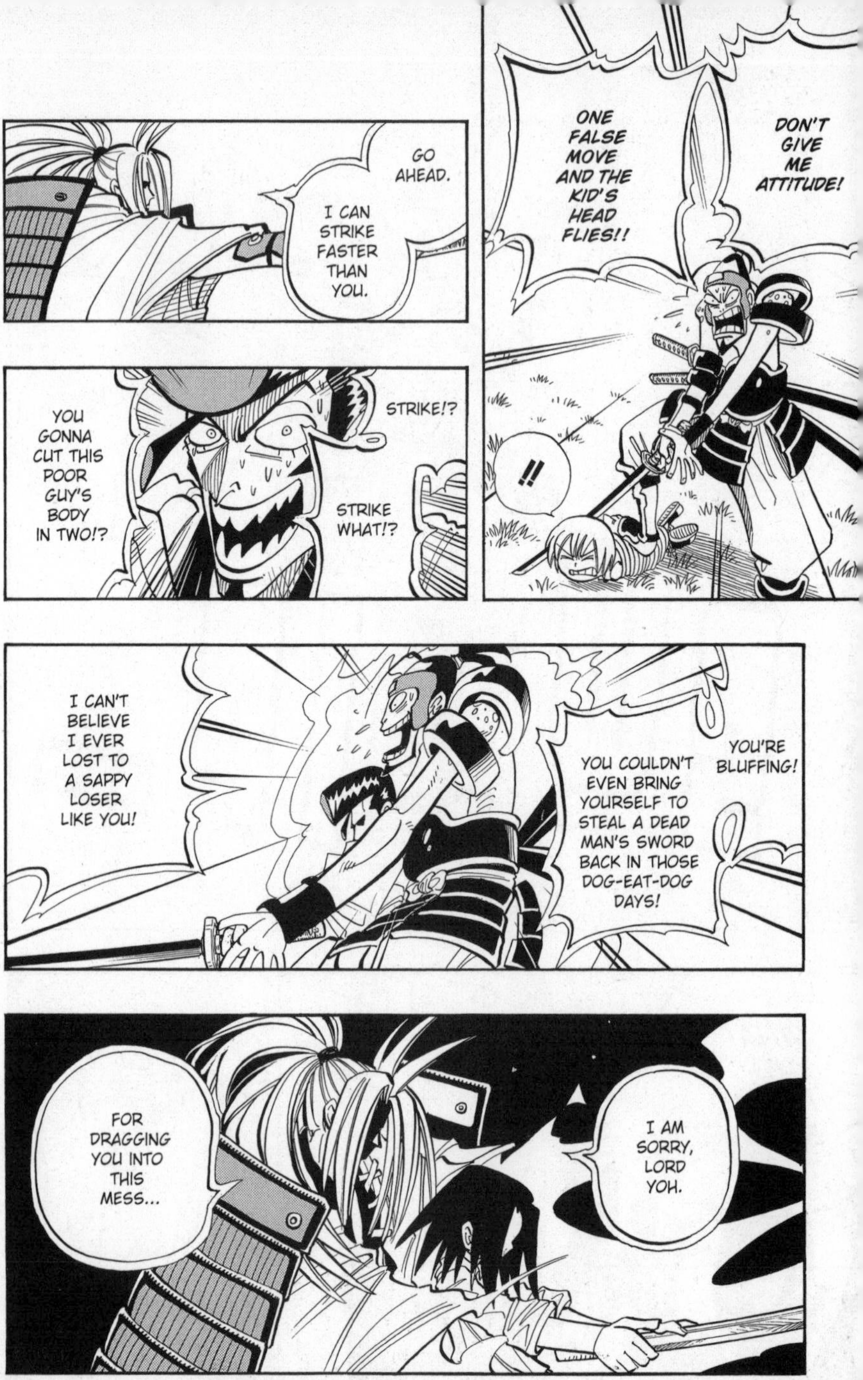
DON'T GIVE ME ATTITUDE!
ONE FALSE MOVE AND THE KID'S HEAD FLIES!!
!!
GO AHEAD.
I CAN STRIKE FASTER THAN YOU.
STRIKE!?
STRIKE WHAT!?
YOU GONNA CUT THIS POOR GUY'S BODY IN TWO!?
YOU'RE BLUFFING!
YOU COULDN'T EVEN BRING YOURSELF TO STEAL A DEAD MAN'S SWORD BACK IN THOSE DOG-EAT-DOG DAYS!
I CAN'T BELIEVE I EVER LOST TO A SAPPY LOSER LIKE YOU!
I AM SORRY, LORD YOH.
FOR DRAGGING YOU INTO THIS MESS...

READ THIS WAY

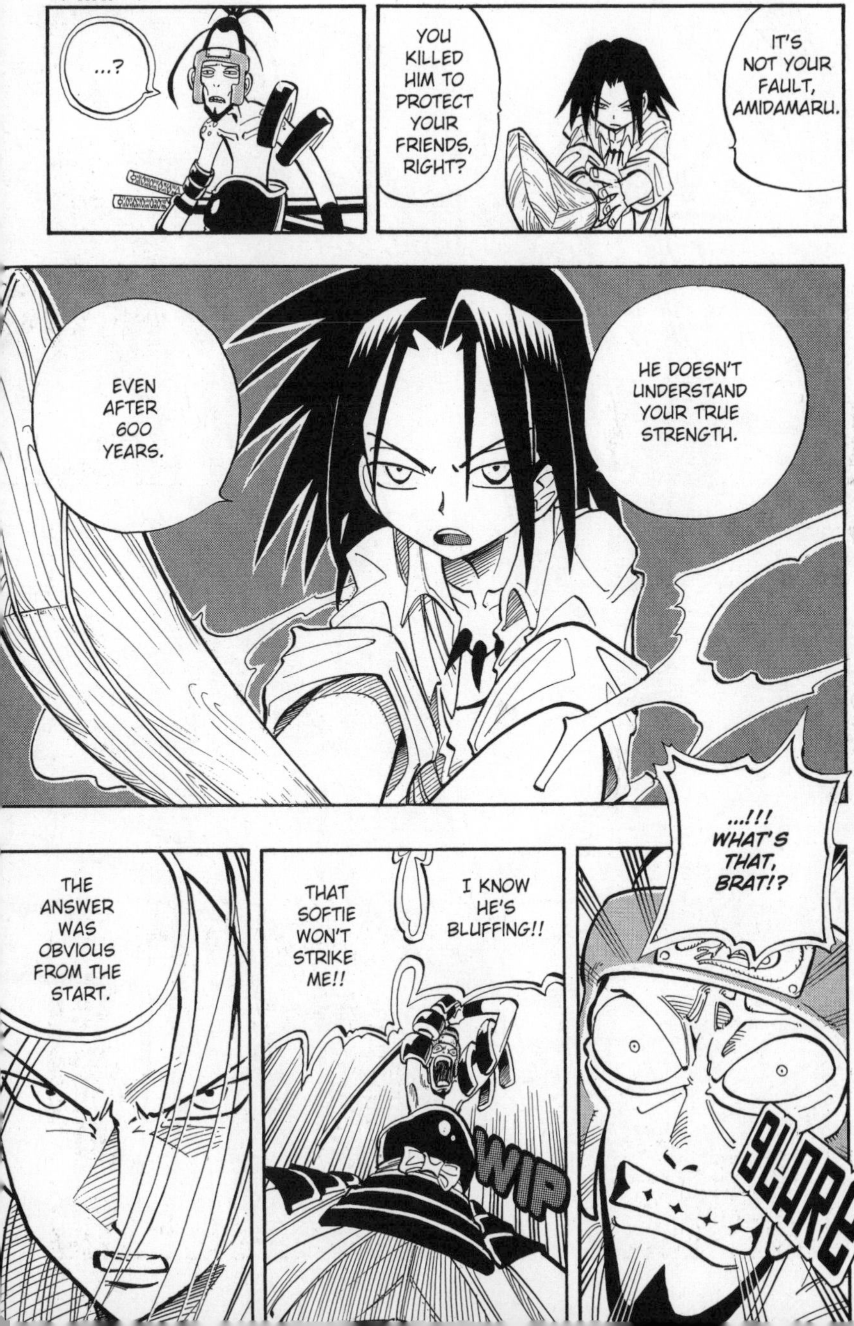
IT'S NOT YOUR FAULT, AMIDAMARU.
YOU KILLED HIM TO PROTECT YOUR FRIENDS, RIGHT?
...?
HE DOESN'T UNDERSTAND YOUR TRUE STRENGTH.
EVEN AFTER 600 YEARS.
...!!! WHAT'S THAT, BRAT!?
GLARE
I KNOW HE'S BLUFFING!!
THAT SOFTIE WON'T STRIKE ME!!
WIP
THE ANSWER WAS OBVIOUS FROM THE START.

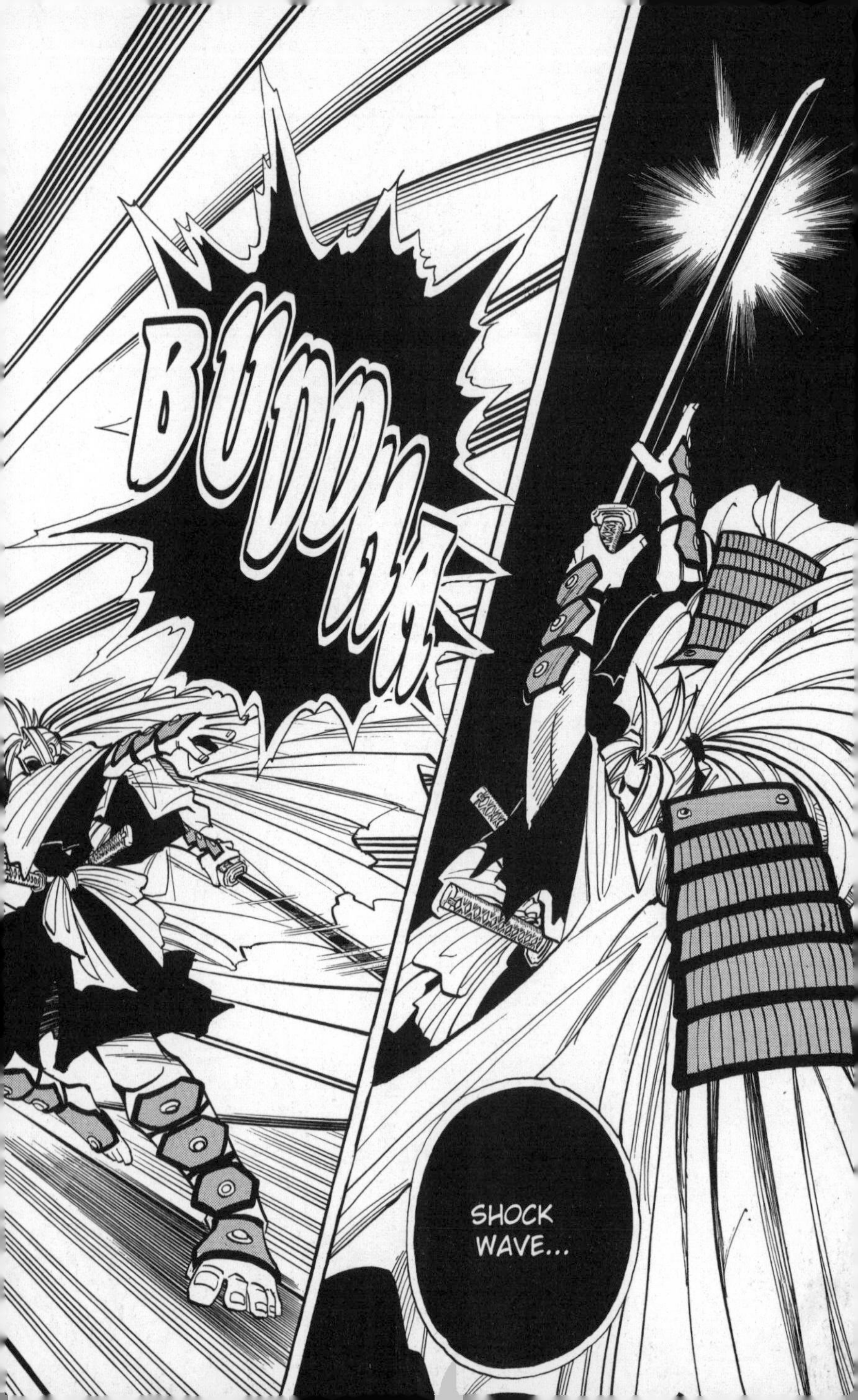

BOOOM
SHOCK WAVE...

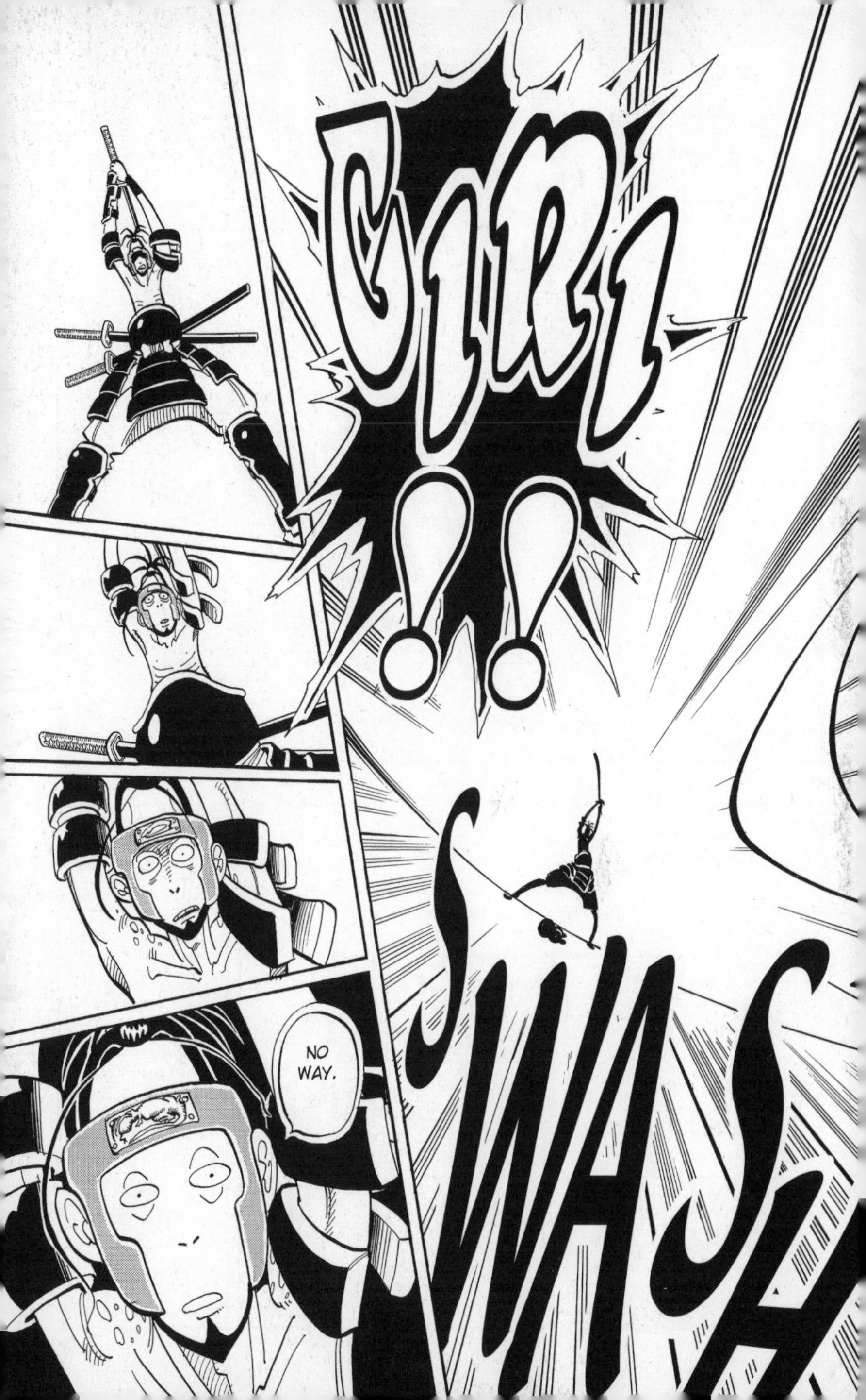
SWASH
NO WAY.

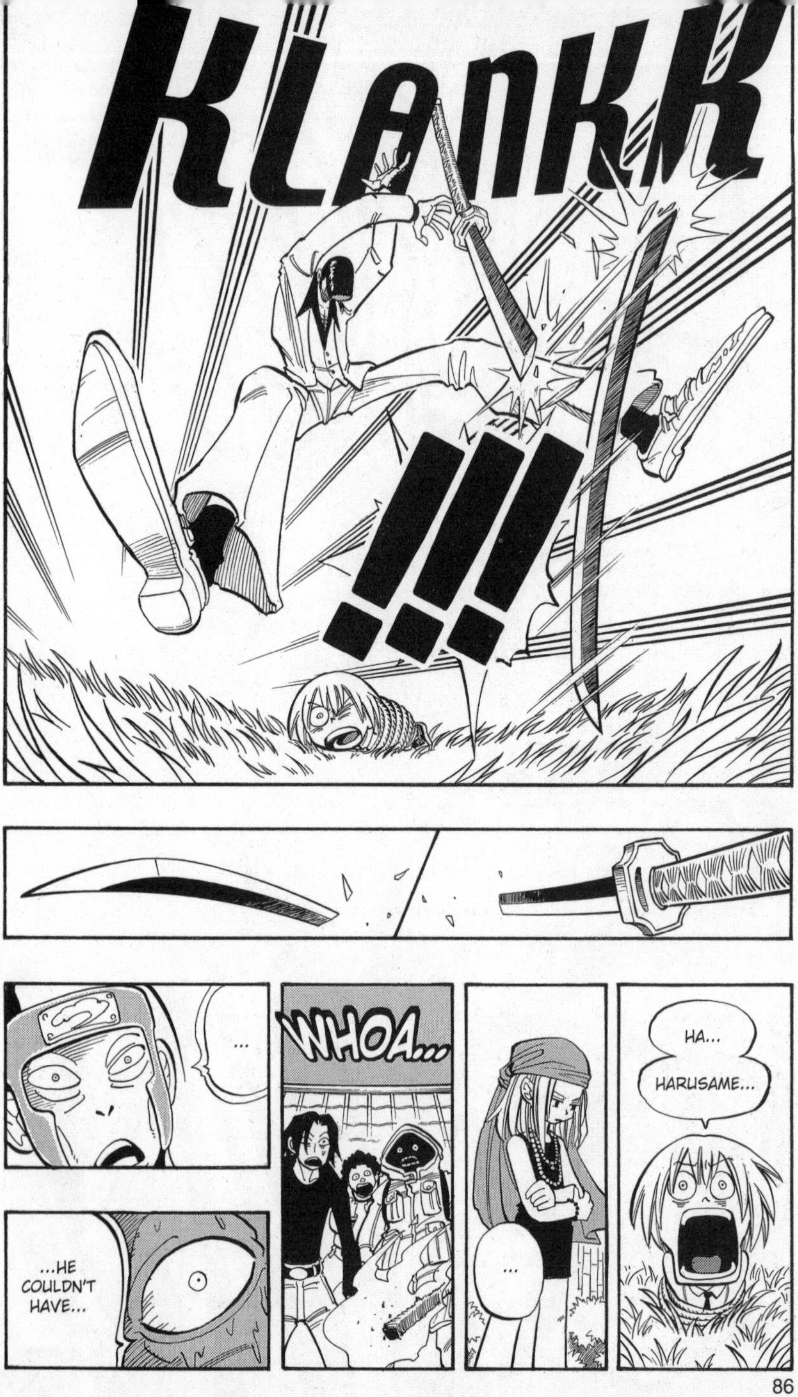
KLANKK
!!!
HA...
HARUSAME...
...
WHOA...
...
...HE COULDN'T HAVE...

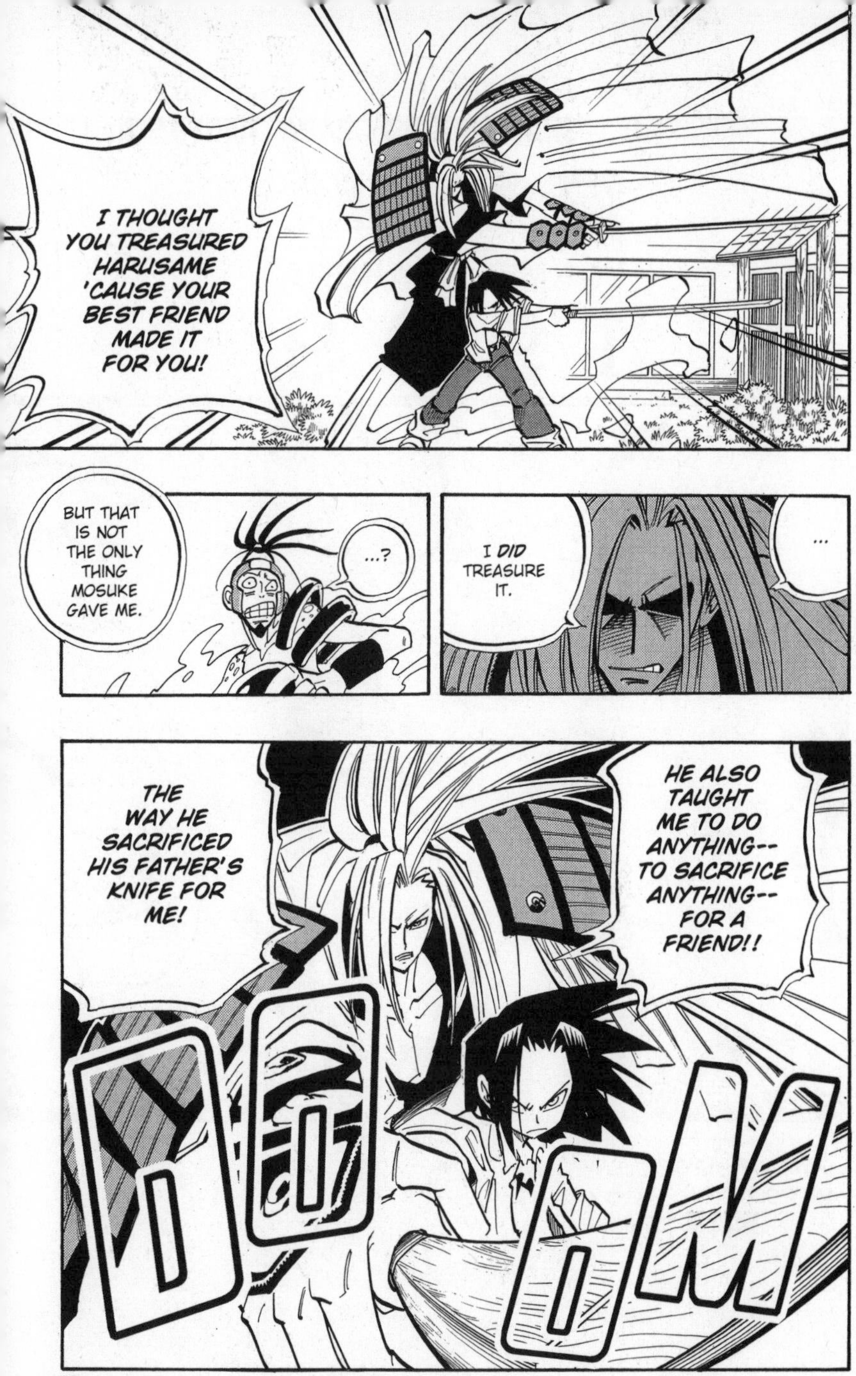
I THOUGHT YOU TREASURED HARUSAME 'CAUSE YOUR BEST FRIEND MADE IT FOR YOU!
...
I DID TREASURE IT.
BUT THAT IS NOT THE ONLY THING MOSUKE GAVE ME.
...?
HE ALSO TAUGHT ME TO DO ANYTHING-- TO SACRIFICE ANYTHING-- FOR A FRIEND!!
THE WAY HE SACRIFICED HIS FATHER'S KNIFE FOR ME!
DOOM

SHAMAN KING CHARACTER FILE No.11

麻倉葉明
YOHMEI ASAKURA
1989

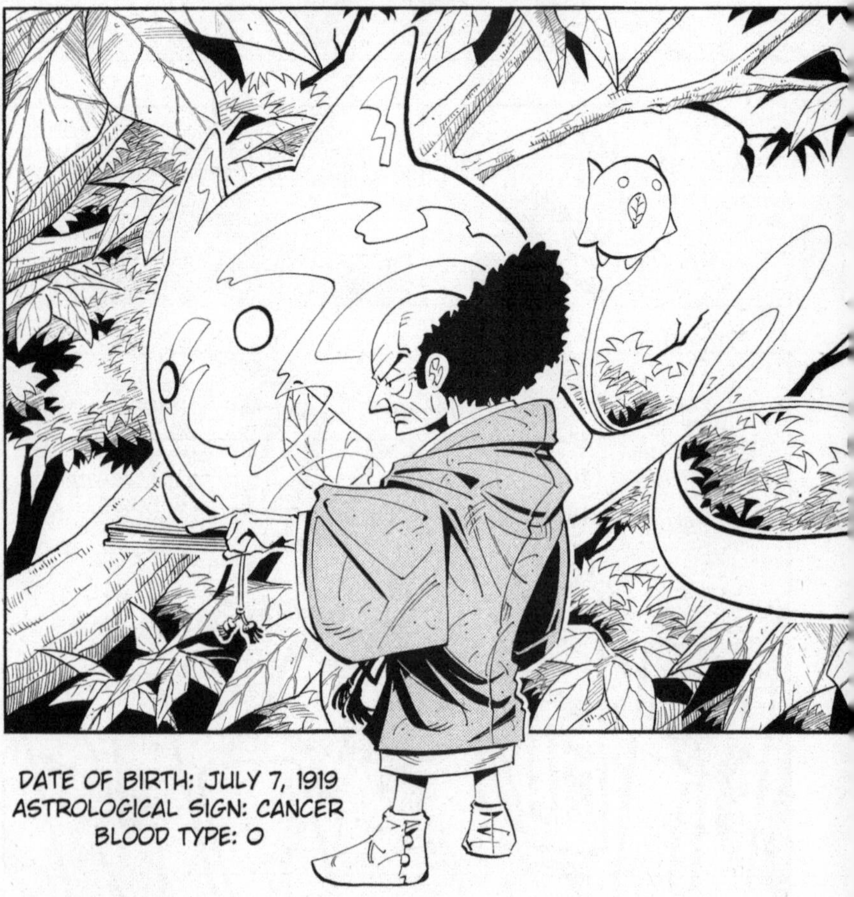

DATE OF BIRTH: JULY 7, 1919
ASTROLOGICAL SIGN: CANCER
BLOOD TYPE: O

READ THIS WAY

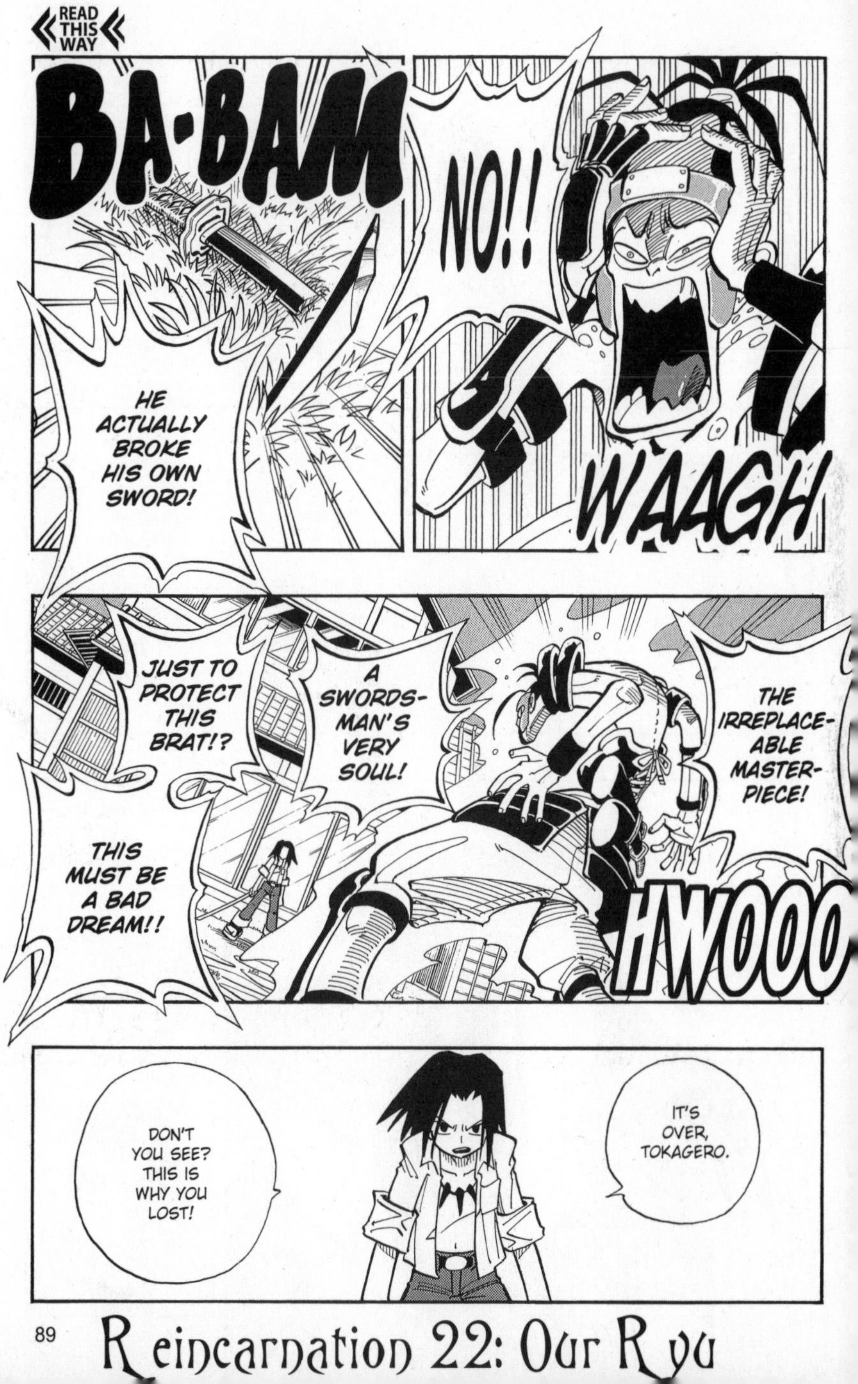

NO!!
WAAGH
BA-BAM
HE ACTUALLY BROKE HIS OWN SWORD!
THE IRREPLACEABLE MASTERPIECE!
A SWORDSMAN'S VERY SOUL!
JUST TO PROTECT THIS BRAT!?
THIS MUST BE A BAD DREAM!!
HWOOO
IT'S OVER, TOKAGERO.
DON'T YOU SEE? THIS IS WHY YOU LOST!

Reincarnation 22: Our Ryu

READ THIS WAY

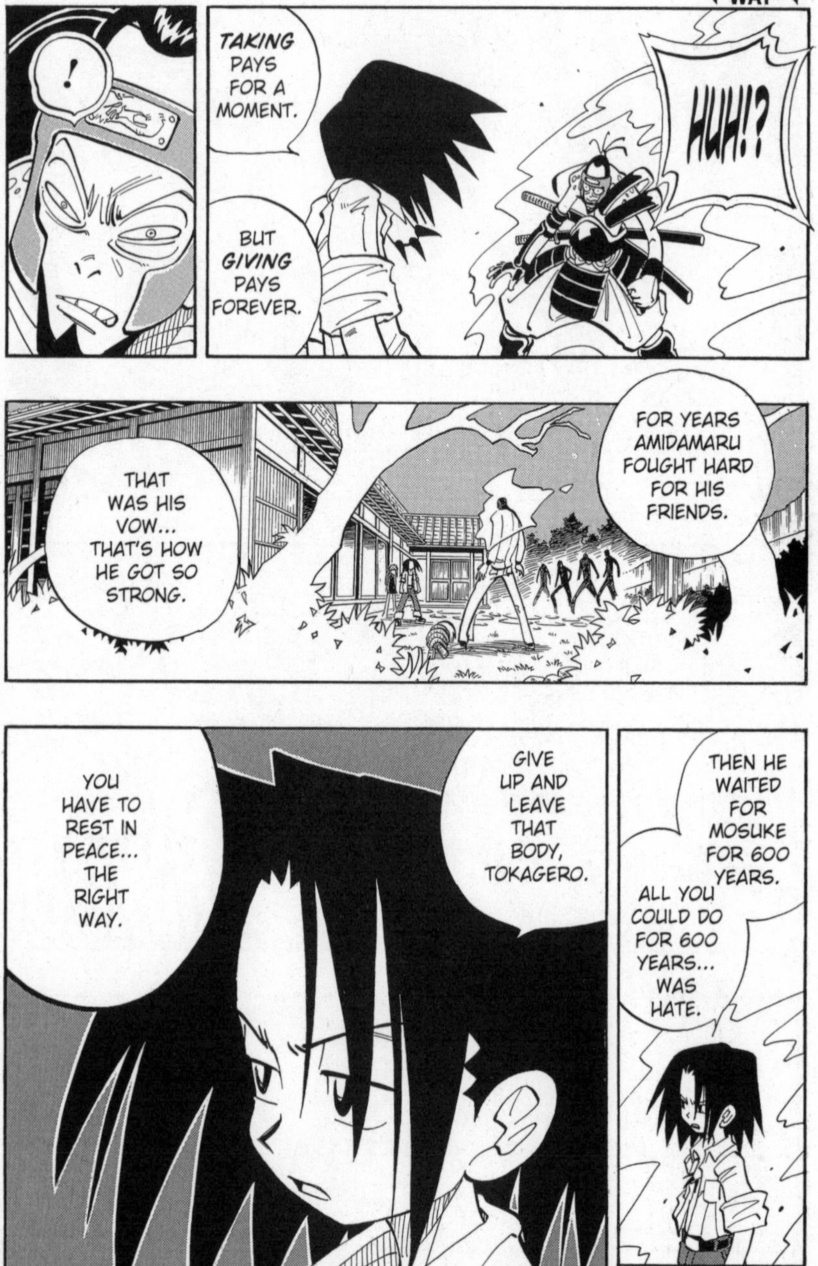
HUH!?
TAKING PAYS FOR A MOMENT.
BUT GIVING PAYS FOREVER.
!
FOR YEARS AMIDAMARU FOUGHT HARD FOR HIS FRIENDS.
THAT WAS HIS VOW... THAT'S HOW HE GOT SO STRONG.
THEN HE WAITED FOR MOSUKE FOR 600 YEARS.
ALL YOU COULD DO FOR 600 YEARS... WAS HATE.
GIVE UP AND LEAVE THAT BODY, TOKAGERO.
YOU HAVE TO REST IN PEACE... THE RIGHT WAY.

Reincarnation 22: Our Ryu

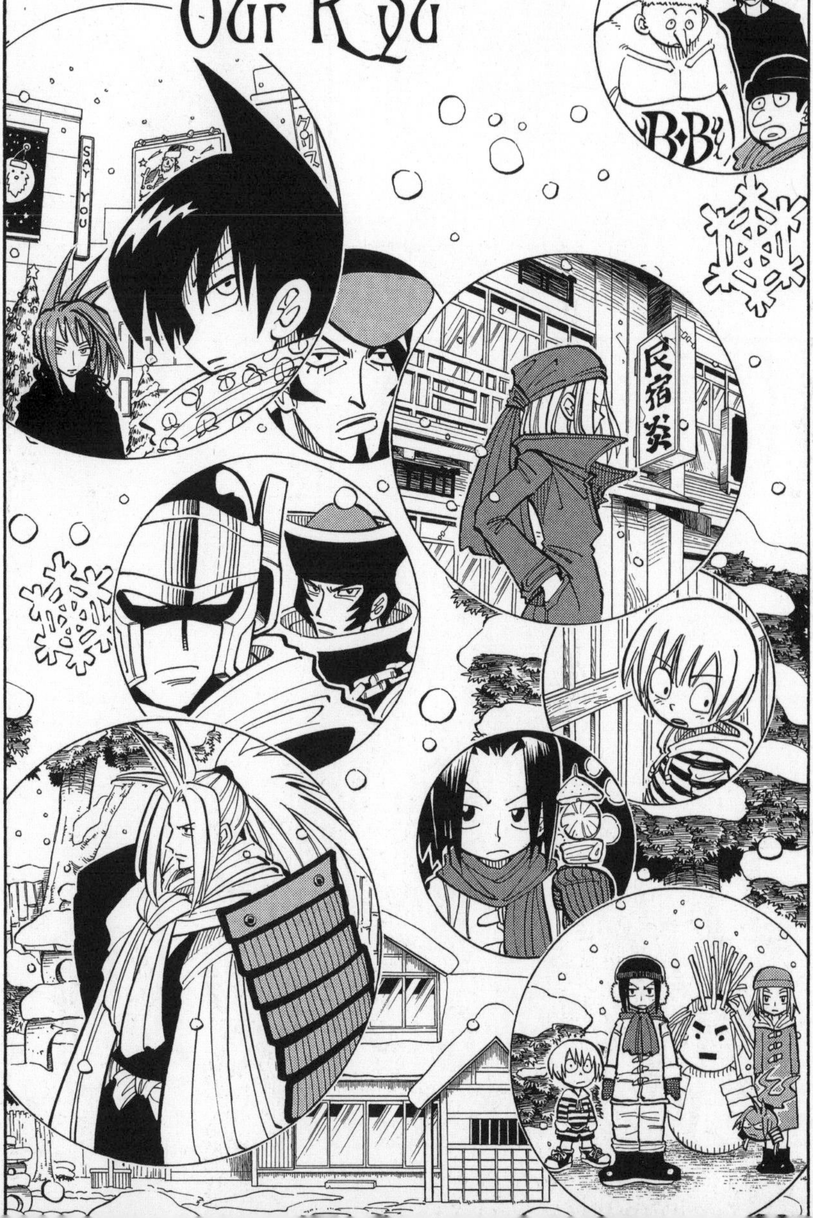
SAY YOU
民宿炎

READ THIS WAY

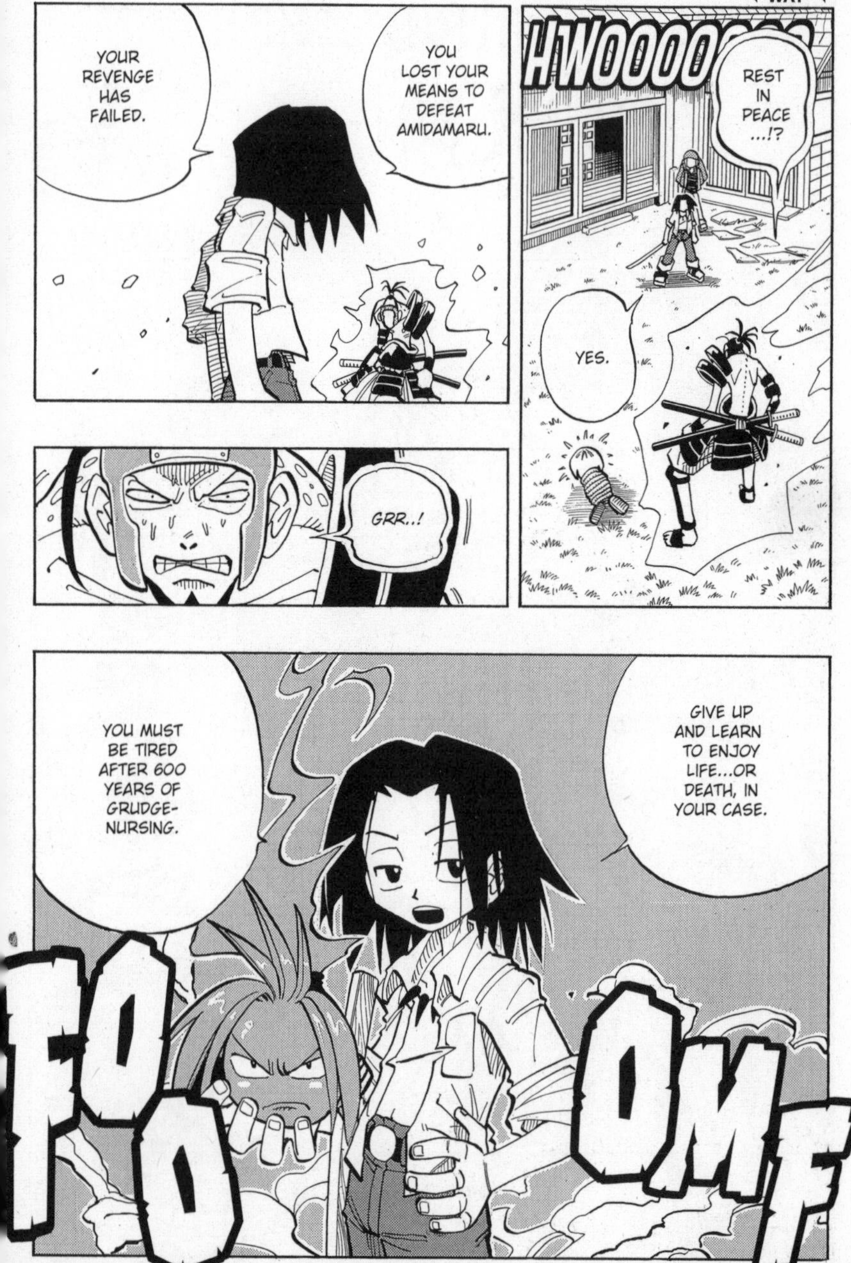

HWOOOOO
REST IN PEACE ...!?
YES.
YOU LOST YOUR MEANS TO DEFEAT AMIDAMARU.
YOUR REVENGE HAS FAILED.
GRR..!
GIVE UP AND LEARN TO ENJOY LIFE...OR DEATH, IN YOUR CASE.
YOU MUST BE TIRED AFTER 600 YEARS OF GRUDGE-NURSING.
FOOOMF

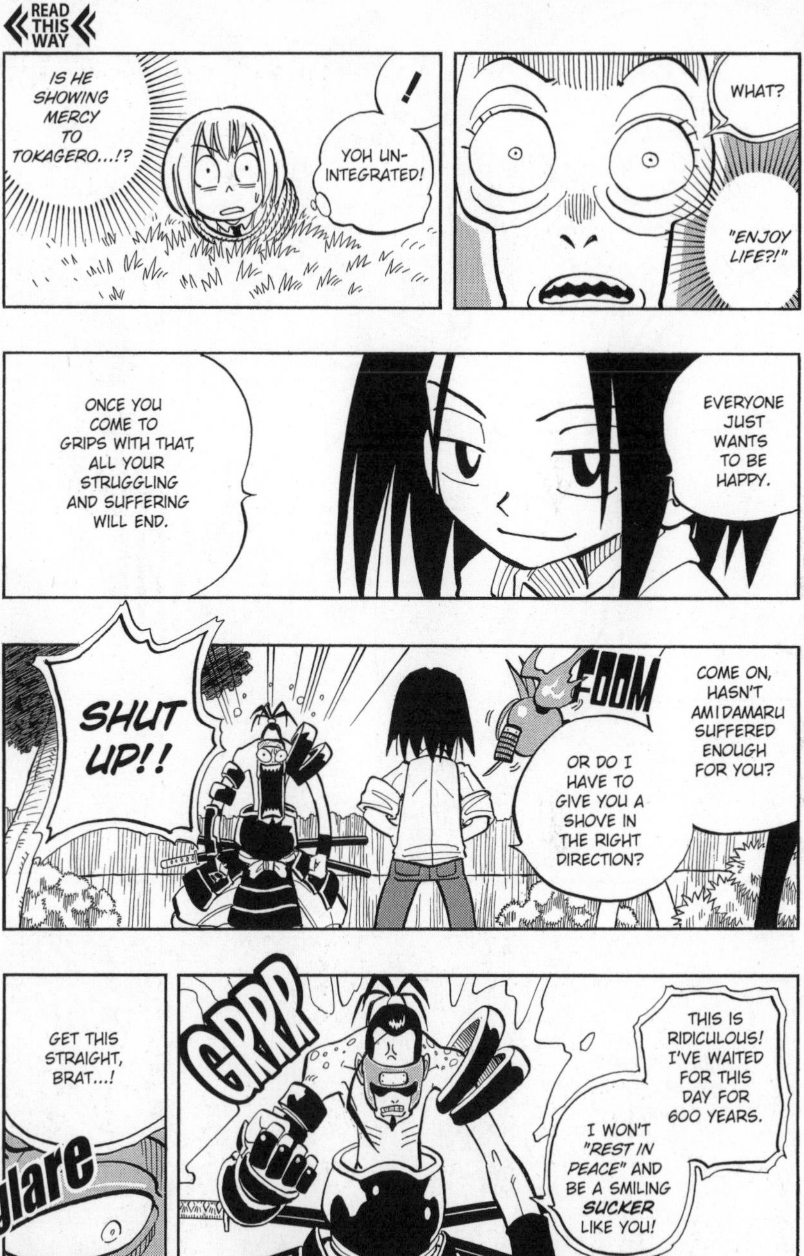
READ THIS WAY
WHAT?
"ENJOY LIFE?!"
!
YOH UN-INTEGRATED!
IS HE SHOWING MERCY TO TOKAGERO...!?
EVERYONE JUST WANTS TO BE HAPPY.
ONCE YOU COME TO GRIPS WITH THAT, ALL YOUR STRUGGLING AND SUFFERING WILL END.
COME ON, HASN'T AMIDAMARU SUFFERED ENOUGH FOR YOU?
FOOM
OR DO I HAVE TO GIVE YOU A SHOVE IN THE RIGHT DIRECTION?
SHUT UP!!
THIS IS RIDICULOUS! I'VE WAITED FOR THIS DAY FOR 600 YEARS.
I WON'T "REST IN PEACE" AND BE A SMILING SUCKER LIKE YOU!
GRRR
GET THIS STRAIGHT, BRAT...!
glare

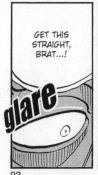

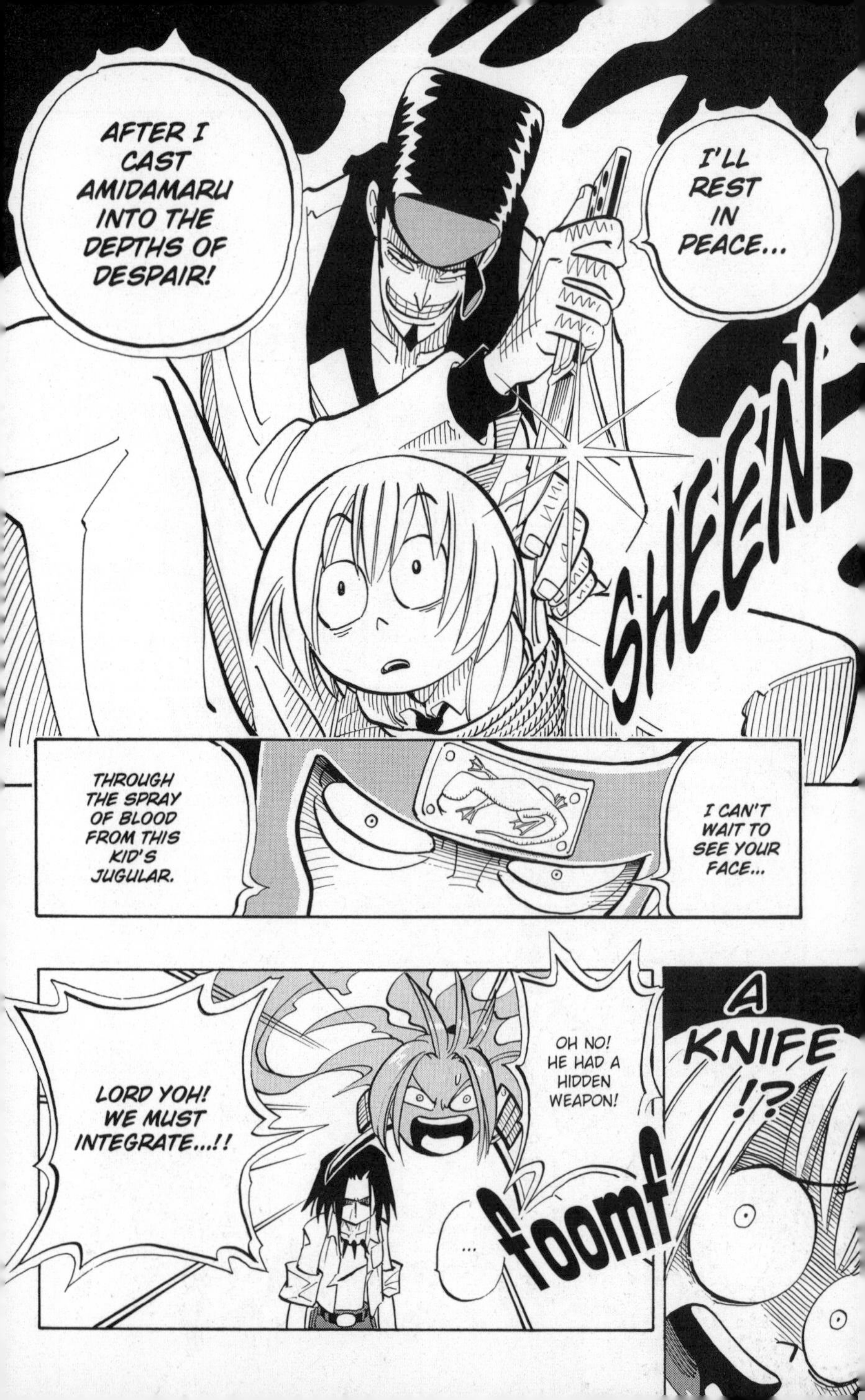
I'LL REST IN PEACE...
AFTER I CAST AMIDAMARU INTO THE DEPTHS OF DESPAIR!
SHEEN
I CAN'T WAIT TO SEE YOUR FACE...
THROUGH THE SPRAY OF BLOOD FROM THIS KID'S JUGULAR.
A KNIFE !?
OH NO! HE HAD A HIDDEN WEAPON!
LORD YOH! WE MUST INTEGRATE...!!
...
foomf

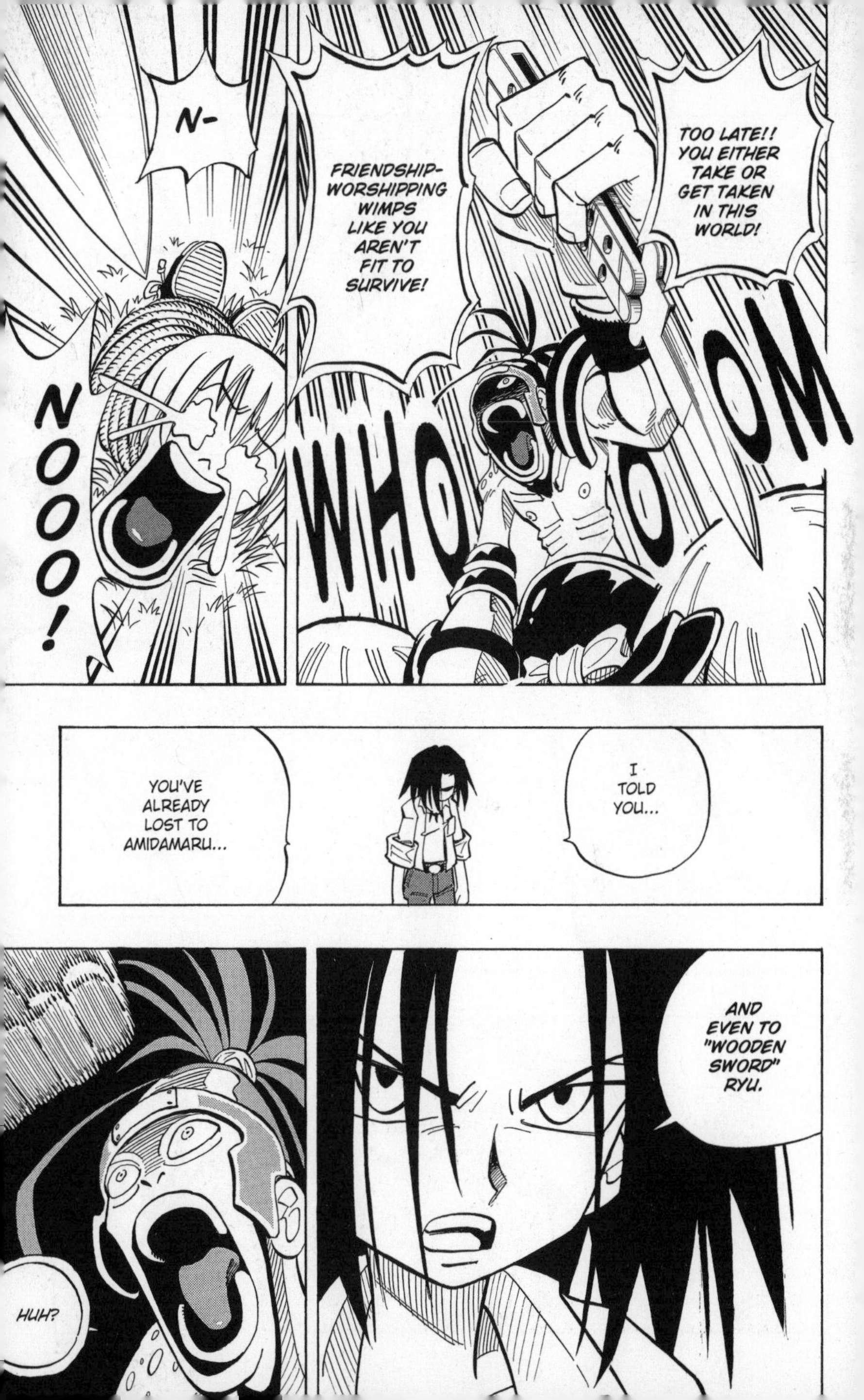
TOO LATE!! YOU EITHER TAKE OR GET TAKEN IN THIS WORLD!
FRIENDSHIP-WORSHIPPING WIMPS LIKE YOU AREN'T FIT TO SURVIVE!
WHOOOOM
N-
NOOOO!
I TOLD YOU...
YOU'VE ALREADY LOST TO AMIDAMARU...
AND EVEN TO "WOODEN SWORD" RYU.
HUH?

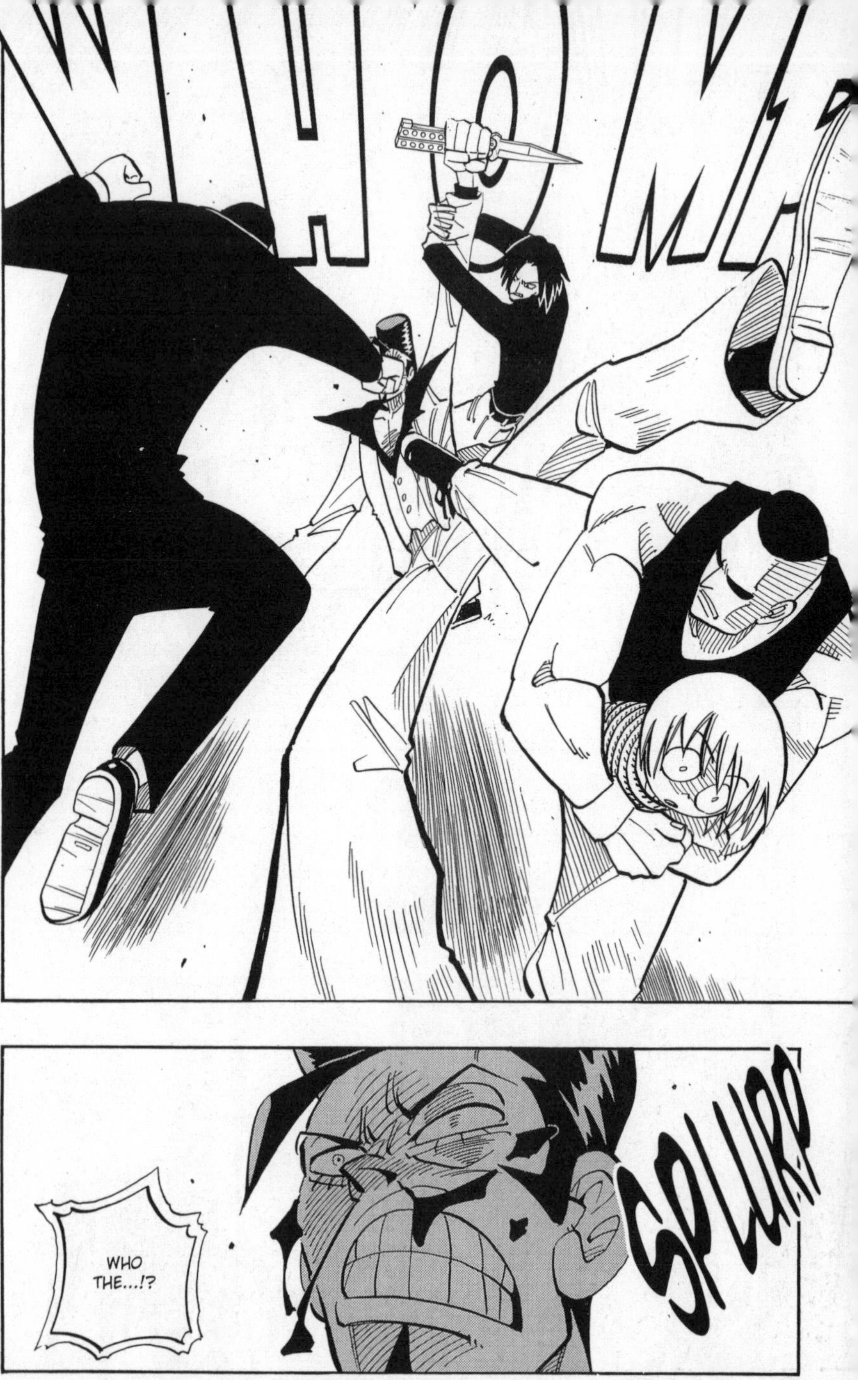
WHOMP
SPLURP
WHO THE...!?

READ THIS WAY

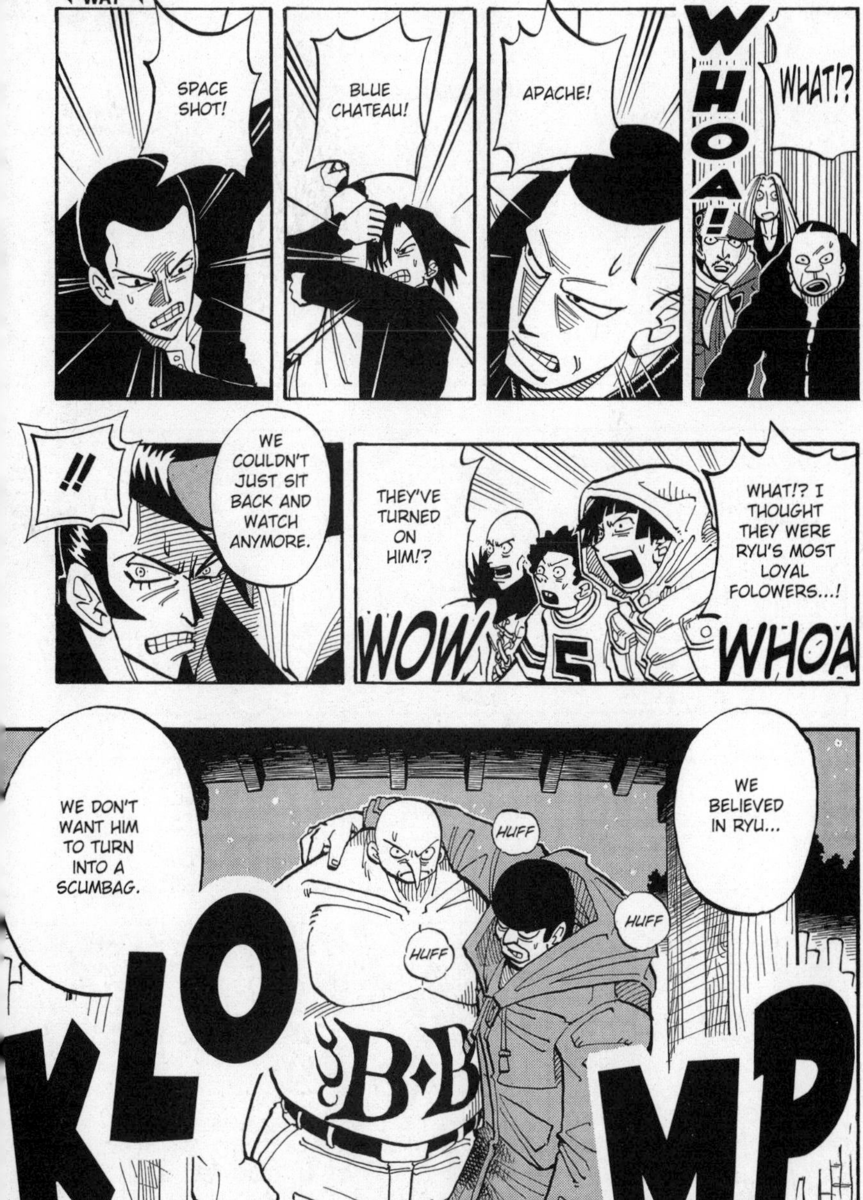

WHOA!
WHAT!?
APACHE!
BLUE CHATEAU!
SPACE SHOT!
WHAT!? I THOUGHT THEY WERE RYU'S MOST LOYAL FOLOWERS...!
WHOA
THEY'VE TURNED ON HIM!?
WOW
WE COULDN'T JUST SIT BACK AND WATCH ANYMORE.
!!
WE BELIEVED IN RYU...
HUFF
HUFF
HUFF
WE DON'T WANT HIM TO TURN INTO A SCUMBAG.
B·B
KLOMP

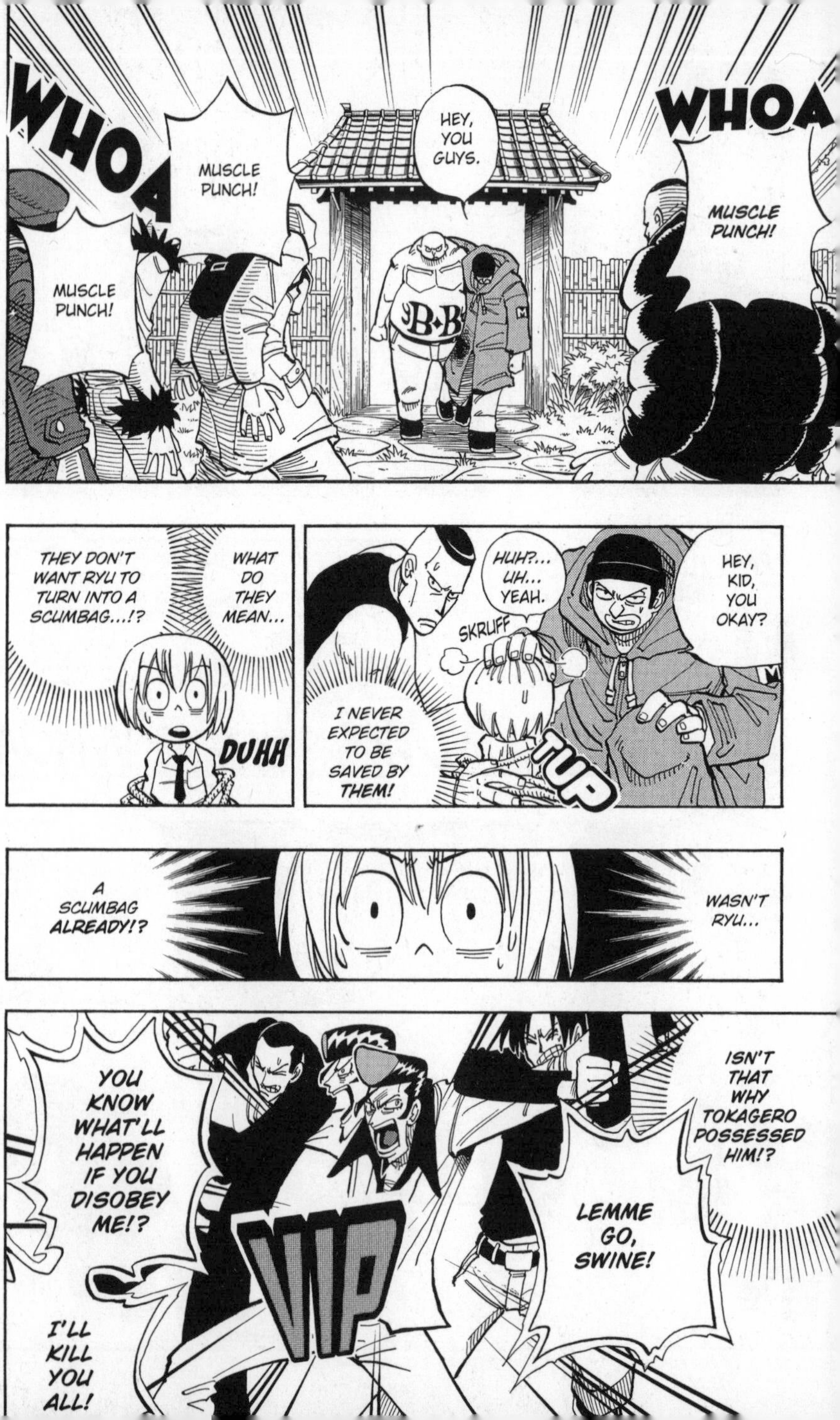
WHOA
MUSCLE PUNCH!
HEY, YOU GUYS.
WHOA
MUSCLE PUNCH!
MUSCLE PUNCH!
HEY, KID, YOU OKAY?
HUH?... UH... YEAH.
SKRUFF
I NEVER EXPECTED TO BE SAVED BY THEM!
TUP
WHAT DO THEY MEAN...
THEY DON'T WANT RYU TO TURN INTO A SCUMBAG...!?
DUHH
WASN'T RYU...
A SCUMBAG ALREADY!?
ISN'T THAT WHY TOKAGERO POSSESSED HIM!?
YOU KNOW WHAT'LL HAPPEN IF YOU DISOBEY ME!?
LEMME GO, SWINE!
VIP
I'LL KILL YOU ALL!

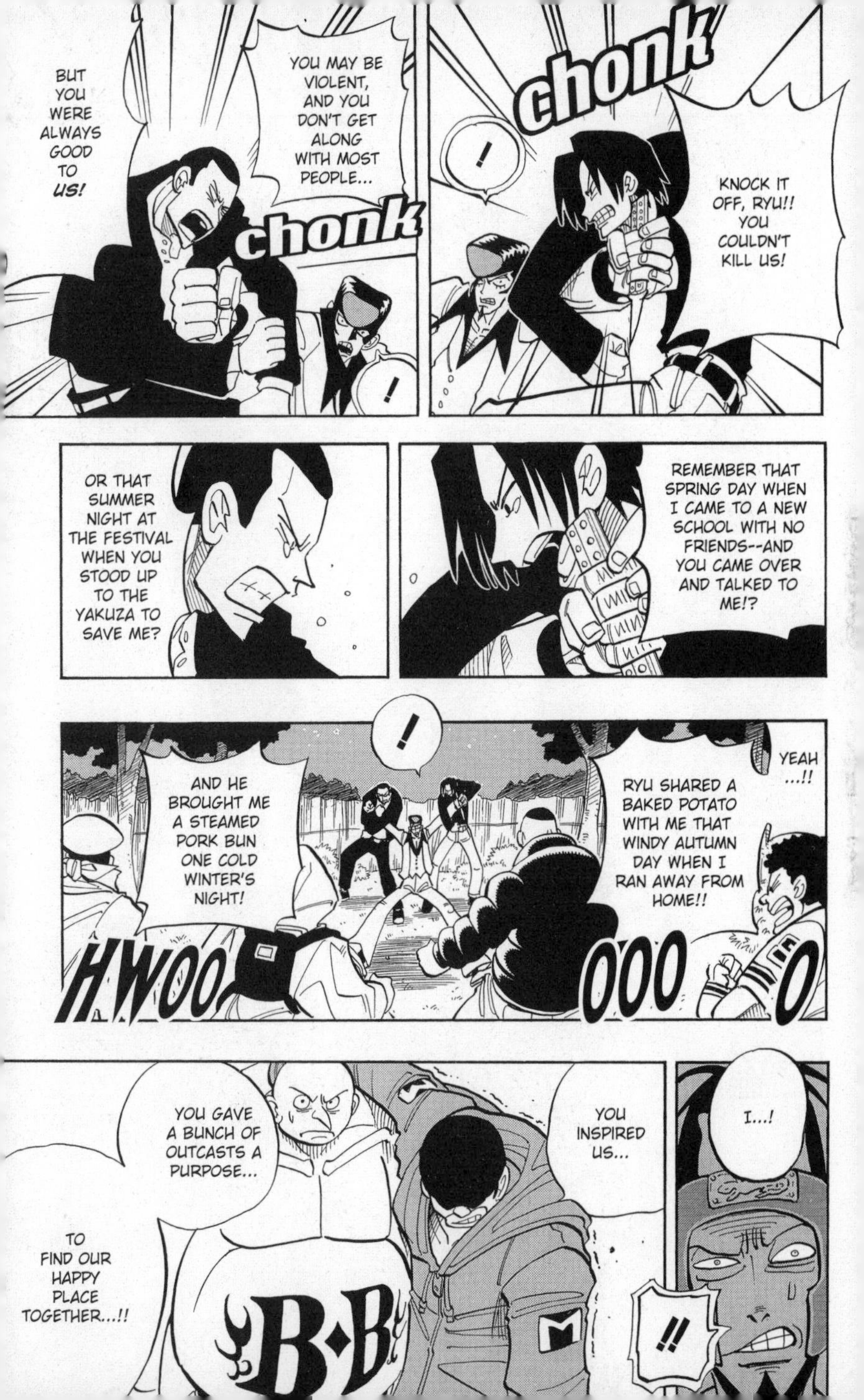
chonk
!
KNOCK IT OFF, RYU!! YOU COULDN'T KILL US!
YOU MAY BE VIOLENT, AND YOU DON'T GET ALONG WITH MOST PEOPLE...
BUT YOU WERE ALWAYS GOOD TO *US!*
chonk
!
REMEMBER THAT SPRING DAY WHEN I CAME TO A NEW SCHOOL WITH NO FRIENDS--AND YOU CAME OVER AND TALKED TO ME!?
OR THAT SUMMER NIGHT AT THE FESTIVAL WHEN YOU STOOD UP TO THE YAKUZA TO SAVE ME?
!
YEAH ...!!
RYU SHARED A BAKED POTATO WITH ME THAT WINDY AUTUMN DAY WHEN I RAN AWAY FROM HOME!!
AND HE BROUGHT ME A STEAMED PORK BUN ONE COLD WINTER'S NIGHT!
HWOOOOOO
I...!
!!
YOU INSPIRED US...
YOU GAVE A BUNCH OF OUTCASTS A PURPOSE...
TO FIND OUR HAPPY PLACE TOGETHER...!!
B•B
M

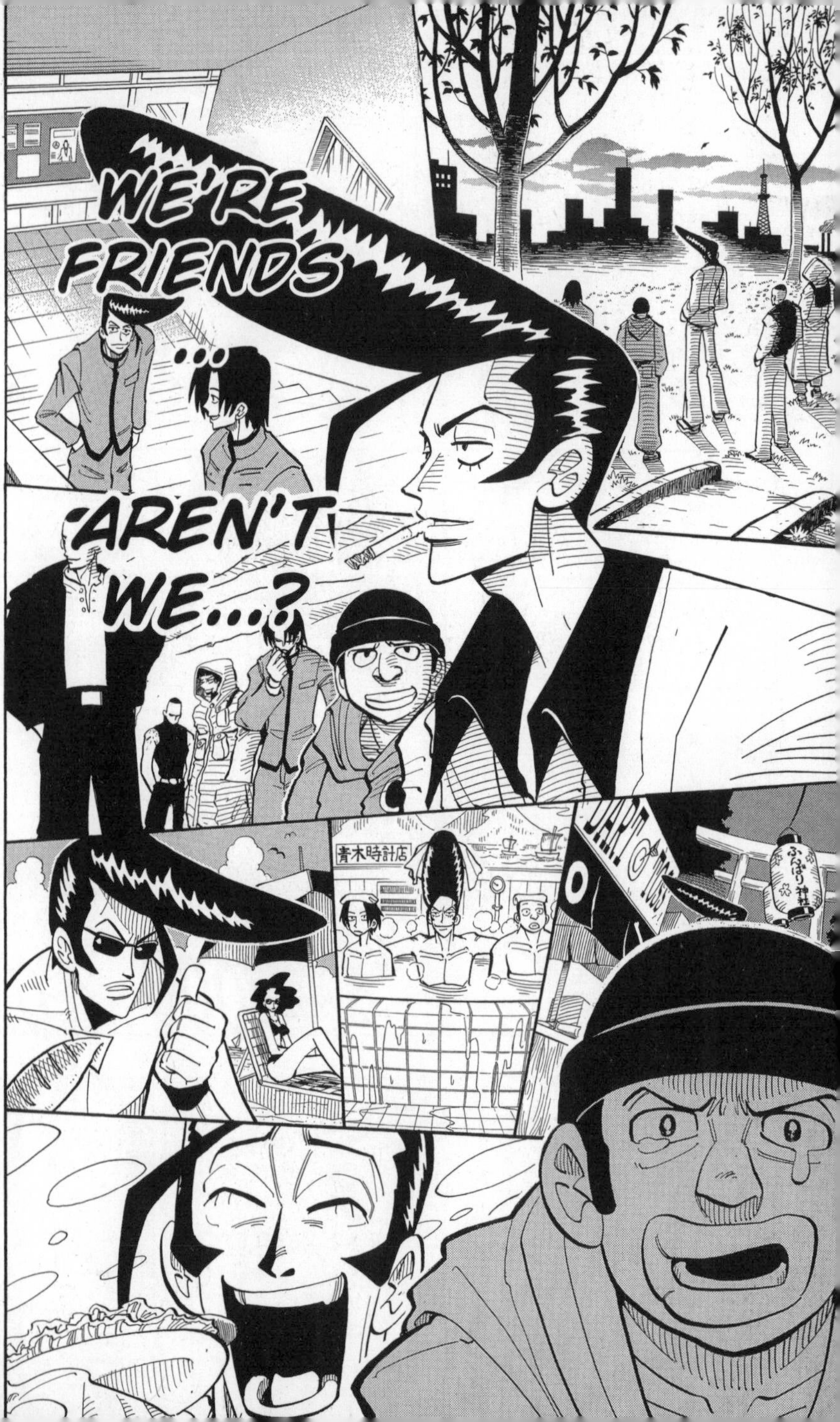

WE'RE FRIENDS
...
AREN'T WE...?
ふんばり神社
DART
青木時計店

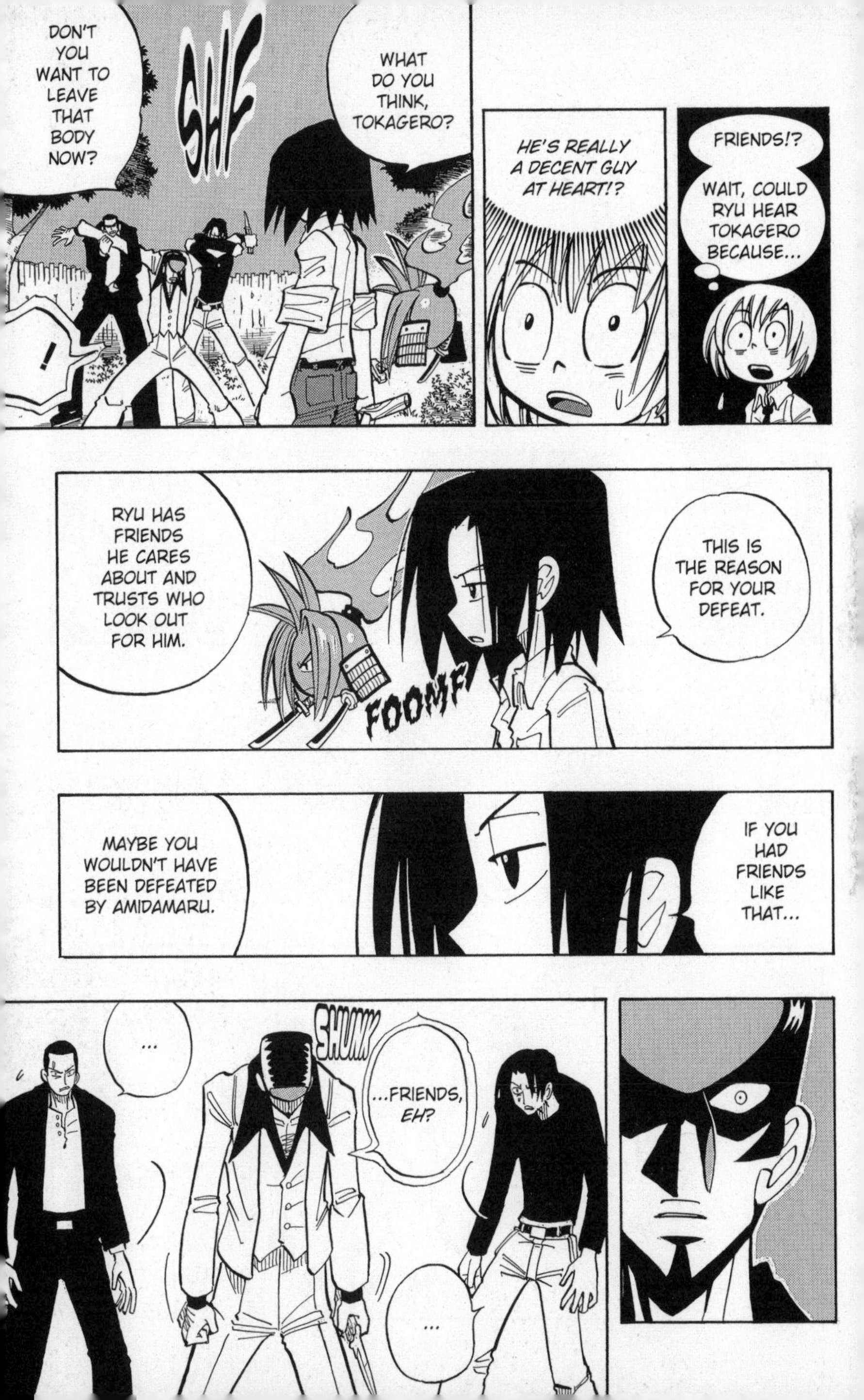

FRIENDS!?
WAIT, COULD RYU HEAR TOKAGERO BECAUSE...
HE'S REALLY A DECENT GUY AT HEART!?
WHAT DO YOU THINK, TOKAGERO?
SHF
DON'T YOU WANT TO LEAVE THAT BODY NOW?
!
THIS IS THE REASON FOR YOUR DEFEAT.
RYU HAS FRIENDS HE CARES ABOUT AND TRUSTS WHO LOOK OUT FOR HIM.
FOOMF
IF YOU HAD FRIENDS LIKE THAT...
MAYBE YOU WOULDN'T HAVE BEEN DEFEATED BY AMIDAMARU.
SHUNK
...FRIENDS, EH?
...
...

READ THIS WAY

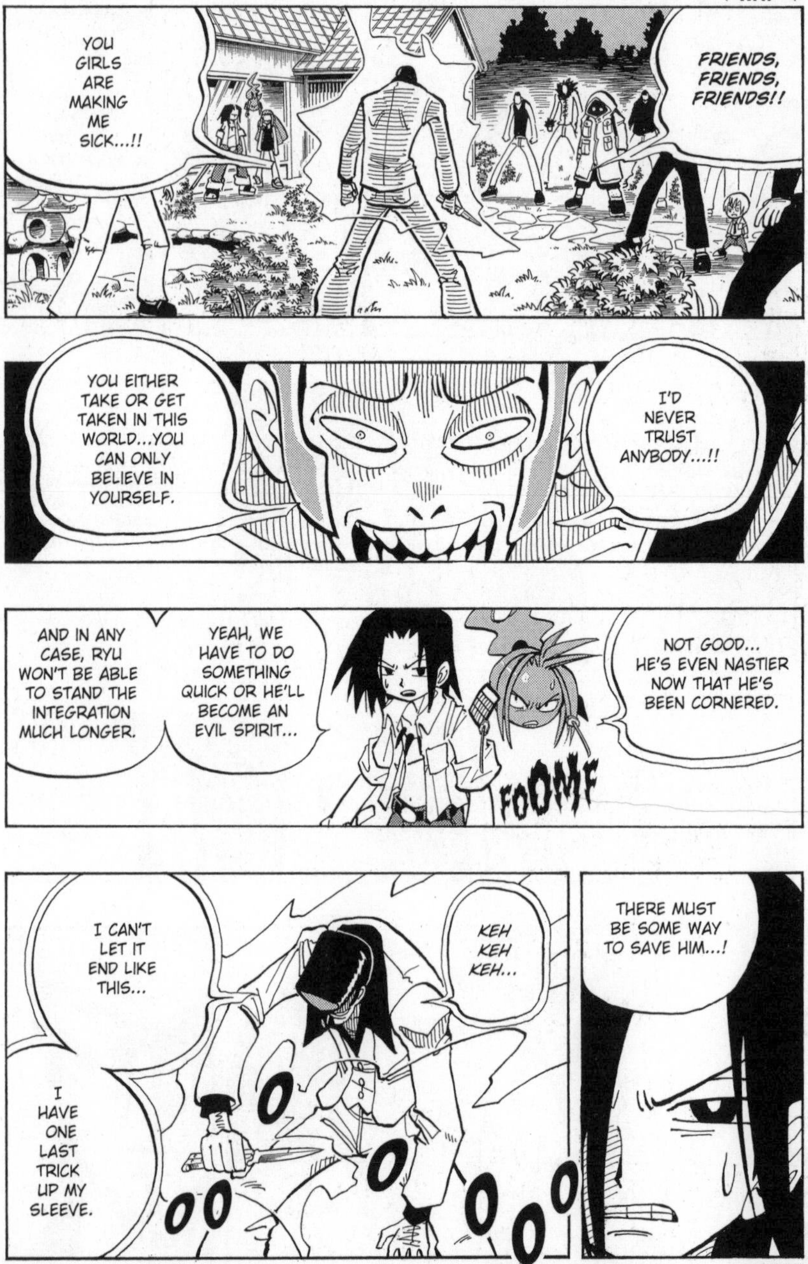

FRIENDS, FRIENDS, FRIENDS!!
YOU GIRLS ARE MAKING ME SICK...!!
I'D NEVER TRUST ANYBODY...!!
YOU EITHER TAKE OR GET TAKEN IN THIS WORLD...YOU CAN ONLY BELIEVE IN YOURSELF.
NOT GOOD... HE'S EVEN NASTIER NOW THAT HE'S BEEN CORNERED.
FOOMF
YEAH, WE HAVE TO DO SOMETHING QUICK OR HE'LL BECOME AN EVIL SPIRIT...
AND IN ANY CASE, RYU WON'T BE ABLE TO STAND THE INTEGRATION MUCH LONGER.
THERE MUST BE SOME WAY TO SAVE HIM...!
KEH KEH KEH...
I CAN'T LET IT END LIKE THIS...
I HAVE ONE LAST TRICK UP MY SLEEVE.

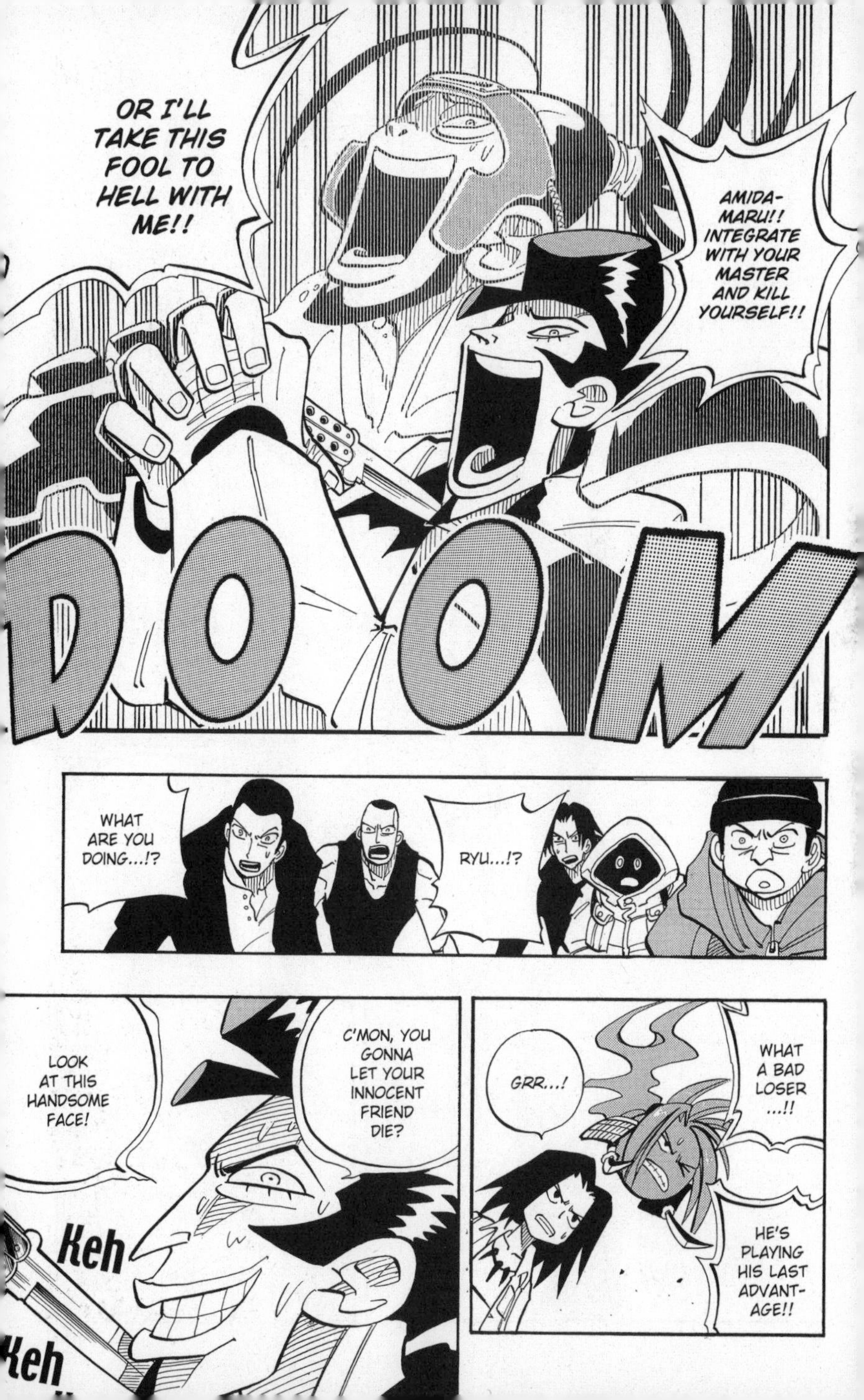
AMIDA-MARU!! INTEGRATE WITH YOUR MASTER AND KILL YOURSELF!!
OR I'LL TAKE THIS FOOL TO HELL WITH ME!!
DOOM
RYU...!?
WHAT ARE YOU DOING...!?
WHAT A BAD LOSER ...!!
GRR...!
HE'S PLAYING HIS LAST ADVANTAGE!!
C'MON, YOU GONNA LET YOUR INNOCENT FRIEND DIE?
LOOK AT THIS HANDSOME FACE!
Keh
Keh

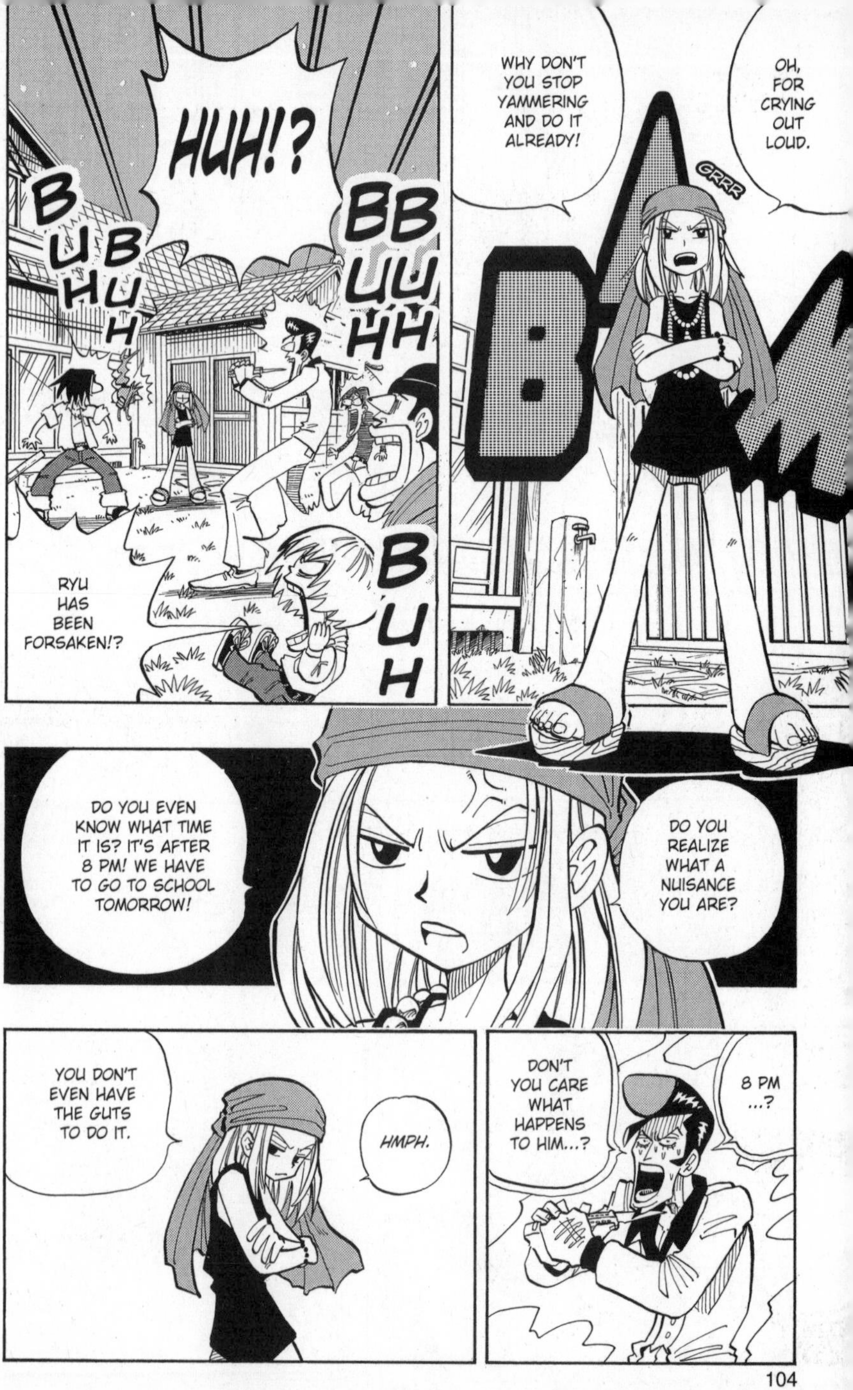
OH, FOR CRYING OUT LOUD.
WHY DON'T YOU STOP YAMMERING AND DO IT ALREADY!
GRRR
BAM
HUH!?
BBUUHH
BUBHUH
BUH
RYU HAS BEEN FORSAKEN!?
DO YOU REALIZE WHAT A NUISANCE YOU ARE?
DO YOU EVEN KNOW WHAT TIME IT IS? IT'S AFTER 8 PM! WE HAVE TO GO TO SCHOOL TOMORROW!
8 PM ...?
DON'T YOU CARE WHAT HAPPENS TO HIM...?
HMPH.
YOU DON'T EVEN HAVE THE GUTS TO DO IT.

READ THIS WAY

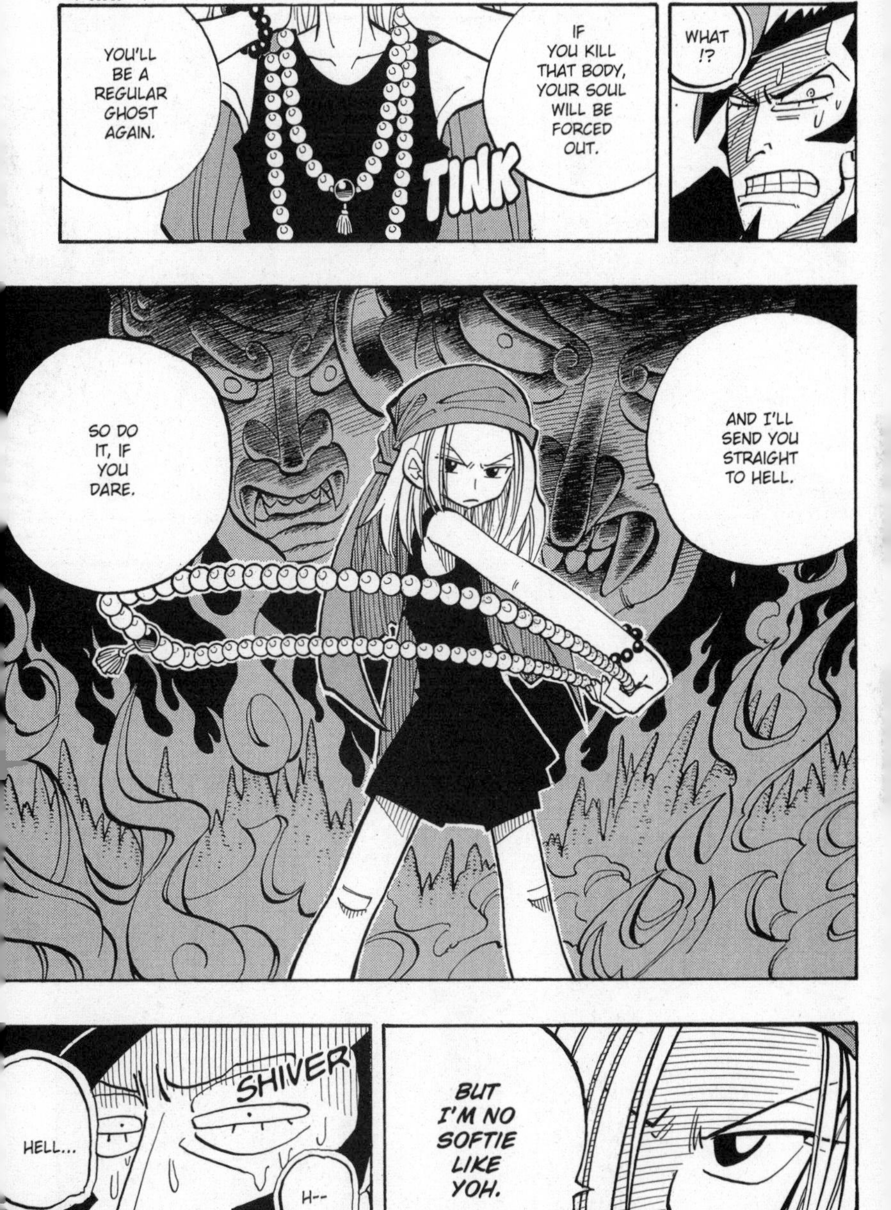
WHAT !?
IF YOU KILL THAT BODY, YOUR SOUL WILL BE FORCED OUT.
TINK
YOU'LL BE A REGULAR GHOST AGAIN.
AND I'LL SEND YOU STRAIGHT TO HELL.
SO DO IT, IF YOU DARE.
BUT I'M NO SOFTIE LIKE YOH.
SHIVER
HELL...
H--

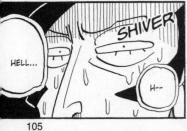

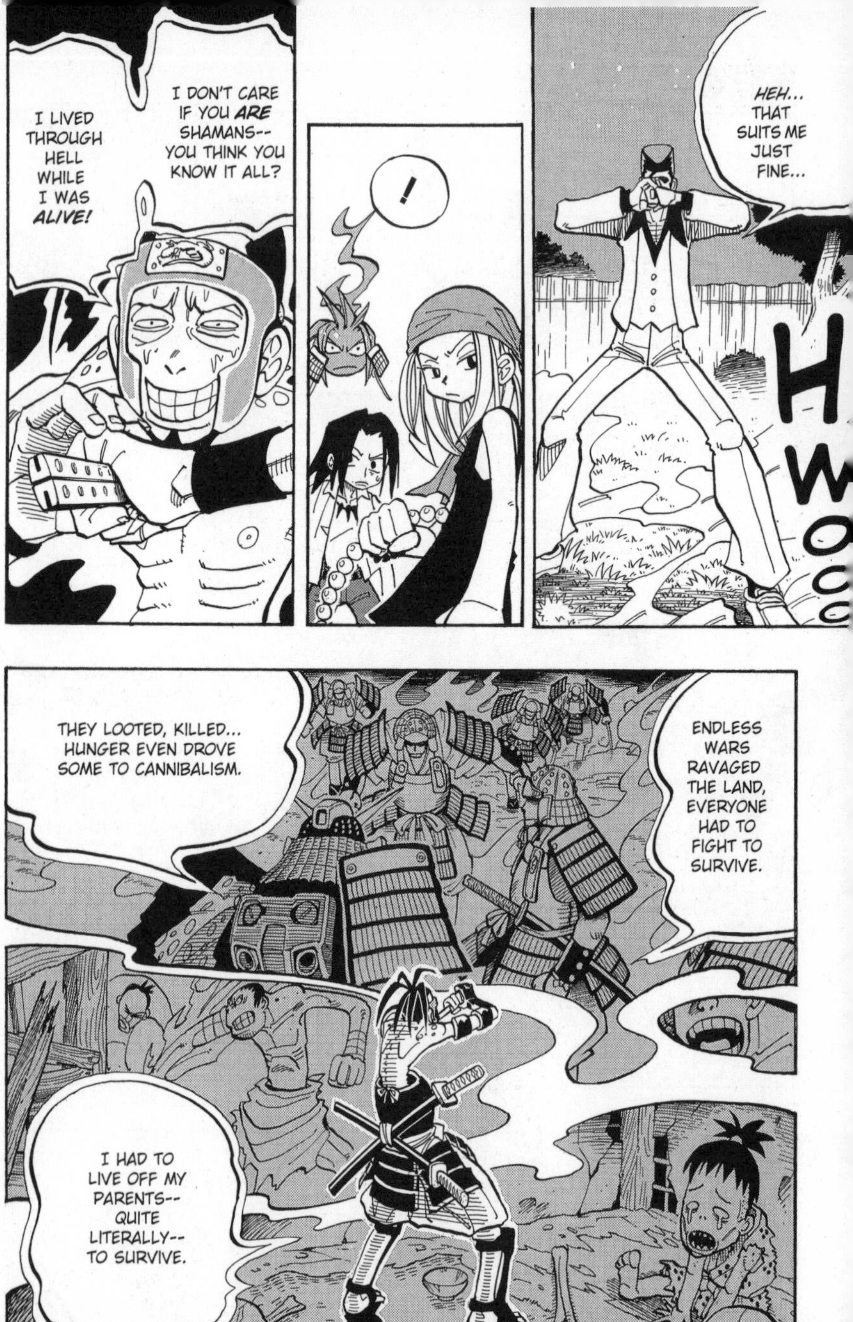
HEH... THAT SUITS ME JUST FINE...
HWOO
!
I DON'T CARE IF YOU ARE SHAMANS-- YOU THINK YOU KNOW IT ALL?
I LIVED THROUGH HELL WHILE I WAS ALIVE!
ENDLESS WARS RAVAGED THE LAND, EVERYONE HAD TO FIGHT TO SURVIVE.
THEY LOOTED, KILLED... HUNGER EVEN DROVE SOME TO CANNIBALISM.
I HAD TO LIVE OFF MY PARENTS-- QUITE LITERALLY-- TO SURVIVE.

READ THIS WAY

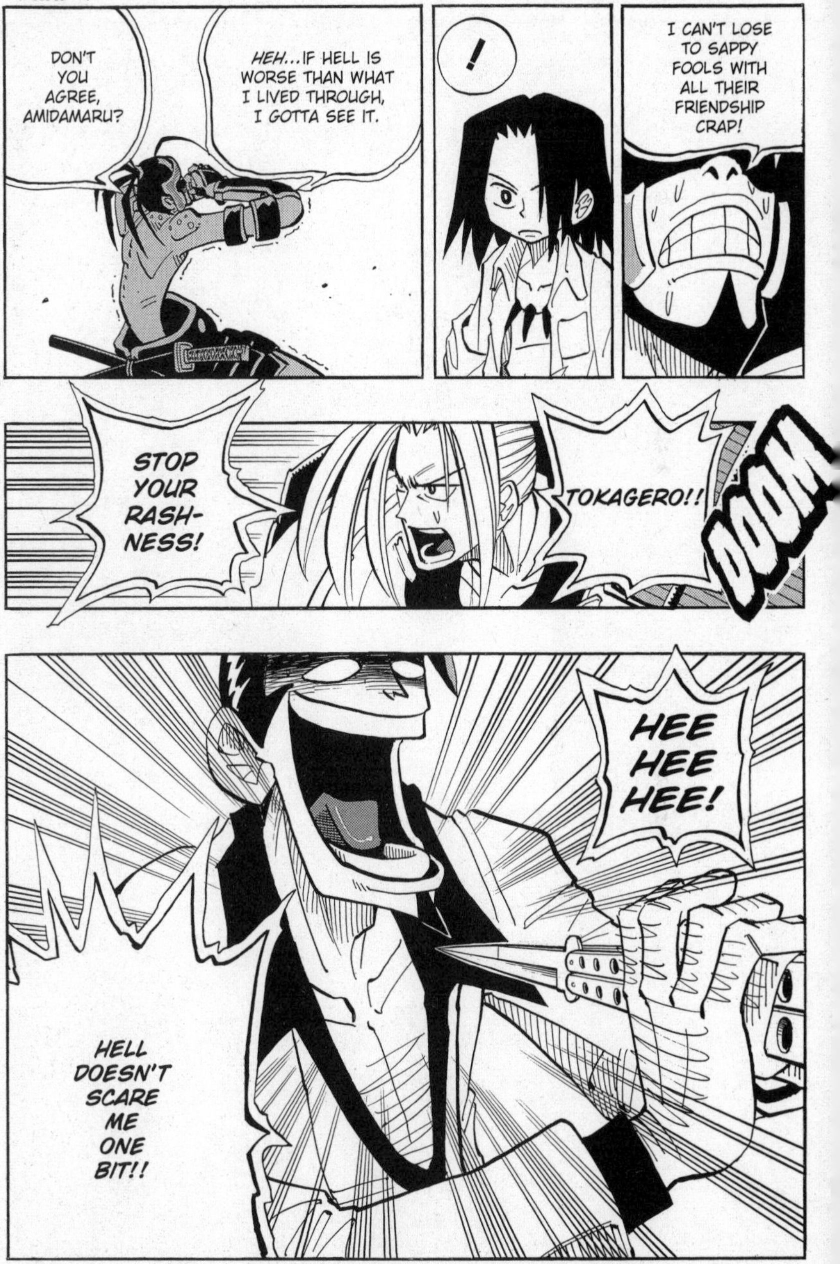
I CAN'T LOSE TO SAPPY FOOLS WITH ALL THEIR FRIENDSHIP CRAP!
!
HEH...IF HELL IS WORSE THAN WHAT I LIVED THROUGH, I GOTTA SEE IT.
DON'T YOU AGREE, AMIDAMARU?
DOOM
TOKAGERO!!
STOP YOUR RASHNESS!
HEE HEE HEE!
HELL DOESN'T SCARE ME ONE BIT!!

SHAMAN
KING
3

ERNIE L. CAKE
TOILET-HAUNTING
SPIRIT

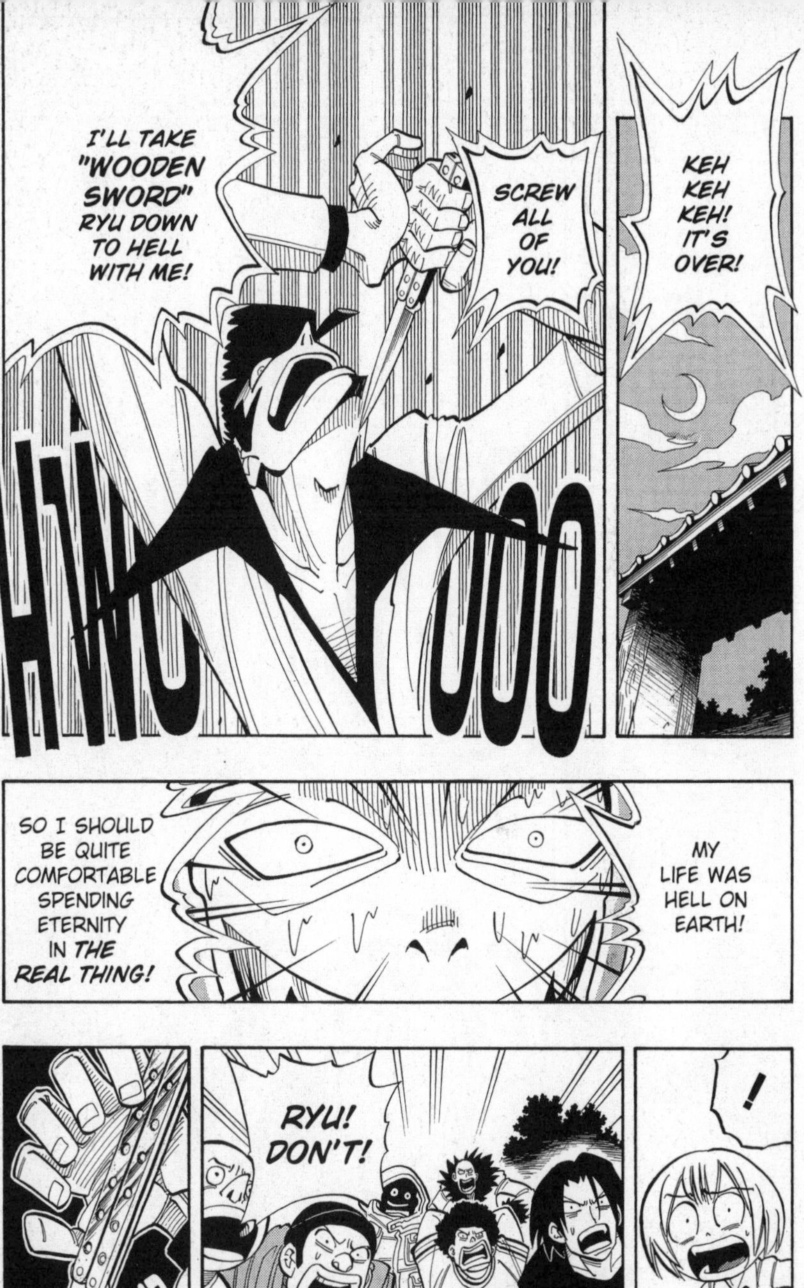
KEH KEH KEH! IT'S OVER!
SCREW ALL OF YOU!
I'LL TAKE "WOODEN SWORD" RYU DOWN TO HELL WITH ME!
MY LIFE WAS HELL ON EARTH!
SO I SHOULD BE QUITE COMFORTABLE SPENDING ETERNITY IN *THE REAL THING!*
!
RYU! DON'T!
SLIP

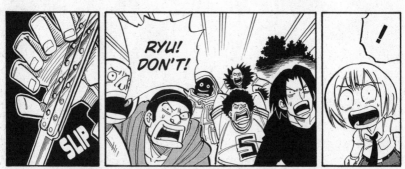

Reincarnation 23: Tokagero Blues

READ THIS WAY

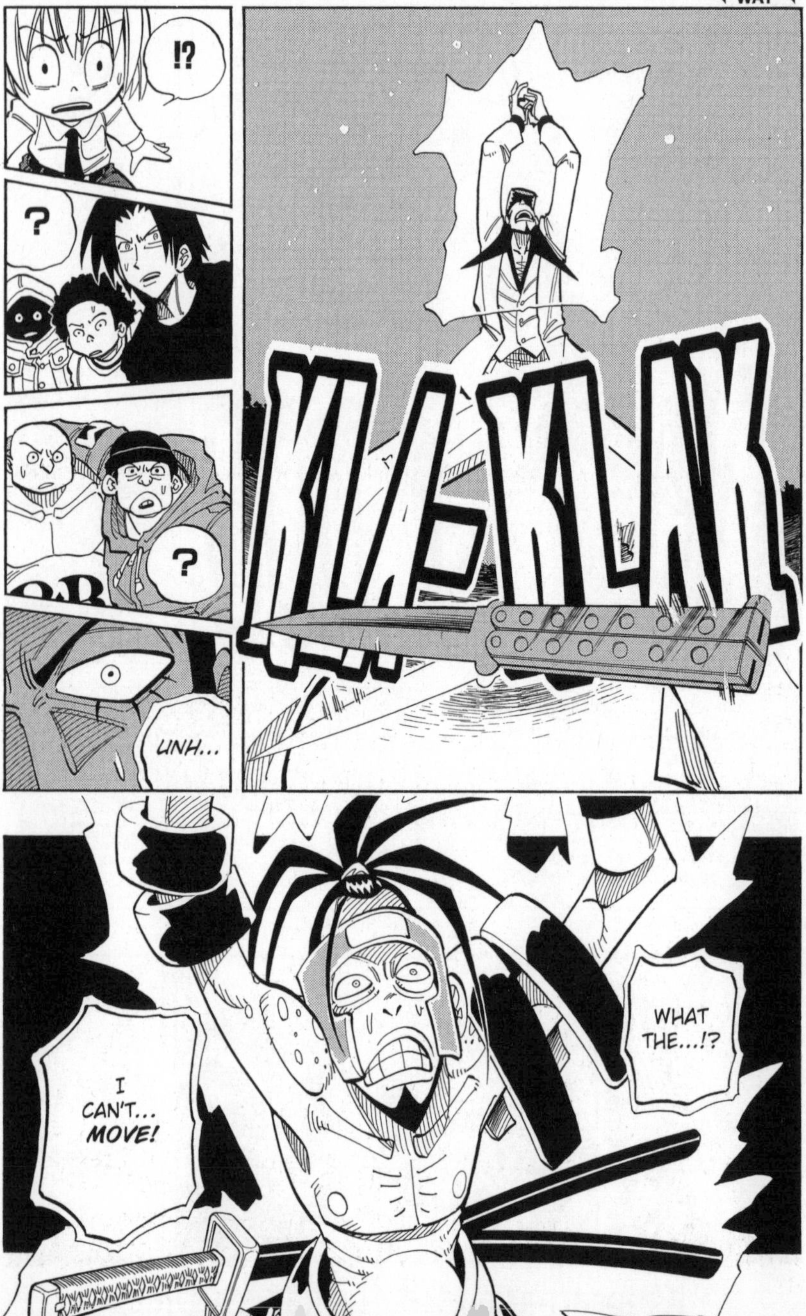
KLA-KLAK
!?
?
?
UNH...
WHAT THE...!?
I CAN'T... MOVE!

READ THIS WAY

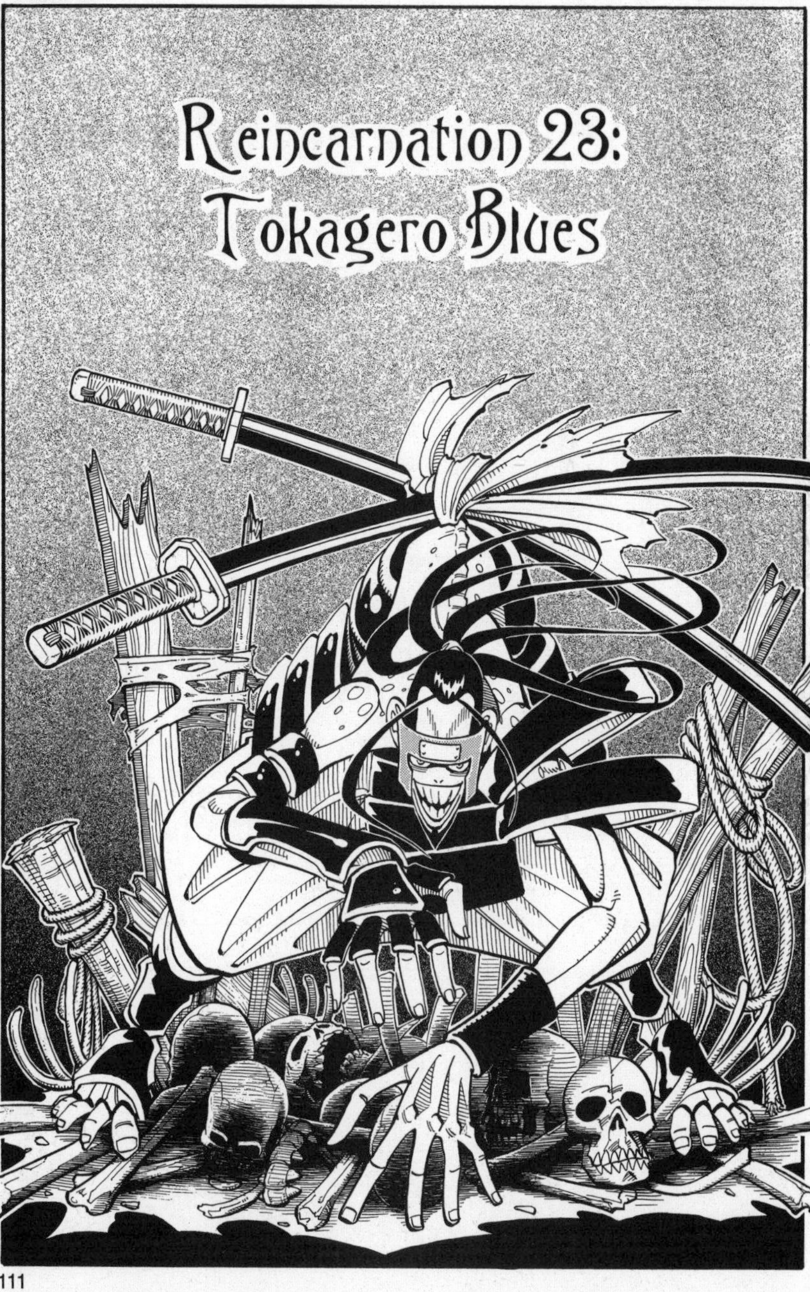
Reincarnation 23:
Tokagero Blues

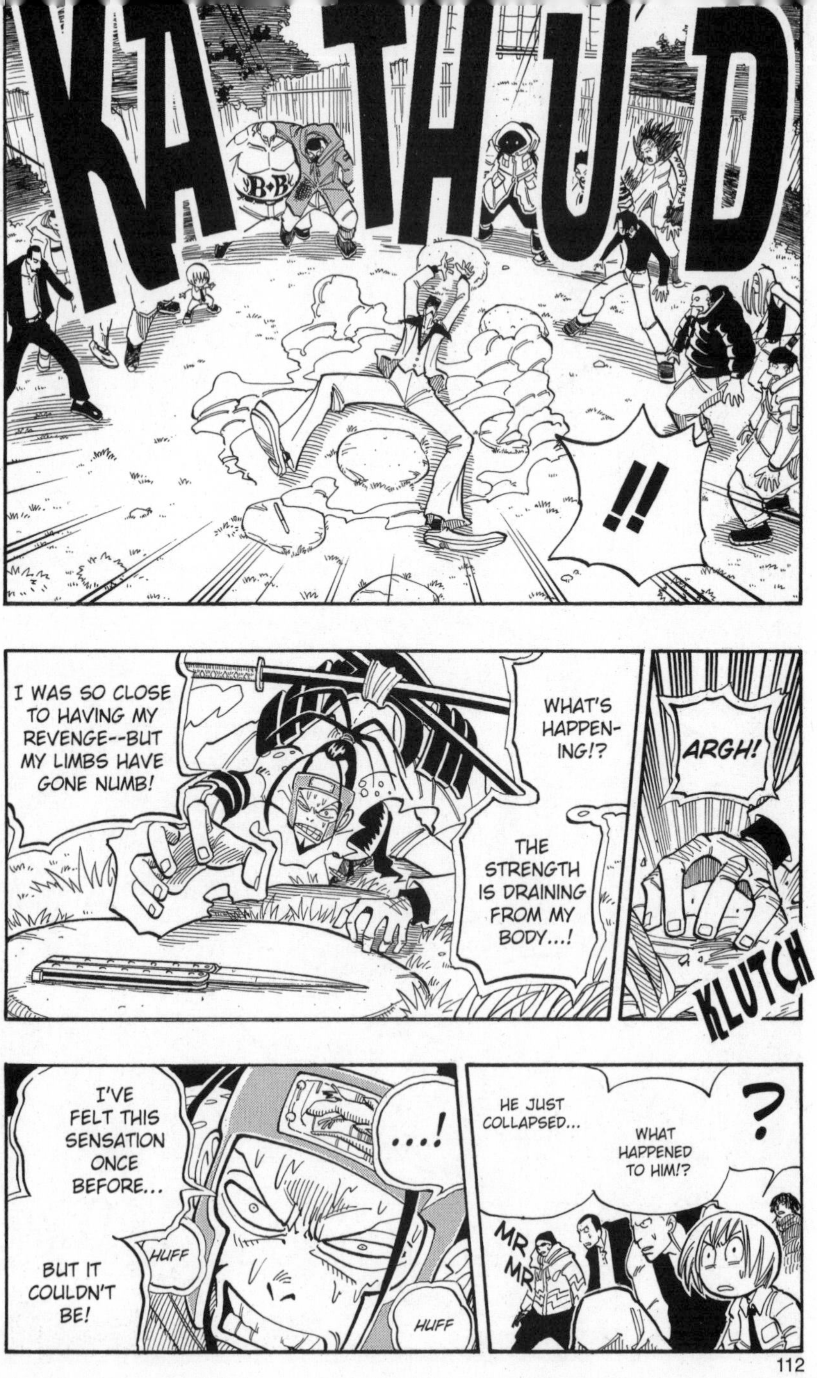
KATHUD
!!
ARGH!
KLUTCH
WHAT'S HAPPEN-ING!?
THE STRENGTH IS DRAINING FROM MY BODY...!
I WAS SO CLOSE TO HAVING MY REVENGE--BUT MY LIMBS HAVE GONE NUMB!
?
WHAT HAPPENED TO HIM!?
HE JUST COLLAPSED...
MR MR
...!
I'VE FELT THIS SENSATION ONCE BEFORE...
HUFF
BUT IT COULDN'T BE!
HUFF

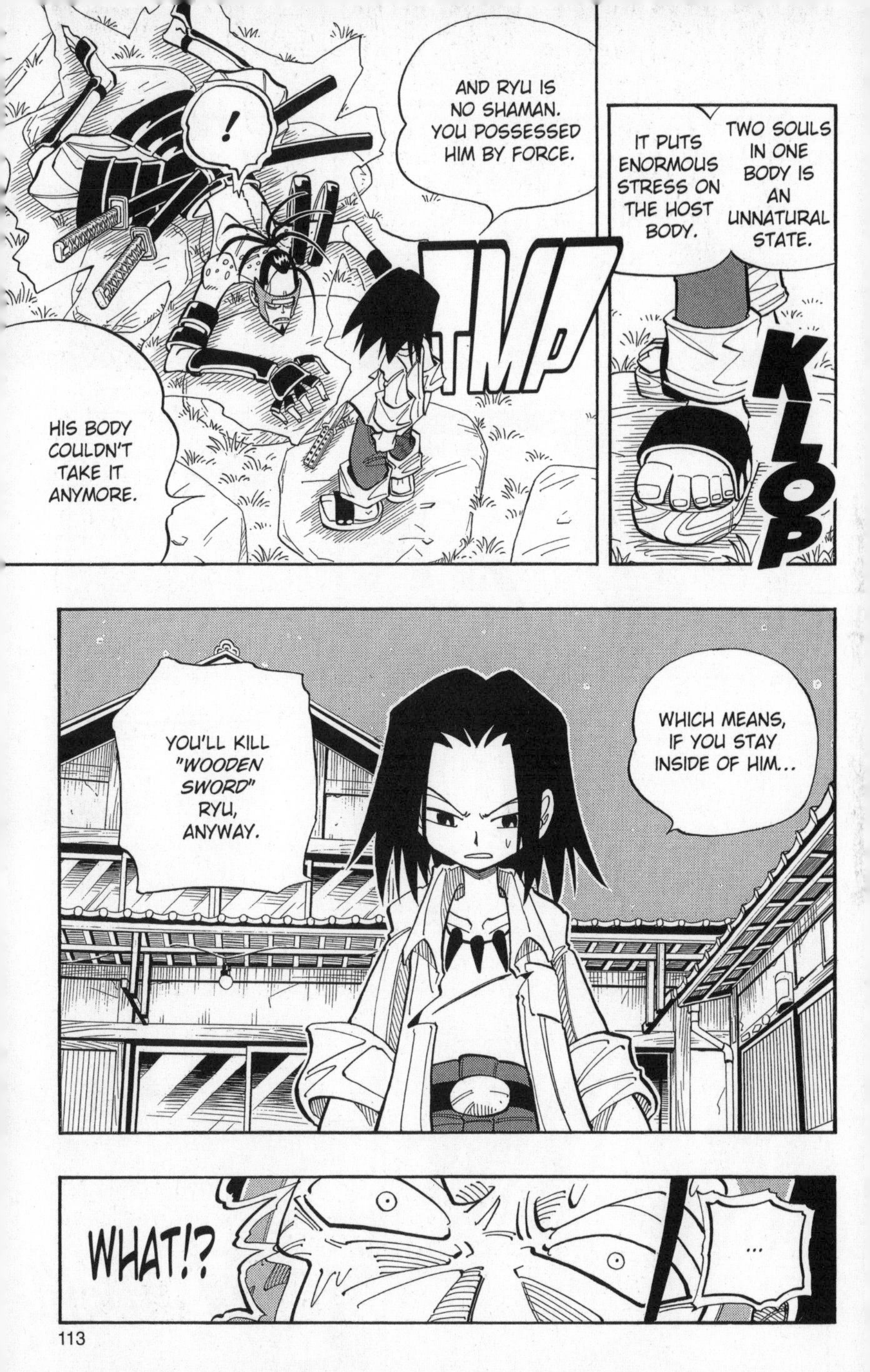
TWO SOULS IN ONE BODY IS AN UNNATURAL STATE.
IT PUTS ENORMOUS STRESS ON THE HOST BODY.
KLOP
AND RYU IS NO SHAMAN. YOU POSSESSED HIM BY FORCE.
TMP
!
HIS BODY COULDN'T TAKE IT ANYMORE.
WHICH MEANS, IF YOU STAY INSIDE OF HIM...
YOU'LL KILL "WOODEN SWORD" RYU, ANYWAY.
...
WHAT!?

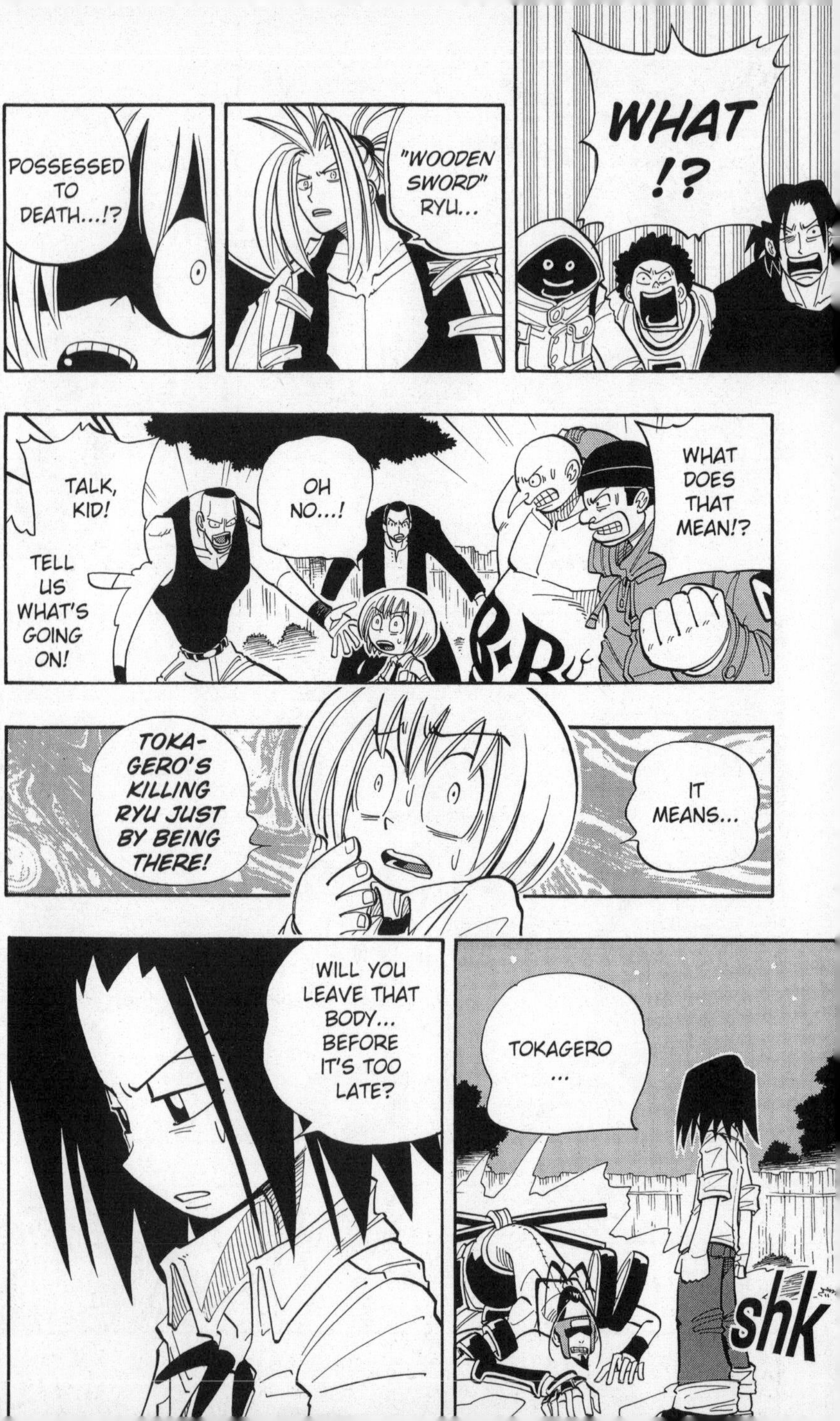
WHAT !?
"WOODEN SWORD" RYU...
POSSESSED TO DEATH...!?
WHAT DOES THAT MEAN!?
OH NO...!
TALK, KID!
TELL US WHAT'S GOING ON!
IT MEANS...
TOKA-GERO'S KILLING RYU JUST BY BEING THERE!
TOKAGERO ...
shk
WILL YOU LEAVE THAT BODY... BEFORE IT'S TOO LATE?

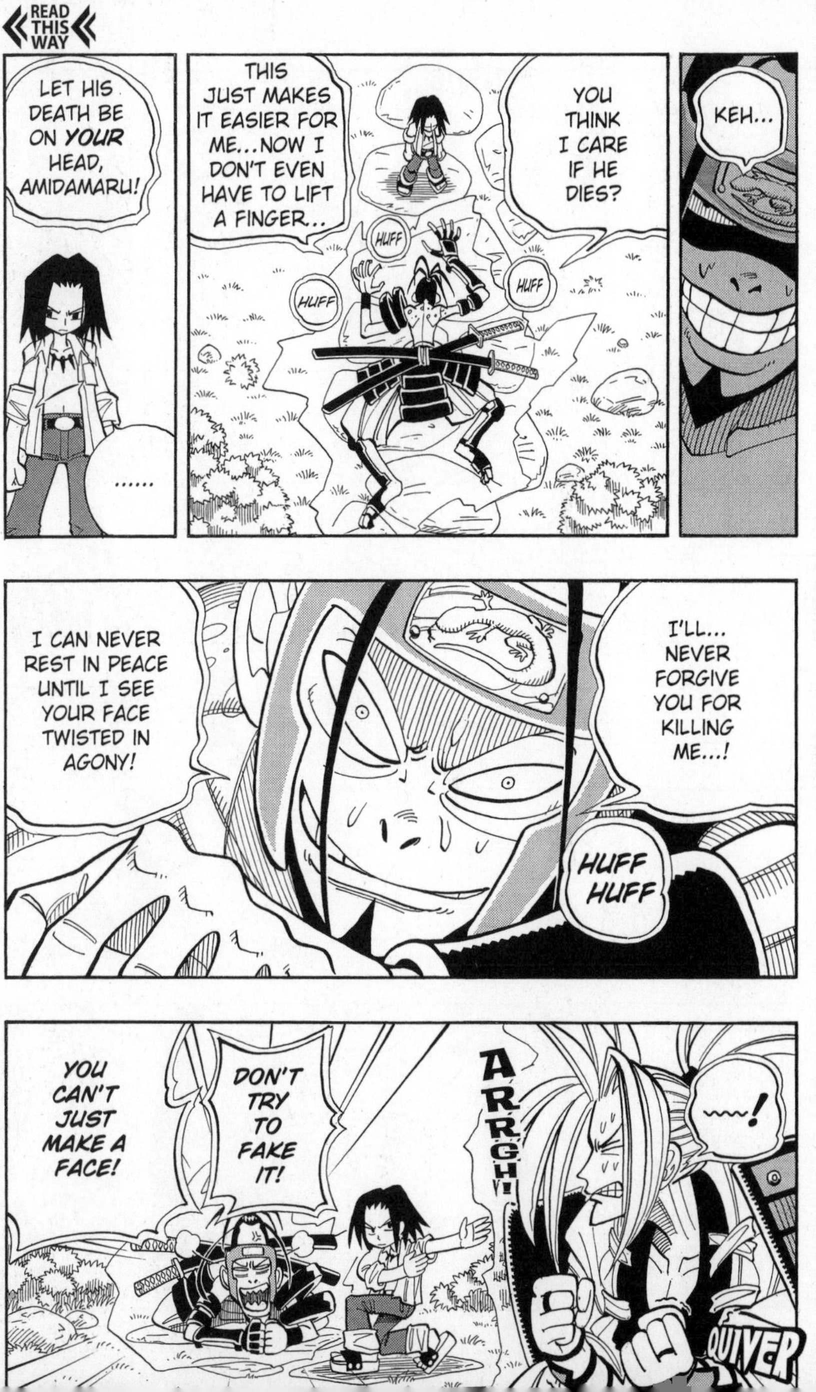
READ THIS WAY
KEH...
YOU THINK I CARE IF HE DIES?
HUFF
HUFF
HUFF
THIS JUST MAKES IT EASIER FOR ME...NOW I DON'T EVEN HAVE TO LIFT A FINGER...
LET HIS DEATH BE ON YOUR HEAD, AMIDAMARU!
......
I'LL... NEVER FORGIVE YOU FOR KILLING ME...!
HUFF HUFF
I CAN NEVER REST IN PEACE UNTIL I SEE YOUR FACE TWISTED IN AGONY!
~~~!
QUIVER
ARRGH!
DON'T TRY TO FAKE IT!
YOU CAN'T JUST MAKE A FACE!
~~~

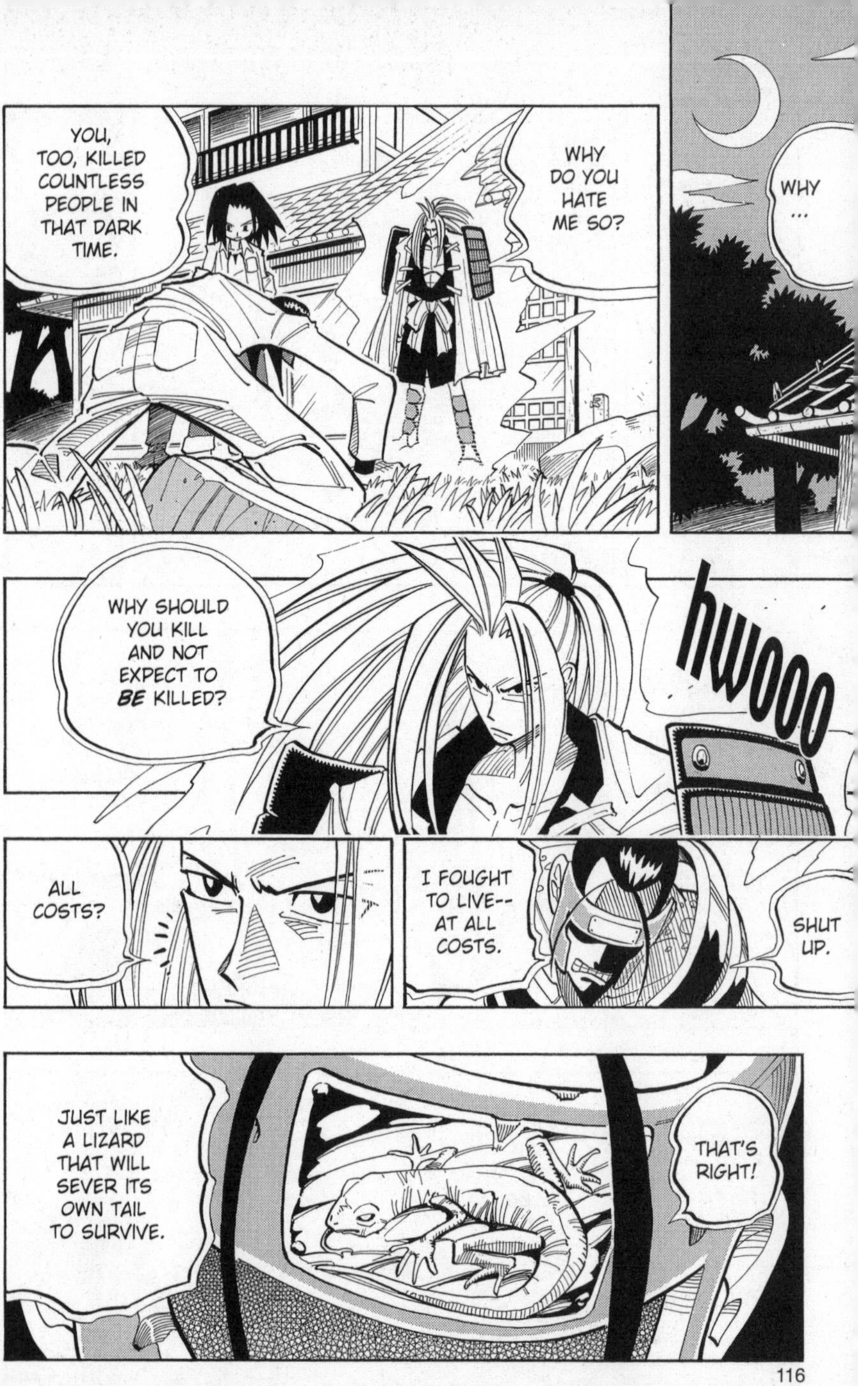
WHY ...
WHY DO YOU HATE ME SO?
YOU, TOO, KILLED COUNTLESS PEOPLE IN THAT DARK TIME.
hwooo
WHY SHOULD YOU KILL AND NOT EXPECT TO *BE* KILLED?
SHUT UP.
I FOUGHT TO LIVE--AT ALL COSTS.
ALL COSTS?
THAT'S RIGHT!
JUST LIKE A LIZARD THAT WILL SEVER ITS OWN TAIL TO SURVIVE.

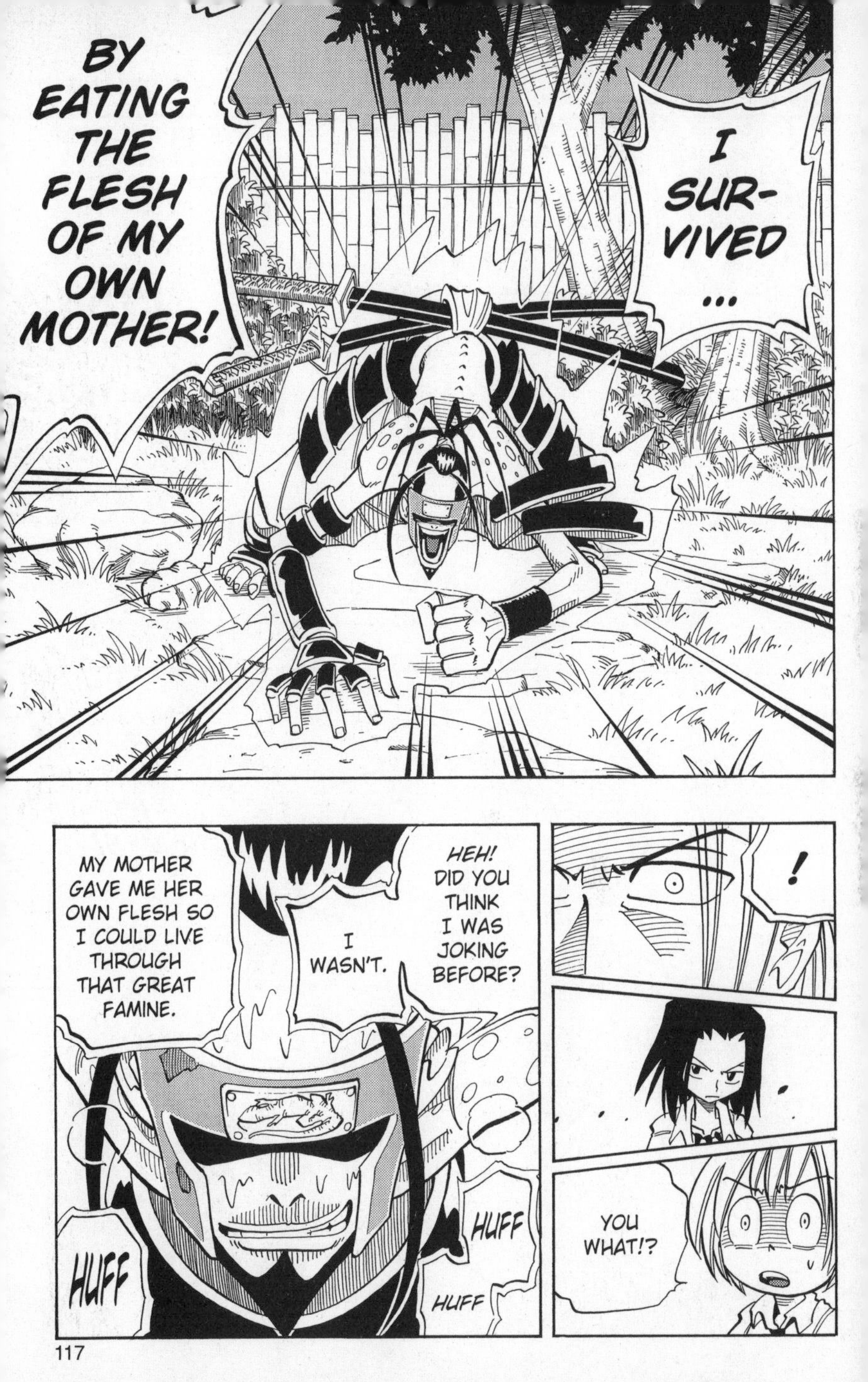
I SURVIVED...
BY EATING THE FLESH OF MY OWN MOTHER!
!
...
YOU WHAT!?
HEH! DID YOU THINK I WAS JOKING BEFORE?
I WASN'T.
MY MOTHER GAVE ME HER OWN FLESH SO I COULD LIVE THROUGH THAT GREAT FAMINE.
HUFF
HUFF
HUFF

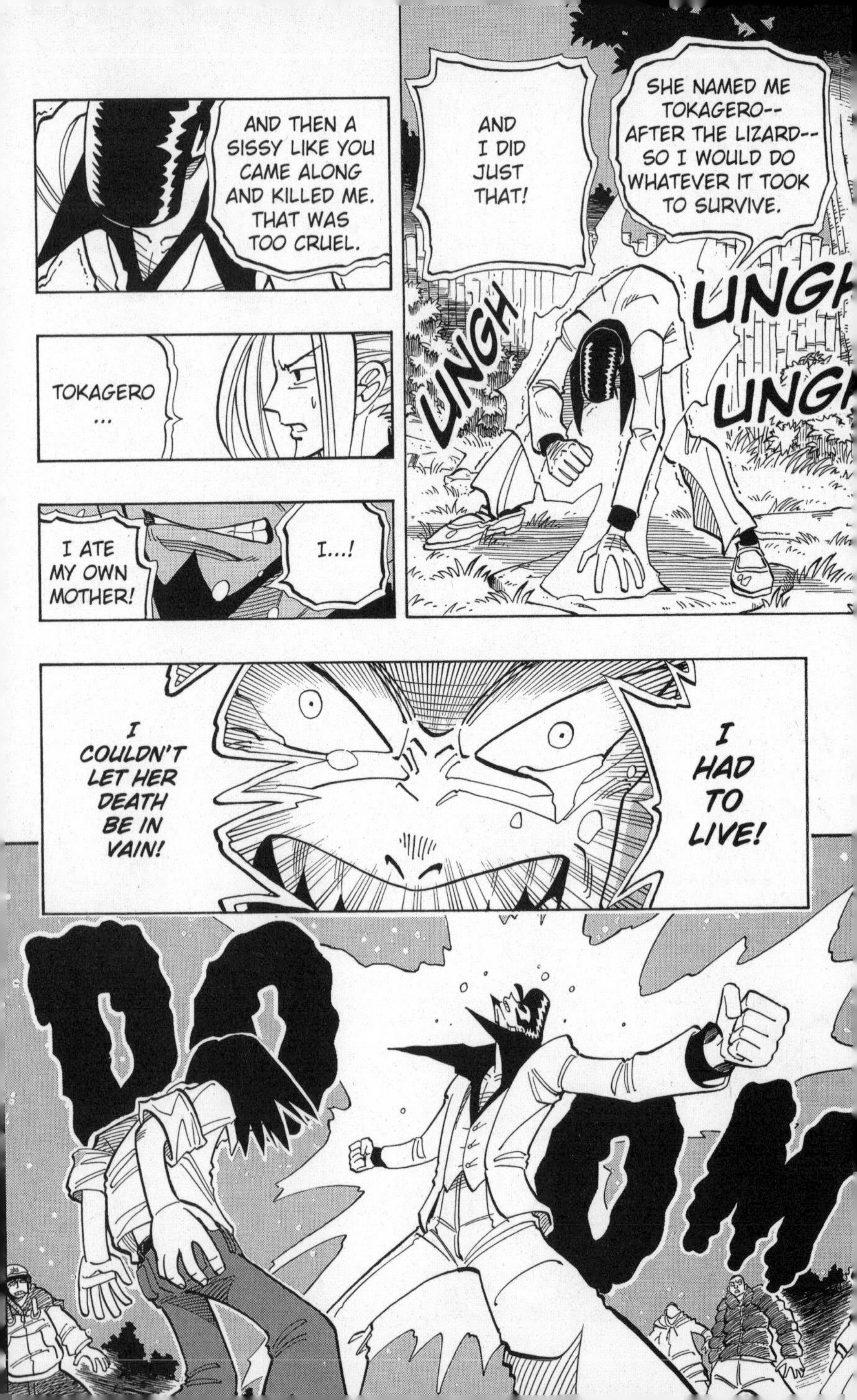
SHE NAMED ME TOKAGERO-- AFTER THE LIZARD-- SO I WOULD DO WHATEVER IT TOOK TO SURVIVE.
AND I DID JUST THAT!
UNGH
UNGH
UNGH
AND THEN A SISSY LIKE YOU CAME ALONG AND KILLED ME. THAT WAS TOO CRUEL.
TOKAGERO ...
I...!
I ATE MY OWN MOTHER!
I HAD TO LIVE!
I COULDN'T LET HER DEATH BE IN VAIN!
DOOM

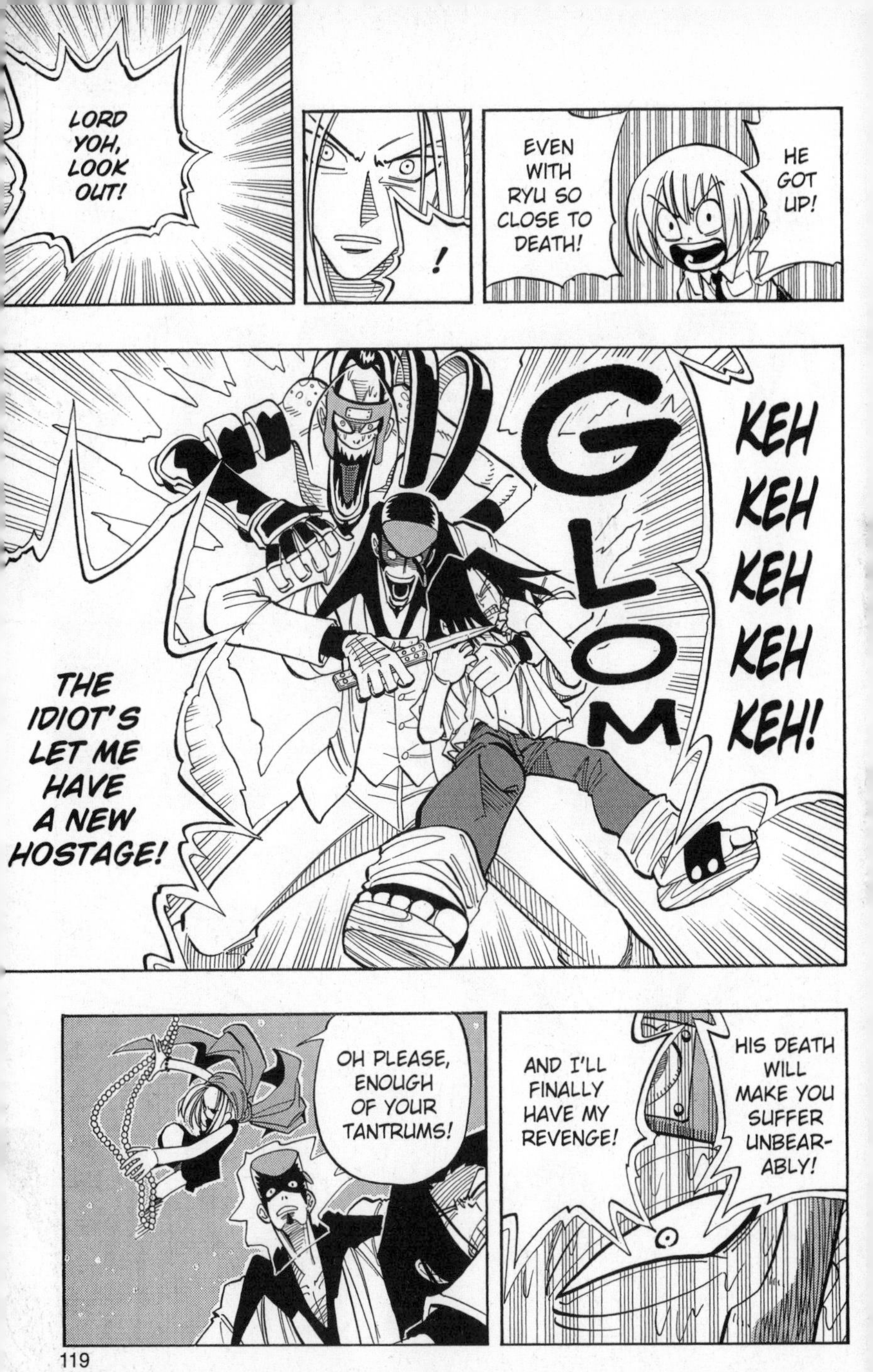
HE GOT UP!
EVEN WITH RYU SO CLOSE TO DEATH!
!
LORD YOH, LOOK OUT!
KEH KEH KEH KEH KEH!
GLOM
THE IDIOT'S LET ME HAVE A NEW HOSTAGE!
HIS DEATH WILL MAKE YOU SUFFER UNBEARABLY!
AND I'LL FINALLY HAVE MY REVENGE!
OH PLEASE, ENOUGH OF YOUR TANTRUMS!

READ THIS WAY

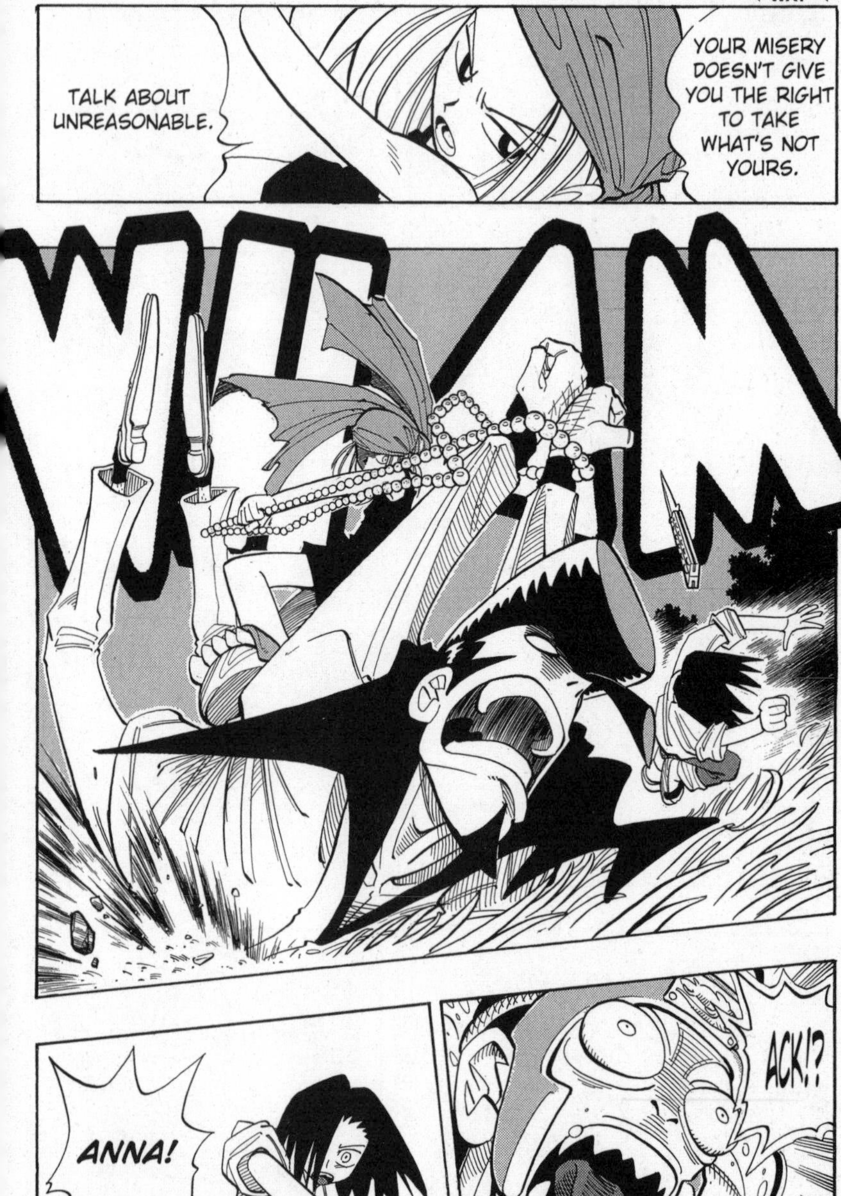

YOUR MISERY DOESN'T GIVE YOU THE RIGHT TO TAKE WHAT'S NOT YOURS.
TALK ABOUT UNREASONABLE.
WHAM
ACK!?
ANNA!

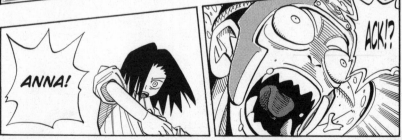

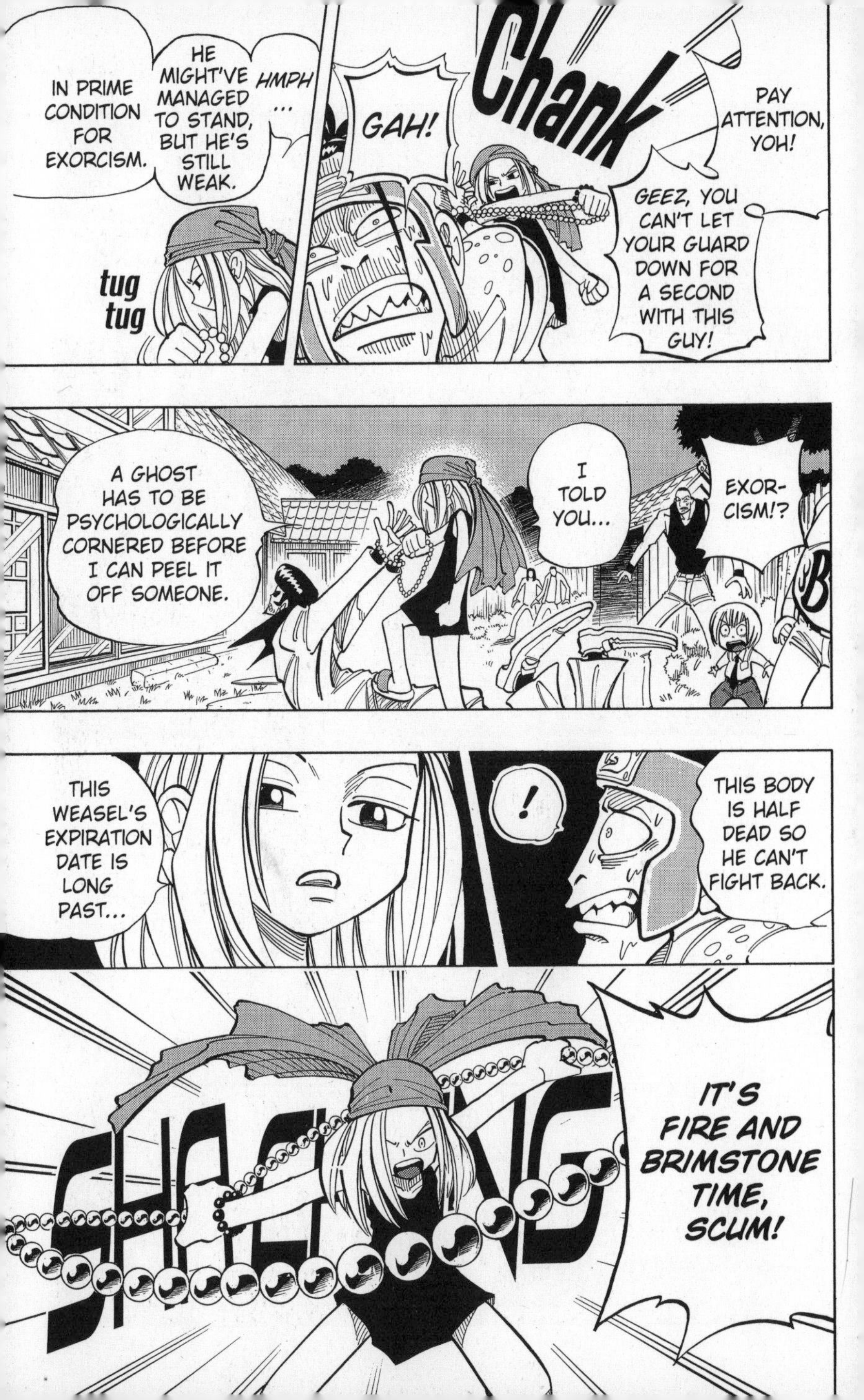
Chank
PAY ATTENTION, YOH!
GEEZ, YOU CAN'T LET YOUR GUARD DOWN FOR A SECOND WITH THIS GUY!
GAH!
HMPH ...
HE MIGHT'VE MANAGED TO STAND, BUT HE'S STILL WEAK.
IN PRIME CONDITION FOR EXORCISM.
tug tug
EXOR-CISM!?
I TOLD YOU...
A GHOST HAS TO BE PSYCHOLOGICALLY CORNERED BEFORE I CAN PEEL IT OFF SOMEONE.
!
THIS BODY IS HALF DEAD SO HE CAN'T FIGHT BACK.
THIS WEASEL'S EXPIRATION DATE IS LONG PAST...
IT'S FIRE AND BRIMSTONE TIME, SCUM!

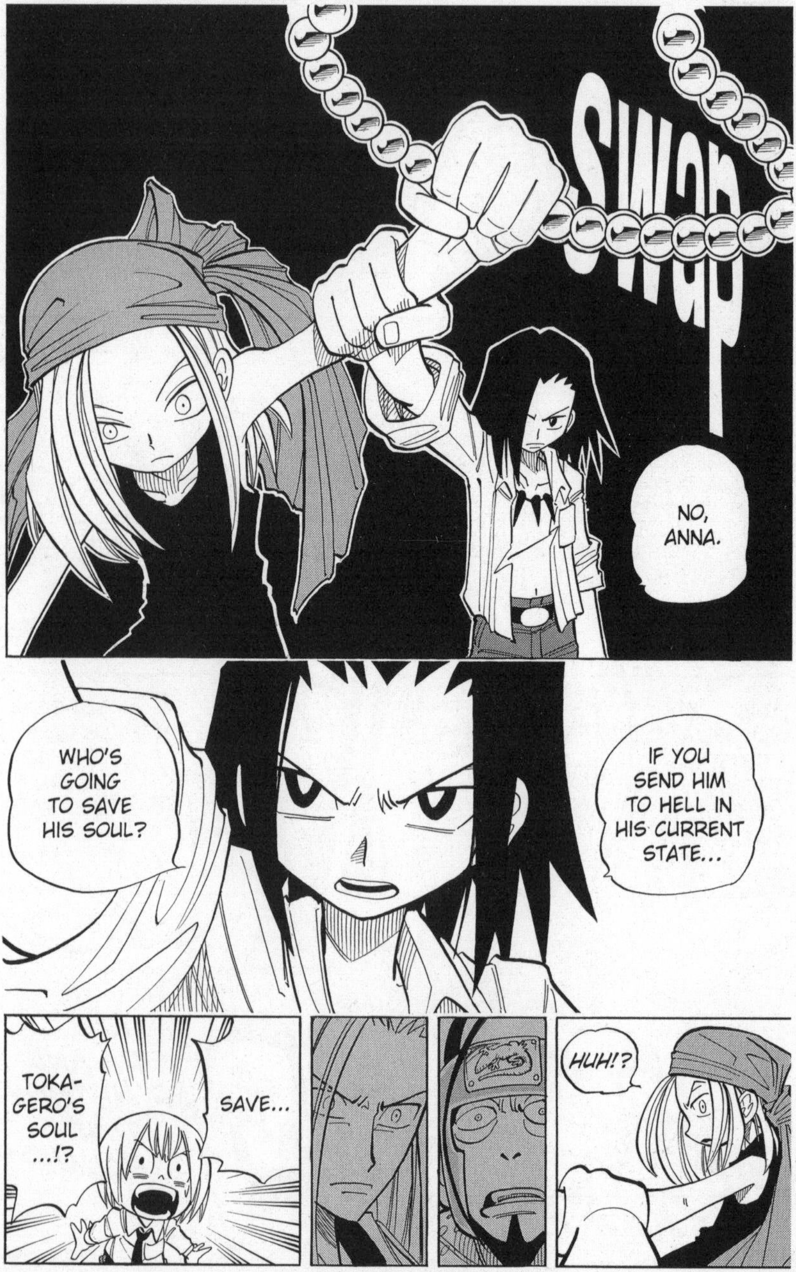
SWAP
NO, ANNA.
IF YOU SEND HIM TO HELL IN HIS CURRENT STATE...
WHO'S GOING TO SAVE HIS SOUL?
HUH!?
SAVE...
TOKA-GERO'S SOUL ...!?

READ THIS WAY

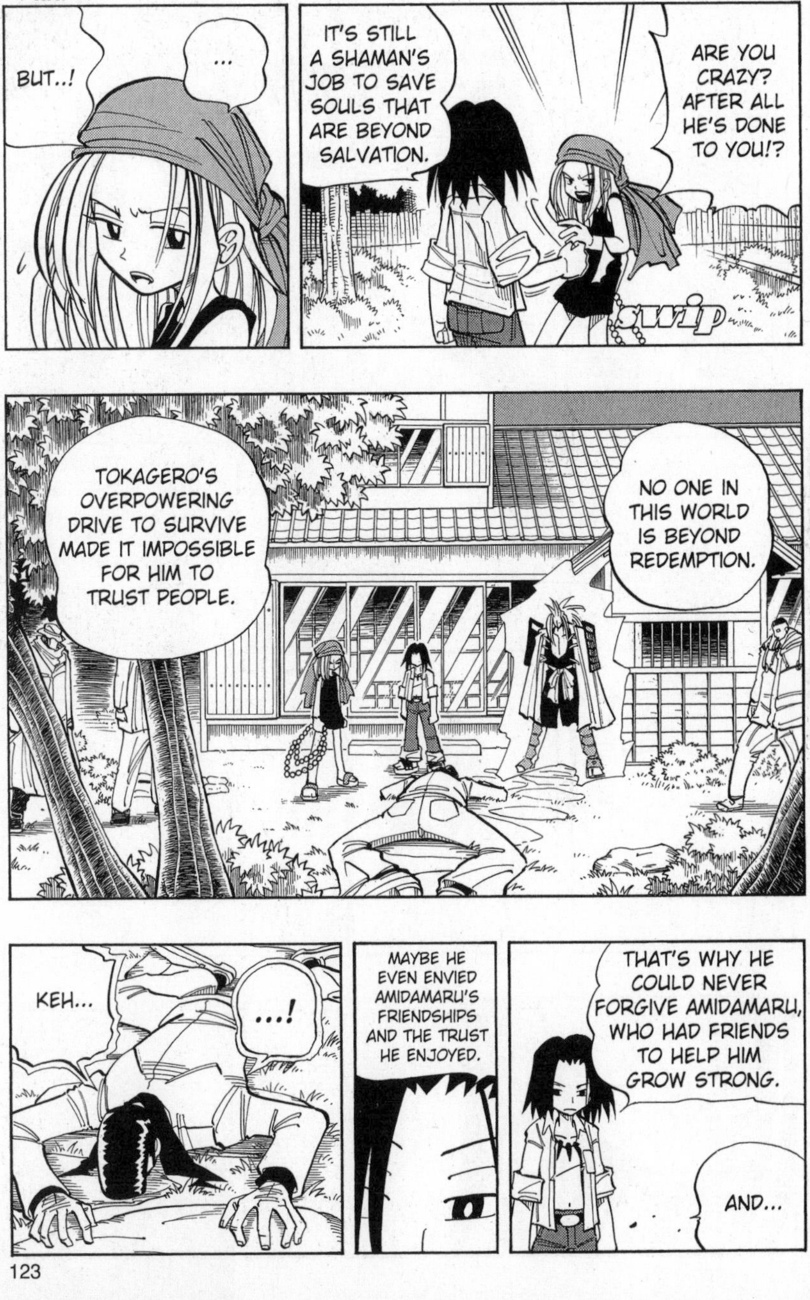

ARE YOU CRAZY? AFTER ALL HE'S DONE TO YOU!?
IT'S STILL A SHAMAN'S JOB TO SAVE SOULS THAT ARE BEYOND SALVATION.
swip
...
BUT..!
NO ONE IN THIS WORLD IS BEYOND REDEMPTION.
TOKAGERO'S OVERPOWERING DRIVE TO SURVIVE MADE IT IMPOSSIBLE FOR HIM TO TRUST PEOPLE.
THAT'S WHY HE COULD NEVER FORGIVE AMIDAMARU, WHO HAD FRIENDS TO HELP HIM GROW STRONG.
AND...
MAYBE HE EVEN ENVIED AMIDAMARU'S FRIENDSHIPS AND THE TRUST HE ENJOYED.
...!
KEH...

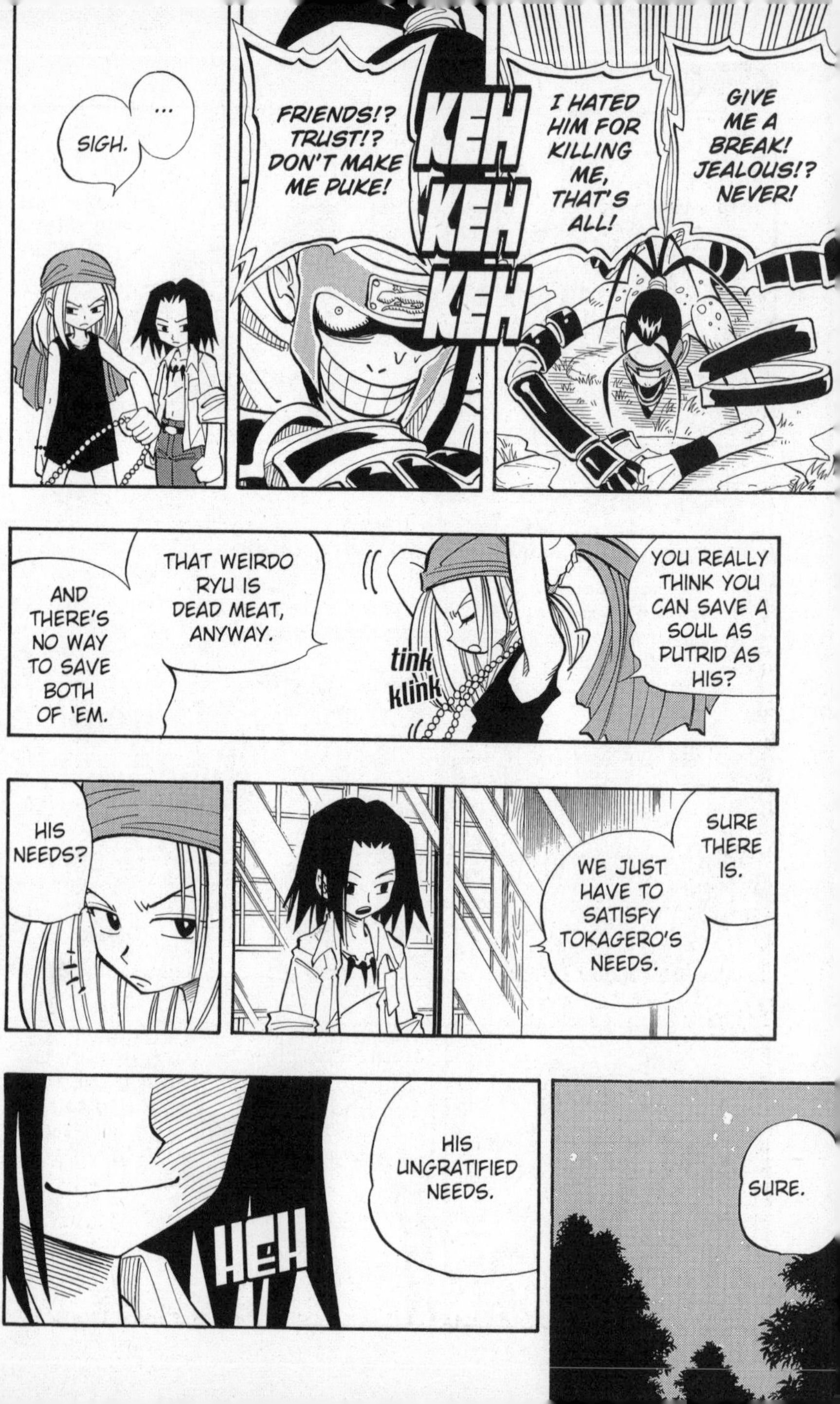
GIVE ME A BREAK! JEALOUS!? NEVER!
I HATED HIM FOR KILLING ME, THAT'S ALL!
KEH KEH KEH
FRIENDS!? TRUST!? DON'T MAKE ME PUKE!
...
SIGH.
YOU REALLY THINK YOU CAN SAVE A SOUL AS PUTRID AS HIS?
tink klink
THAT WEIRDO RYU IS DEAD MEAT, ANYWAY.
AND THERE'S NO WAY TO SAVE BOTH OF 'EM.
SURE THERE IS.
WE JUST HAVE TO SATISFY TOKAGERO'S NEEDS.
HIS NEEDS?
SURE.
HIS UNGRATIFIED NEEDS.
HEH

READ THIS WAY

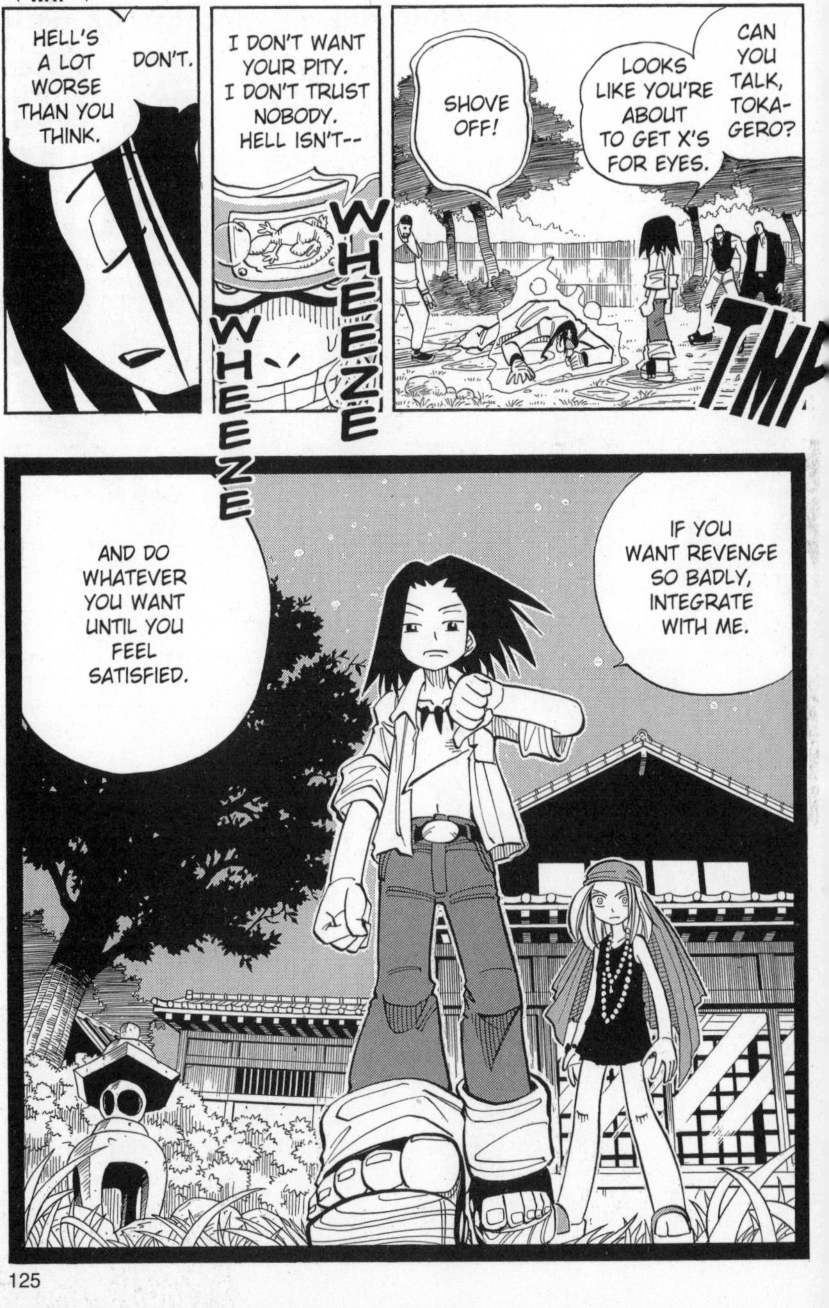
CAN YOU TALK, TOKA-GERO?
LOOKS LIKE YOU'RE ABOUT TO GET X'S FOR EYES.
SHOVE OFF!
TMP
I DON'T WANT YOUR PITY. I DON'T TRUST NOBODY. HELL ISN'T--
WHEEZE
WHEEZE
DON'T.
HELL'S A LOT WORSE THAN YOU THINK.
IF YOU WANT REVENGE SO BADLY, INTEGRATE WITH ME.
AND DO WHATEVER YOU WANT UNTIL YOU FEEL SATISFIED.

SHAMAN KING CHARACTER FILE No.12

喪助
MOSUKE
1999

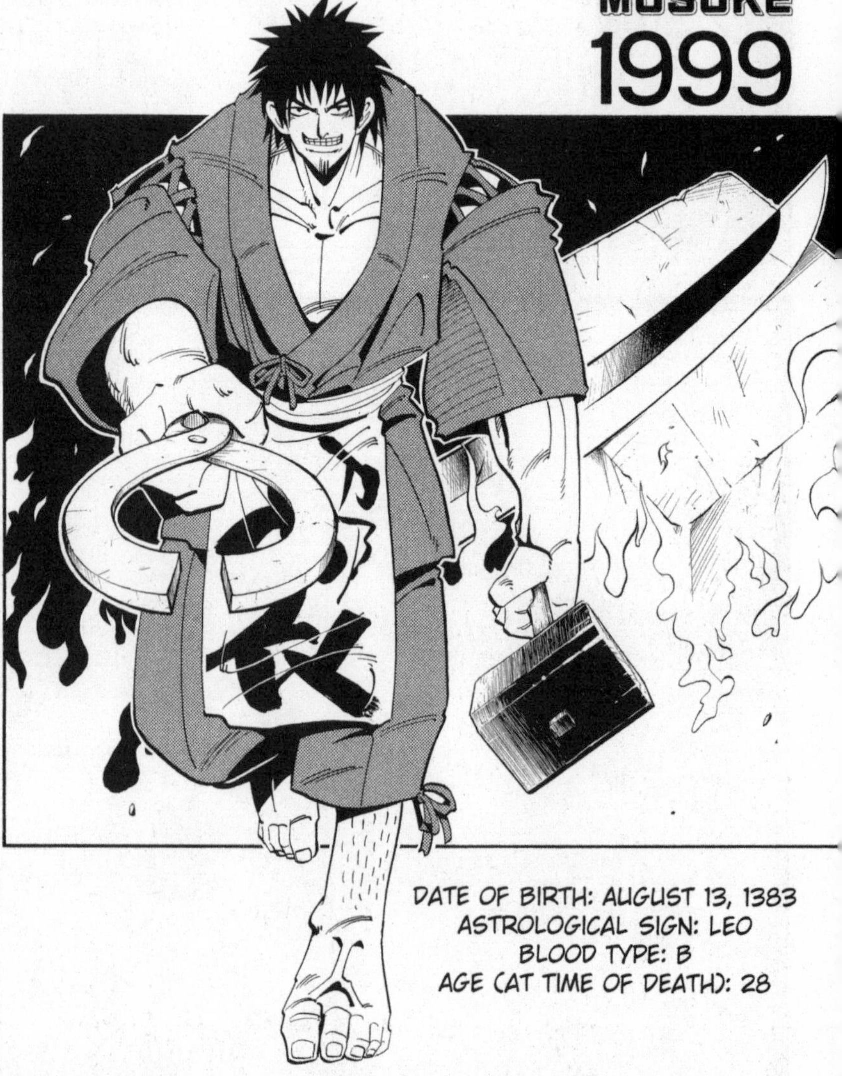

DATE OF BIRTH: AUGUST 13, 1383
ASTROLOGICAL SIGN: LEO
BLOOD TYPE: B
AGE (AT TIME OF DEATH): 28

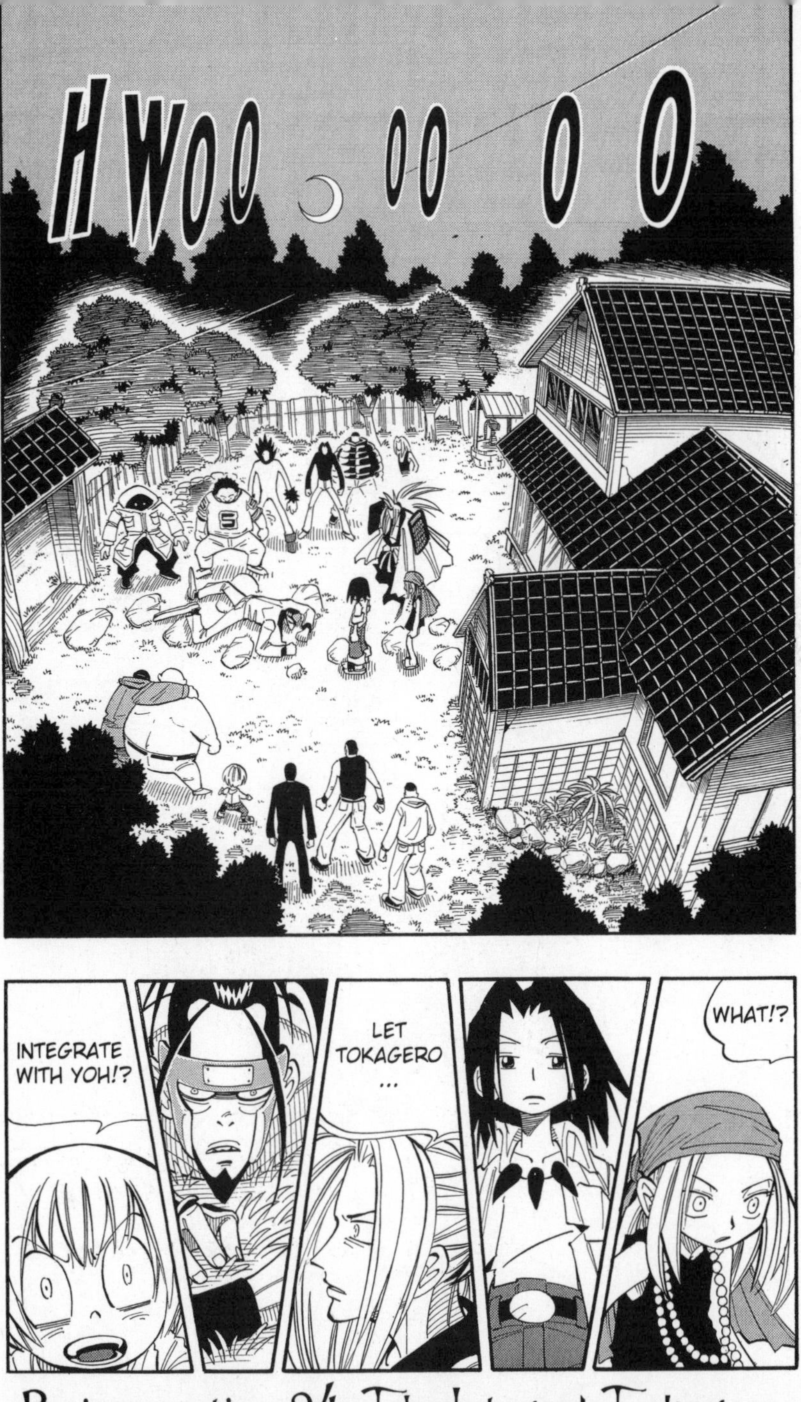
HWOO OO O O
WHAT!?
LET TOKAGERO ...
INTEGRATE WITH YOH!?

Reincarnation 24: The Integral Tokagero

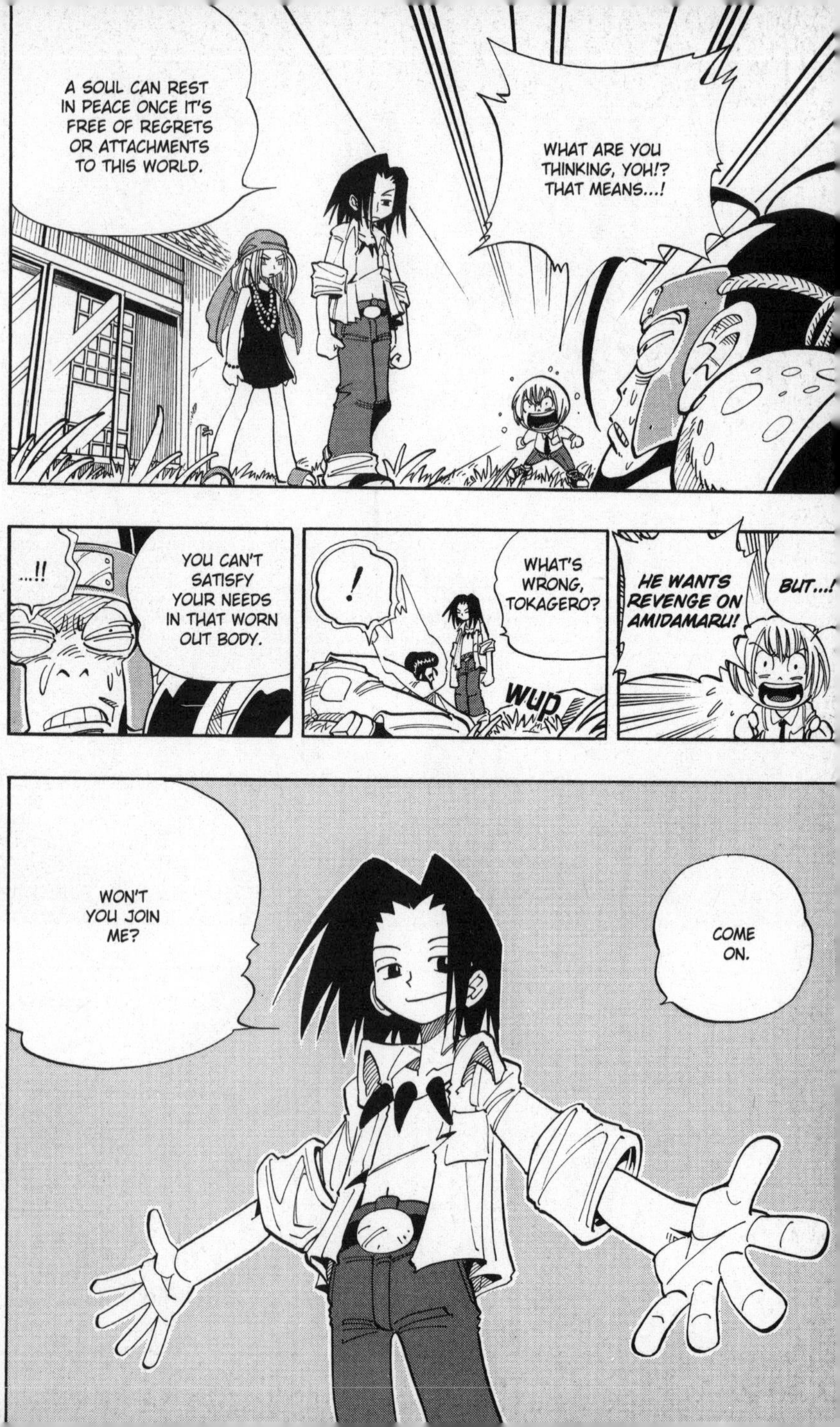
A SOUL CAN REST IN PEACE ONCE IT'S FREE OF REGRETS OR ATTACHMENTS TO THIS WORLD.
WHAT ARE YOU THINKING, YOH!? THAT MEANS...!
BUT...!
HE WANTS REVENGE ON AMIDAMARU!
WHAT'S WRONG, TOKAGERO?
!
wup
YOU CAN'T SATISFY YOUR NEEDS IN THAT WORN OUT BODY.
...!!
COME ON.
WON'T YOU JOIN ME?

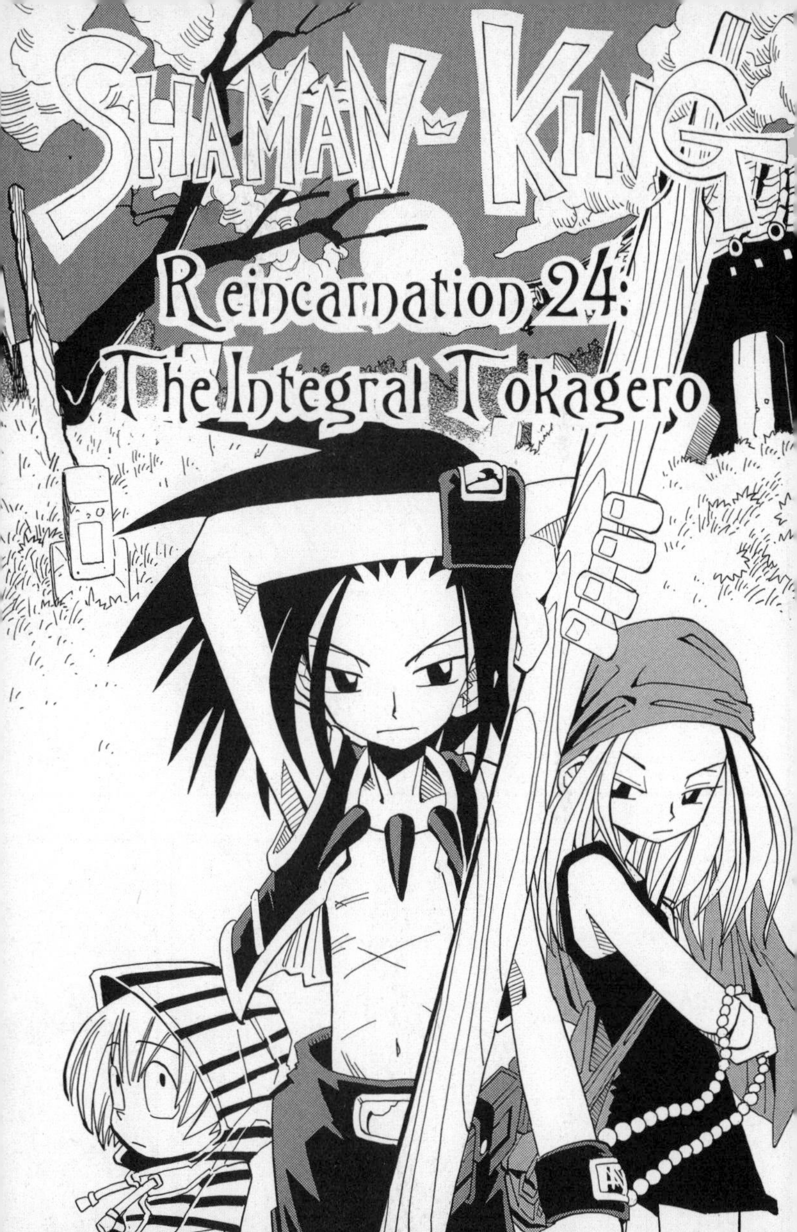
SHAMAN KING
Reincarnation 24:
The Integral Tokagero

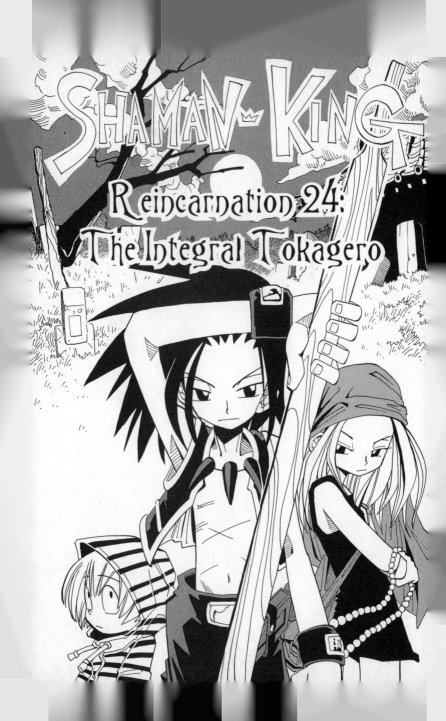

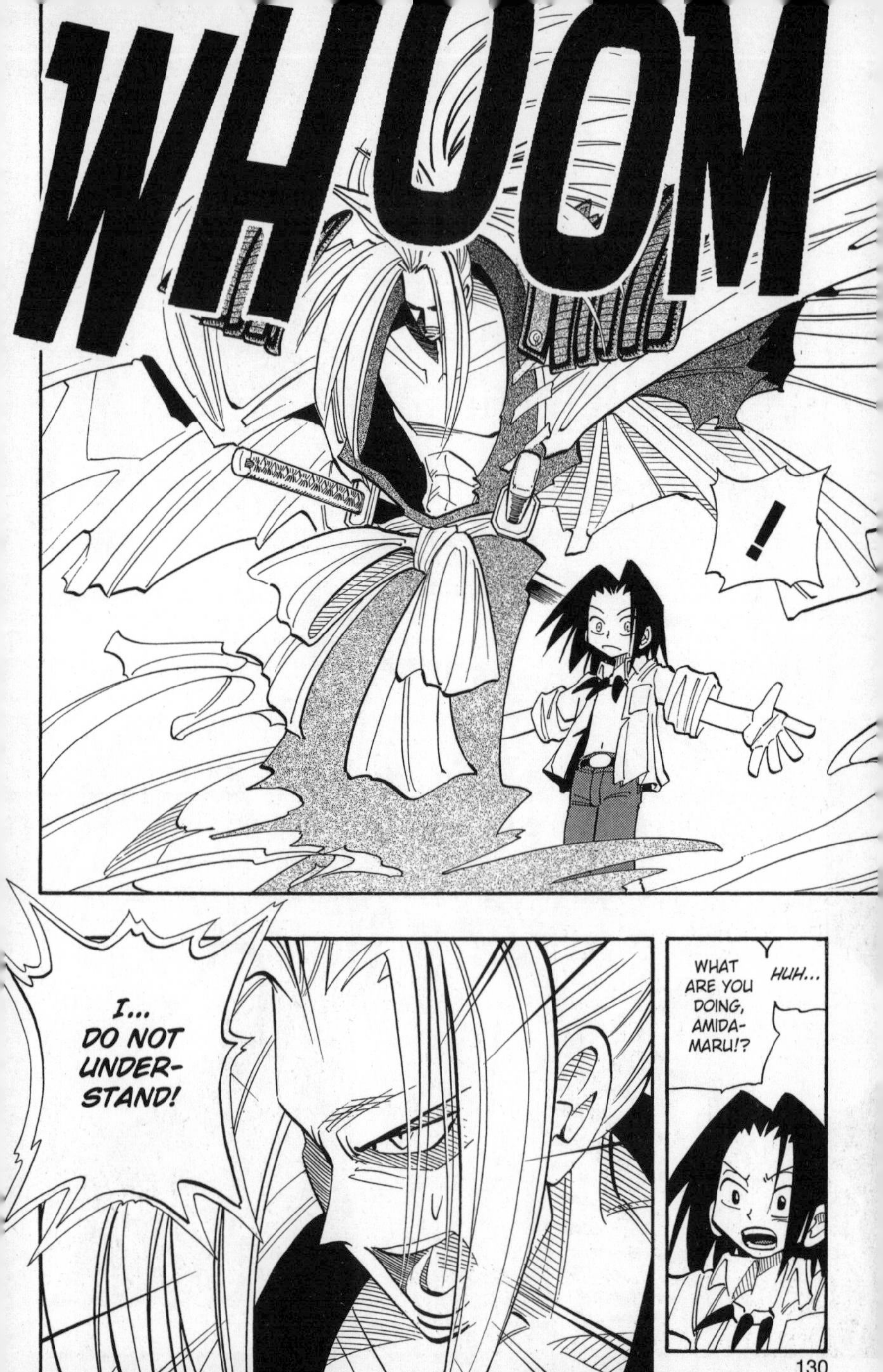
WHOOM
!
HUH...
WHAT ARE YOU DOING, AMIDA-MARU!?
I... DO NOT UNDER-STAND!

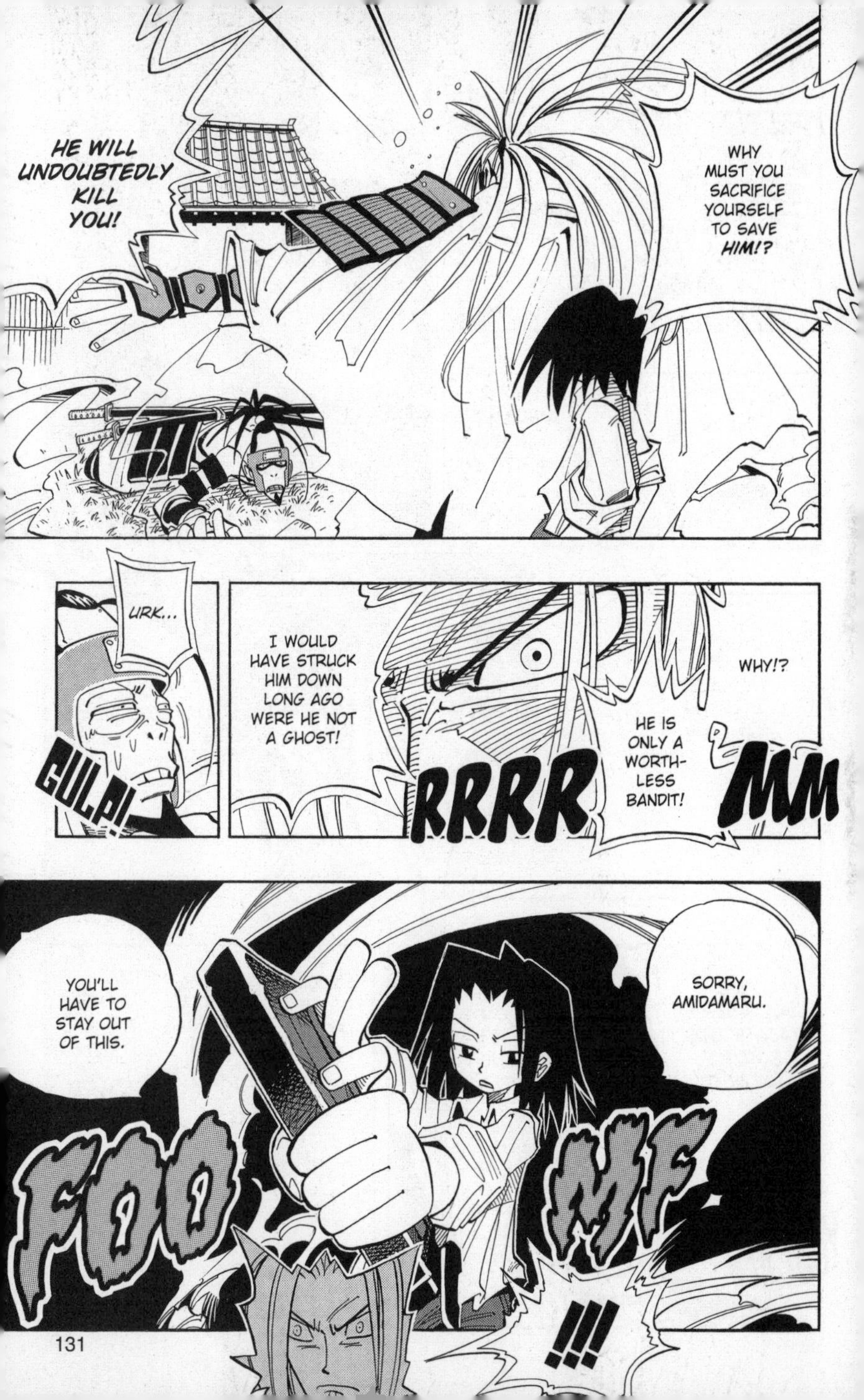
WHY MUST YOU SACRIFICE YOURSELF TO SAVE HIM!?
HE WILL UNDOUBTEDLY KILL YOU!
WHY!?
HE IS ONLY A WORTH-LESS BANDIT!
I WOULD HAVE STRUCK HIM DOWN LONG AGO WERE HE NOT A GHOST!
RRRRMM
URK...
GULP!
SORRY, AMIDAMARU.
YOU'LL HAVE TO STAY OUT OF THIS.
FOOMF
!!!

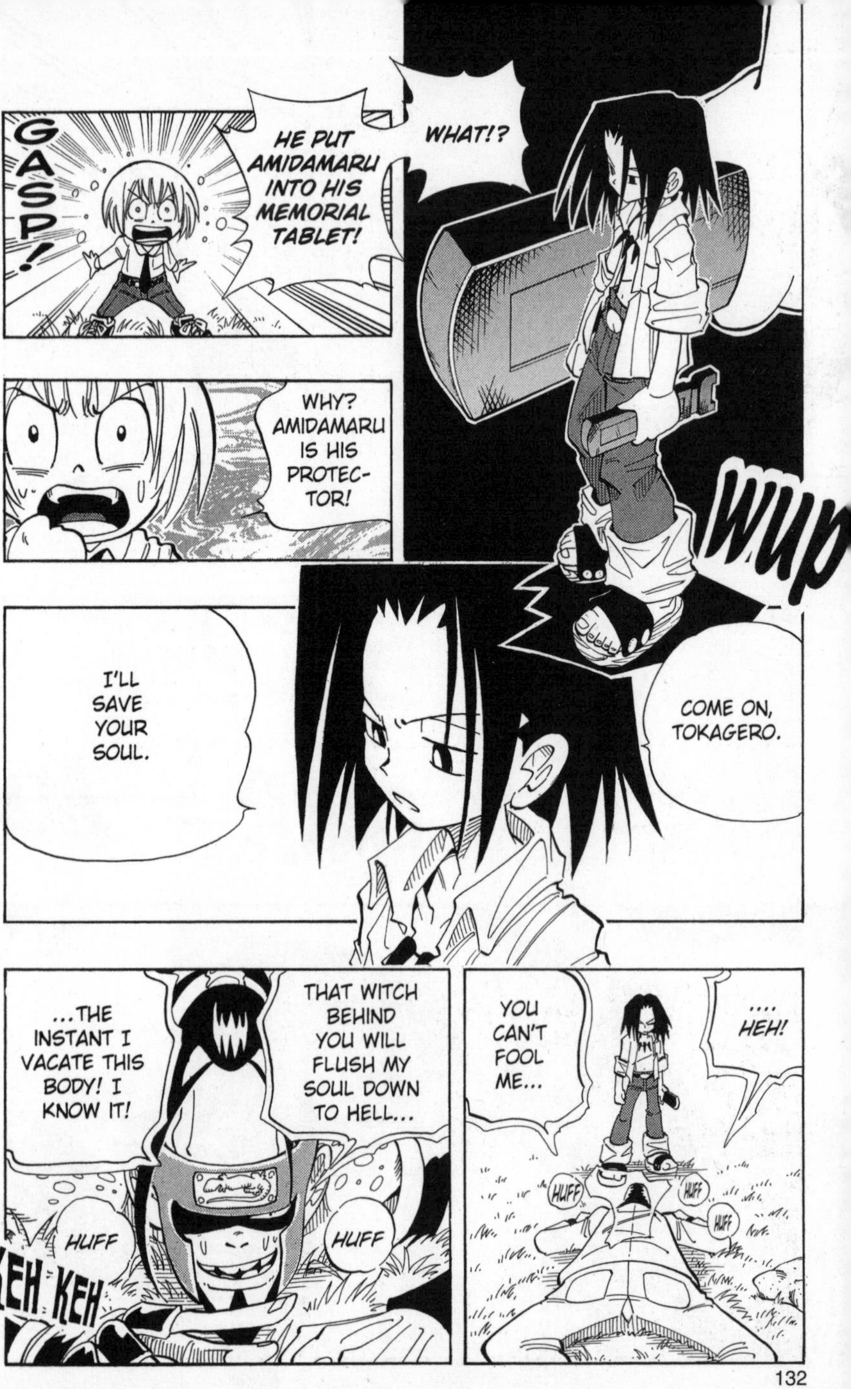
WHAT!?
WUP
GASP!
HE PUT AMIDAMARU INTO HIS MEMORIAL TABLET!
WHY? AMIDAMARU IS HIS PROTECTOR!
COME ON, TOKAGERO.
I'LL SAVE YOUR SOUL.
.... HEH!
YOU CAN'T FOOL ME...
HUFF
HUFF
HUFF
THAT WITCH BEHIND YOU WILL FLUSH MY SOUL DOWN TO HELL...
...THE INSTANT I VACATE THIS BODY! I KNOW IT!
HUFF
HUFF
KEH KEH

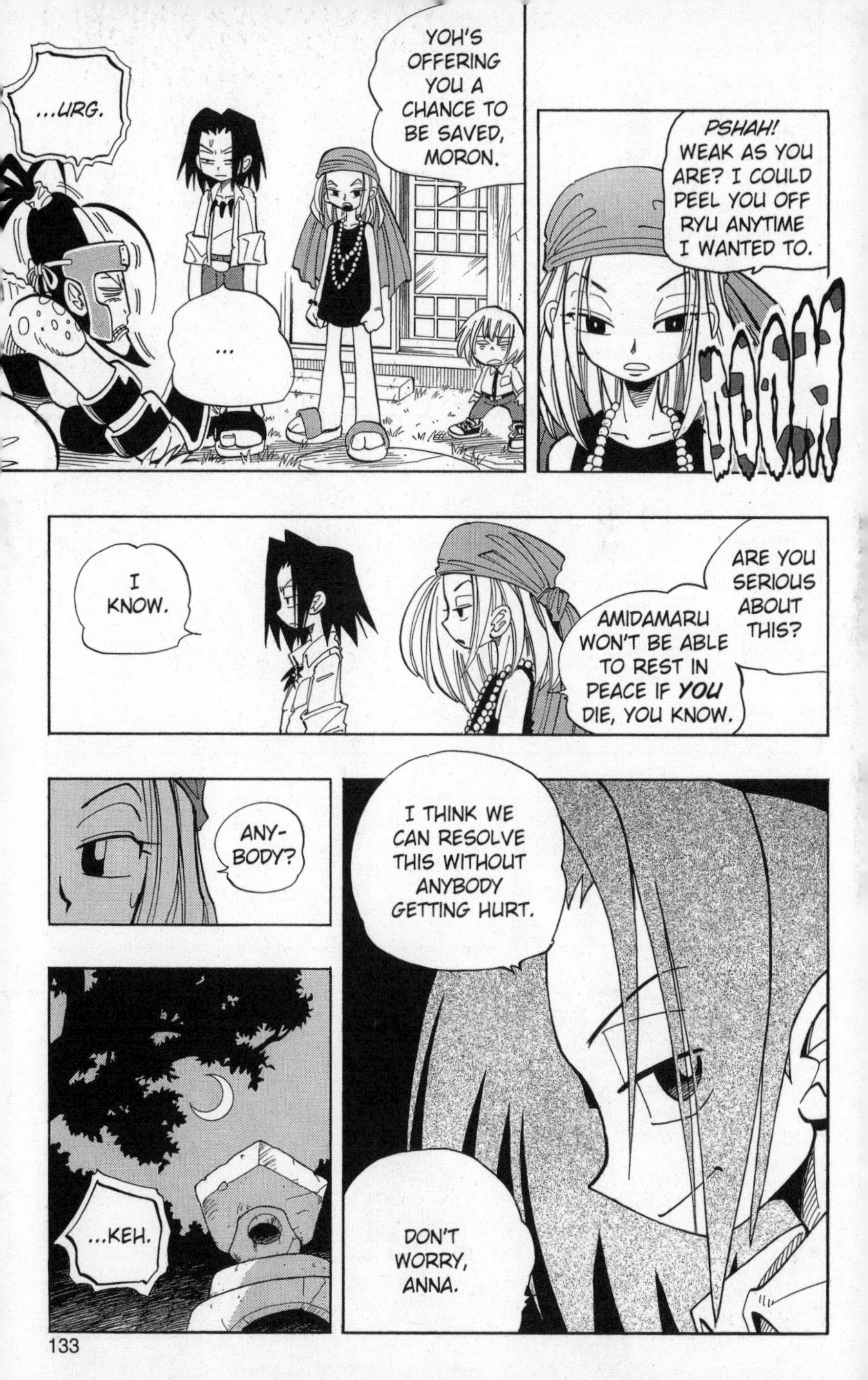
PSHAH! WEAK AS YOU ARE? I COULD PEEL YOU OFF RYU ANYTIME I WANTED TO.
YOH'S OFFERING YOU A CHANCE TO BE SAVED, MORON.
...URG.
...
ARE YOU SERIOUS ABOUT THIS?
AMIDAMARU WON'T BE ABLE TO REST IN PEACE IF YOU DIE, YOU KNOW.
I KNOW.
I THINK WE CAN RESOLVE THIS WITHOUT ANYBODY GETTING HURT.
DON'T WORRY, ANNA.
ANY-BODY?
...KEH.

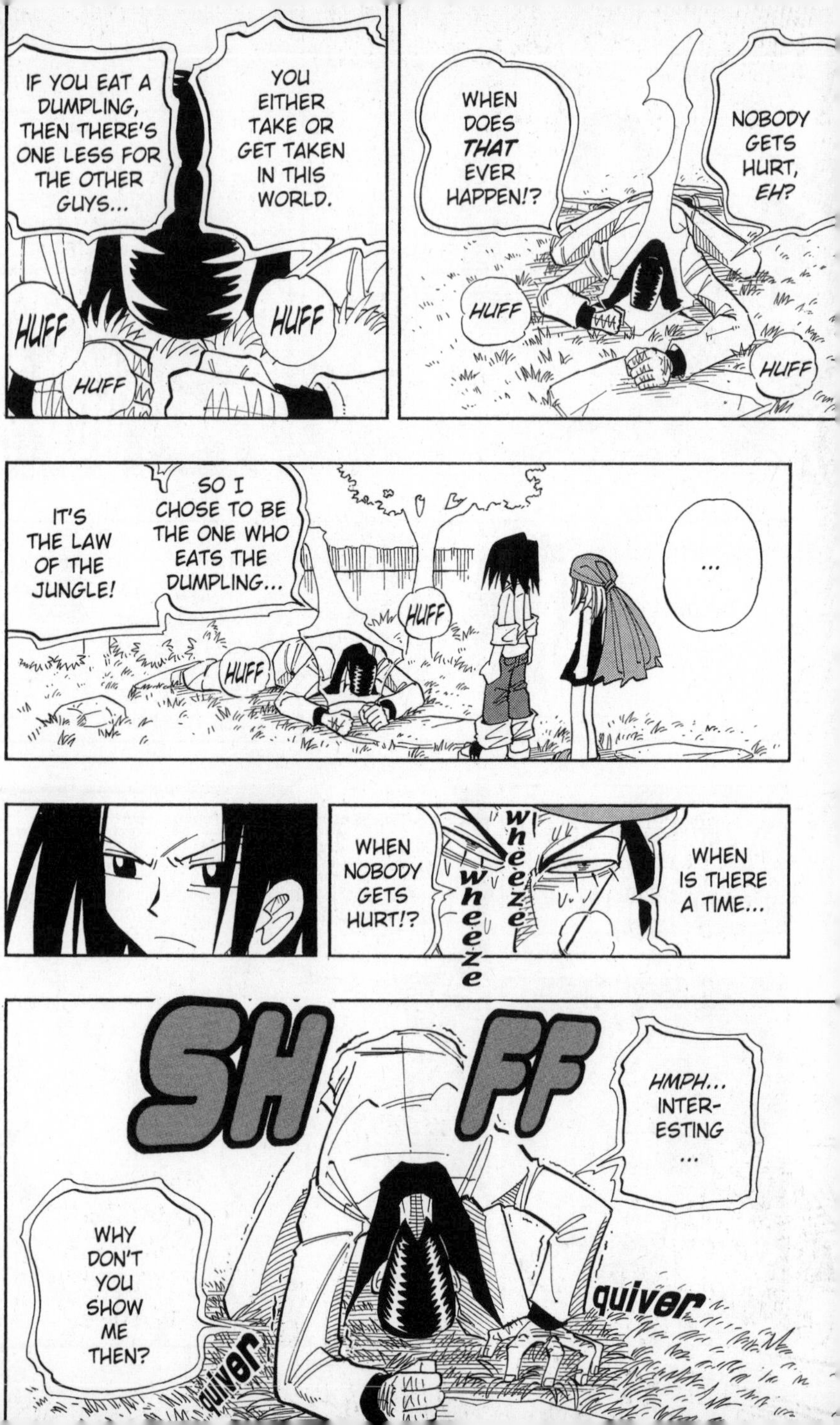
NOBODY GETS HURT, *EH?*
WHEN DOES ***THAT*** EVER HAPPEN!?
HUFF
HUFF
YOU EITHER TAKE OR GET TAKEN IN THIS WORLD.
IF YOU EAT A DUMPLING, THEN THERE'S ONE LESS FOR THE OTHER GUYS...
HUFF
HUFF
HUFF
...
SO I CHOSE TO BE THE ONE WHO EATS THE DUMPLING...
IT'S THE LAW OF THE JUNGLE!
HUFF
HUFF
WHEN IS THERE A TIME...
wheeze
wheeze
WHEN NOBODY GETS HURT!?
SH FF
HMPH... INTER-ESTING ...
quiver
WHY DON'T YOU SHOW ME THEN?
quiver

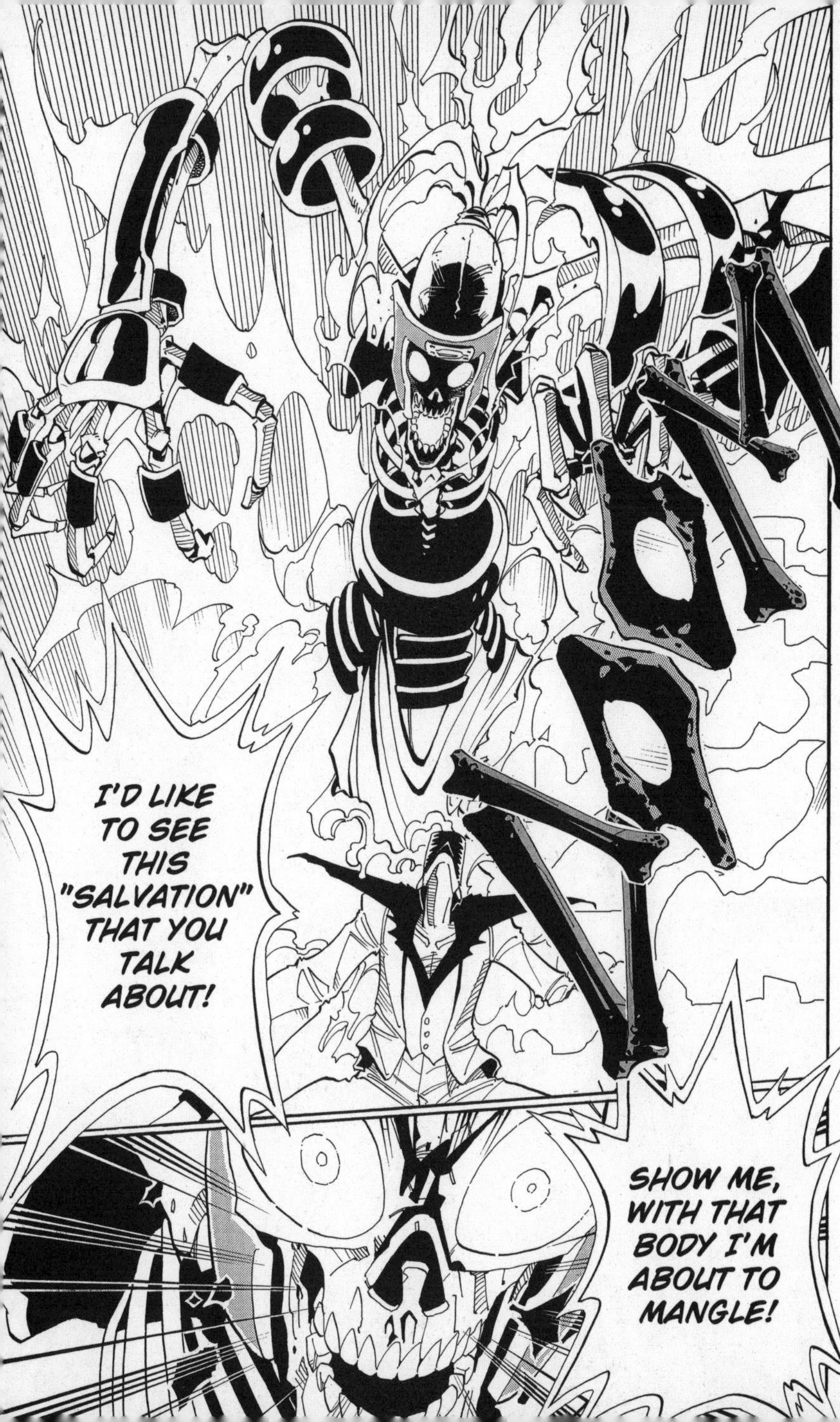
I'D LIKE TO SEE THIS "SALVATION" THAT YOU TALK ABOUT!
SHOW ME, WITH THAT BODY I'M ABOUT TO MANGLE!

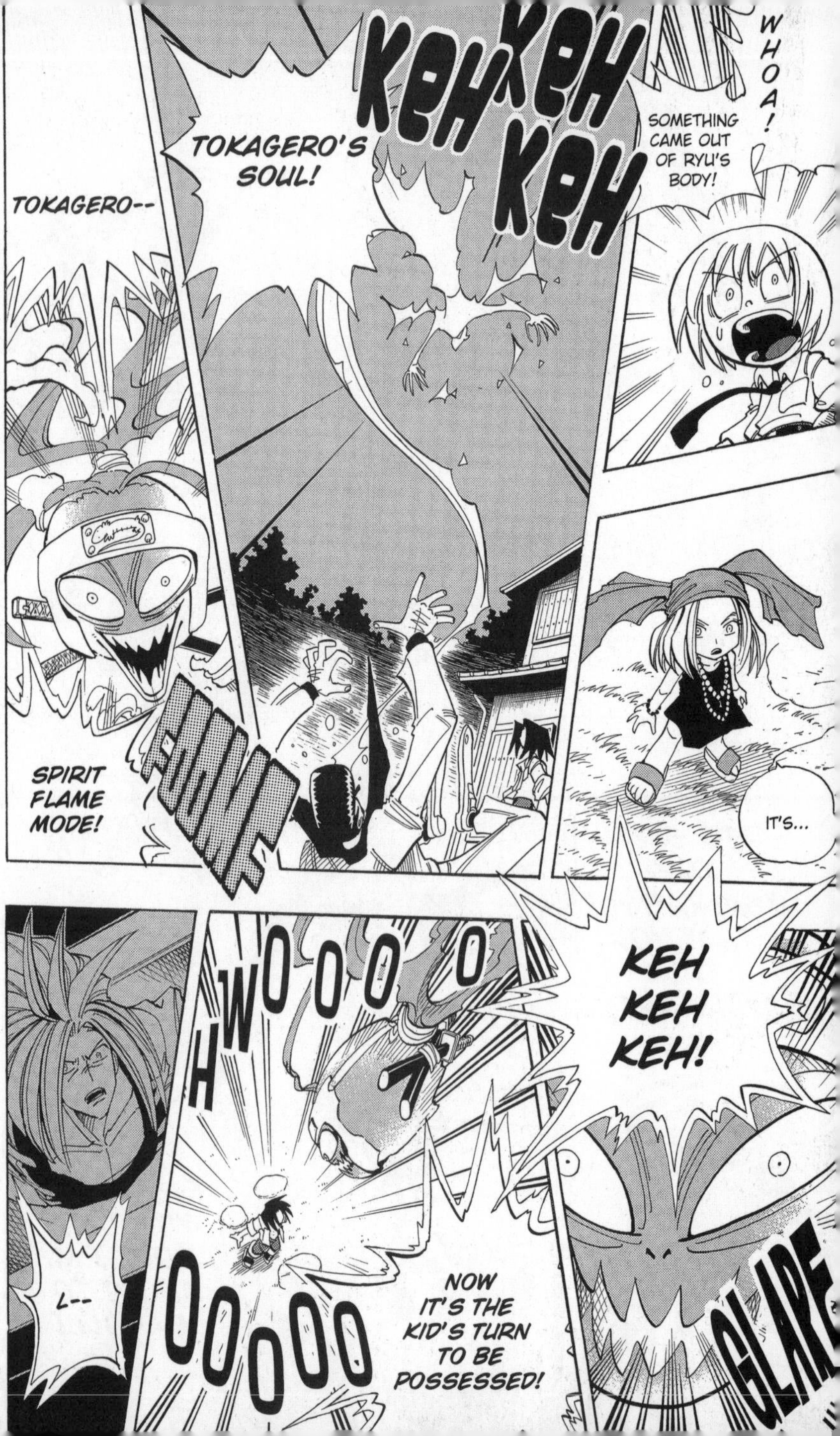
WHOA!
SOMETHING CAME OUT OF RYU'S BODY!
IT'S...
KEH KEH KEH KEH
TOKAGERO'S SOUL!
TOKAGERO--
SPIRIT FLAME MODE!
KEH KEH KEH!
GLARE
NOW IT'S THE KID'S TURN TO BE POSSESSED!
WHOOOO
OOOOOO
L--

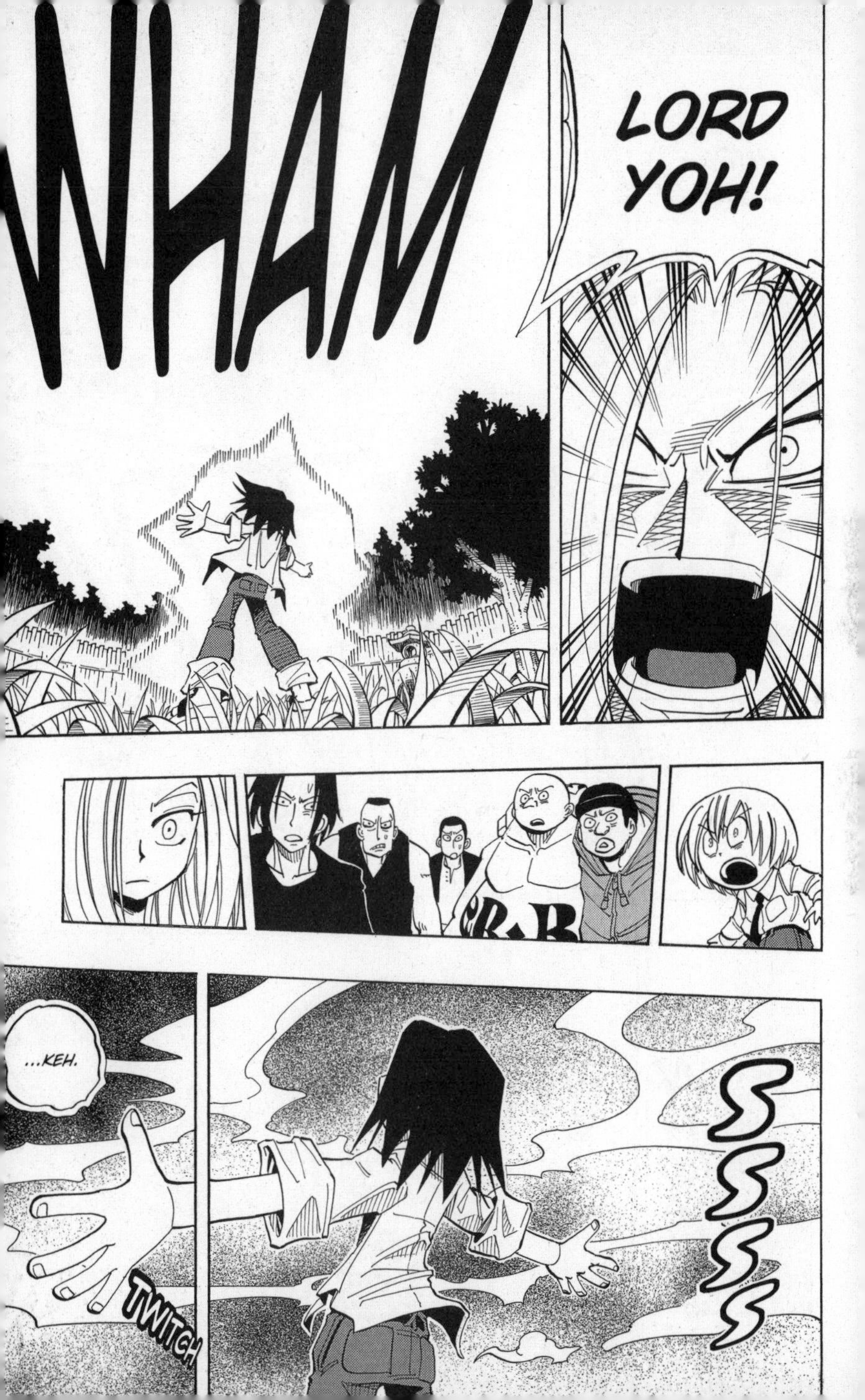
LORD YOH!
WHAM
SSSS
...KEH.
TWITCH

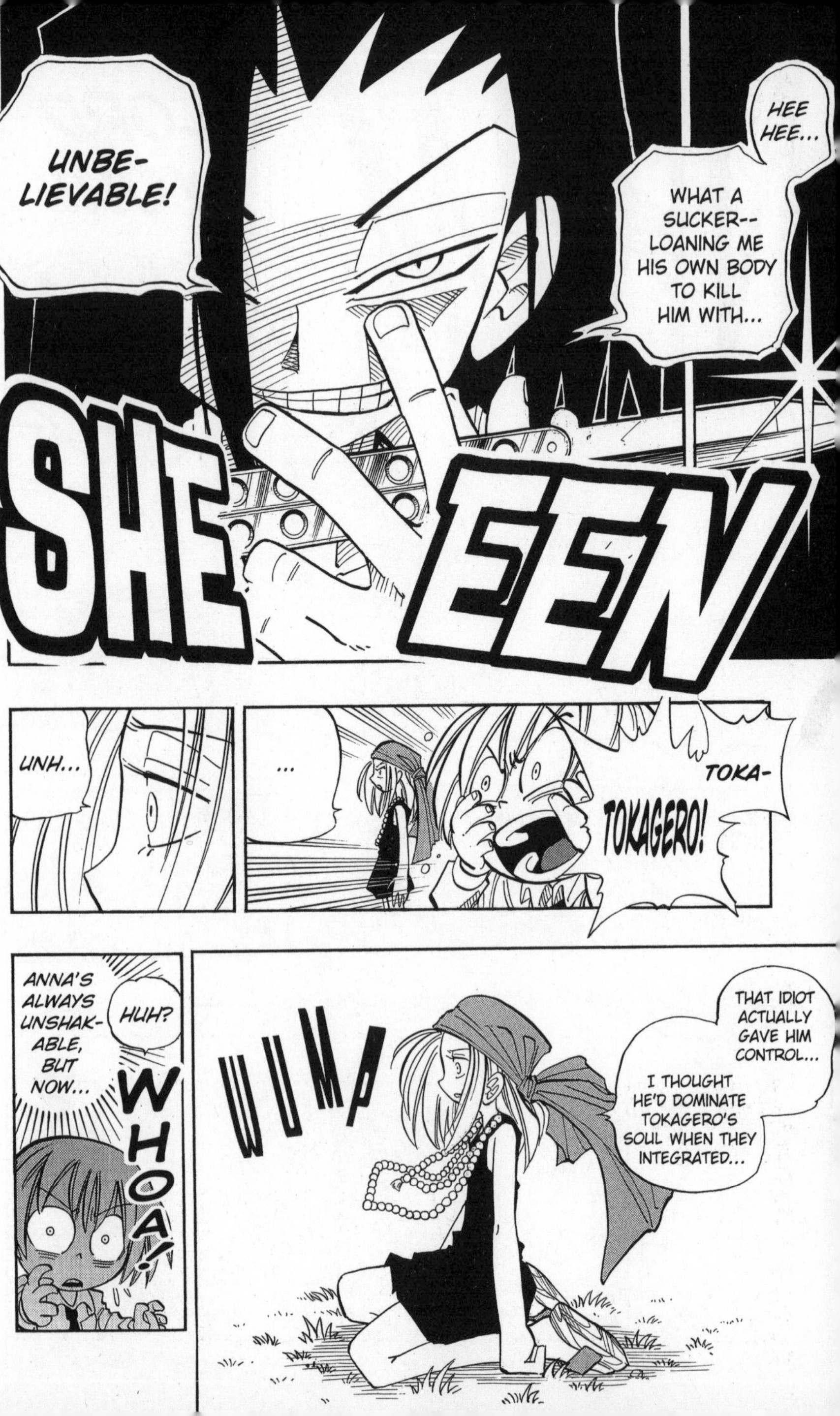
HEE HEE...
WHAT A SUCKER-- LOANING ME HIS OWN BODY TO KILL HIM WITH...
UNBE-LIEVABLE!
SHE EEN
TOKA-
TOKAGERO!
...
UNH...
THAT IDIOT ACTUALLY GAVE HIM CONTROL...
I THOUGHT HE'D DOMINATE TOKAGERO'S SOUL WHEN THEY INTEGRATED...
WUUMP
HUH?
ANNA'S ALWAYS UNSHAK-ABLE, BUT NOW...
WHOA!

READ THIS WAY

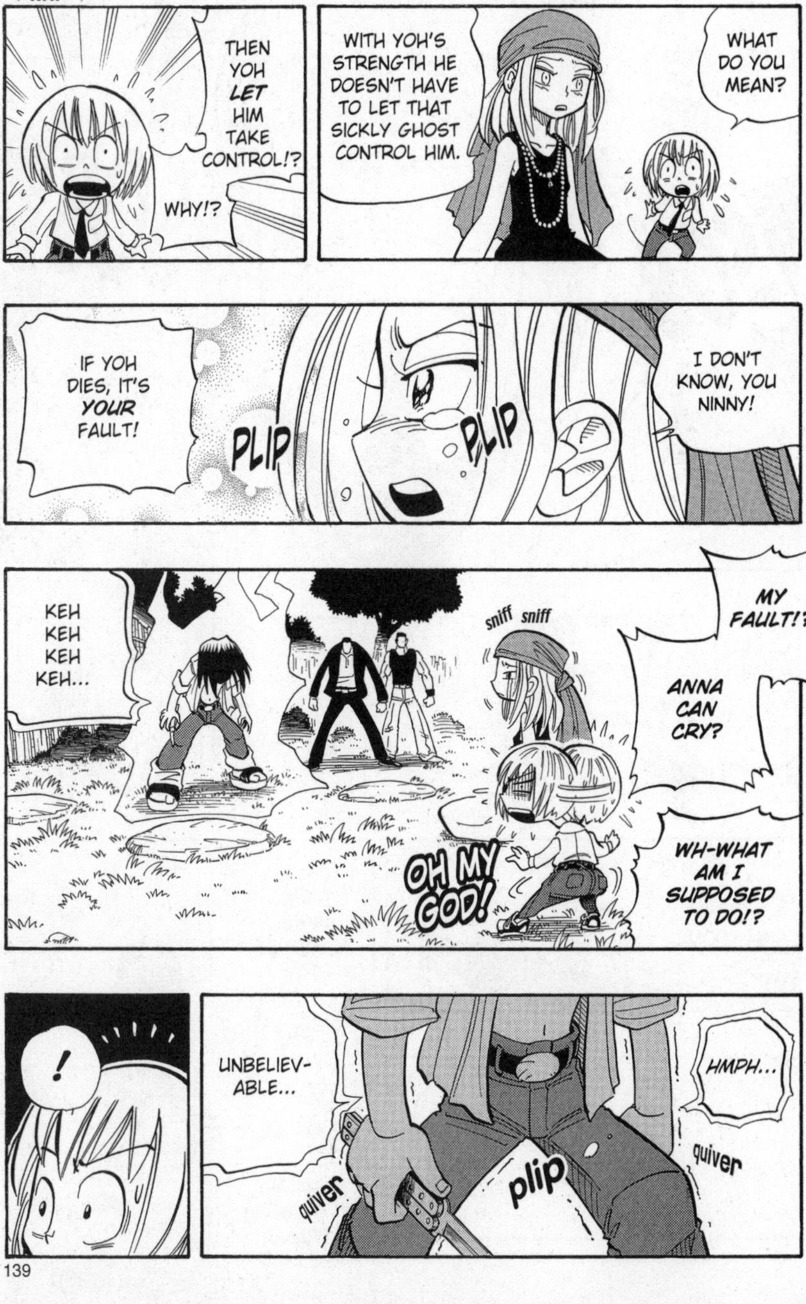

WHAT DO YOU MEAN?
WITH YOH'S STRENGTH HE DOESN'T HAVE TO LET THAT SICKLY GHOST CONTROL HIM.
THEN YOH *LET* HIM TAKE CONTROL!?
WHY!?
I DON'T KNOW, YOU NINNY!
PLIP
PLIP
IF YOH DIES, IT'S *YOUR* FAULT!
MY FAULT!?
sniff sniff
ANNA CAN CRY?
WH-WHAT AM I SUPPOSED TO DO!?
OH MY GOD!
KEH KEH KEH KEH...
HMPH...
quiver
plip
UNBELIEVABLE...
quiver
!

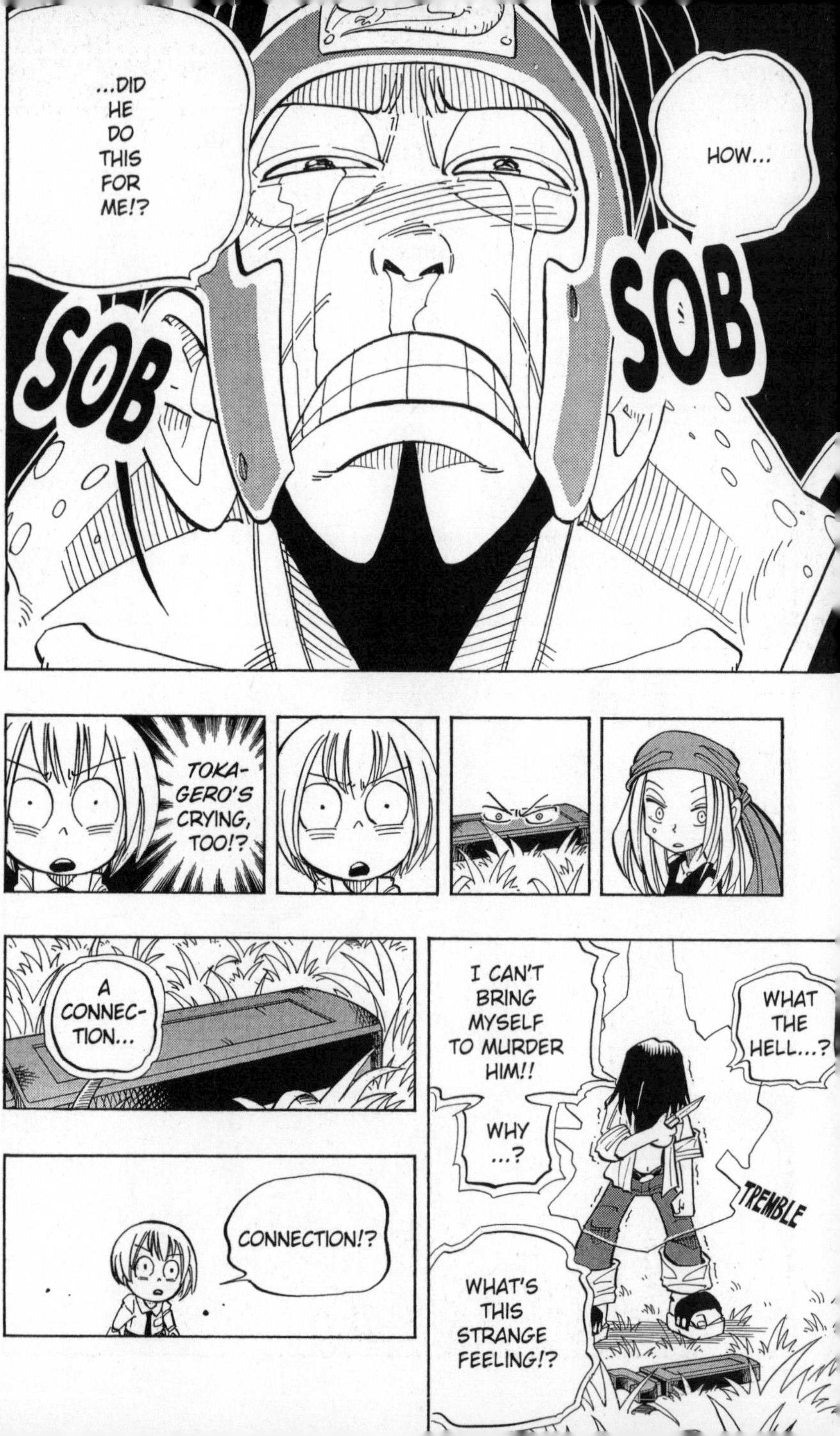
HOW...
SOB
...DID HE DO THIS FOR ME!?
SOB
TOKA-GERO'S CRYING, TOO!?
WHAT THE HELL...?
I CAN'T BRING MYSELF TO MURDER HIM!!
WHY ...?
TREMBLE
WHAT'S THIS STRANGE FEELING!?
A CONNECTION...
CONNECTION!?

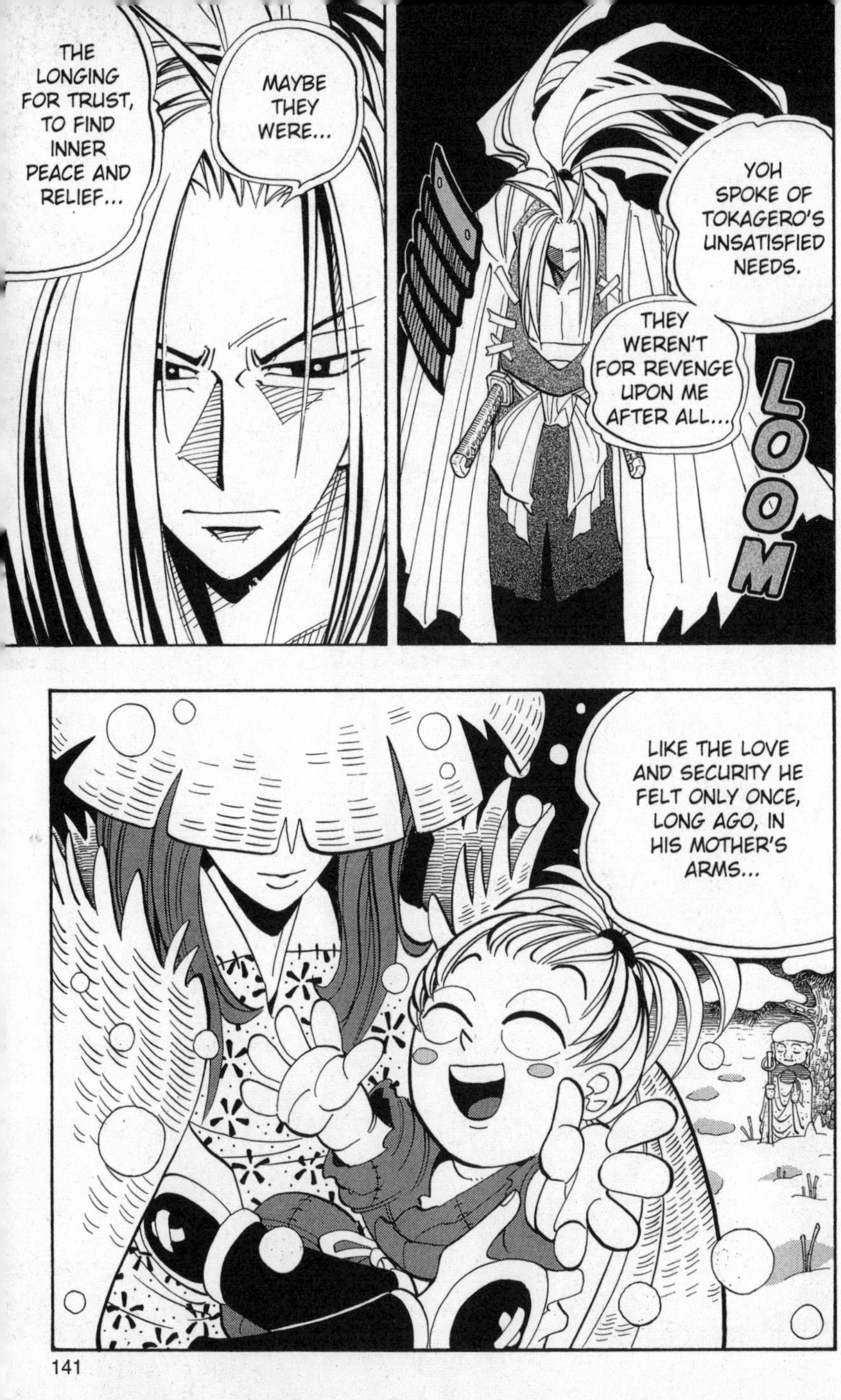
YOH SPOKE OF TOKAGERO'S UNSATISFIED NEEDS.
THEY WEREN'T FOR REVENGE UPON ME AFTER ALL...
LOOOM
MAYBE THEY WERE...
THE LONGING FOR TRUST, TO FIND INNER PEACE AND RELIEF...
LIKE THE LOVE AND SECURITY HE FELT ONLY ONCE, LONG AGO, IN HIS MOTHER'S ARMS...

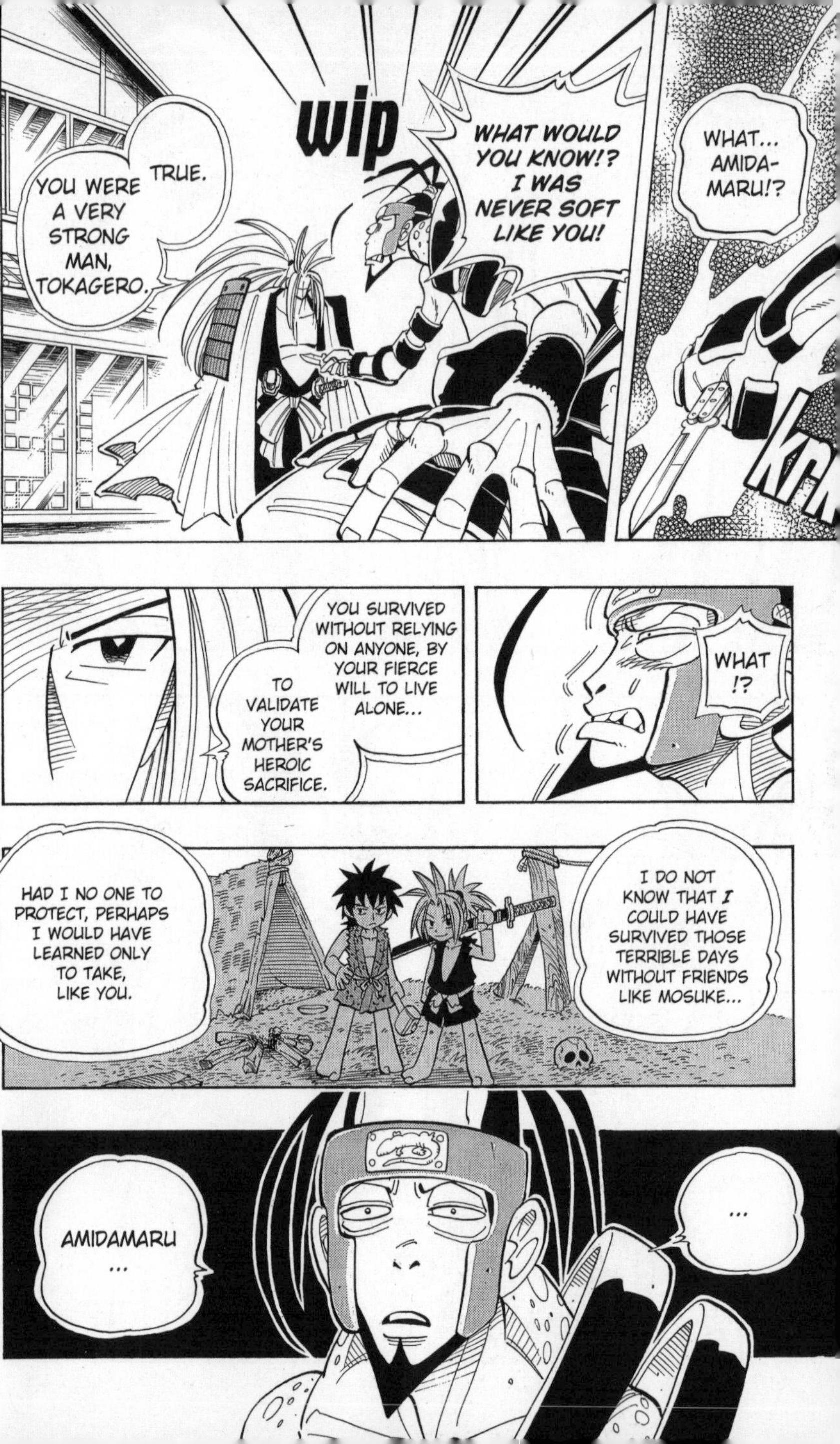
WHAT... AMIDA-MARU!?
wip
WHAT WOULD YOU KNOW!? I WAS NEVER SOFT LIKE YOU!
TRUE.
YOU WERE A VERY STRONG MAN, TOKAGERO.
WHAT !?
YOU SURVIVED WITHOUT RELYING ON ANYONE, BY YOUR FIERCE WILL TO LIVE ALONE...
TO VALIDATE YOUR MOTHER'S HEROIC SACRIFICE.
I DO NOT KNOW THAT I COULD HAVE SURVIVED THOSE TERRIBLE DAYS WITHOUT FRIENDS LIKE MOSUKE...
HAD I NO ONE TO PROTECT, PERHAPS I WOULD HAVE LEARNED ONLY TO TAKE, LIKE YOU.
...
AMIDAMARU ...

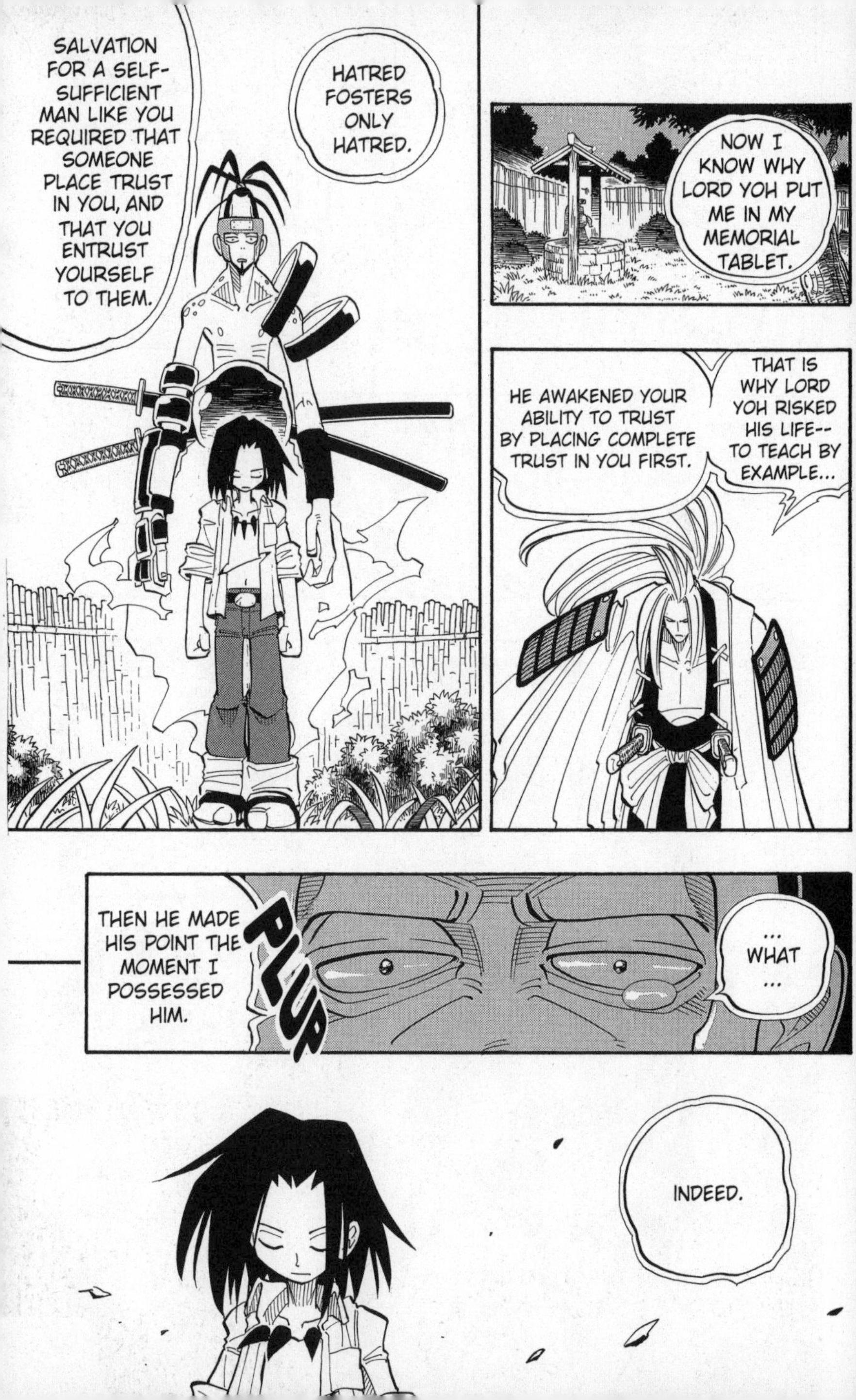
NOW I KNOW WHY LORD YOH PUT ME IN MY MEMORIAL TABLET.
THAT IS WHY LORD YOH RISKED HIS LIFE-- TO TEACH BY EXAMPLE...
HE AWAKENED YOUR ABILITY TO TRUST BY PLACING COMPLETE TRUST IN YOU FIRST.
HATRED FOSTERS ONLY HATRED.
SALVATION FOR A SELF-SUFFICIENT MAN LIKE YOU REQUIRED THAT SOMEONE PLACE TRUST IN YOU, AND THAT YOU ENTRUST YOURSELF TO THEM.
... WHAT ...
PLUP
THEN HE MADE HIS POINT THE MOMENT I POSSESSED HIM.
INDEED.

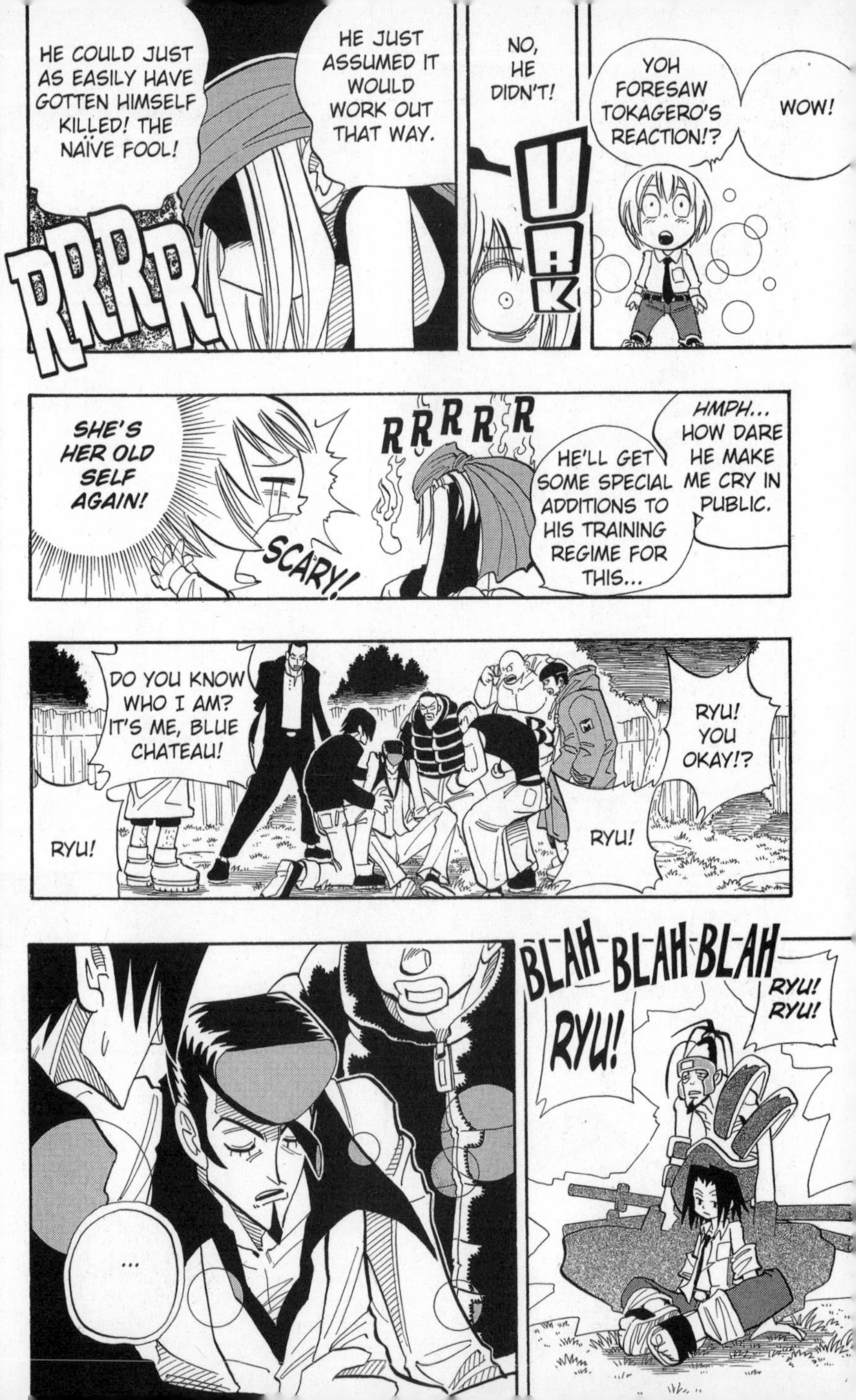
WOW!
YOH FORESAW TOKAGERO'S REACTION!?
NO, HE DIDN'T!
URK
HE JUST ASSUMED IT WOULD WORK OUT THAT WAY.
HE COULD JUST AS EASILY HAVE GOTTEN HIMSELF KILLED! THE NAÏVE FOOL!
RRRR
HMPH... HOW DARE HE MAKE ME CRY IN PUBLIC.
HE'LL GET SOME SPECIAL ADDITIONS TO HIS TRAINING REGIME FOR THIS...
RRRRR
SCARY!
SHE'S HER OLD SELF AGAIN!
RYU! YOU OKAY!?
RYU!
DO YOU KNOW WHO I AM? IT'S ME, BLUE CHATEAU!
RYU!
RYU! RYU!
BLAH-BLAH-BLAH
RYU!
...

READ THIS WAY

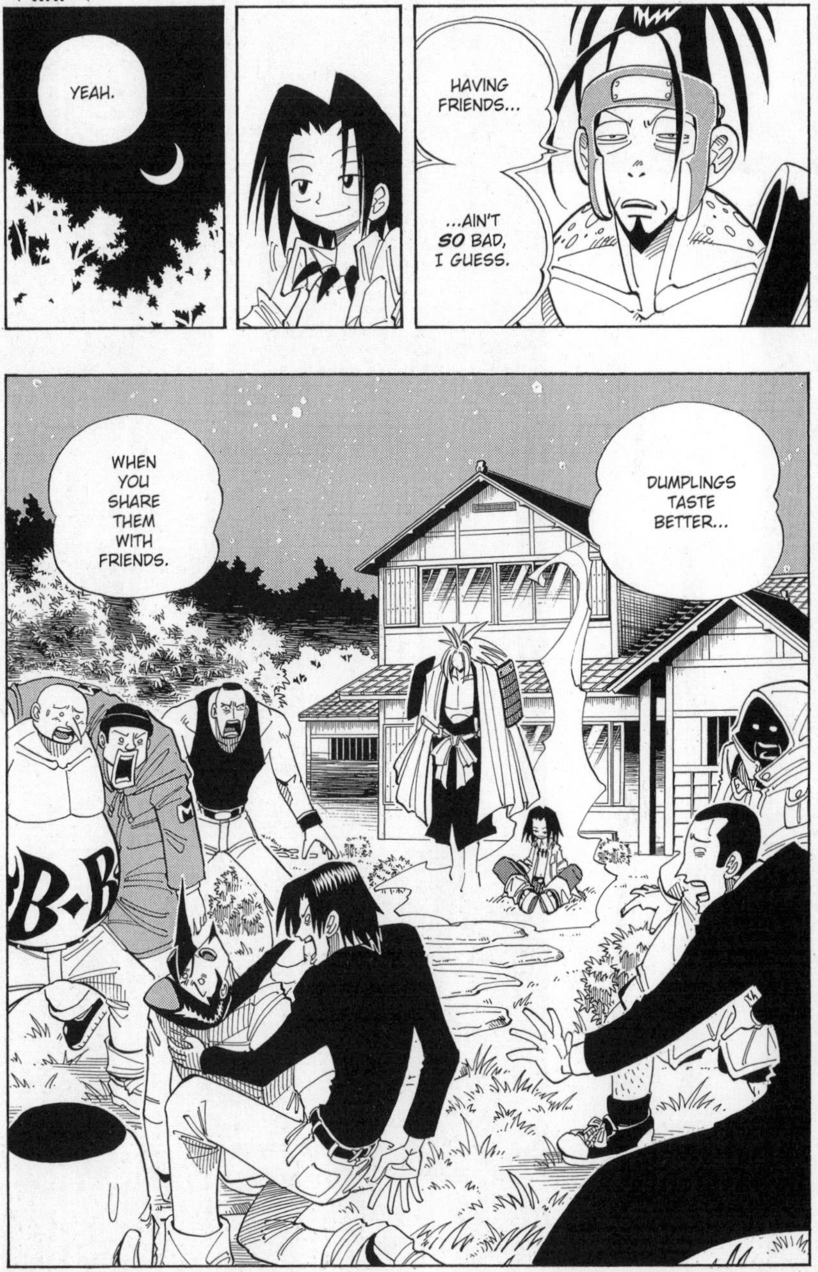
HAVING FRIENDS...
...AIN'T SO BAD, I GUESS.
YEAH.
DUMPLINGS TASTE BETTER...
WHEN YOU SHARE THEM WITH FRIENDS.

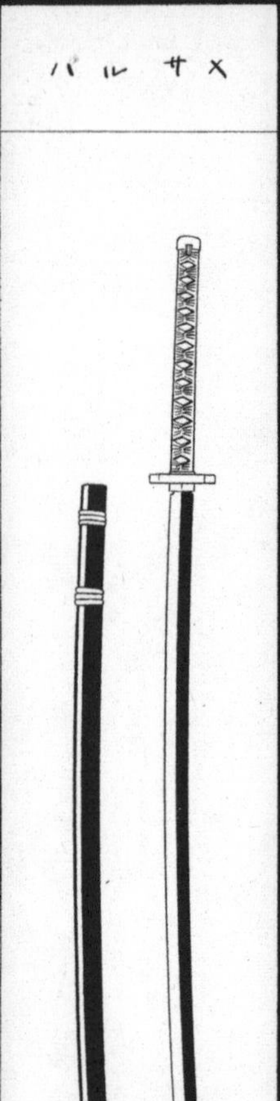
ハルサメ

SHAMAN
KING
3

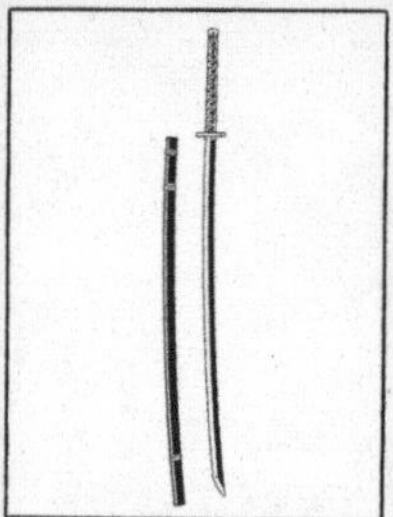

HARUSAME: THE SWORD MADE BY MOSUKE

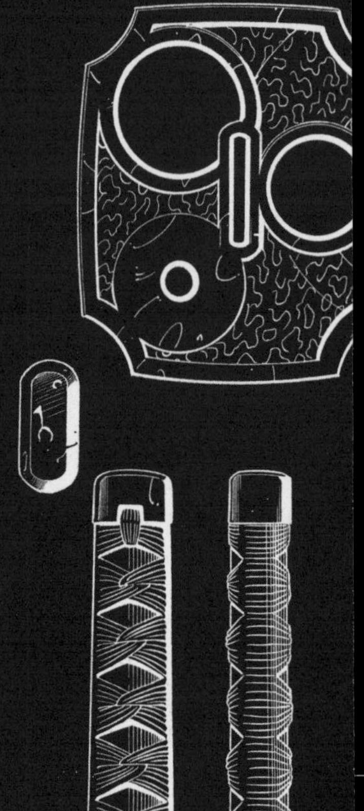

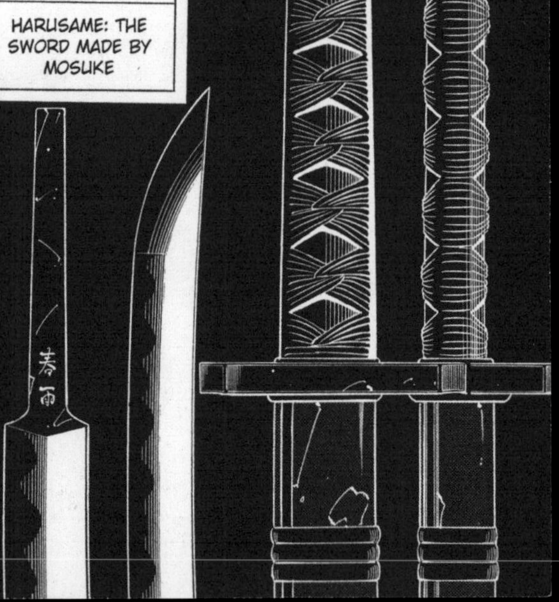

Reincarnation 25: The Dragon's Gratitude

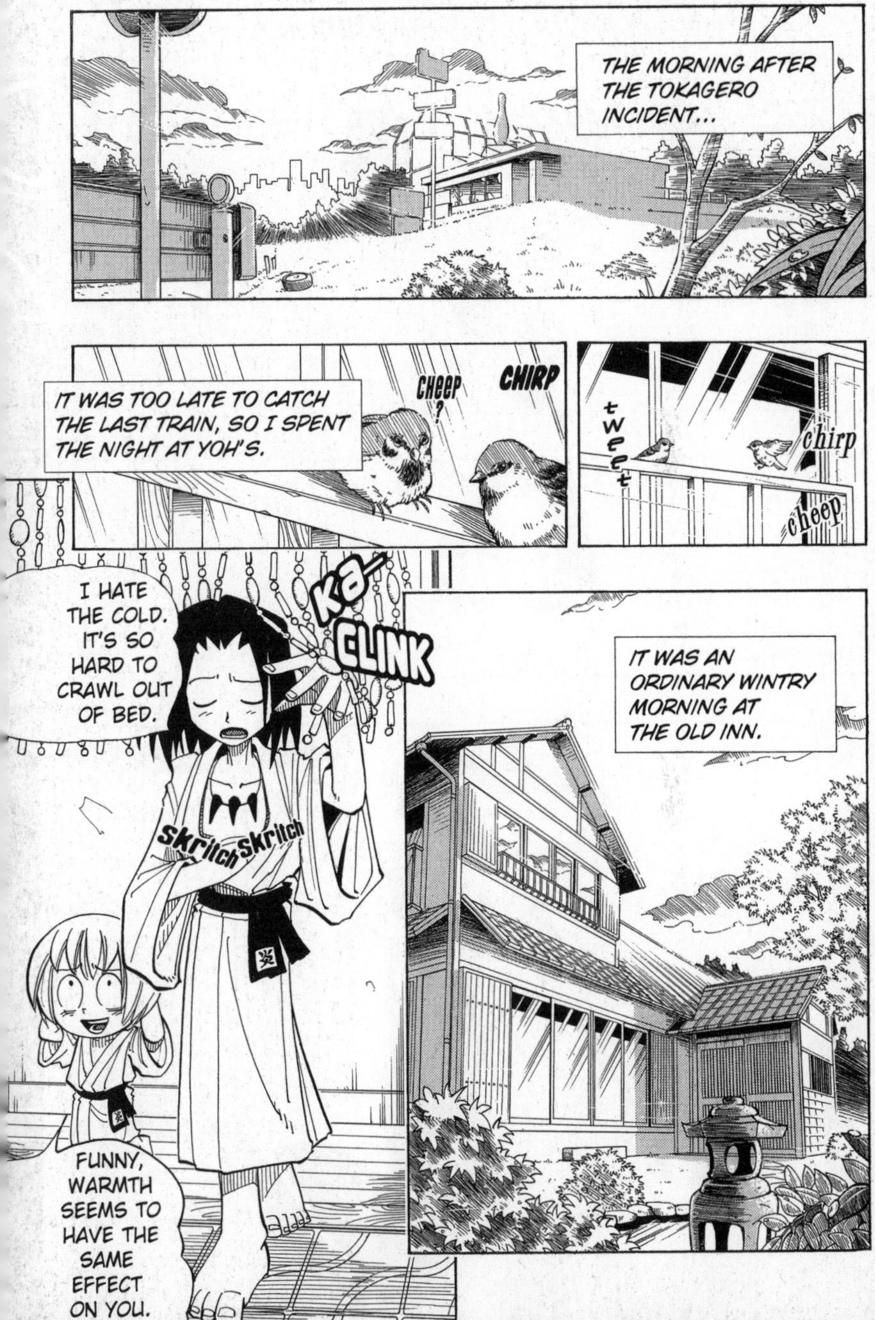
THE MORNING AFTER THE TOKAGERO INCIDENT...
tweet
chirp
cheep
CHIRP
CHEEP ?
IT WAS TOO LATE TO CATCH THE LAST TRAIN, SO I SPENT THE NIGHT AT YOH'S.
IT WAS AN ORDINARY WINTRY MORNING AT THE OLD INN.
KA-CLINK
I HATE THE COLD. IT'S SO HARD TO CRAWL OUT OF BED.
SKRITCH SKRITCH
FUNNY, WARMTH SEEMS TO HAVE THE SAME EFFECT ON YOU.

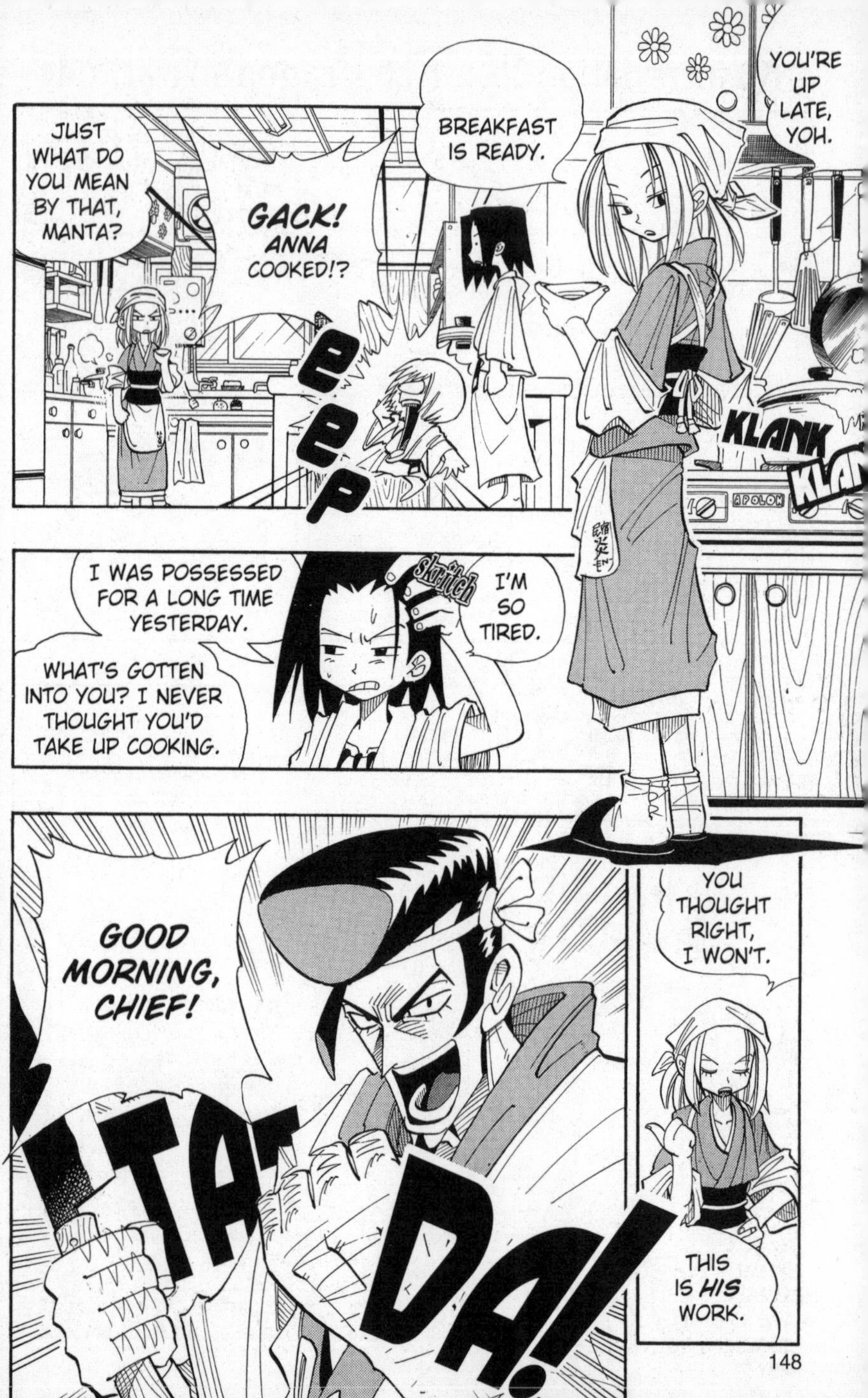
YOU'RE UP LATE, YOH.
KLANK
KLAN
BREAKFAST IS READY.
GACK! ANNA COOKED!?
eeep
JUST WHAT DO YOU MEAN BY THAT, MANTA?
APOLON
I'M SO TIRED.
skritch
I WAS POSSESSED FOR A LONG TIME YESTERDAY.
WHAT'S GOTTEN INTO YOU? I NEVER THOUGHT YOU'D TAKE UP COOKING.
YOU THOUGHT RIGHT, I WON'T.
THIS IS *HIS* WORK.
GOOD MORNING, CHIEF!
TA-DA!

READ THIS WAY

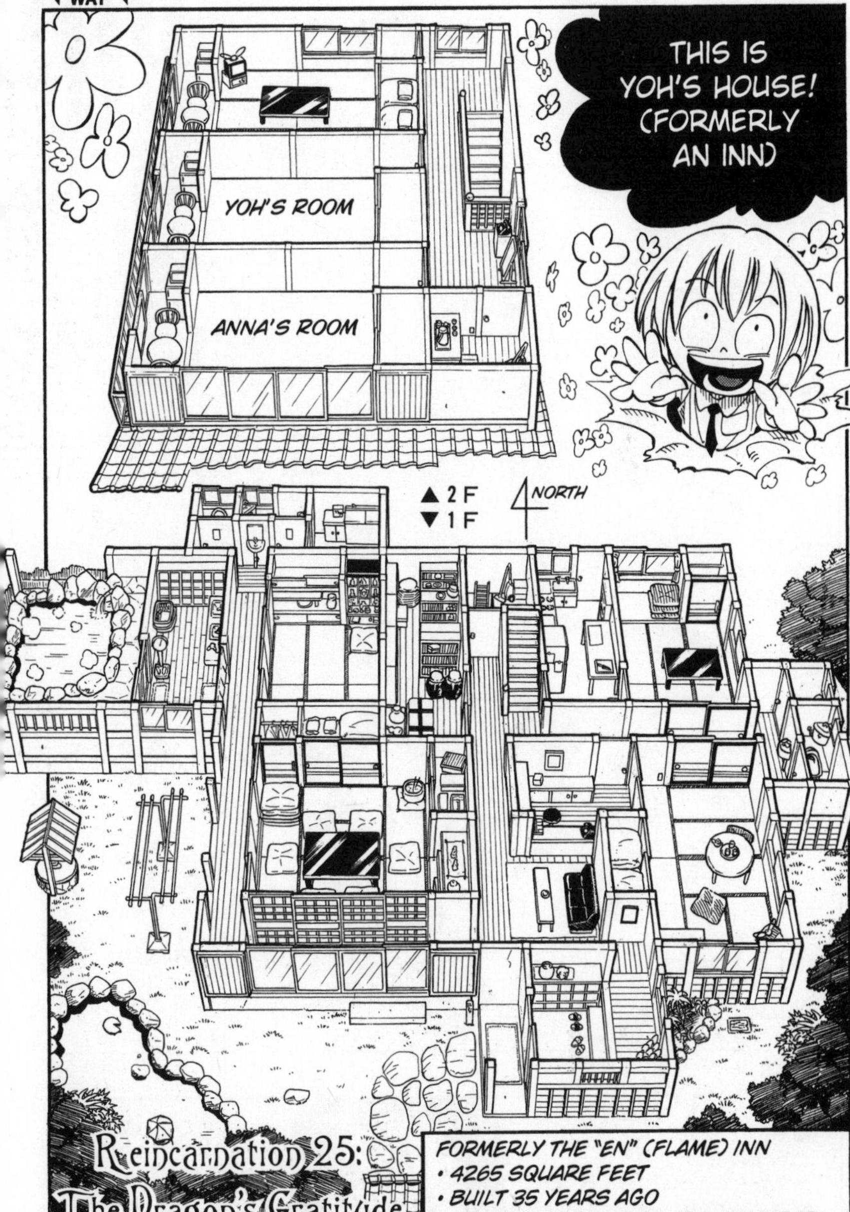
THIS IS YOH'S HOUSE! (FORMERLY AN INN)
YOH'S ROOM
ANNA'S ROOM
▲2 F
▼1 F
NORTH
Reincarnation 25: The Dragon's Gratitude
FORMERLY THE "EN" (FLAME) INN
• 4265 SQUARE FEET
• BUILT 35 YEARS AGO
• 30-MINUTE BUS RIDE FROM FUNBARI HILL STATION, THEN AN 18-MINUTE WALK

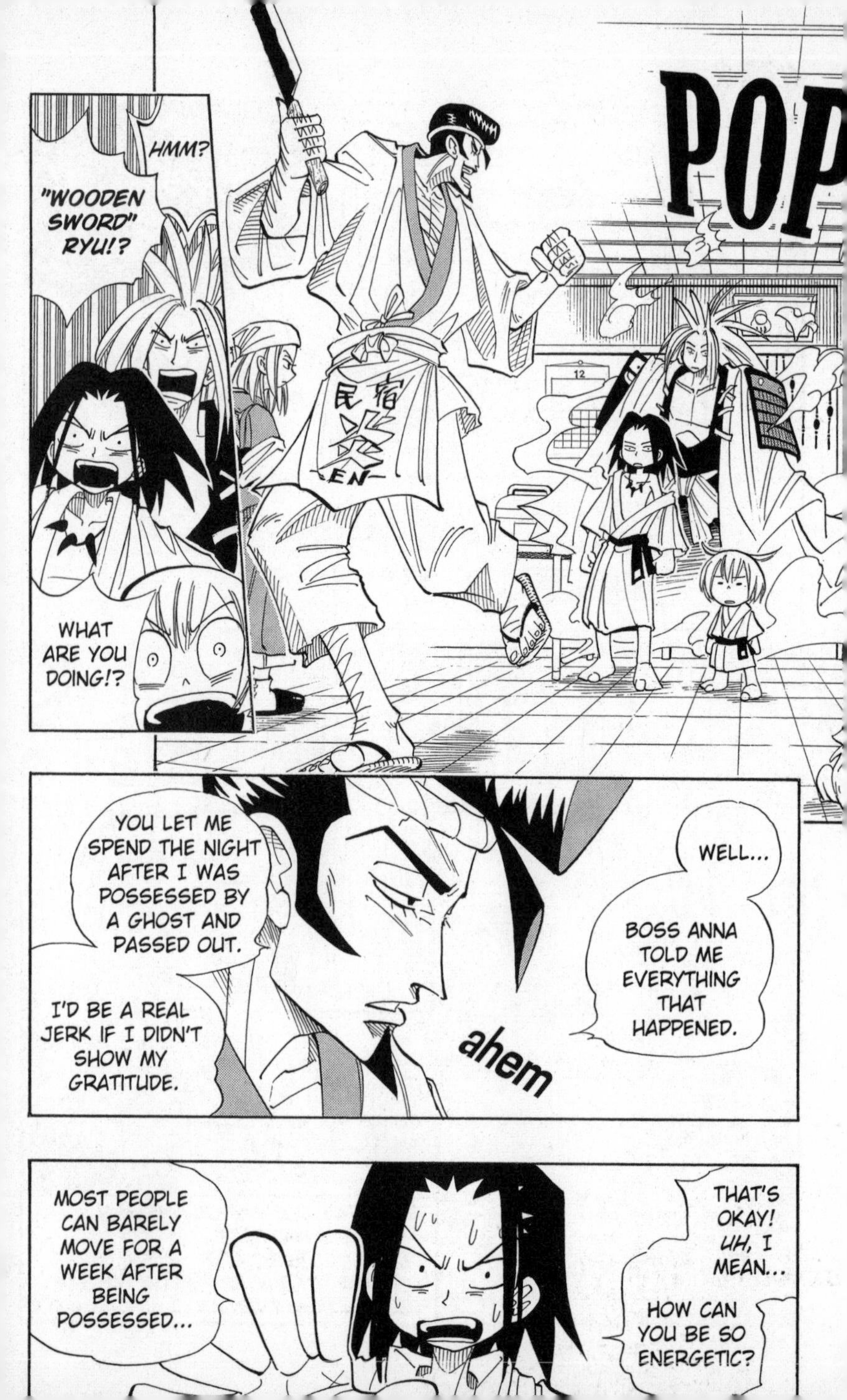
POP
HMM?
"WOODEN SWORD" RYU!?
WHAT ARE YOU DOING!?
WELL...
BOSS ANNA TOLD ME EVERYTHING THAT HAPPENED.
ahem
YOU LET ME SPEND THE NIGHT AFTER I WAS POSSESSED BY A GHOST AND PASSED OUT.
I'D BE A REAL JERK IF I DIDN'T SHOW MY GRATITUDE.
THAT'S OKAY! UH, I MEAN...
HOW CAN YOU BE SO ENERGETIC?
MOST PEOPLE CAN BARELY MOVE FOR A WEEK AFTER BEING POSSESSED...

READ THIS WAY

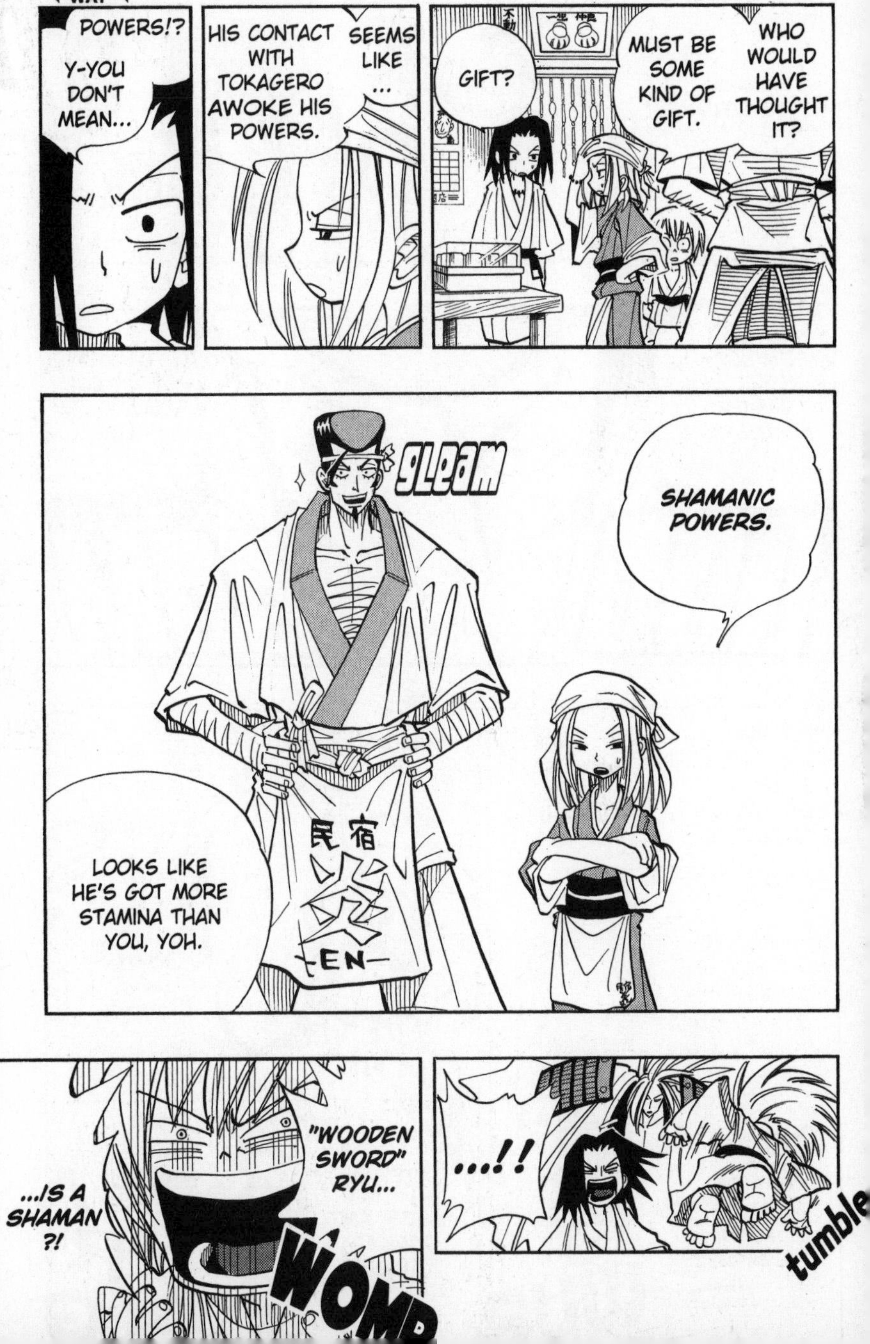
WHO WOULD HAVE THOUGHT IT?
MUST BE SOME KIND OF GIFT.
GIFT?
SEEMS LIKE ...
HIS CONTACT WITH TOKAGERO AWOKE HIS POWERS.
POWERS!?
Y-YOU DON'T MEAN...
SHAMANIC POWERS.
GLEAM
民宿
炎
EN
LOOKS LIKE HE'S GOT MORE STAMINA THAN YOU, YOH.
...!!
tumble
"WOODEN SWORD" RYU...
...IS A SHAMAN ?!
WOMP

READ THIS WAY

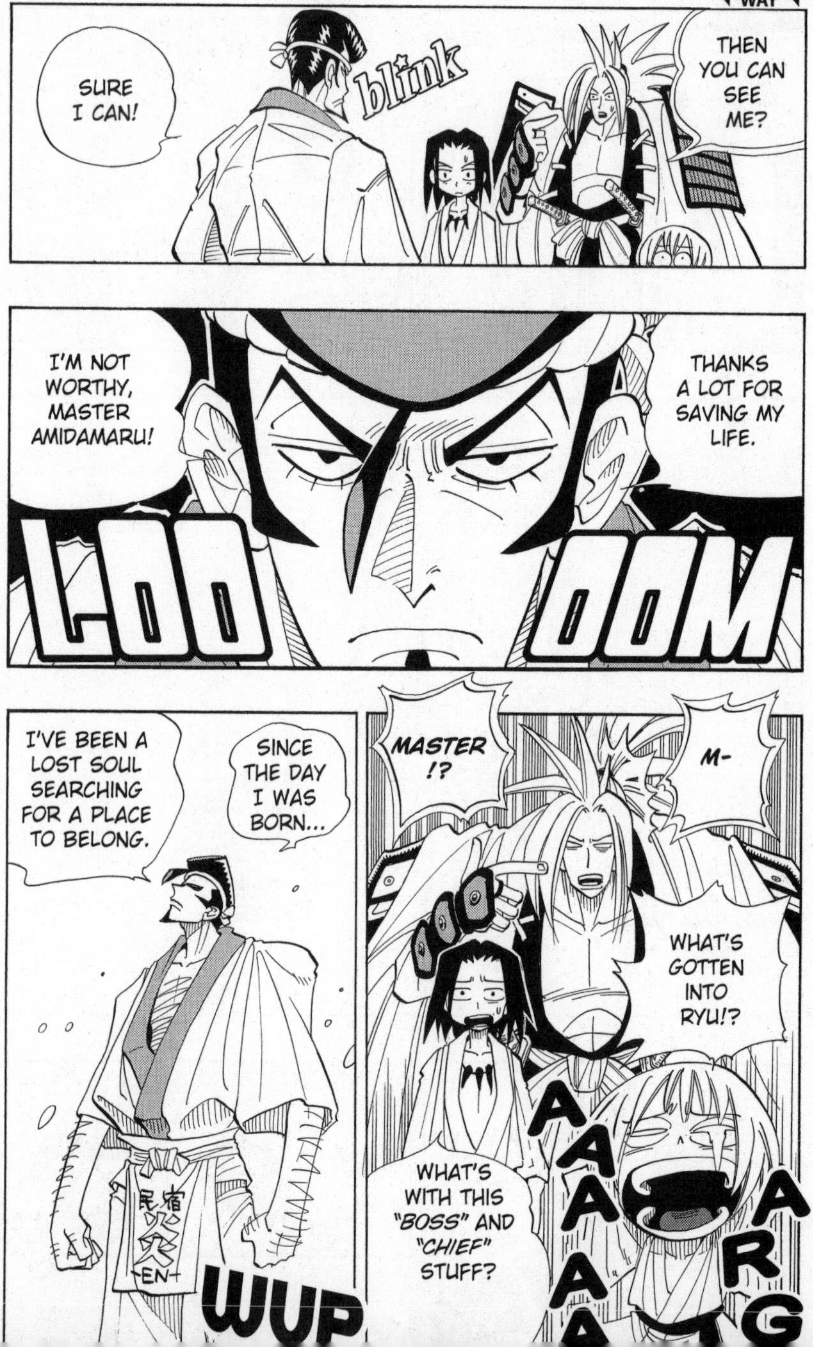
THEN YOU CAN SEE ME?
blink
SURE I CAN!
THANKS A LOT FOR SAVING MY LIFE.
I'M NOT WORTHY, MASTER AMIDAMARU!
LOO OOM
M-
MASTER !?
WHAT'S GOTTEN INTO RYU!?
AAAAA
ARG
WHAT'S WITH THIS "BOSS" AND "CHIEF" STUFF?
SINCE THE DAY I WAS BORN...
I'VE BEEN A LOST SOUL SEARCHING FOR A PLACE TO BELONG.
民宿 炎 EN
WUP

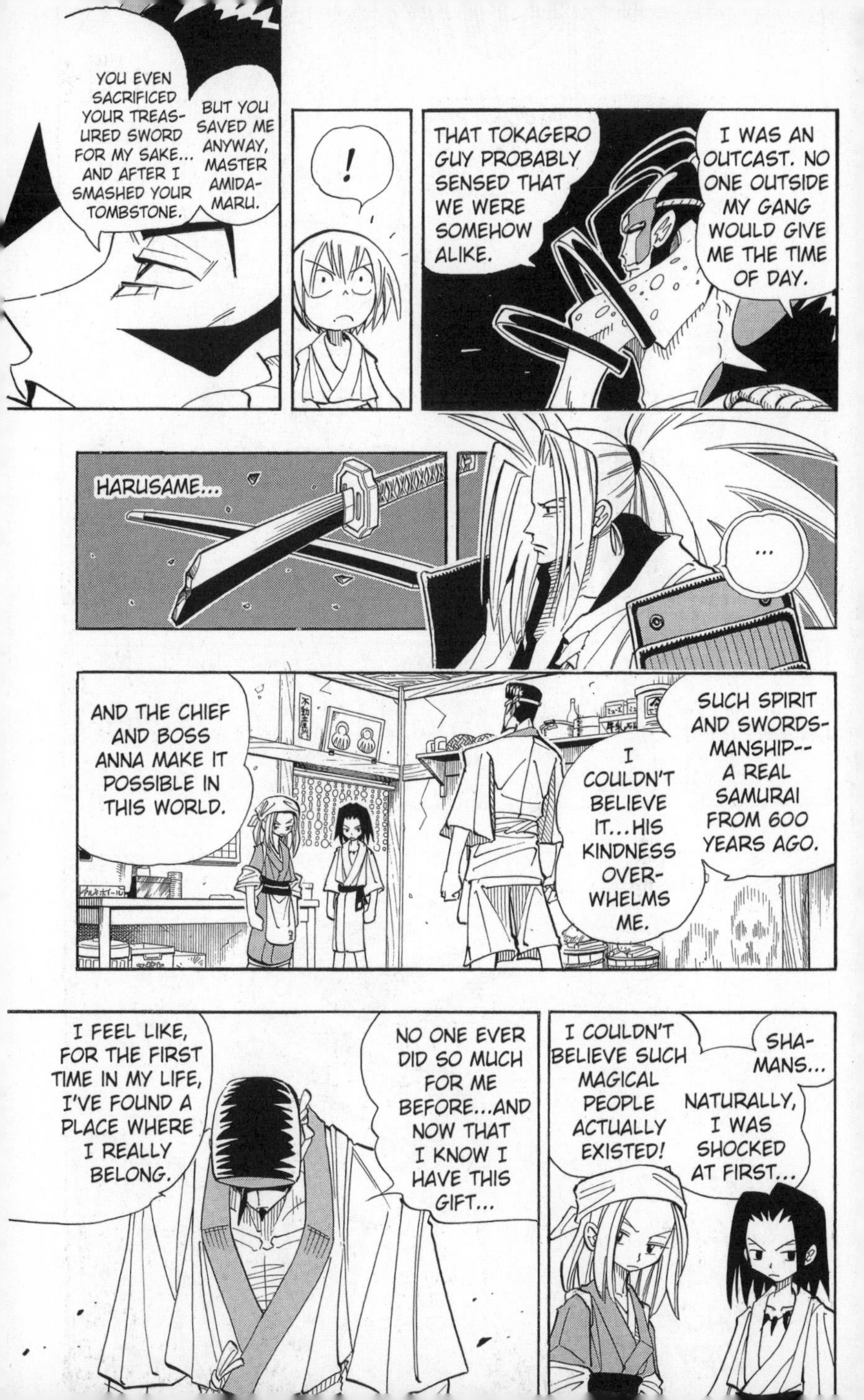
I WAS AN OUTCAST. NO ONE OUTSIDE MY GANG WOULD GIVE ME THE TIME OF DAY.
THAT TOKAGERO GUY PROBABLY SENSED THAT WE WERE SOMEHOW ALIKE.
!
BUT YOU SAVED ME ANYWAY, MASTER AMIDA-MARU.
YOU EVEN SACRIFICED YOUR TREAS-URED SWORD FOR MY SAKE... AND AFTER I SMASHED YOUR TOMBSTONE.
...
HARUSAME...
SUCH SPIRIT AND SWORDS-MANSHIP-- A REAL SAMURAI FROM 600 YEARS AGO.
I COULDN'T BELIEVE IT...HIS KINDNESS OVER-WHELMS ME.
AND THE CHIEF AND BOSS ANNA MAKE IT POSSIBLE IN THIS WORLD.
SHA-MANS...
NATURALLY, I WAS SHOCKED AT FIRST...
I COULDN'T BELIEVE SUCH MAGICAL PEOPLE ACTUALLY EXISTED!
NO ONE EVER DID SO MUCH FOR ME BEFORE...AND NOW THAT I KNOW I HAVE THIS GIFT...
I FEEL LIKE, FOR THE FIRST TIME IN MY LIFE, I'VE FOUND A PLACE WHERE I REALLY BELONG.

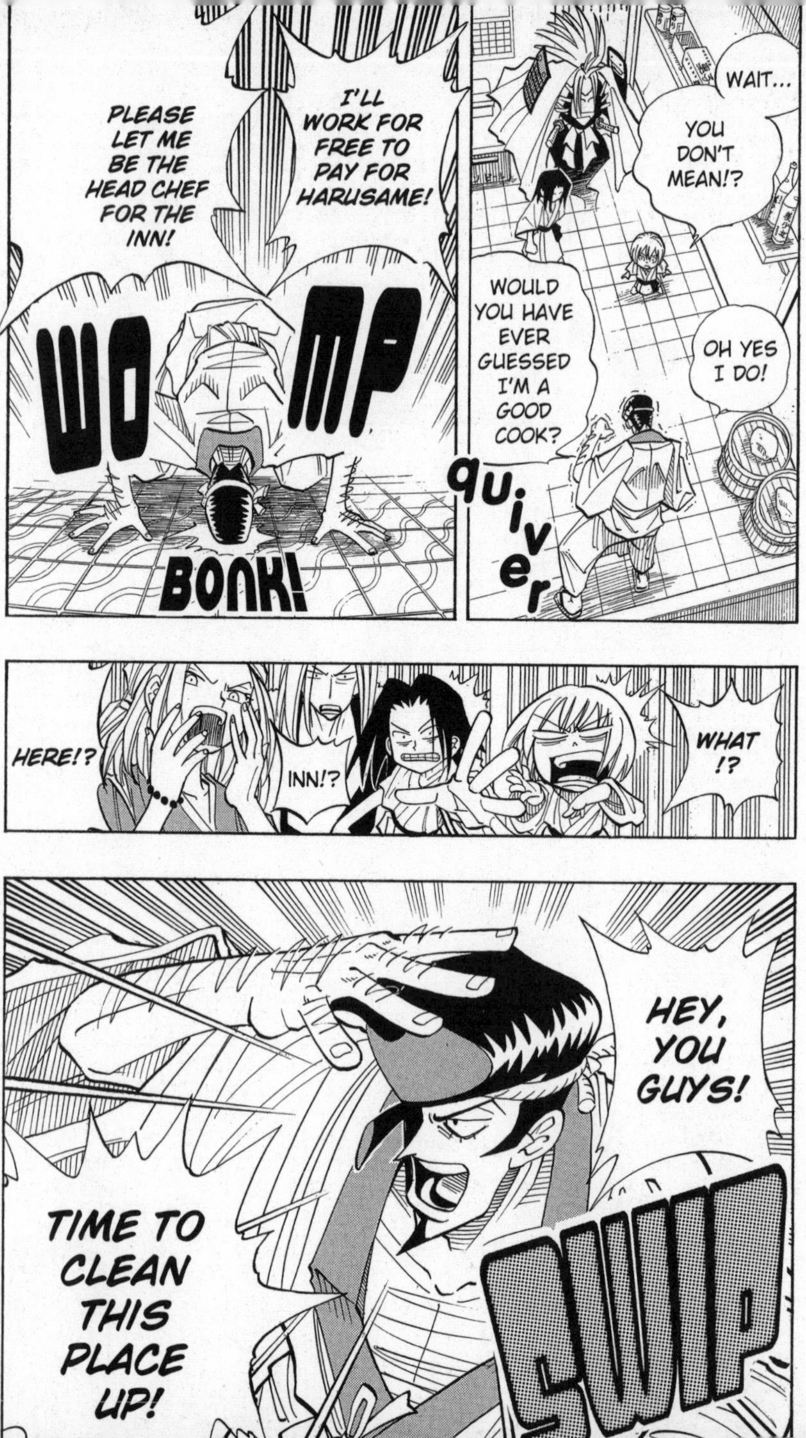
WAIT...
YOU DON'T MEAN!?
WOULD YOU HAVE EVER GUESSED I'M A GOOD COOK?
OH YES I DO!
quiver
I'LL WORK FOR FREE TO PAY FOR HARUSAME!
PLEASE LET ME BE THE HEAD CHEF FOR THE INN!
WOMP
BONK!
WHAT!?
INN!?
HERE!?
HEY, YOU GUYS!
SWIP
TIME TO CLEAN THIS PLACE UP!

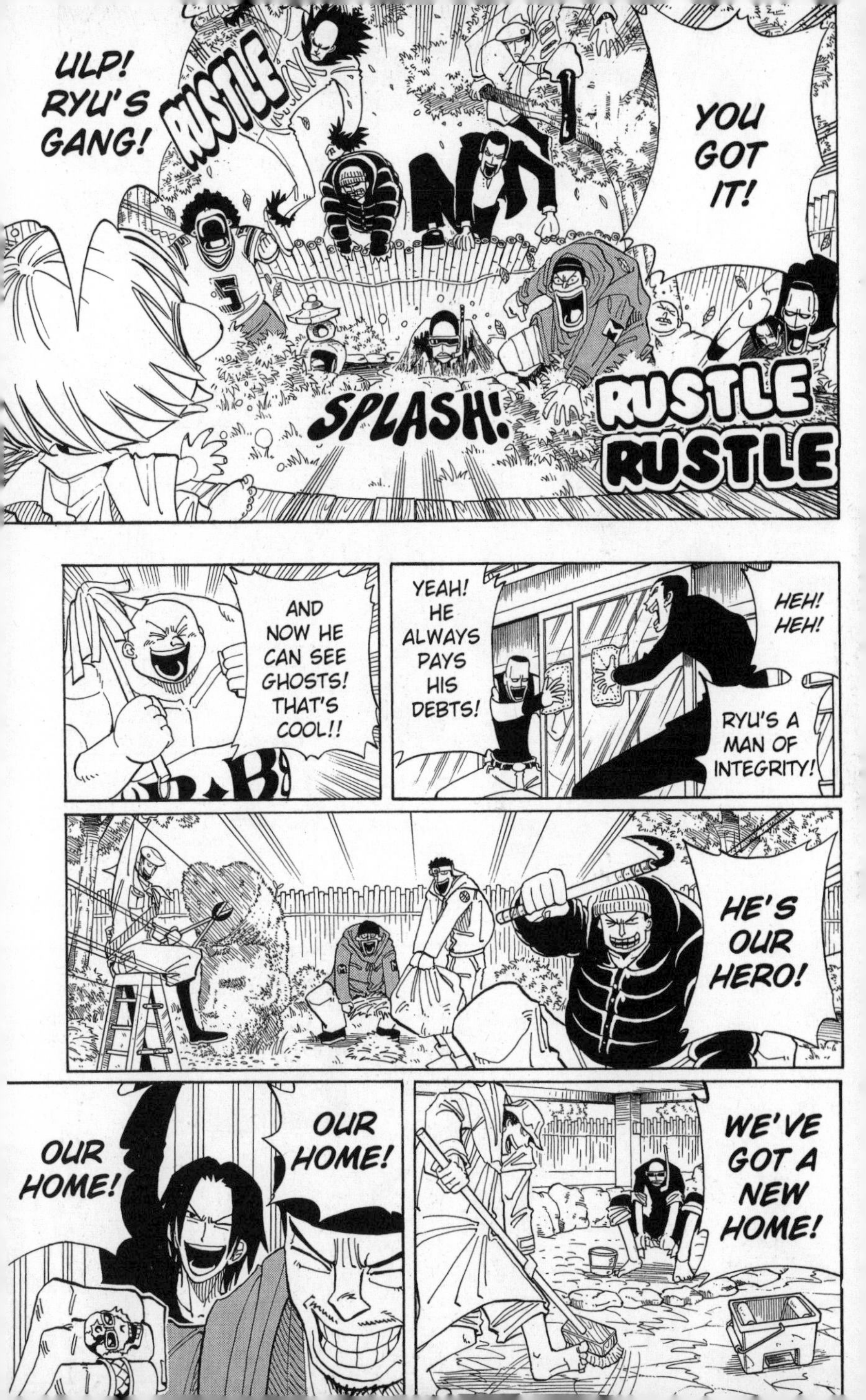
YOU GOT IT!
RUSTLE
ULP! RYU'S GANG!
RUSTLE RUSTLE
SPLASH!
HEH! HEH!
YEAH! HE ALWAYS PAYS HIS DEBTS!
RYU'S A MAN OF INTEGRITY!
AND NOW HE CAN SEE GHOSTS! THAT'S COOL!!
HE'S OUR HERO!
WE'VE GOT A NEW HOME!
OUR HOME!
OUR HOME!

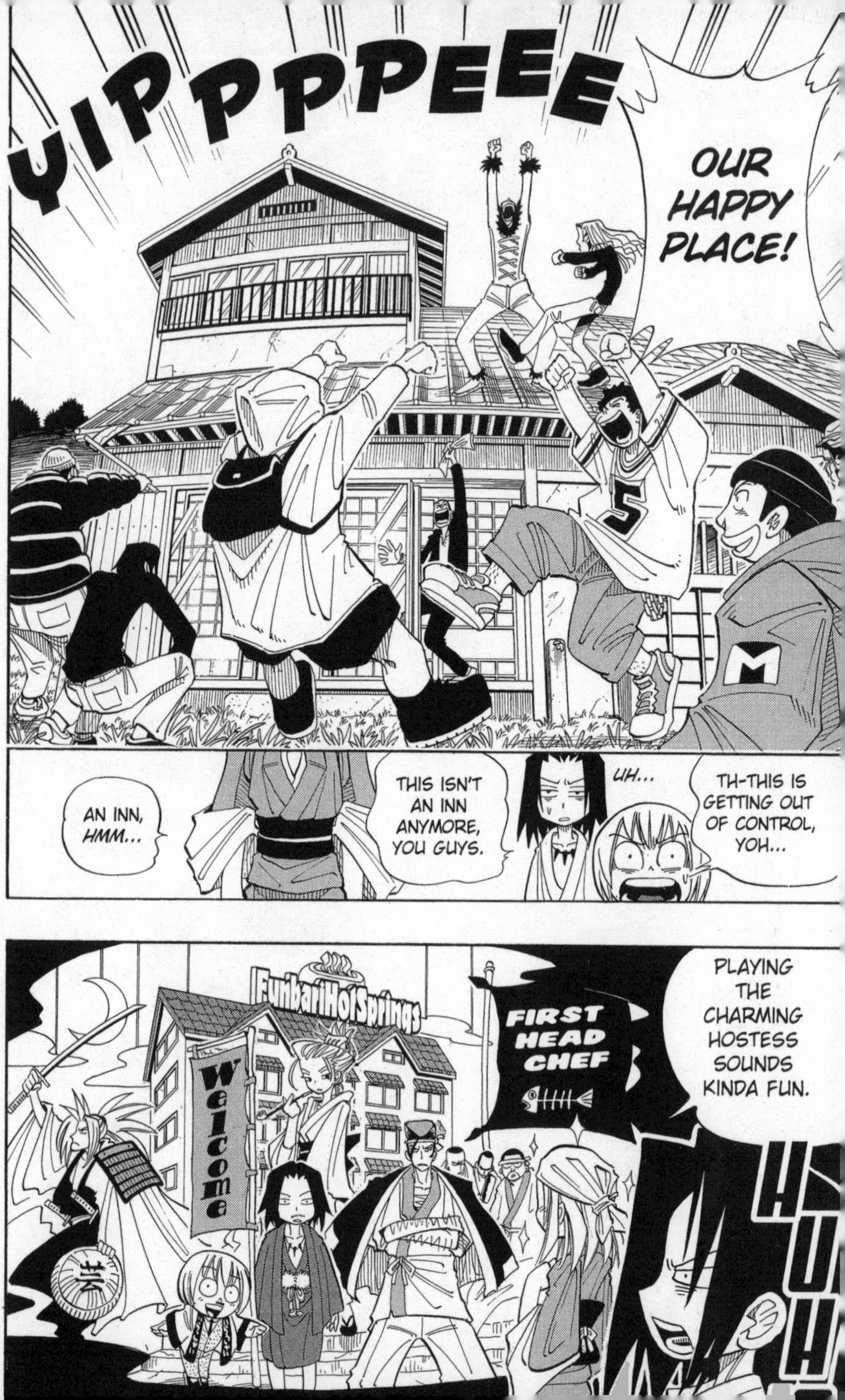
OUR HAPPY PLACE!
YIPPPPEEE
TH-THIS IS GETTING OUT OF CONTROL, YOH...
UH...
THIS ISN'T AN INN ANYMORE, YOU GUYS.
AN INN, HMM...
PLAYING THE CHARMING HOSTESS SOUNDS KINDA FUN.
FIRST HEAD CHEF
FunbariHotSprings
Welcome

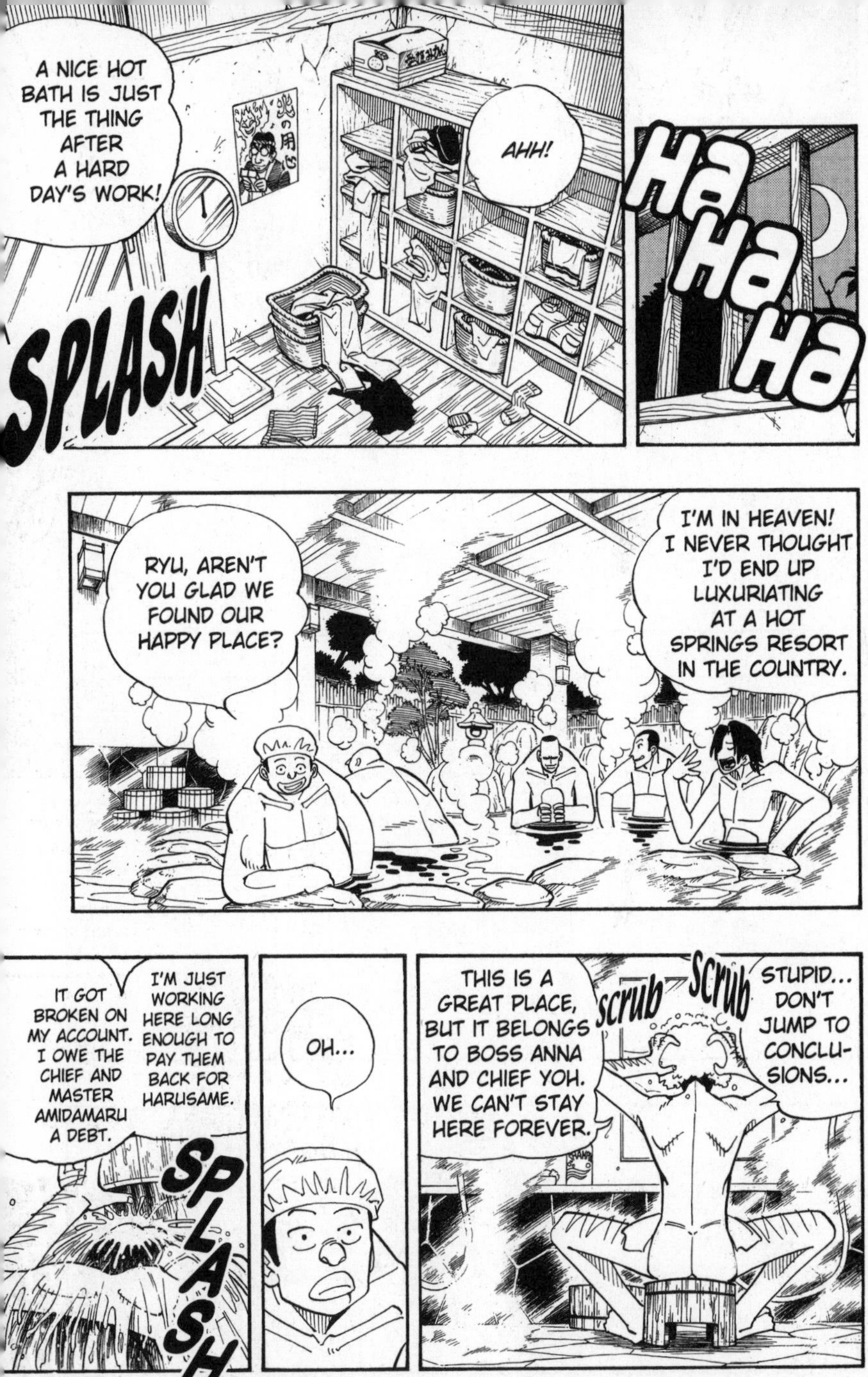
HA HA HA HA
AHH!
A NICE HOT BATH IS JUST THE THING AFTER A HARD DAY'S WORK!
SPLASH
I'M IN HEAVEN! I NEVER THOUGHT I'D END UP LUXURIATING AT A HOT SPRINGS RESORT IN THE COUNTRY.
RYU, AREN'T YOU GLAD WE FOUND OUR HAPPY PLACE?
STUPID... DON'T JUMP TO CONCLUSIONS...
SCRUB
SCRUB
THIS IS A GREAT PLACE, BUT IT BELONGS TO BOSS ANNA AND CHIEF YOH. WE CAN'T STAY HERE FOREVER.
OH...
I'M JUST WORKING HERE LONG ENOUGH TO PAY THEM BACK FOR HARUSAME.
IT GOT BROKEN ON MY ACCOUNT. I OWE THE CHIEF AND MASTER AMIDAMARU A DEBT.
SPLASH

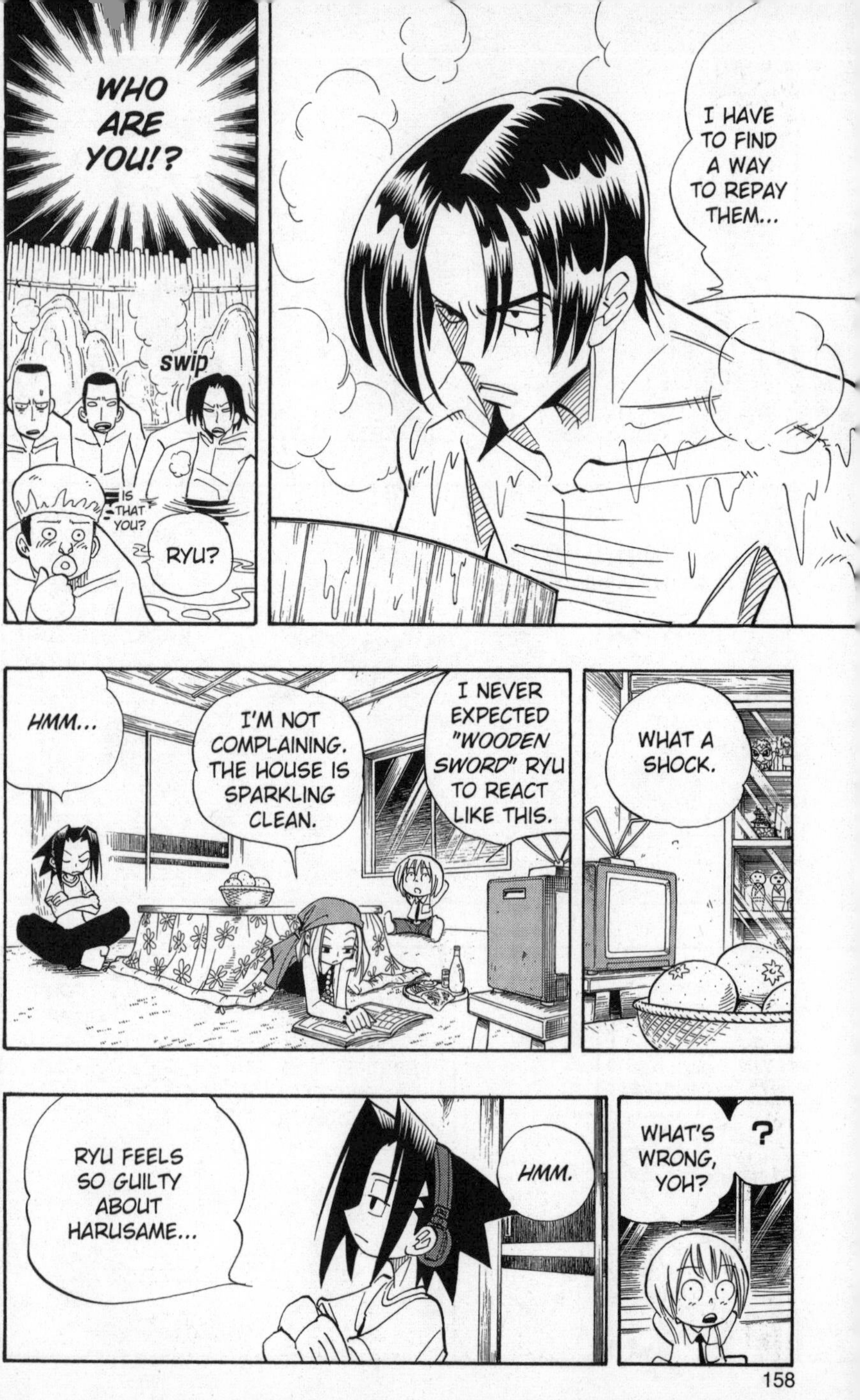
I HAVE TO FIND A WAY TO REPAY THEM...
WHO ARE YOU!?
swip
RYU?
IS THAT YOU?
WHAT A SHOCK.
I NEVER EXPECTED "WOODEN SWORD" RYU TO REACT LIKE THIS.
I'M NOT COMPLAINING. THE HOUSE IS SPARKLING CLEAN.
HMM...
WHAT'S WRONG, YOH?
?
HMM.
RYU FEELS SO GUILTY ABOUT HARUSAME...

READ THIS WAY

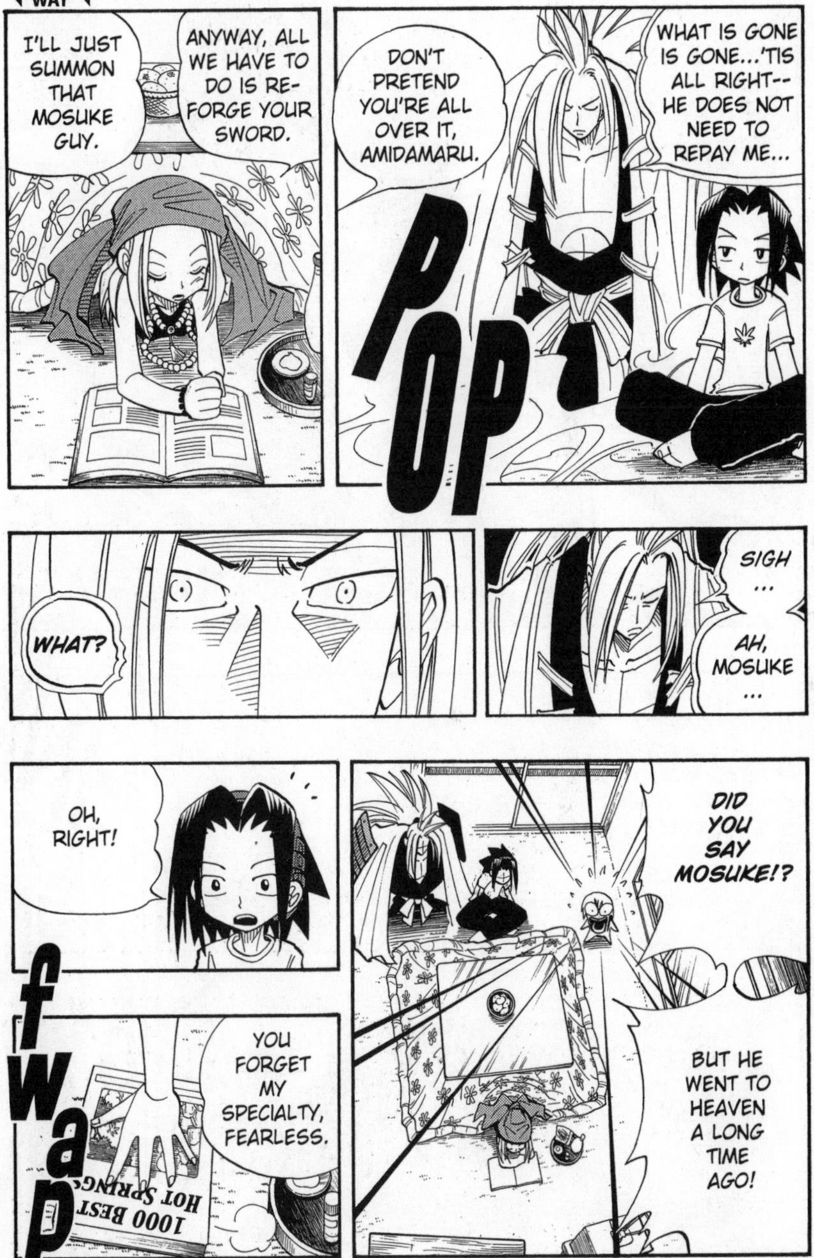
WHAT IS GONE IS GONE...'TIS ALL RIGHT--HE DOES NOT NEED TO REPAY ME...
DON'T PRETEND YOU'RE ALL OVER IT, AMIDAMARU.
POP
ANYWAY, ALL WE HAVE TO DO IS RE-FORGE YOUR SWORD.
I'LL JUST SUMMON THAT MOSUKE GUY.
SIGH ...
AH, MOSUKE ...
WHAT?
DID YOU SAY MOSUKE!?
BUT HE WENT TO HEAVEN A LONG TIME AGO!
OH, RIGHT!
YOU FORGET MY SPECIALTY, FEARLESS.
fwap
1000 BEST HOT SPRINGS

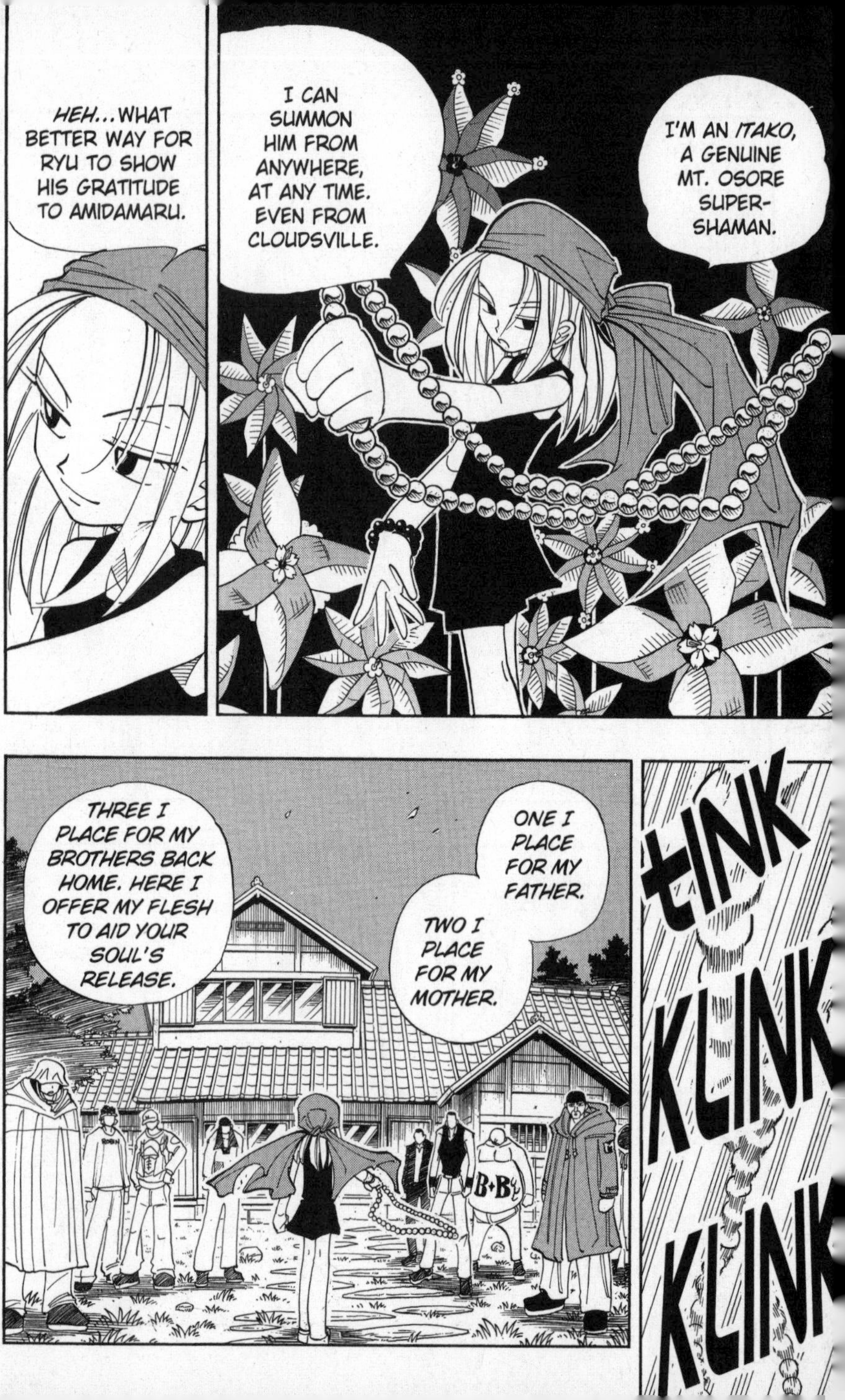
I'M AN *ITAKO*, A GENUINE MT. OSORE SUPER-SHAMAN.
I CAN SUMMON HIM FROM ANYWHERE, AT ANY TIME. EVEN FROM CLOUDSVILLE.
HEH... WHAT BETTER WAY FOR RYU TO SHOW HIS GRATITUDE TO AMIDAMARU.
tINK
KLINK
KLINK
ONE I PLACE FOR MY FATHER.
TWO I PLACE FOR MY MOTHER.
THREE I PLACE FOR MY BROTHERS BACK HOME. HERE I OFFER MY FLESH TO AID YOUR SOUL'S RELEASE.

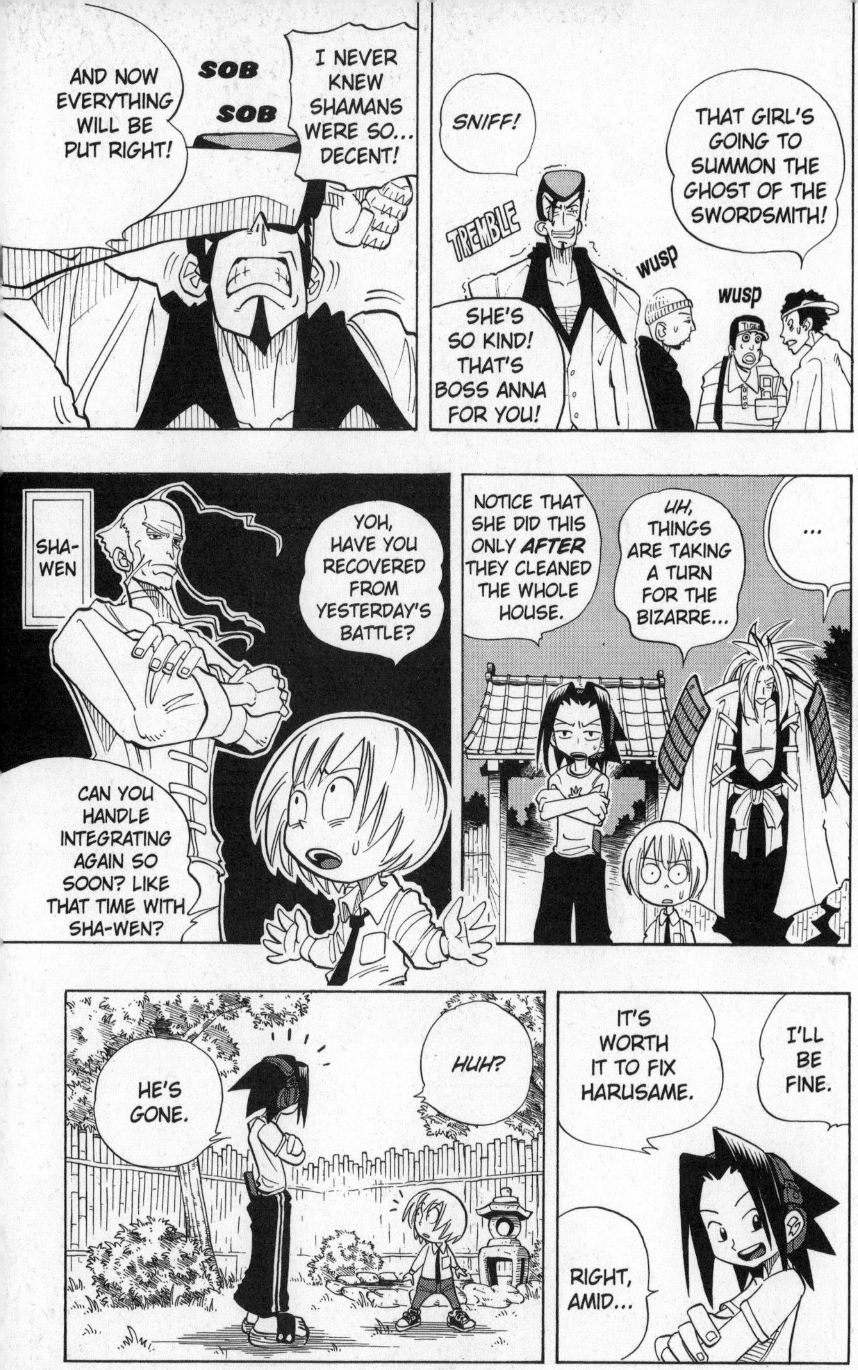
THAT GIRL'S GOING TO SUMMON THE GHOST OF THE SWORDSMITH!
SNIFF!
TREMBLE
WUSP
WUSP
SHE'S SO KIND! THAT'S BOSS ANNA FOR YOU!
I NEVER KNEW SHAMANS WERE SO... DECENT!
SOB
SOB
AND NOW EVERYTHING WILL BE PUT RIGHT!
...
UH, THINGS ARE TAKING A TURN FOR THE BIZARRE...
NOTICE THAT SHE DID THIS ONLY *AFTER* THEY CLEANED THE WHOLE HOUSE.
YOH, HAVE YOU RECOVERED FROM YESTERDAY'S BATTLE?
SHA-WEN
CAN YOU HANDLE INTEGRATING AGAIN SO SOON? LIKE THAT TIME WITH SHA-WEN?
I'LL BE FINE.
IT'S WORTH IT TO FIX HARUSAME.
RIGHT, AMID...
HUH?
HE'S GONE.

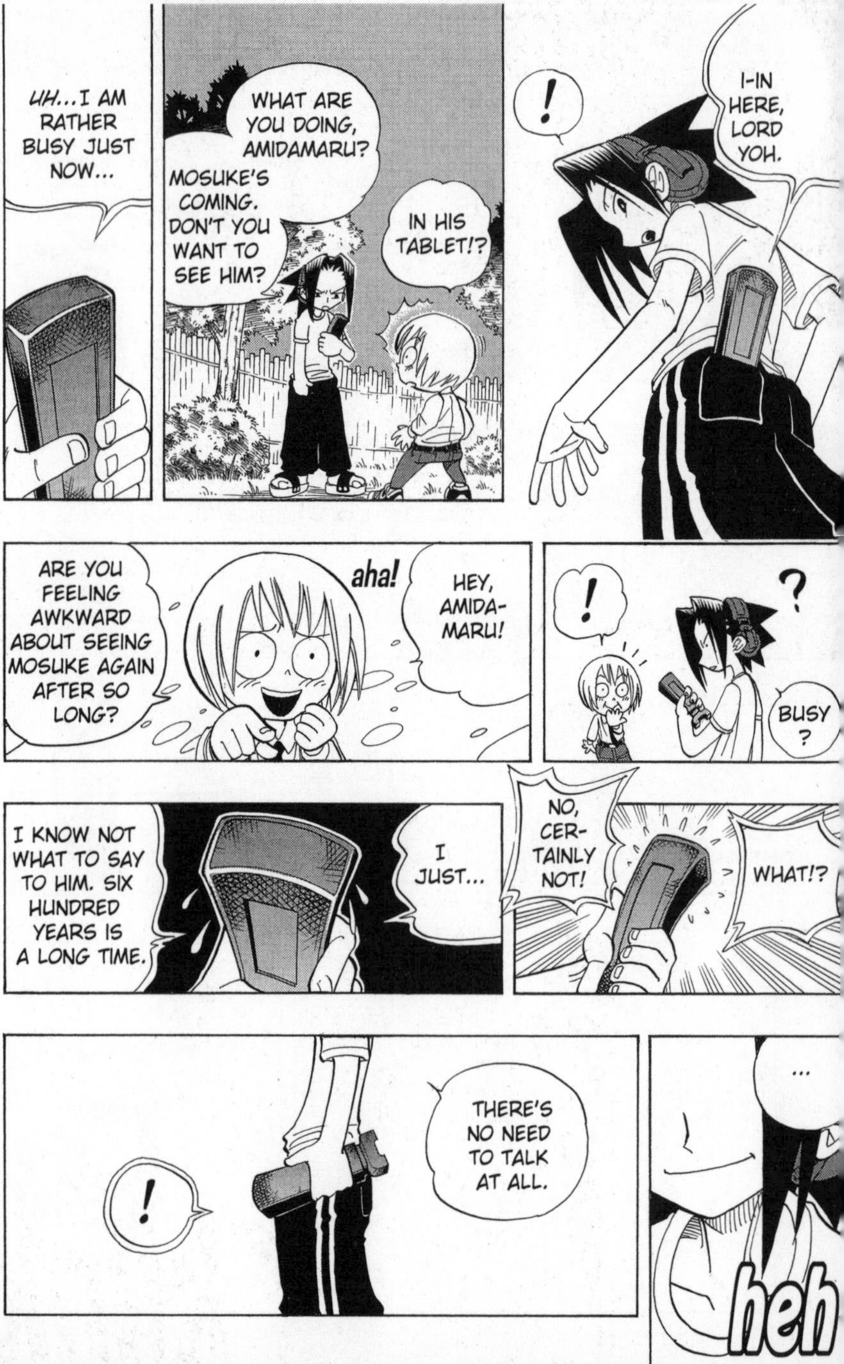
!
I-IN HERE, LORD YOH.
IN HIS TABLET!?
WHAT ARE YOU DOING, AMIDAMARU?
MOSUKE'S COMING. DON'T YOU WANT TO SEE HIM?
UH...I AM RATHER BUSY JUST NOW...
!
?
BUSY ?
HEY, AMIDA-MARU!
aha!
ARE YOU FEELING AWKWARD ABOUT SEEING MOSUKE AGAIN AFTER SO LONG?
WHAT!?
NO, CER-TAINLY NOT!
I JUST...
I KNOW NOT WHAT TO SAY TO HIM. SIX HUNDRED YEARS IS A LONG TIME.
...
heh
THERE'S NO NEED TO TALK AT ALL.
!

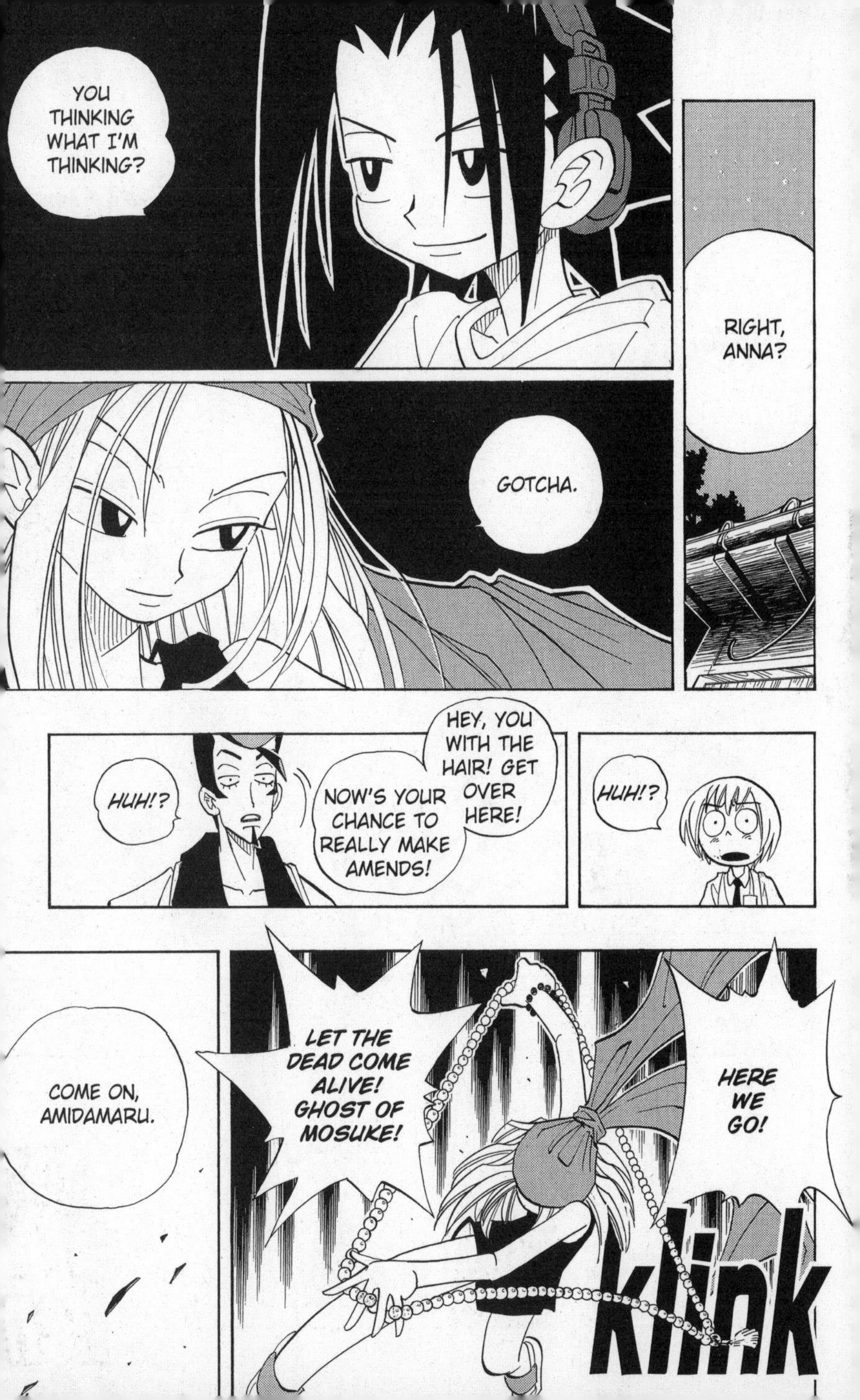
RIGHT, ANNA?
YOU THINKING WHAT I'M THINKING?
GOTCHA.
HUH!?
HEY, YOU WITH THE HAIR! GET OVER HERE!
NOW'S YOUR CHANCE TO REALLY MAKE AMENDS!
HUH!?
HERE WE GO!
LET THE DEAD COME ALIVE! GHOST OF MOSUKE!
klink
COME ON, AMIDAMARU.

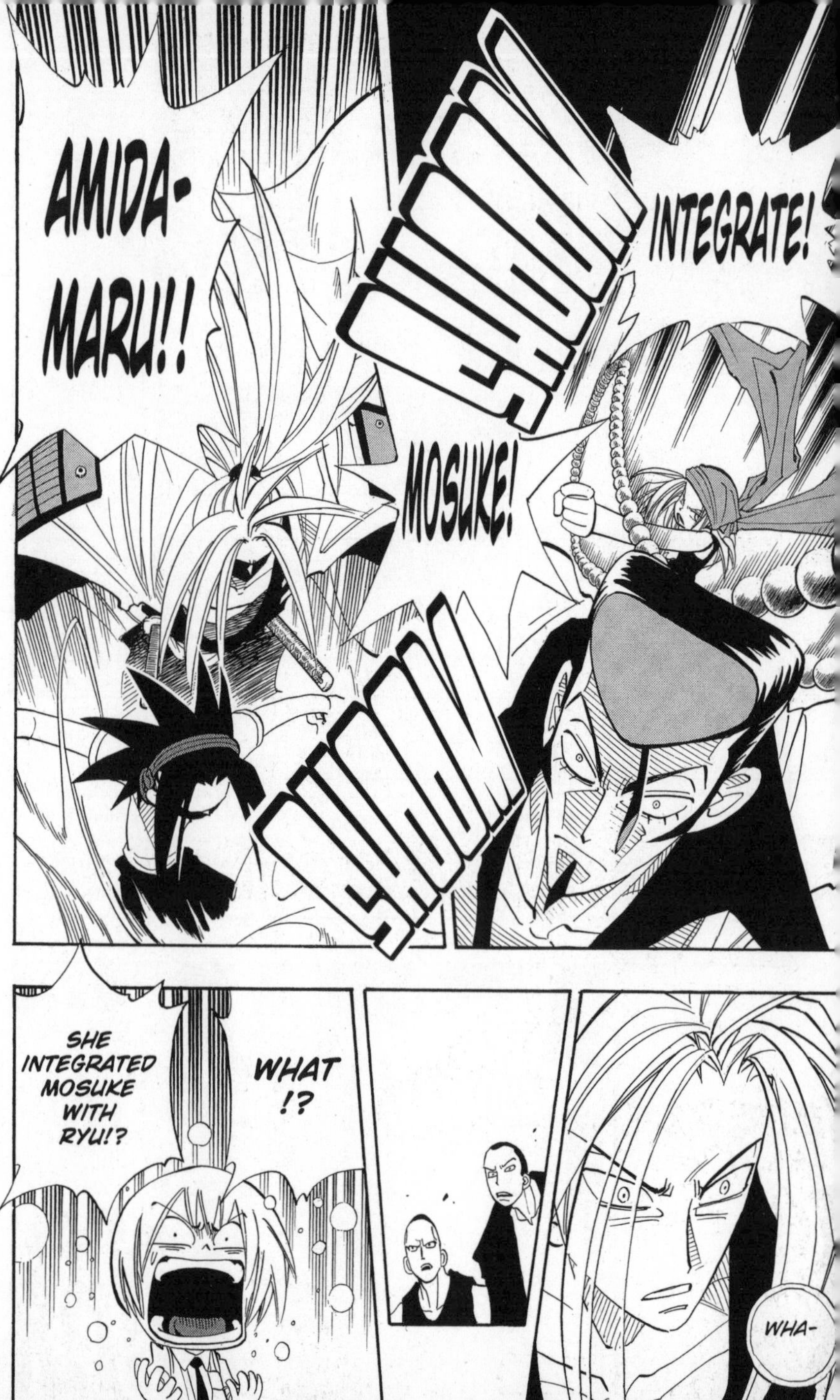
INTEGRATE!
SHOOM
MOSUKE!
AMIDA-MARU!!
SHOOM
WHA-
WHAT!?
SHE INTEGRATED MOSUKE WITH RYU!?

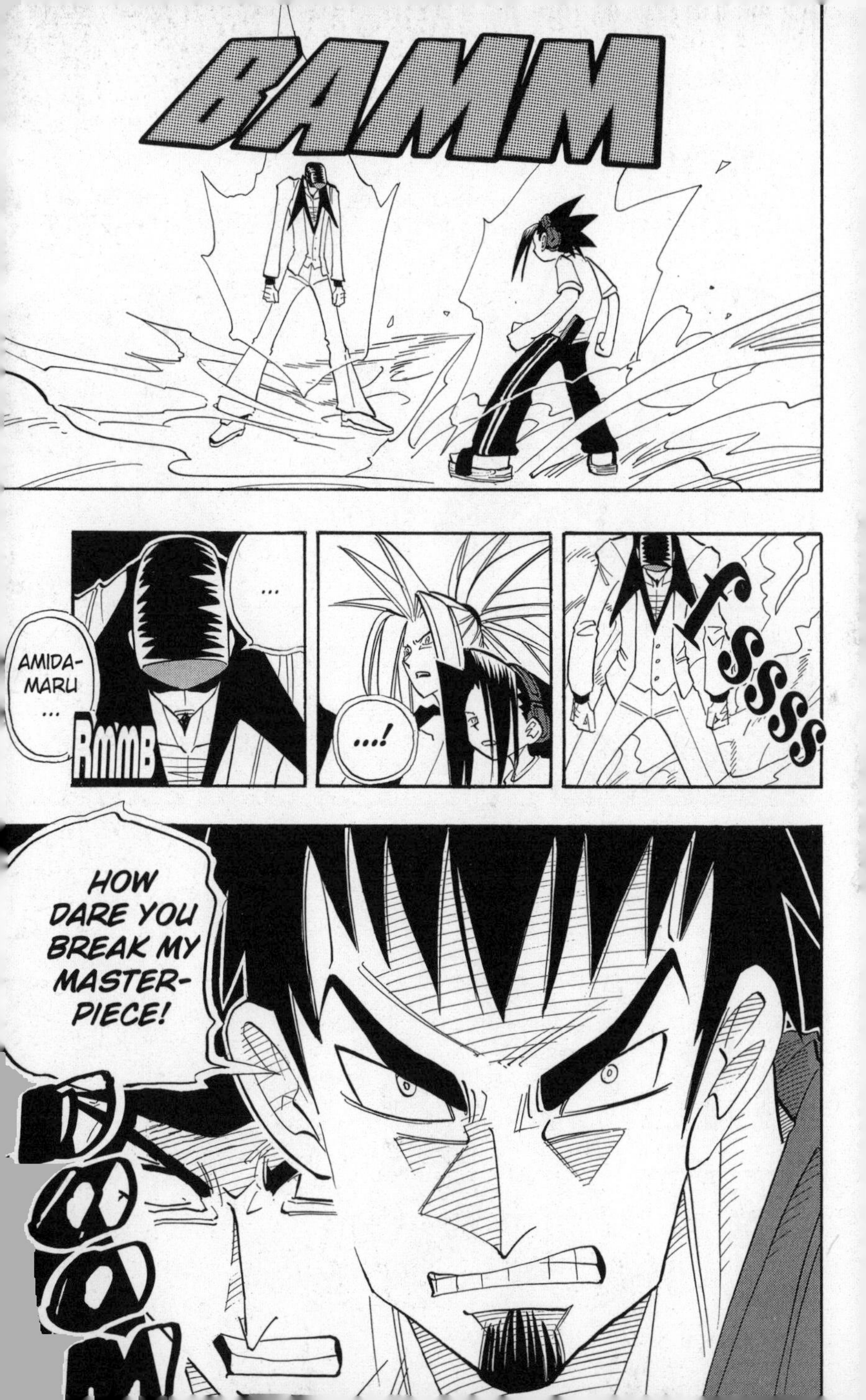
BAMM
fSSSSS
...!
...
AMIDA-MARU ...
RMMB
HOW DARE YOU BREAK MY MASTER-PIECE!
DOOM

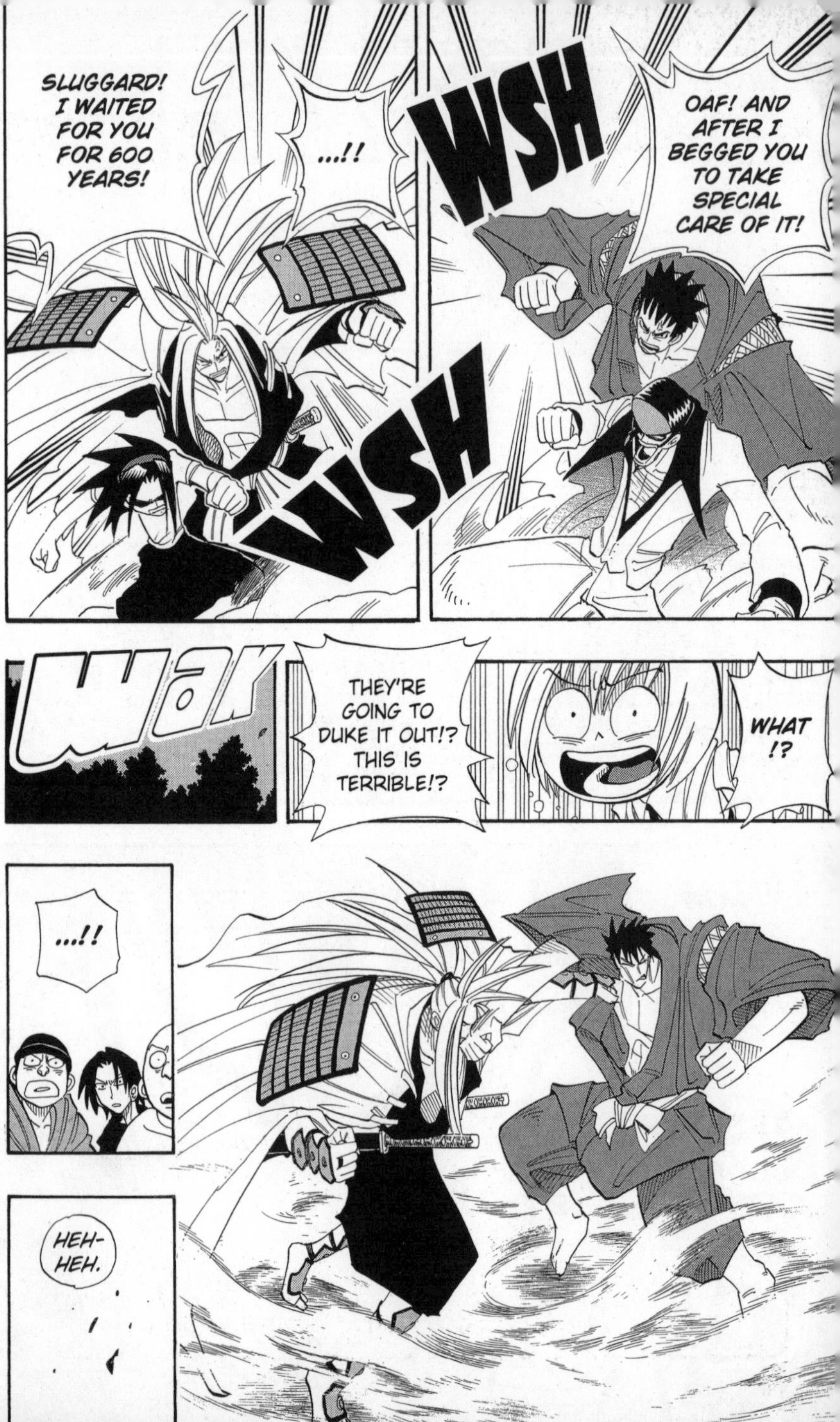
OAF! AND AFTER I BEGGED YOU TO TAKE SPECIAL CARE OF IT!
WSH
...!!
SLUGGARD! I WAITED FOR YOU FOR 600 YEARS!
WSH
WHAT !?
THEY'RE GOING TO DUKE IT OUT!? THIS IS TERRIBLE!?
WAK
...!!
HEH-HEH.

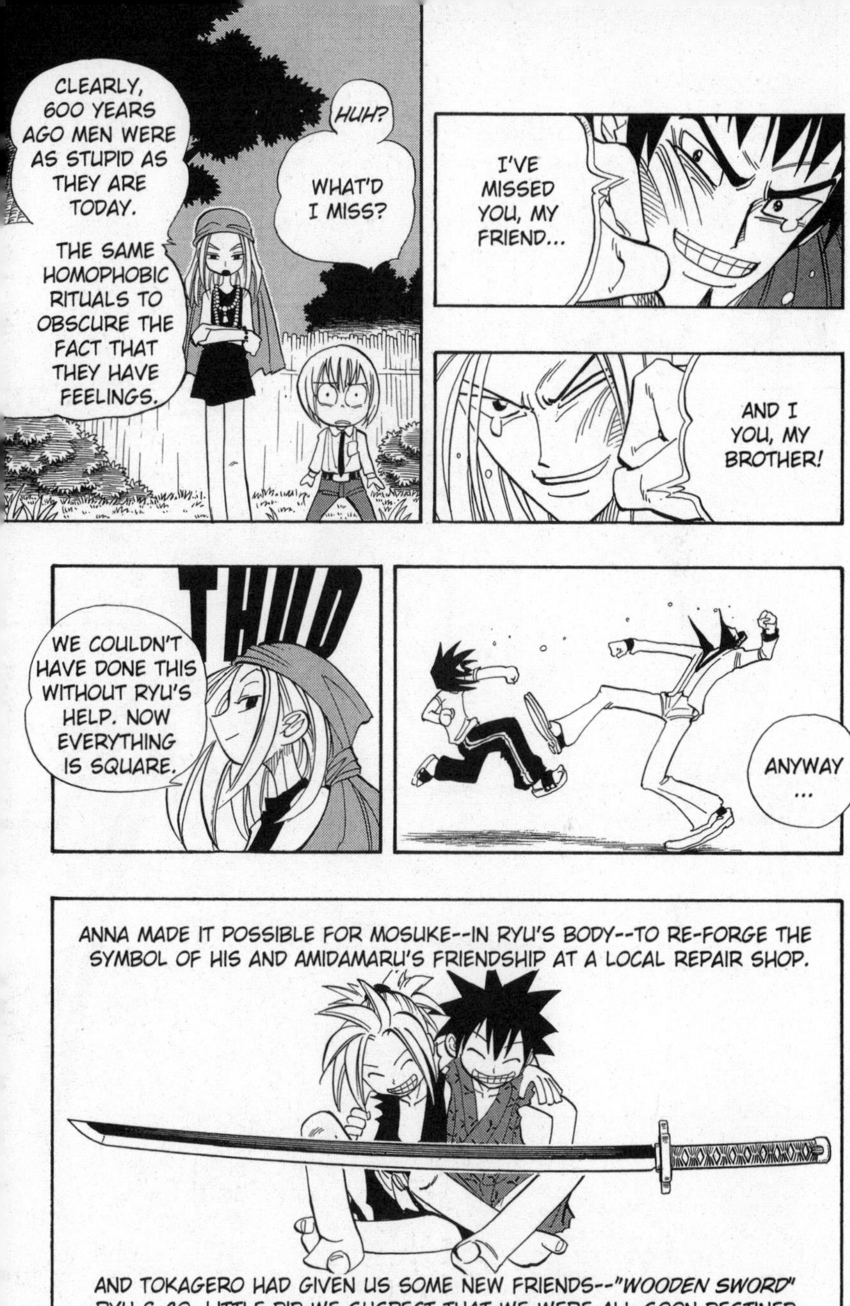
I'VE MISSED YOU, MY FRIEND...
AND I YOU, MY BROTHER!
HUH?
WHAT'D I MISS?
CLEARLY, 600 YEARS AGO MEN WERE AS STUPID AS THEY ARE TODAY.
THE SAME HOMOPHOBIC RITUALS TO OBSCURE THE FACT THAT THEY HAVE FEELINGS.
ANYWAY ...
THUD
WE COULDN'T HAVE DONE THIS WITHOUT RYU'S HELP. NOW EVERYTHING IS SQUARE.
ANNA MADE IT POSSIBLE FOR MOSUKE--IN RYU'S BODY--TO RE-FORGE THE SYMBOL OF HIS AND AMIDAMARU'S FRIENDSHIP AT A LOCAL REPAIR SHOP.
AND TOKAGERO HAD GIVEN US SOME NEW FRIENDS--"WOODEN SWORD" RYU & CO. LITTLE DID WE SUSPECT THAT WE WERE ALL SOON DESTINED FOR AN EVEN MORE HARROWING ADVENTURE...

SHAMAN KING CHARACTER FILE No.13

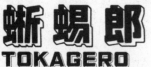

蜥蜴郎
TOKAGERO
1999

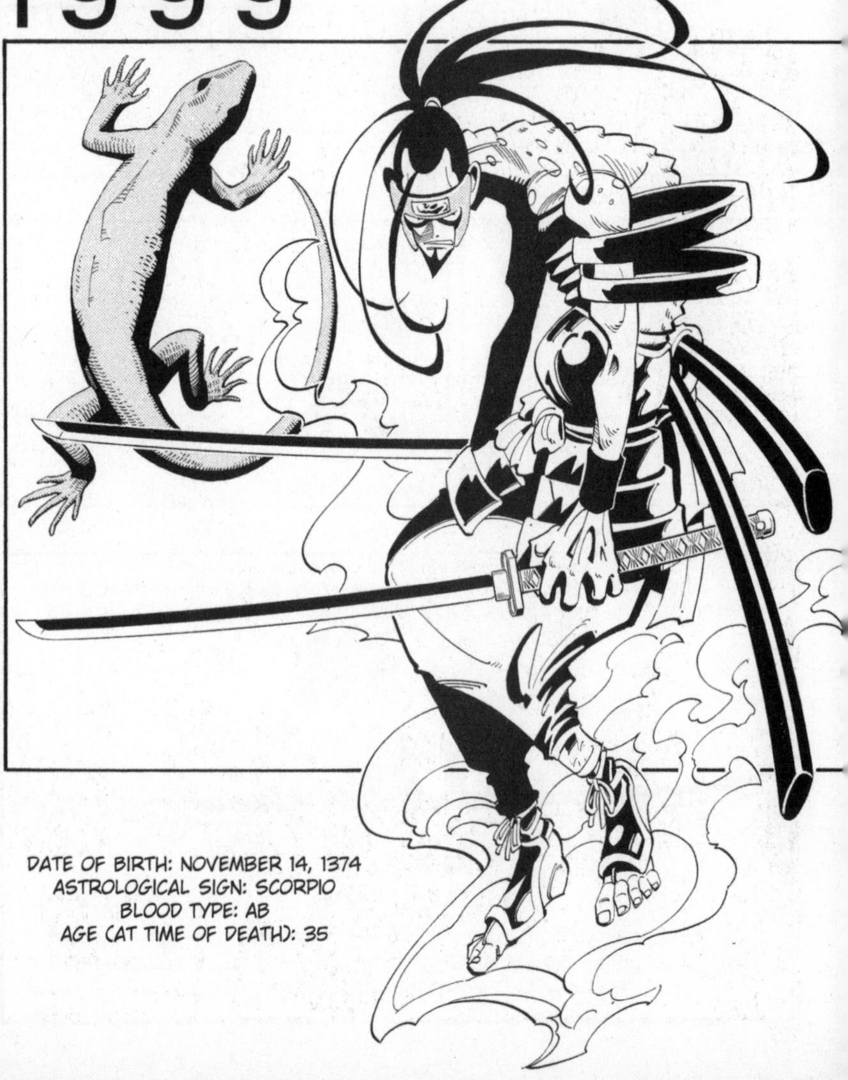

DATE OF BIRTH: NOVEMBER 14, 1374
ASTROLOGICAL SIGN: SCORPIO
BLOOD TYPE: AB
AGE (AT TIME OF DEATH): 35

« READ THIS WAY «

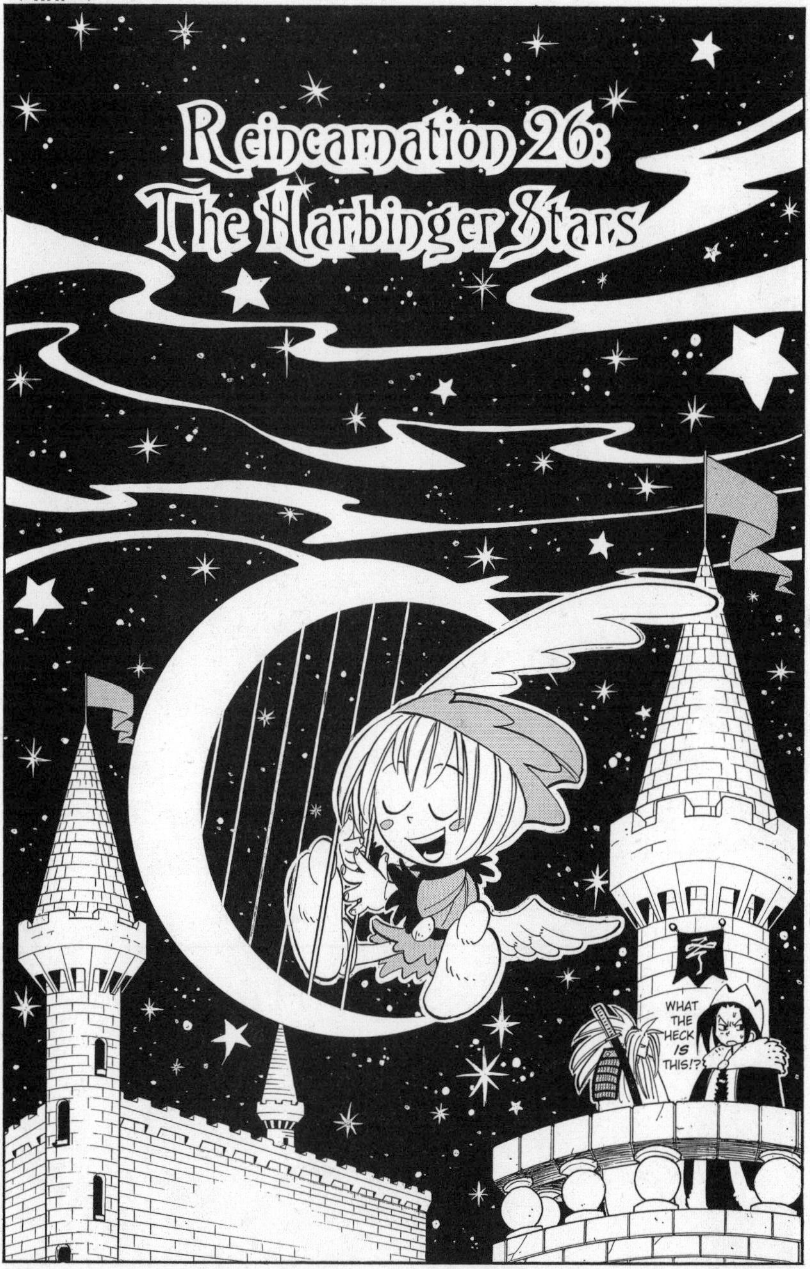
Reincarnation 26:
The Harbinger Stars
WHAT THE HECK *IS* THIS!?

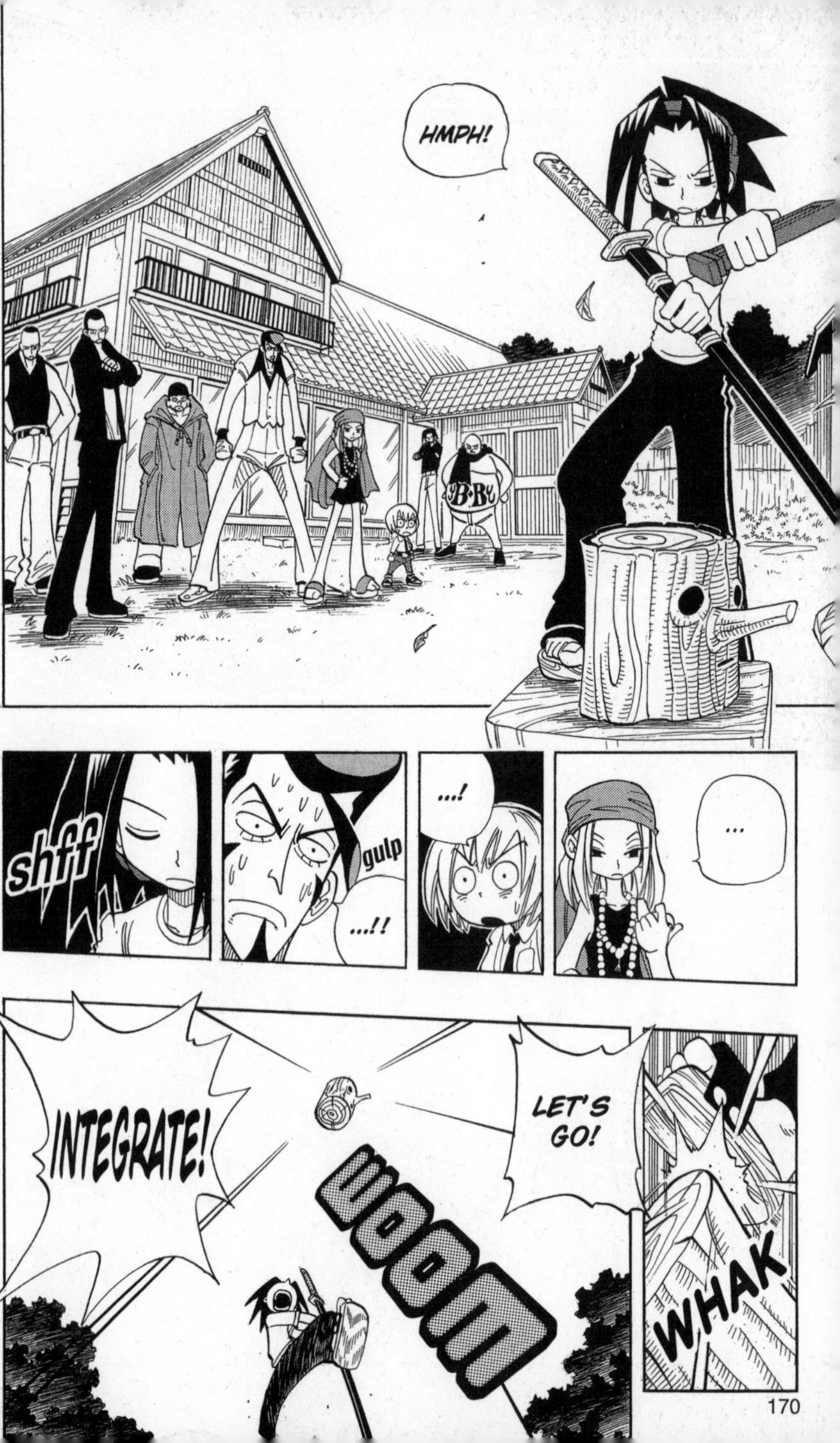
HMPH!
...
...!
gulp
...!!
shff
WHAK
LET'S GO!
INTEGRATE!
WOOM

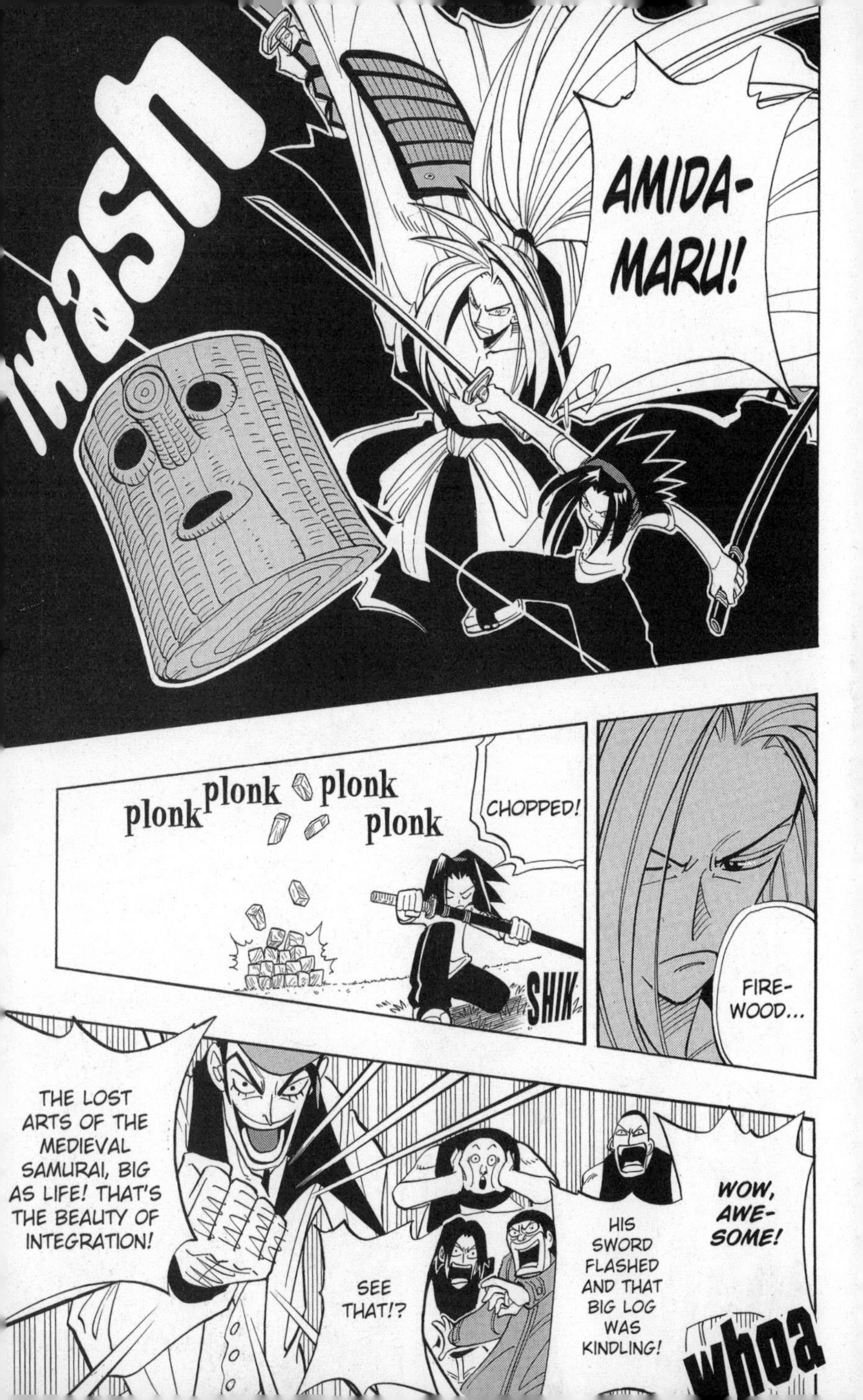
AMIDA-MARU!
whash
FIRE-WOOD...
CHOPPED!
plonk plonk plonk plonk
SHIK
whoa
WOW, AWE-SOME!
HIS SWORD FLASHED AND THAT BIG LOG WAS KINDLING!
SEE THAT!?
THE LOST ARTS OF THE MEDIEVAL SAMURAI, BIG AS LIFE! THAT'S THE BEAUTY OF INTEGRATION!

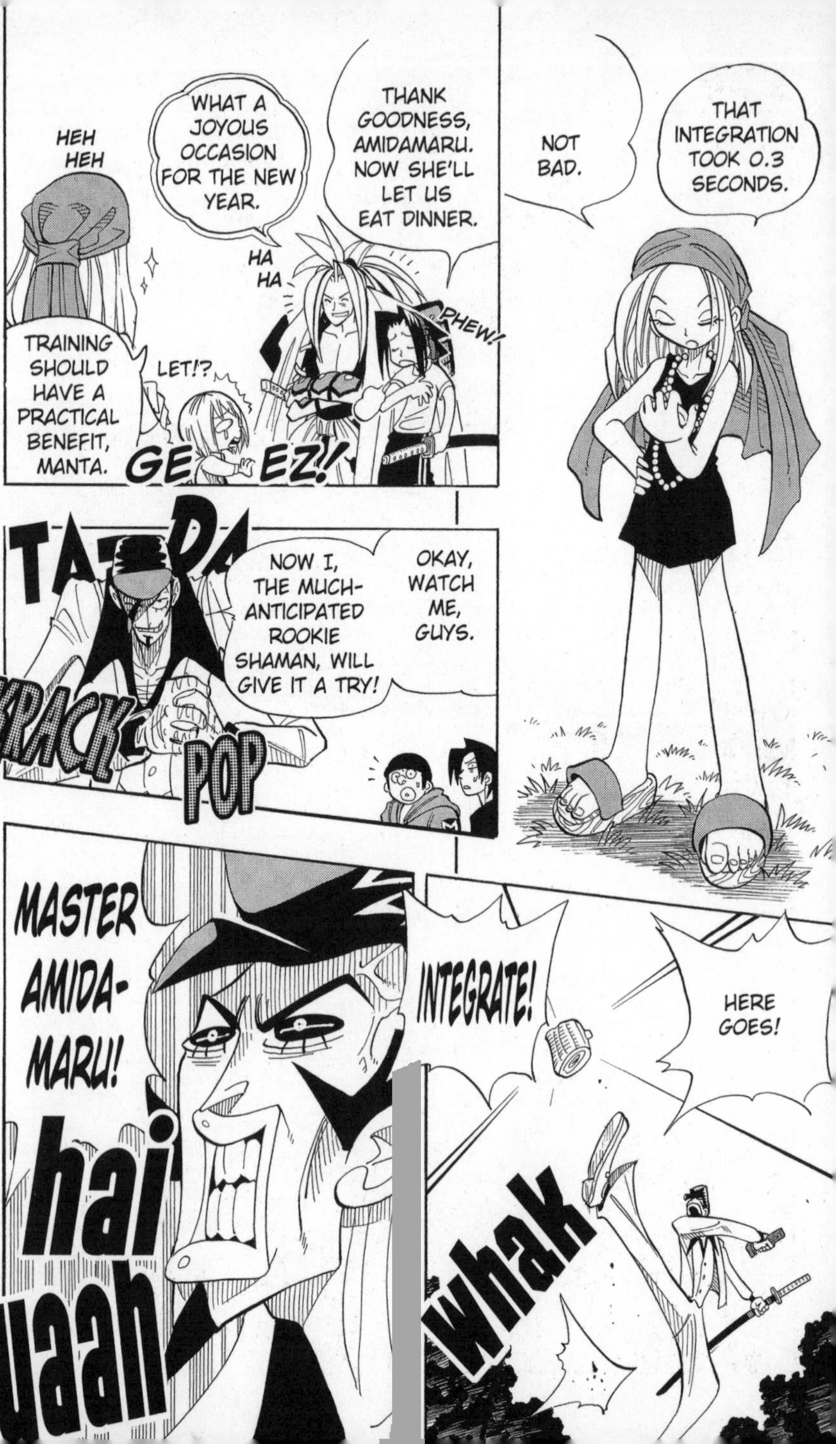
THAT INTEGRATION TOOK 0.3 SECONDS.
NOT BAD.
THANK GOODNESS, AMIDAMARU. NOW SHE'LL LET US EAT DINNER.
WHAT A JOYOUS OCCASION FOR THE NEW YEAR.
HEH HEH
HA HA
PHEW!
TRAINING SHOULD HAVE A PRACTICAL BENEFIT, MANTA.
LET!?
GEEZ!!
TA DA
OKAY, WATCH ME, GUYS.
NOW I, THE MUCH-ANTICIPATED ROOKIE SHAMAN, WILL GIVE IT A TRY!
KRACK
POP
HERE GOES!
WHAK
INTEGRATE!
MASTER AMIDA-MARU!
haiuaah

READ THIS WAY

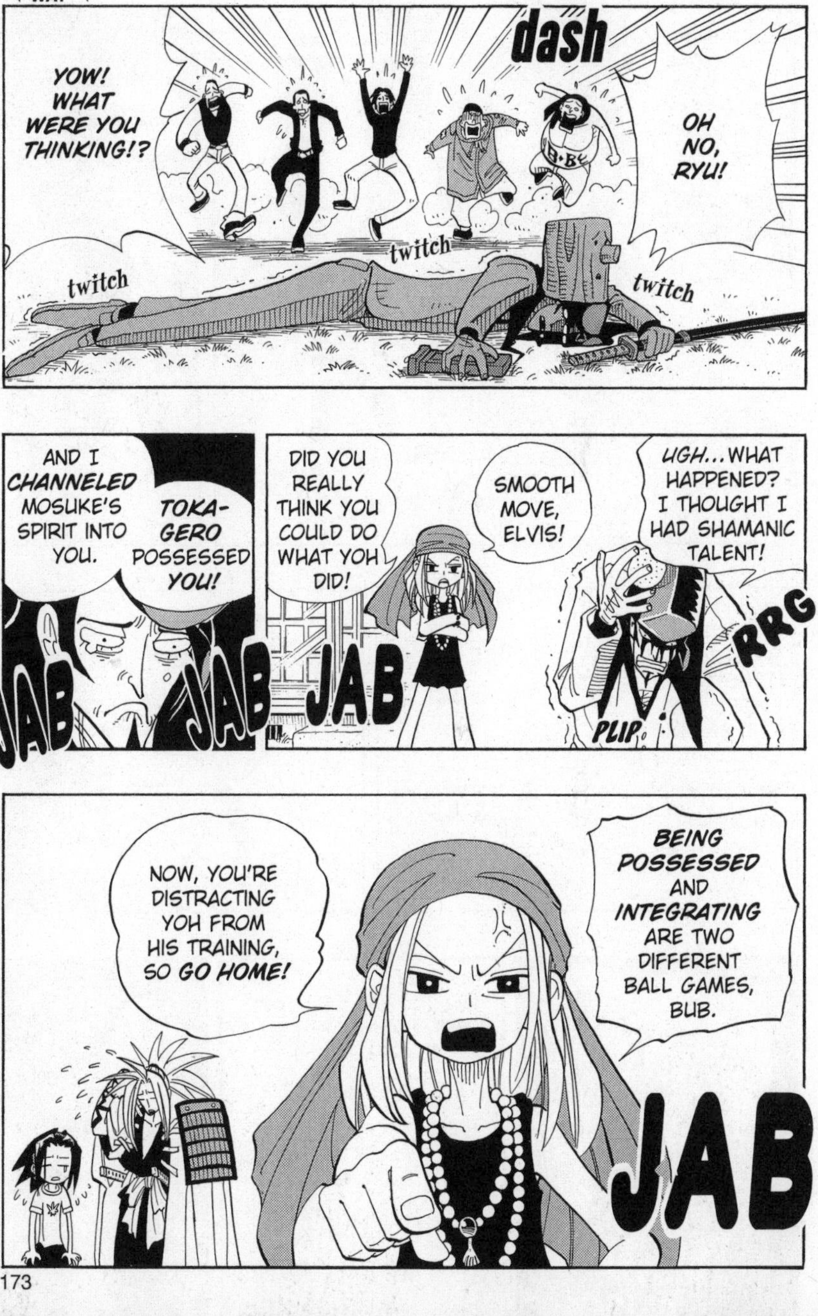
dash
OH NO, RYU!
YOW! WHAT WERE YOU THINKING!?
twitch
twitch
twitch
UGH... WHAT HAPPENED? I THOUGHT I HAD SHAMANIC TALENT!
RRG
SMOOTH MOVE, ELVIS!
DID YOU REALLY THINK YOU COULD DO WHAT YOH DID!
PLIP
JAB
TOKA-GERO POSSESSED YOU!
AND I CHANNELED MOSUKE'S SPIRIT INTO YOU.
JAB
JAB
BEING POSSESSED AND INTEGRATING ARE TWO DIFFERENT BALL GAMES, BUB.
NOW, YOU'RE DISTRACTING YOH FROM HIS TRAINING, SO GO HOME!
JAB

READ THIS WAY

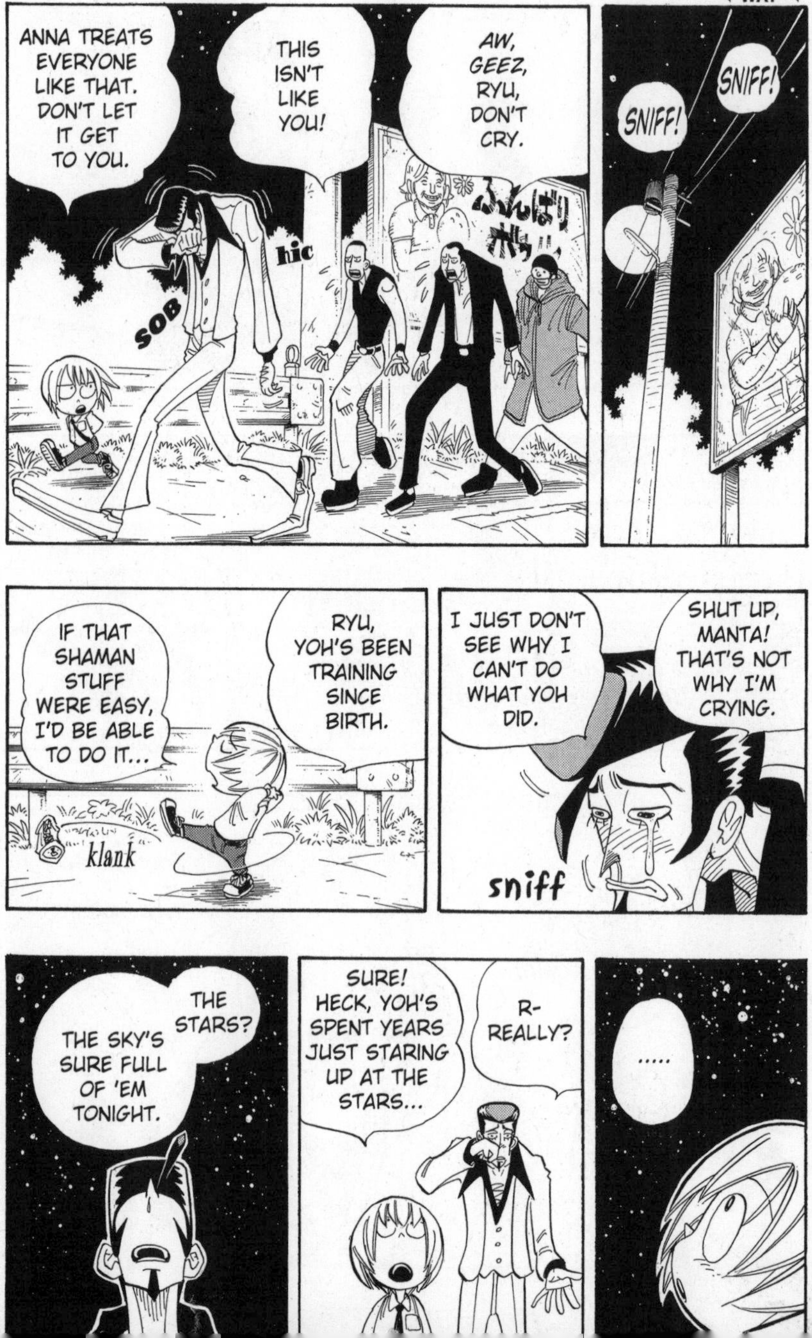
SNIFF!
SNIFF!
AW, GEEZ, RYU, DON'T CRY.
THIS ISN'T LIKE YOU!
ANNA TREATS EVERYONE LIKE THAT. DON'T LET IT GET TO YOU.
hic
SOB
SHUT UP, MANTA! THAT'S NOT WHY I'M CRYING.
I JUST DON'T SEE WHY I CAN'T DO WHAT YOH DID.
sniff
RYU, YOH'S BEEN TRAINING SINCE BIRTH.
IF THAT SHAMAN STUFF WERE EASY, I'D BE ABLE TO DO IT...
klank
.....
R-REALLY?
SURE! HECK, YOH'S SPENT YEARS JUST STARING UP AT THE STARS...
THE STARS?
THE SKY'S SURE FULL OF 'EM TONIGHT.

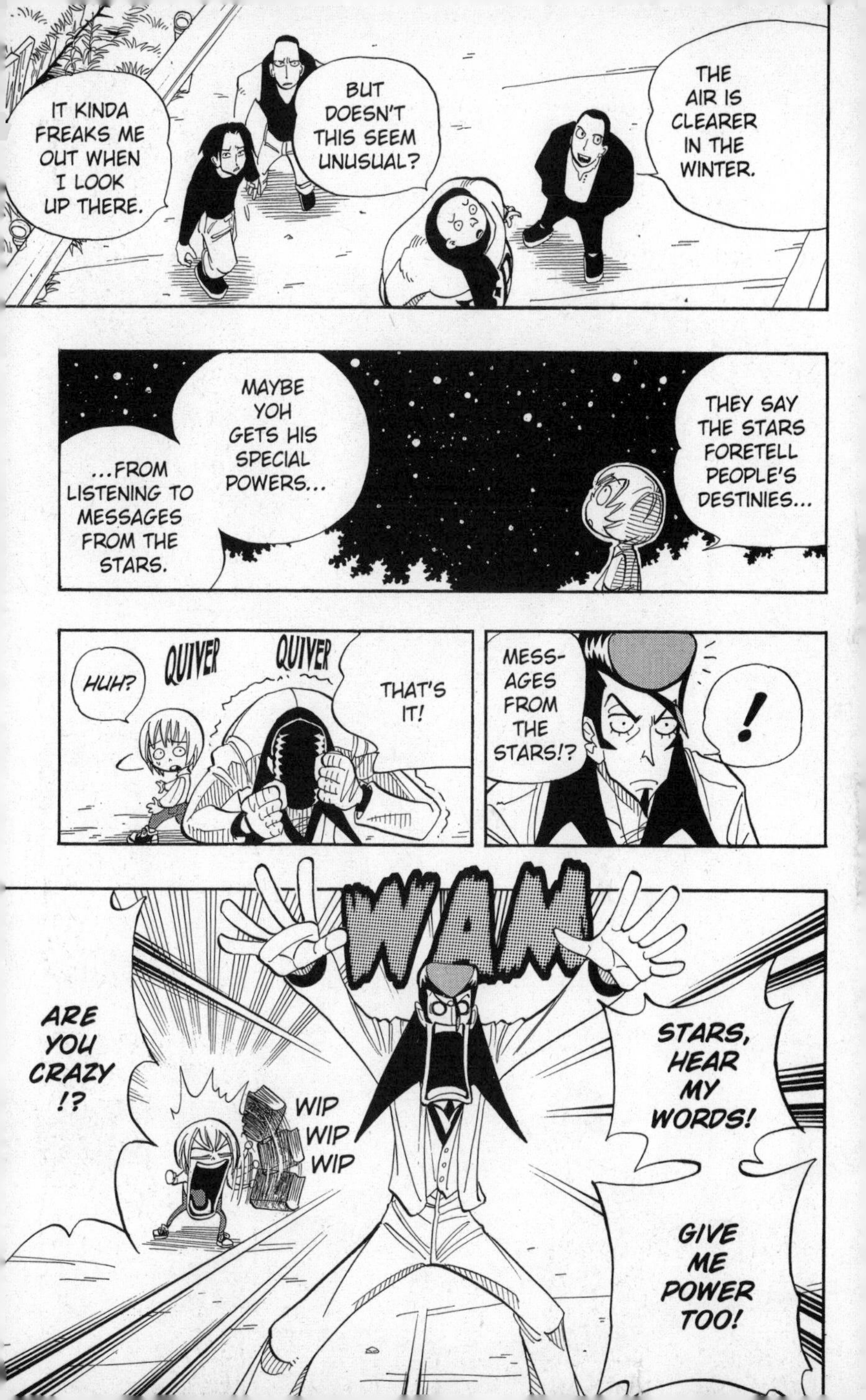
THE AIR IS CLEARER IN THE WINTER.
BUT DOESN'T THIS SEEM UNUSUAL?
IT KINDA FREAKS ME OUT WHEN I LOOK UP THERE.
THEY SAY THE STARS FORETELL PEOPLE'S DESTINIES...
MAYBE YOH GETS HIS SPECIAL POWERS...
...FROM LISTENING TO MESSAGES FROM THE STARS.
!
MESS-AGES FROM THE STARS!?
THAT'S IT!
QUIVER
QUIVER
HUH?
WAM
STARS, HEAR MY WORDS!
GIVE ME POWER TOO!
WIP WIP WIP
ARE YOU CRAZY!?

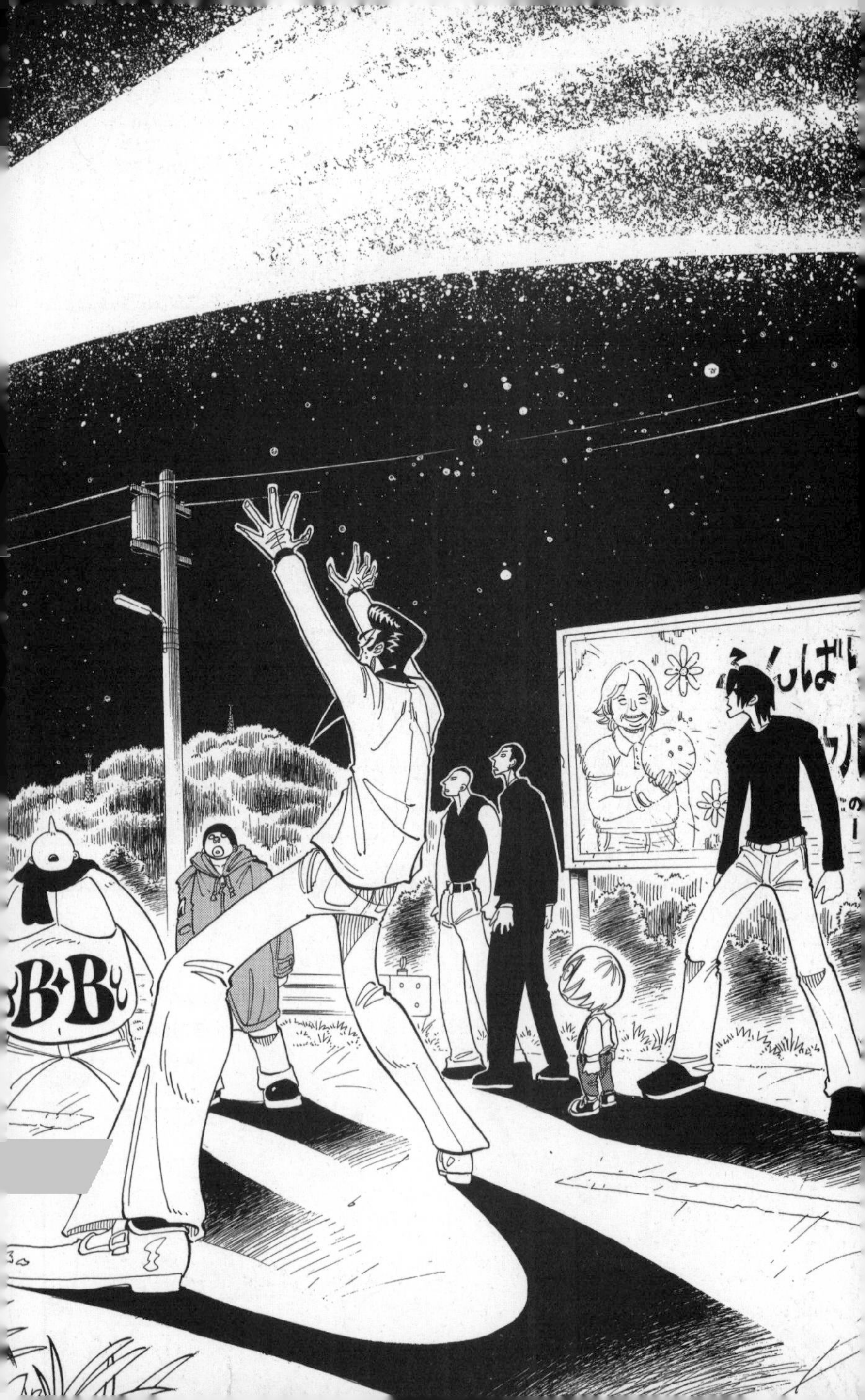

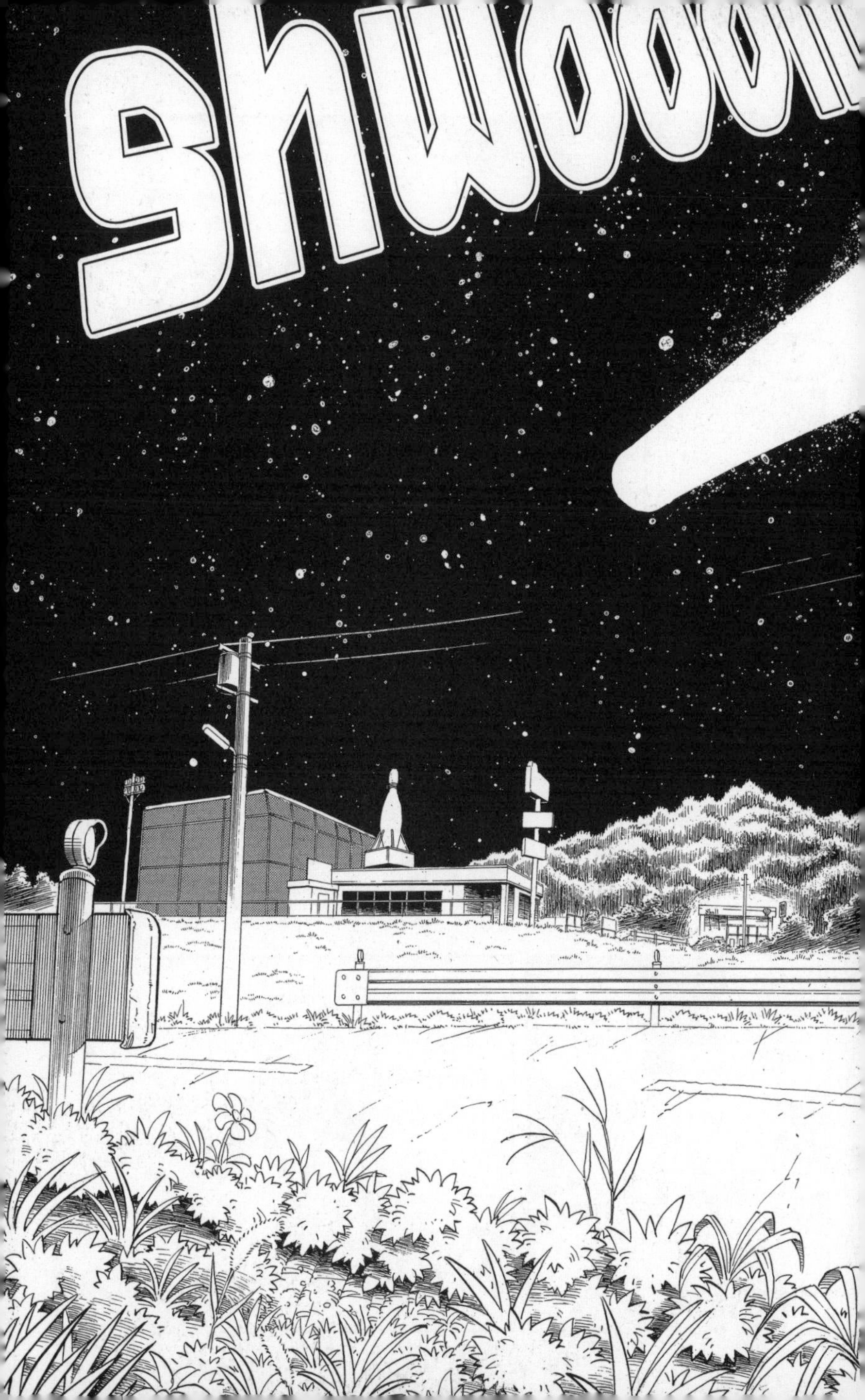
Shwooo

READ THIS WAY

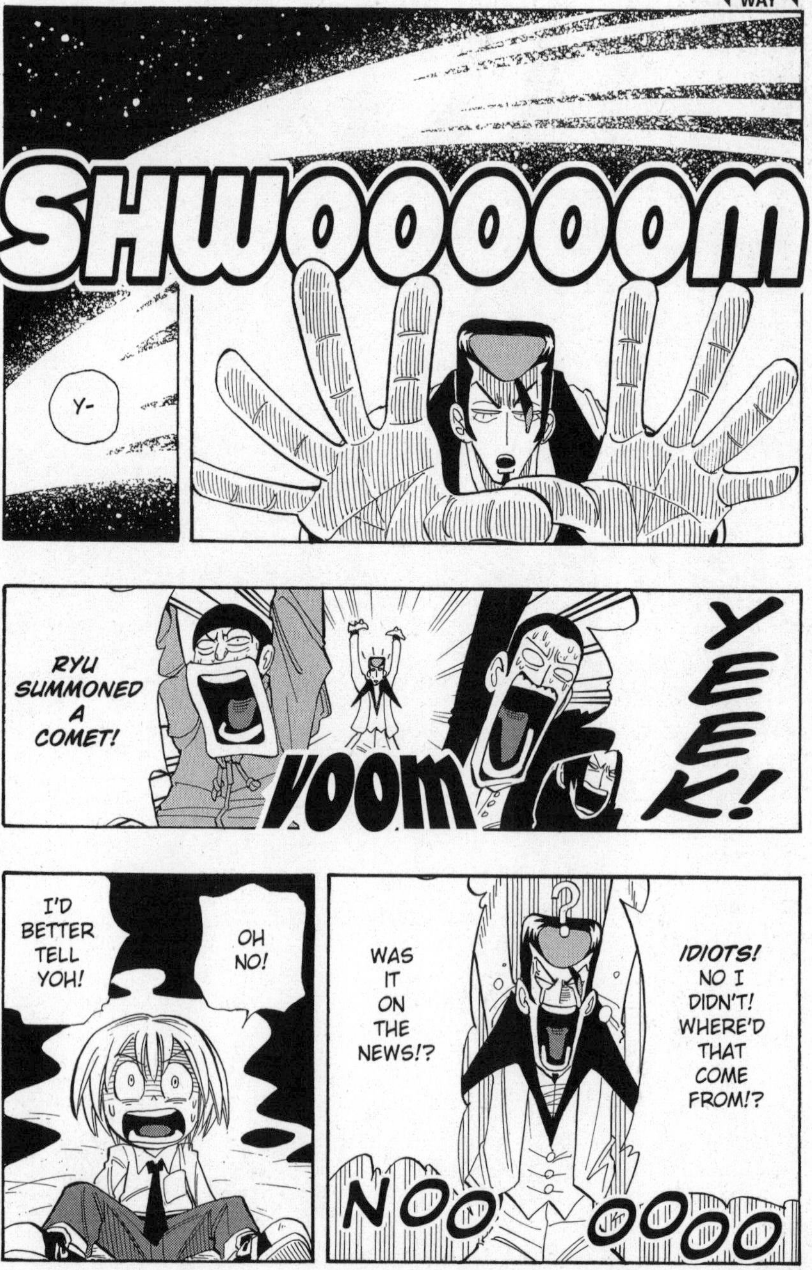
SHWOOOOOM
Y-
YEEK!
VOOM
RYU SUMMONED A COMET!
IDIOTS! NO I DIDN'T! WHERE'D THAT COME FROM!?
WAS IT ON THE NEWS!?
NOO OOOO
OH NO!
I'D BETTER TELL YOH!

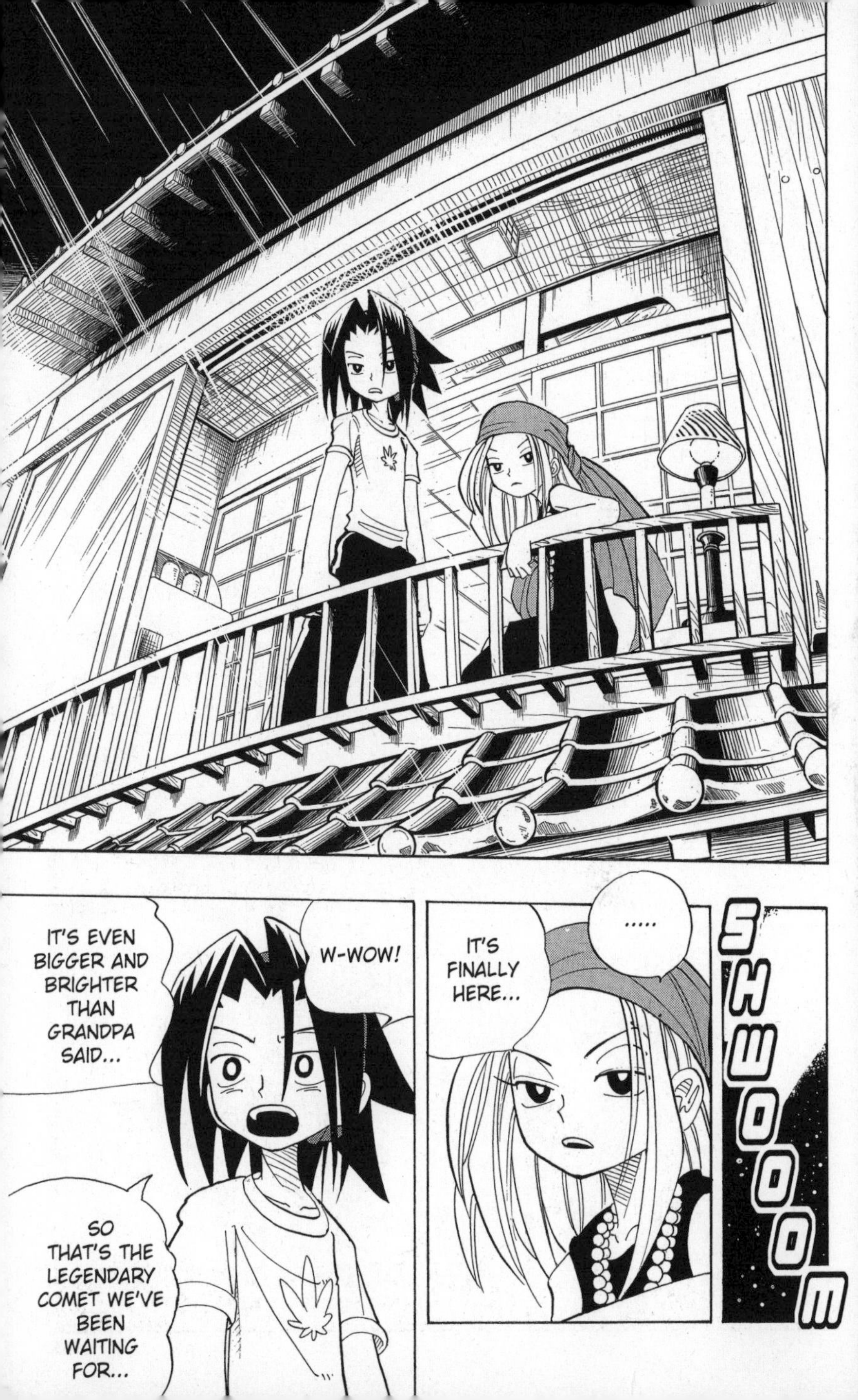
SHWOOOOM
.....
IT'S FINALLY HERE...
W-WOW!
IT'S EVEN BIGGER AND BRIGHTER THAN GRANDPA SAID...
SO THAT'S THE LEGENDARY COMET WE'VE BEEN WAITING FOR...

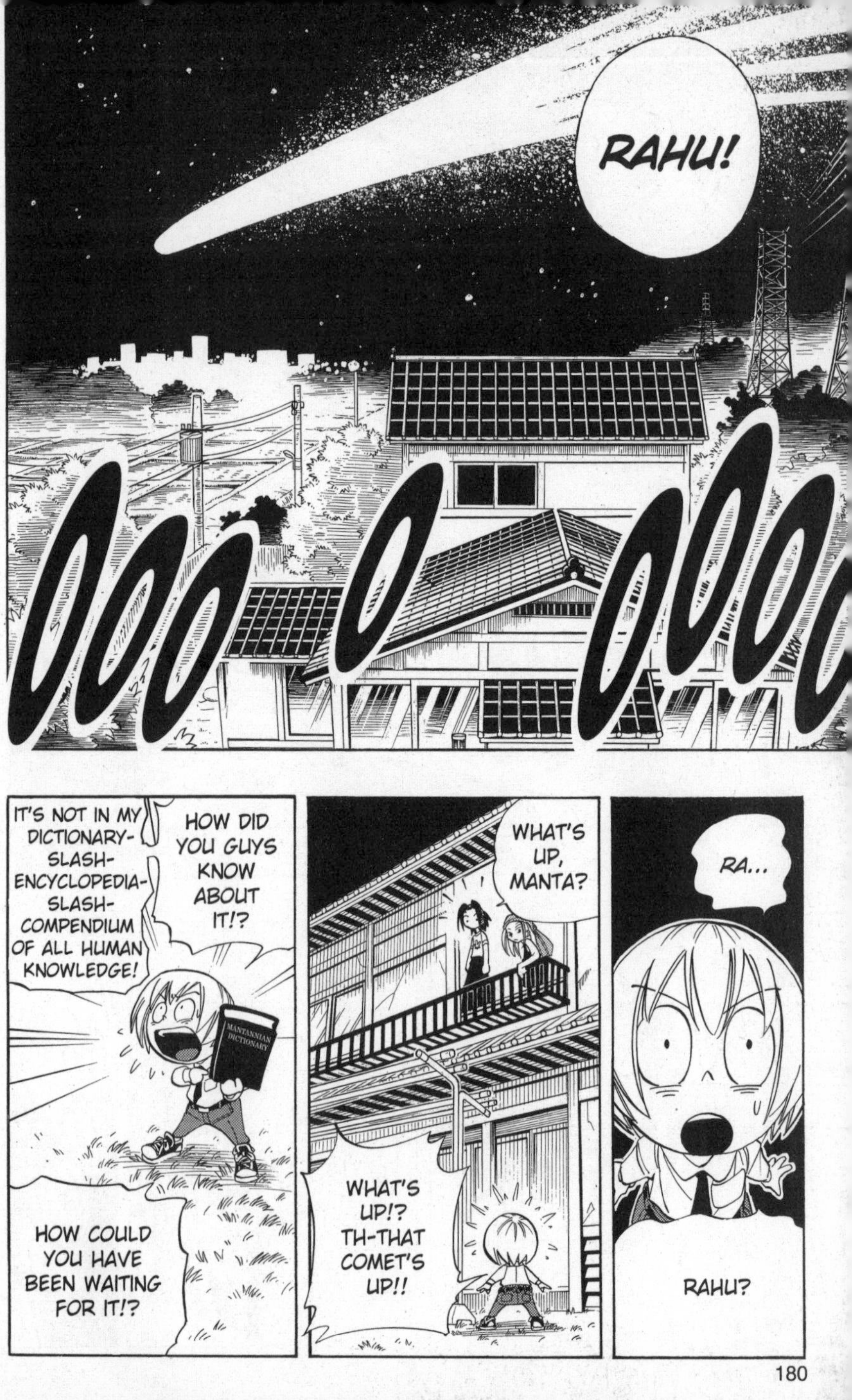
RAHU!
RA...
RAHU?
WHAT'S UP, MANTA?
WHAT'S UP!? TH-THAT COMET'S UP!!
HOW DID YOU GUYS KNOW ABOUT IT!?
IT'S NOT IN MY DICTIONARY-SLASH-ENCYCLOPEDIA-SLASH-COMPENDIUM OF ALL HUMAN KNOWLEDGE!
MANTANNIAN DICTIONARY
HOW COULD YOU HAVE BEEN WAITING FOR IT!?

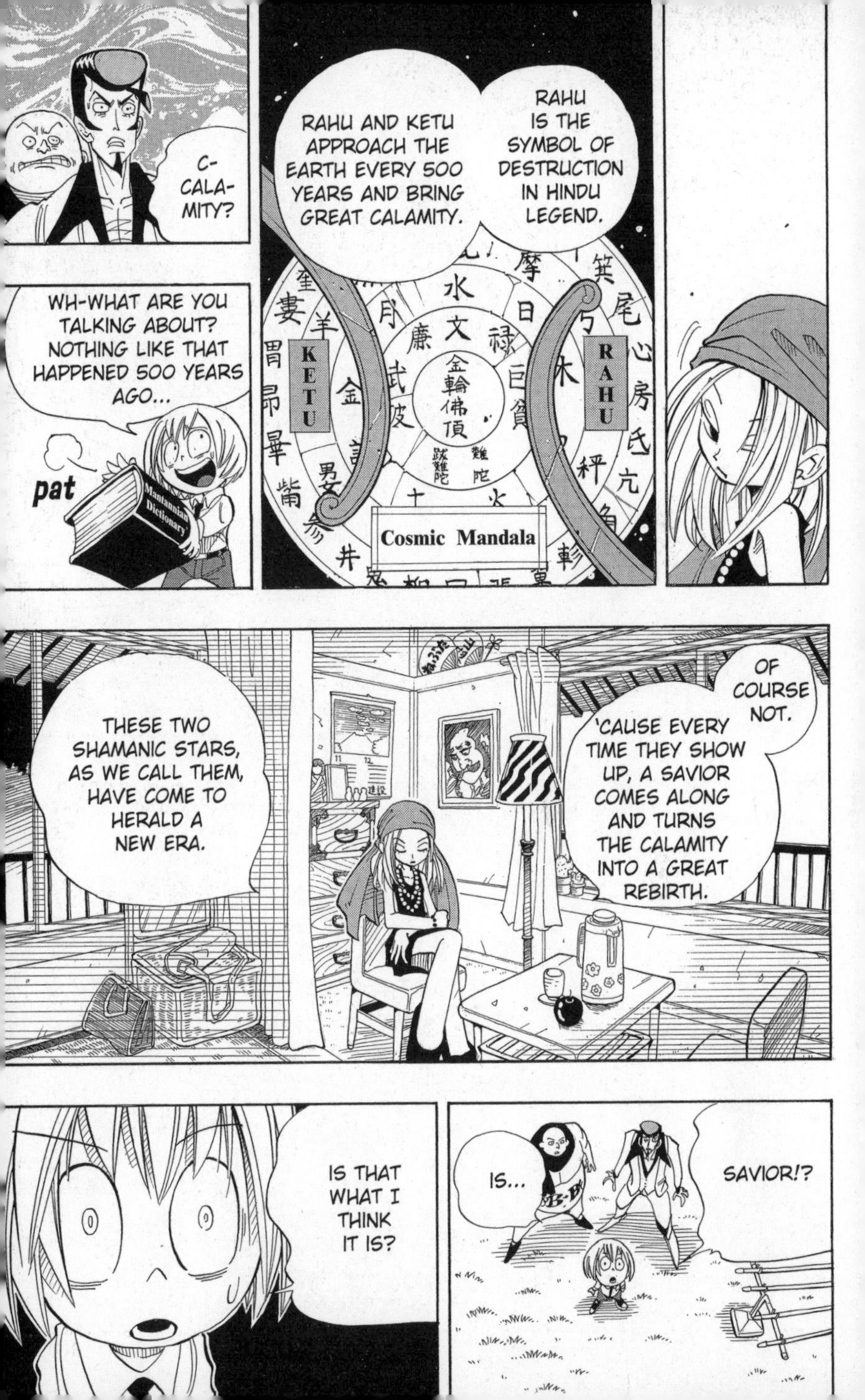
RAHU IS THE SYMBOL OF DESTRUCTION IN HINDU LEGEND.
RAHU AND KETU APPROACH THE EARTH EVERY 500 YEARS AND BRING GREAT CALAMITY.
RAHU
KETU
Cosmic Mandala
C-CALA-MITY?
WH-WHAT ARE YOU TALKING ABOUT? NOTHING LIKE THAT HAPPENED 500 YEARS AGO...
pat
Mantannian Dictionary
OF COURSE NOT.
'CAUSE EVERY TIME THEY SHOW UP, A SAVIOR COMES ALONG AND TURNS THE CALAMITY INTO A GREAT REBIRTH.
THESE TWO SHAMANIC STARS, AS WE CALL THEM, HAVE COME TO HERALD A NEW ERA.
SAVIOR!?
IS...
IS THAT WHAT I THINK IT IS?

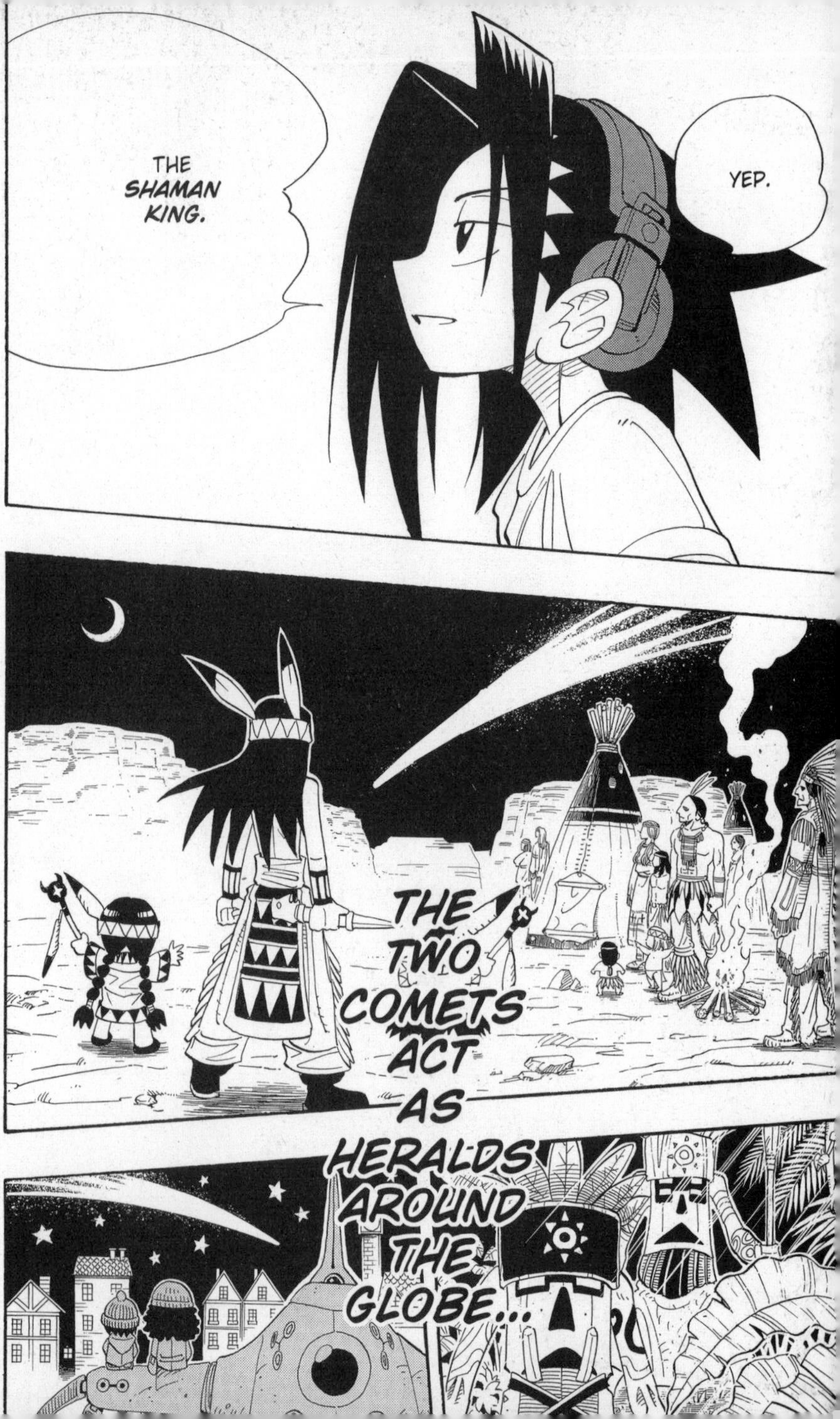
YEP.
THE SHAMAN KING.
THE TWO COMETS ACT AS HERALDS AROUND THE GLOBE...

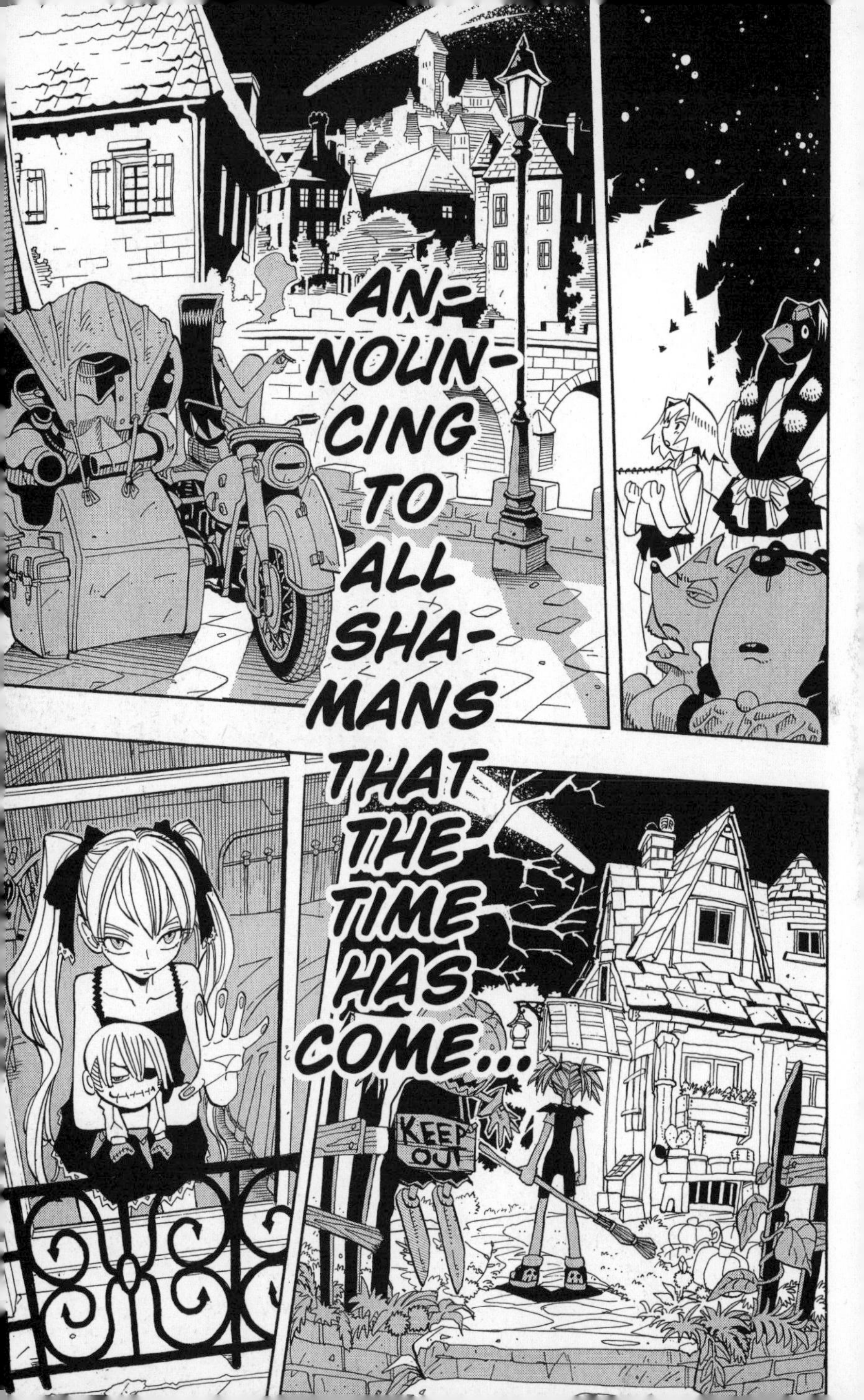
ANNOUNCING TO ALL SHAMANS THAT THE TIME HAS COME...
KEEP OUT

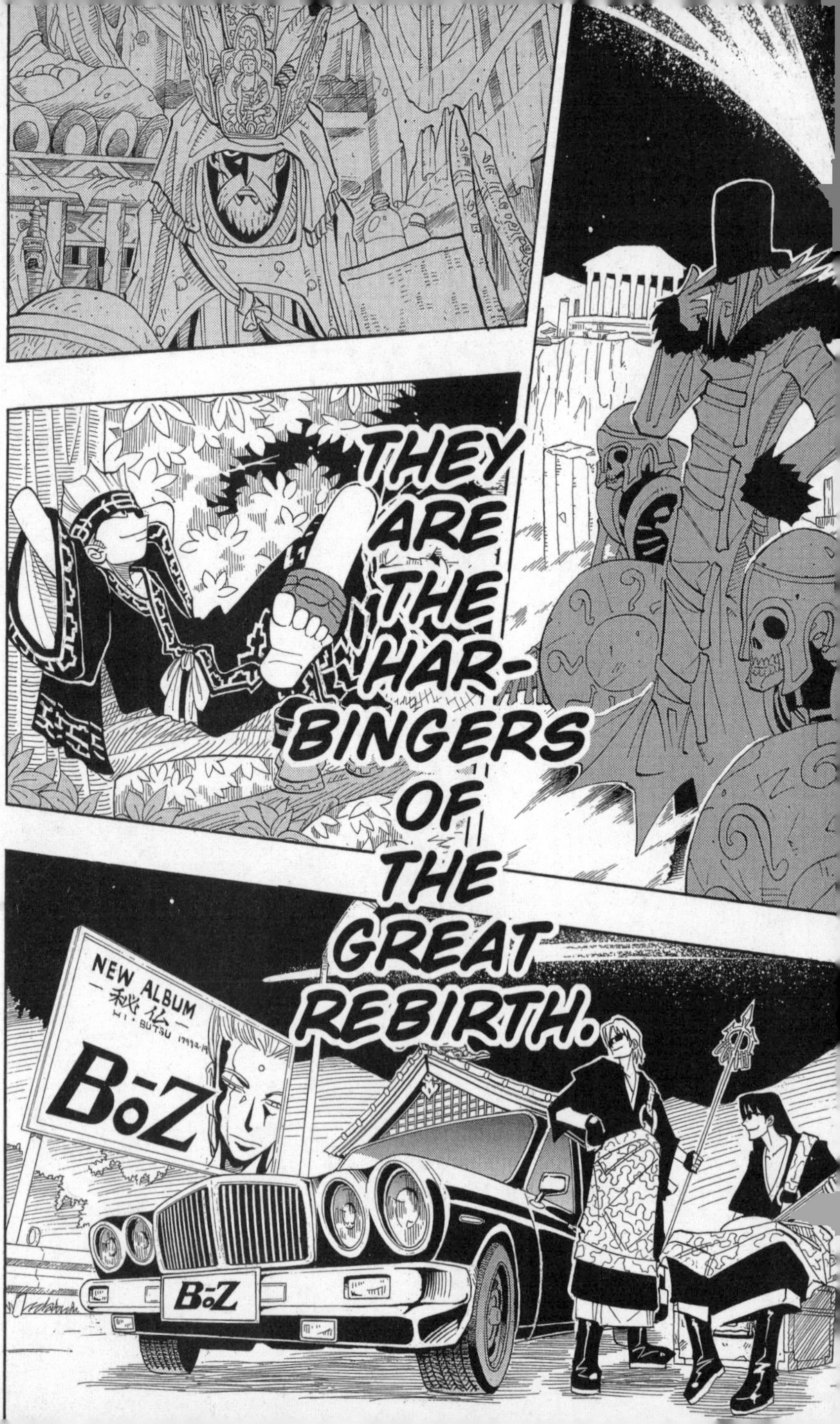
THEY ARE THE HAR-BINGERS OF THE GREAT REBIRTH.
NEW ALBUM
—秘仏—
HI・BUTSU

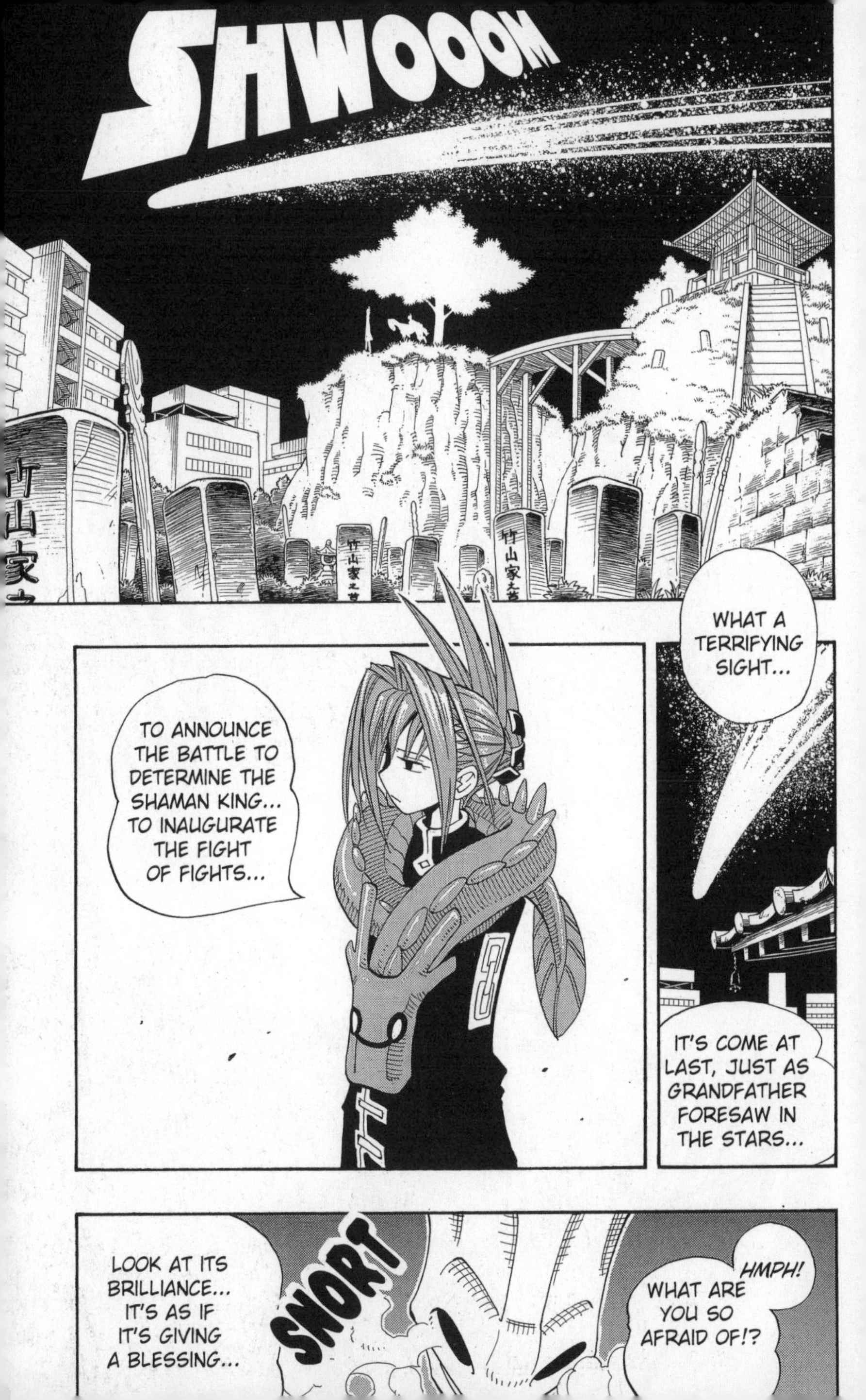
SHWOOOM
WHAT A TERRIFYING SIGHT...
IT'S COME AT LAST, JUST AS GRANDFATHER FORESAW IN THE STARS...
TO ANNOUNCE THE BATTLE TO DETERMINE THE SHAMAN KING... TO INAUGURATE THE FIGHT OF FIGHTS...
HMPH!
WHAT ARE YOU SO AFRAID OF!?
SNORT
LOOK AT ITS BRILLIANCE... IT'S AS IF IT'S GIVING A BLESSING...

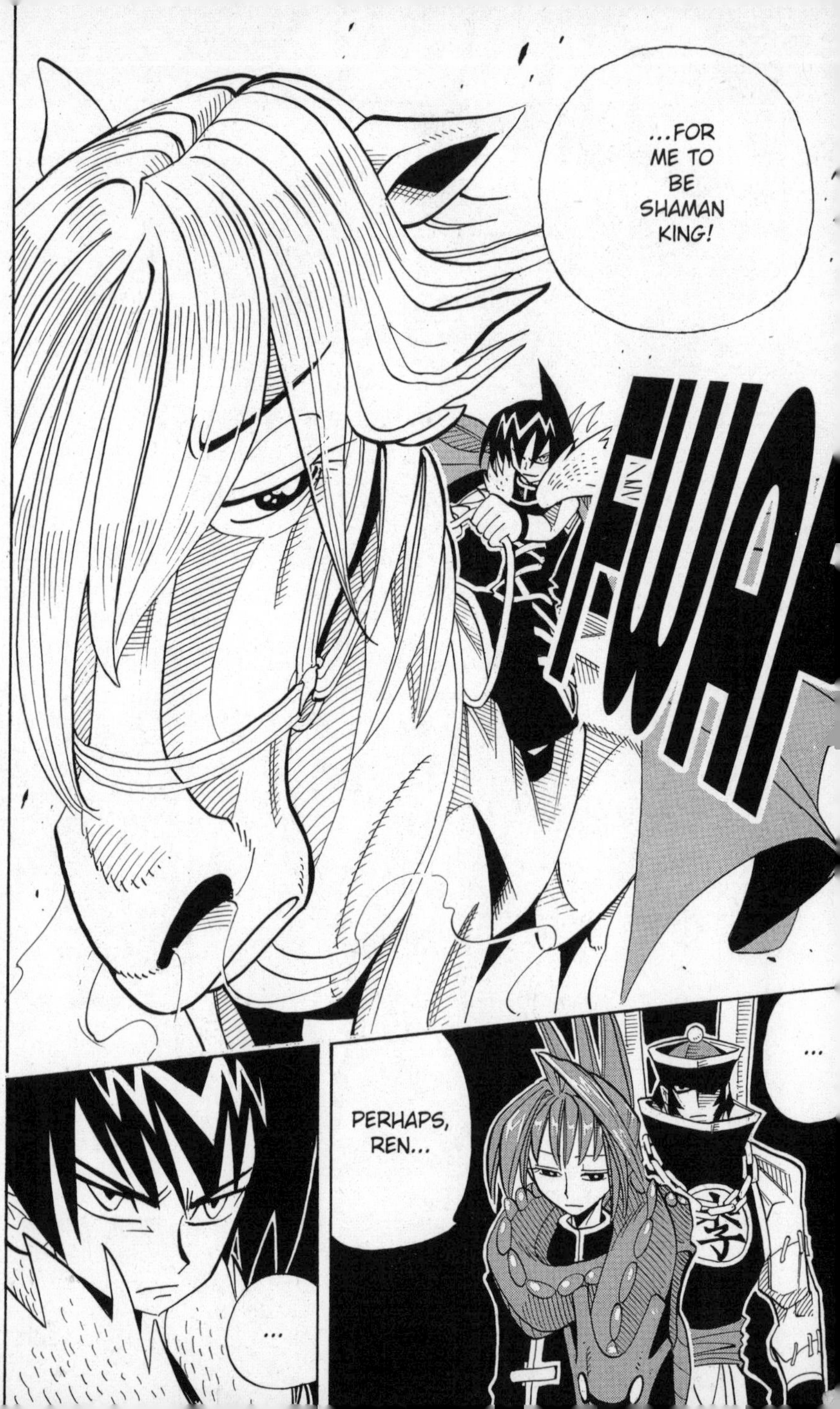
...FOR ME TO BE SHAMAN KING!
...
PERHAPS, REN...
...

READ THIS WAY

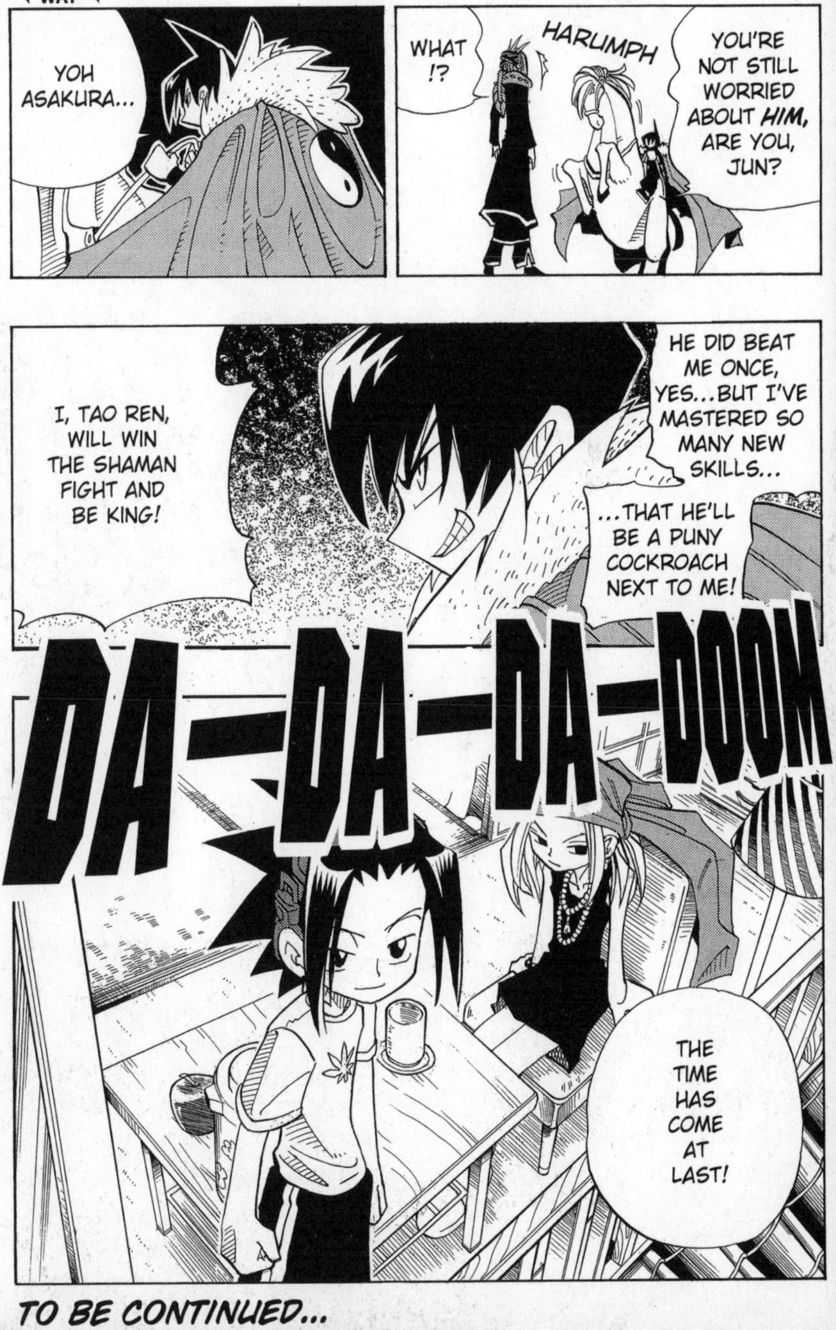
YOU'RE NOT STILL WORRIED ABOUT HIM, ARE YOU, JUN?
HARUMPH
WHAT !?
YOH ASAKURA...
HE DID BEAT ME ONCE, YES...BUT I'VE MASTERED SO MANY NEW SKILLS...
...THAT HE'LL BE A PUNY COCKROACH NEXT TO ME!
I, TAO REN, WILL WIN THE SHAMAN FIGHT AND BE KING!
DA-DA-DA-DOOM
THE TIME HAS COME AT LAST!

TO BE CONTINUED...

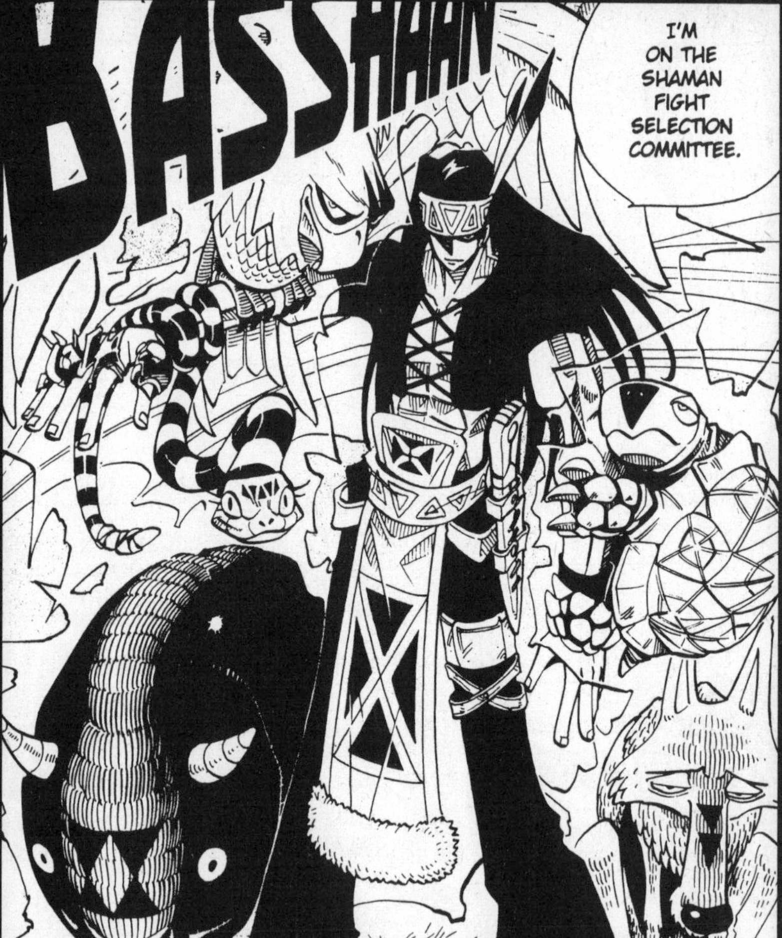
BASSHAAN
I'M ON THE SHAMAN FIGHT SELECTION COMMITTEE.

IN THE NEXT VOLUME...

The "Shaman Fight in Tokyo" is approaching, and talent scouts are scouring the world for contestants. Who's doing the scouting? The Patch, the Native American people who have overseen the Shaman Fight since the dawn of time. But to try and fail means more than just a sharp put-down: if Yoh can't beat Silva and his five animal spirits, he won't get another chance for 500 years! But how can a human ghost defeat these incredible forces of nature?

AVAILABLE NOW!

NARUTO

Story and Art by
Masashi Kishimoto

Naruto is determined to become the greatest ninja ever!

Twelve years ago the Village Hidden in the Leaves was attacked by a fearsome threat. A nine-tailed fox spirit claimed the life of the village leader, the Hokage, and many others. Today, the village is at peace and a troublemaking kid named Naruto is struggling to graduate from Ninja Academy. His goal may be to become the next Hokage, but his true destiny will be much more complicated. The adventure begins now!

WORLD'S BEST SELLING MANGA!

NARUTO © 1999 by Masashi Kishimoto/SHUEISHA Inc.

www.shonenjump.com

www.viz.com

BLEACH

ブリーチ

Story and Art by Tite Kubo

TAKING ON THE AFTERLIFE
ONE SOUL AT A TIME

Ichigo Kurosaki never asked for the ability to see
ghosts—he was born with the gift. When his
family is attacked by a Hollow—a malevolent
lost soul—Ichigo becomes a Soul Reaper,
dedicating his life to protecting the innocent
and helping the tortured spirits themselves find
peace. Find out why Tite Kubo's Bleach has
become an international manga smash-hit!

www.viz.com

www.shonenjump.com

RATED
T
TEEN
ratings.viz.com

BLEACH © 2001 by Tite Kubo/SHUEISHA Inc.